BLUEPRINT FOR DISASTER

Other books by Darby Conley

The Dog Is Not a Toy (House Rule #4)

Fuzzy Logic: Get Fuzzy 2

Groovitude: A Get Fuzzy Treasury

The Get Fuzzy Experience: Are You Bucksperienced

I Would Have Bought You a Cat, But . . .

BLUEPRINT FOR DISASTER

A GET FUZZY Collection

by darby conley

Andrews McMeel
Publishing

Kansas City

Get Fuzzy is distributed internationally by United Feature Syndicate.

Blueprint for Disaster copyright © 2003 by Darby Conley. All rights reserved. Printed in the United States of America. No part of this book may be used or reproduced in any manner whatsoever without written permission except in the case of reprints in the context of reviews. For information, write Andrews McMeel Publishing, an Andrews McMeel Universal company, 4520 Main Street, Kansas City, Missouri 64111.

 03 04 05 06 07 BBG 10 9 8 7 6 5 4 3 2 1

ISBN: 0-7407-3808-9

Library of Congress Control Number: 2003106588

Get Fuzzy can be viewed on the Internet at:

www.comics.com/comics/getfuzzy

ATTENTION: SCHOOLS AND BUSINESSES

Andrews McMeel books are available at quantity discounts with bulk purchase for educational, business, or sales promotional use. For information, please write to: Special Sales Department, Andrews McMeel Publishing, 4520 Main Street, Kansas City, Missouri 64111.

**To Laura
with love**

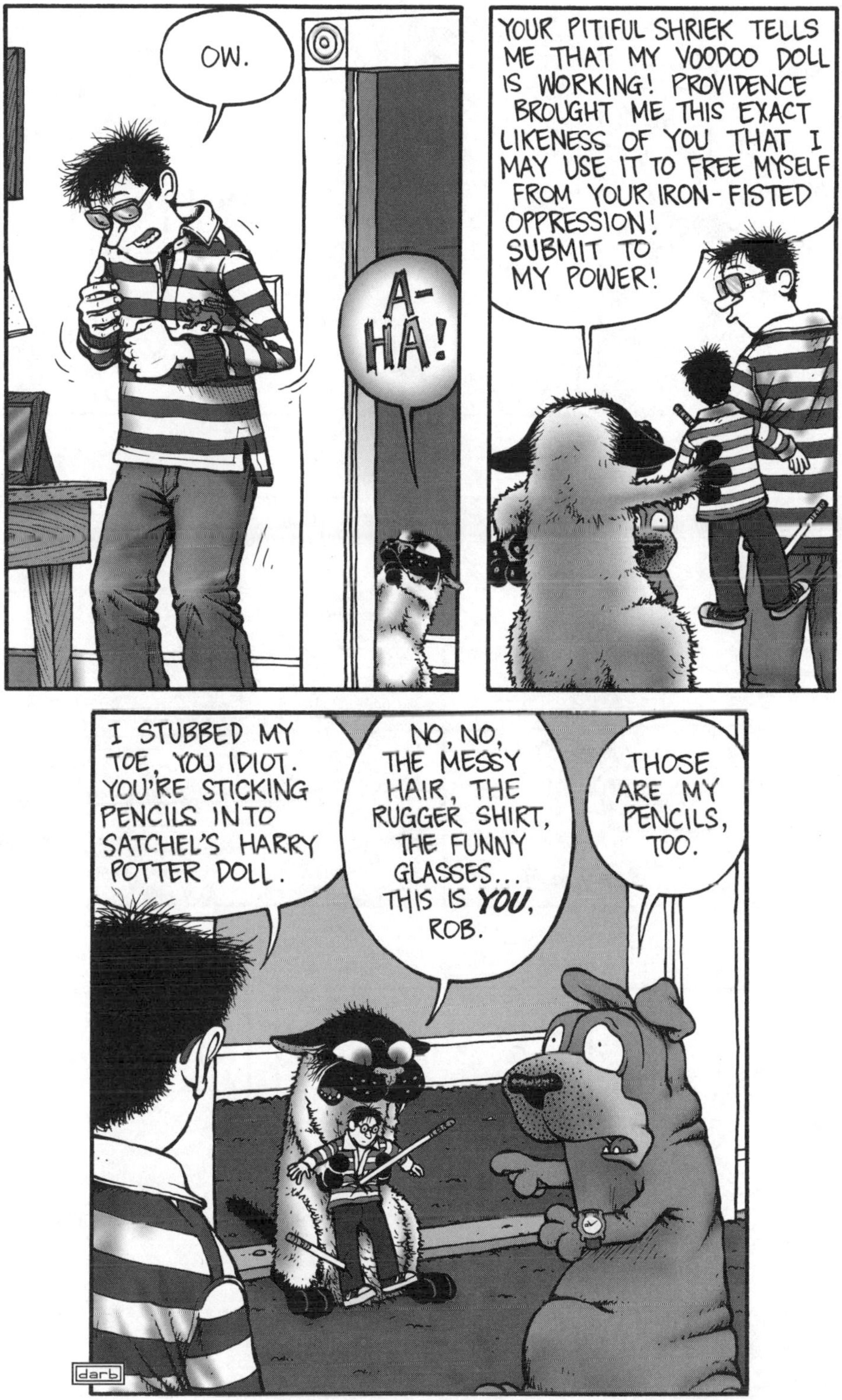
OW.
A-HA!
YOUR PITIFUL SHRIEK TELLS ME THAT MY VOODOO DOLL IS WORKING! PROVIDENCE BROUGHT ME THIS EXACT LIKENESS OF YOU THAT I MAY USE IT TO FREE MYSELF FROM YOUR IRON-FISTED OPPRESSION! SUBMIT TO MY POWER!
I STUBBED MY TOE, YOU IDIOT. YOU'RE STICKING PENCILS INTO SATCHEL'S HARRY POTTER DOLL.
NO, NO, THE MESSY HAIR, THE RUGGER SHIRT, THE FUNNY GLASSES... THIS IS ***YOU***, ROB.
THOSE ARE MY PENCILS, TOO.
darb

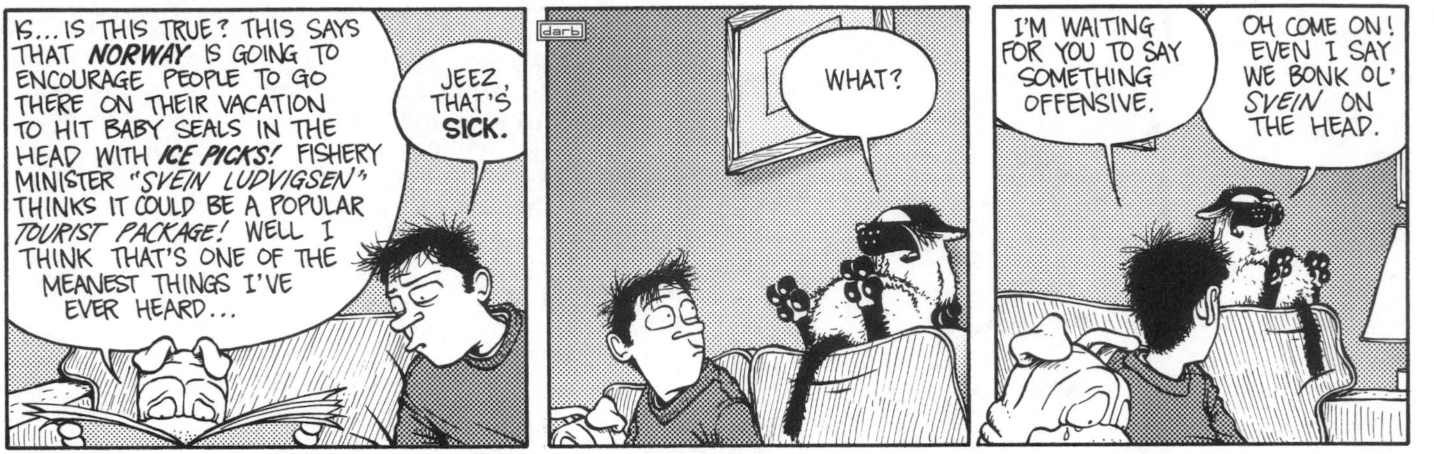
IS... IS THIS TRUE? THIS SAYS THAT **NORWAY** IS GOING TO ENCOURAGE PEOPLE TO GO THERE ON THEIR VACATION TO HIT BABY SEALS IN THE HEAD WITH ***ICE PICKS!*** FISHERY MINISTER *"SVEIN LUDVIGSEN"* THINKS IT COULD BE A POPULAR *TOURIST PACKAGE!* WELL I THINK THAT'S ONE OF THE MEANEST THINGS I'VE EVER HEARD...
JEEZ, THAT'S **SICK.**
darb
WHAT?
I'M WAITING FOR YOU TO SAY SOMETHING OFFENSIVE.
OH COME ON! EVEN I SAY WE BONK OL' *SVEIN* ON THE HEAD.

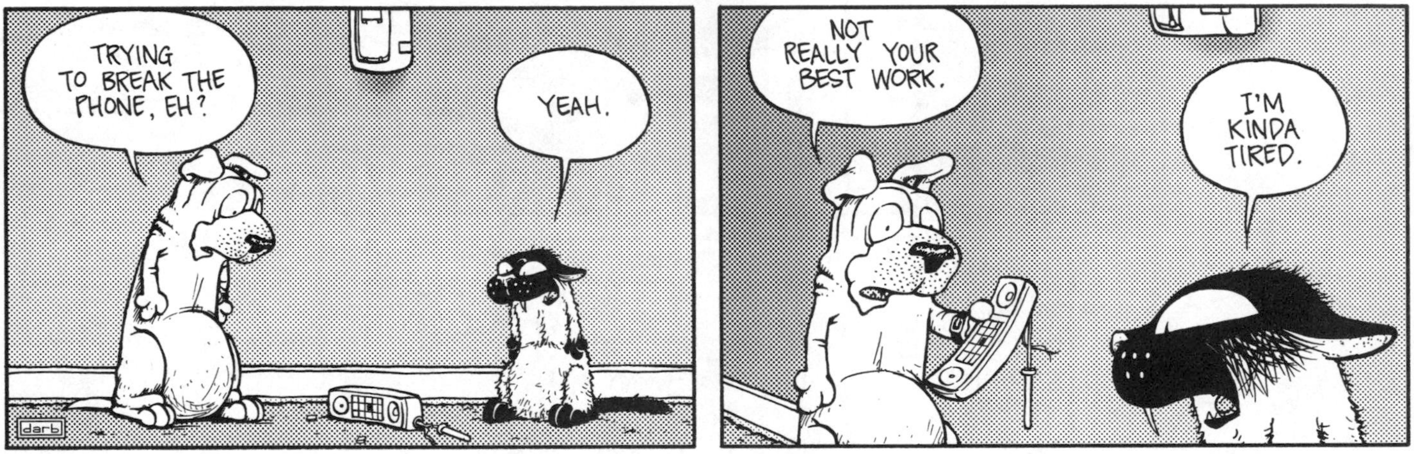
TRYING TO BREAK THE PHONE, EH?
YEAH.
darb
NOT REALLY YOUR BEST WORK.
I'M KINDA TIRED.

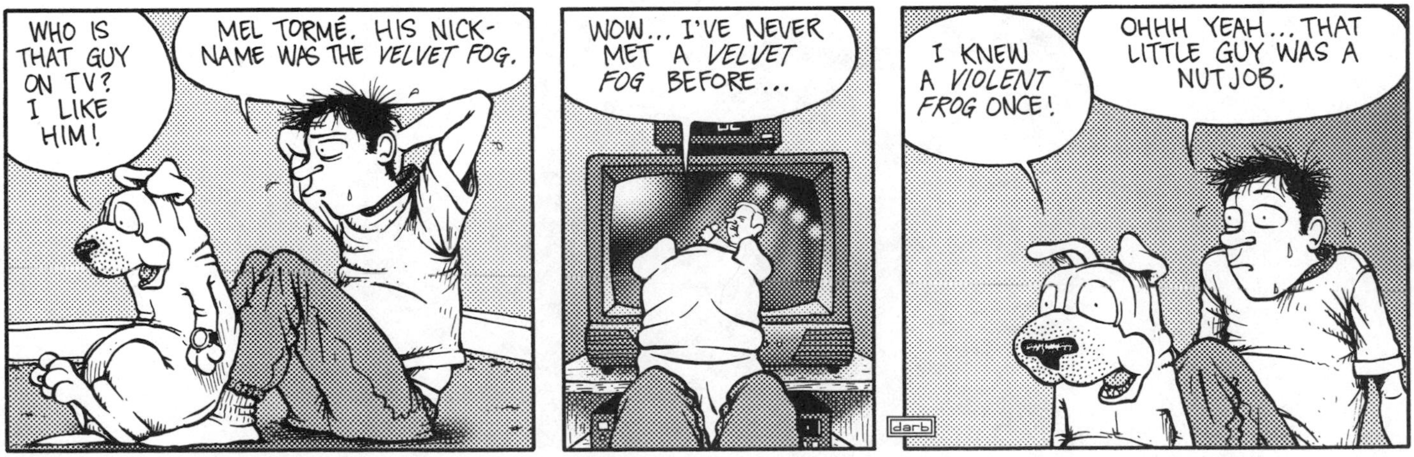
WHO IS THAT GUY ON TV? I LIKE HIM!
MEL TORMÉ. HIS NICK-NAME WAS THE *VELVET FOG.*
WOW... I'VE NEVER MET A *VELVET FOG* BEFORE...
I KNEW A *VIOLENT FROG* ONCE!
OHHH YEAH... THAT LITTLE GUY WAS A NUTJOB.
darb

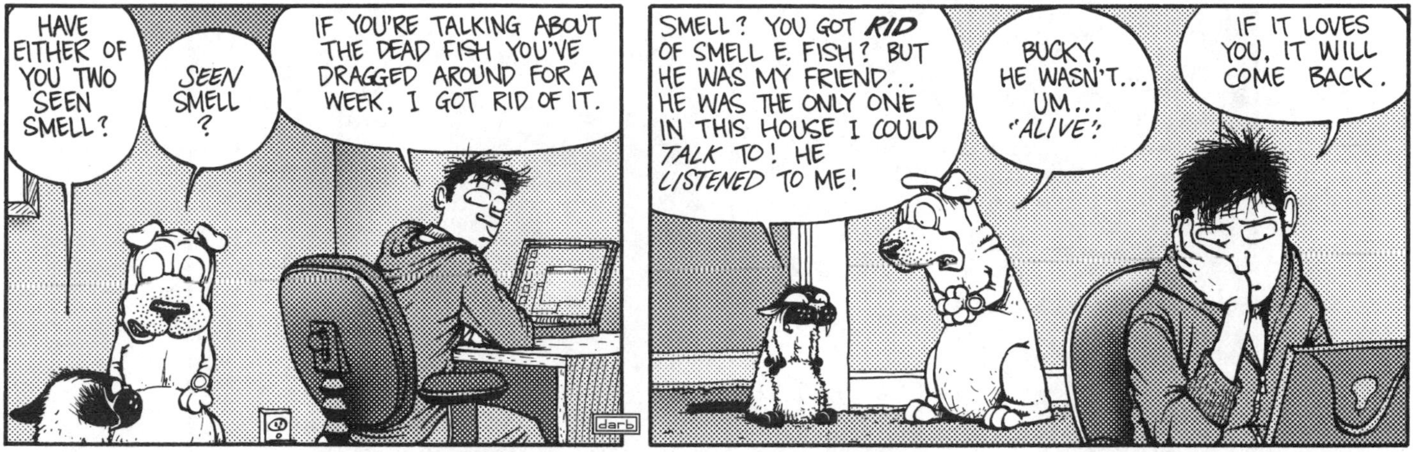
HAVE EITHER OF YOU TWO SEEN SMELL?
SEEN SMELL?
IF YOU'RE TALKING ABOUT THE DEAD FISH YOU'VE DRAGGED AROUND FOR A WEEK, I GOT RID OF IT.
darb
SMELL? YOU GOT RID OF SMELL E. FISH? BUT HE WAS MY FRIEND... HE WAS THE ONLY ONE IN THIS HOUSE I COULD TALK TO! HE LISTENED TO ME!
BUCKY, HE WASN'T... UM... "ALIVE".
IF IT LOVES YOU, IT WILL COME BACK.

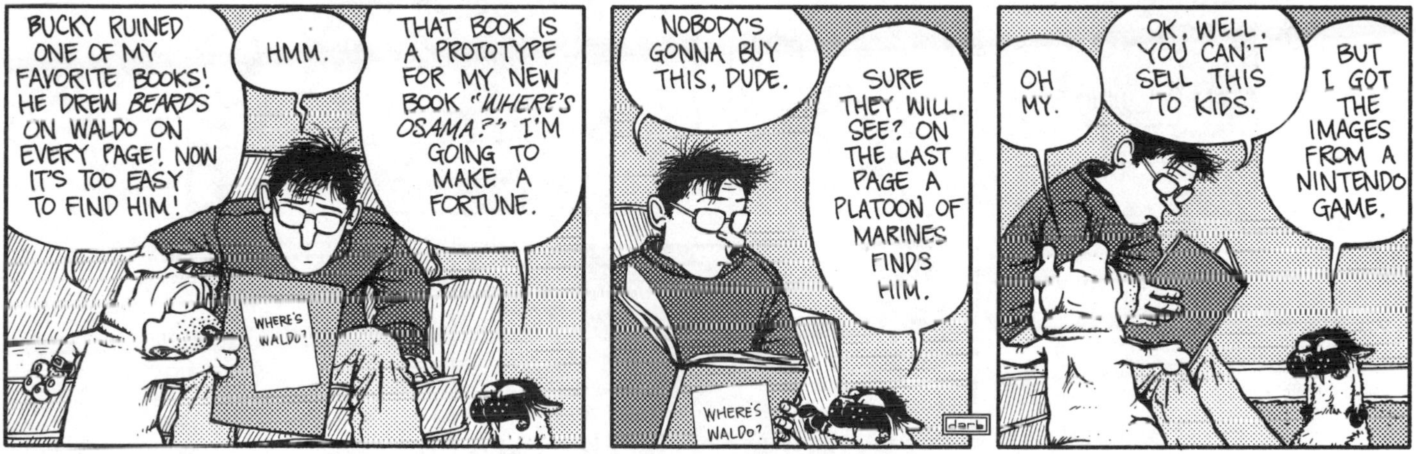
BUCKY RUINED ONE OF MY FAVORITE BOOKS! HE DREW BEARDS ON WALDO ON EVERY PAGE! NOW IT'S TOO EASY TO FIND HIM!
HMM.
THAT BOOK IS A PROTOTYPE FOR MY NEW BOOK "WHERE'S OSAMA?" I'M GOING TO MAKE A FORTUNE.
WHERE'S WALDO?
NOBODY'S GONNA BUY THIS, DUDE.
SURE THEY WILL. SEE? ON THE LAST PAGE A PLATOON OF MARINES FINDS HIM.
WHERE'S WALDO?
darb
OH MY.
OK, WELL, YOU CAN'T SELL THIS TO KIDS.
BUT I GOT THE IMAGES FROM A NINTENDO GAME.

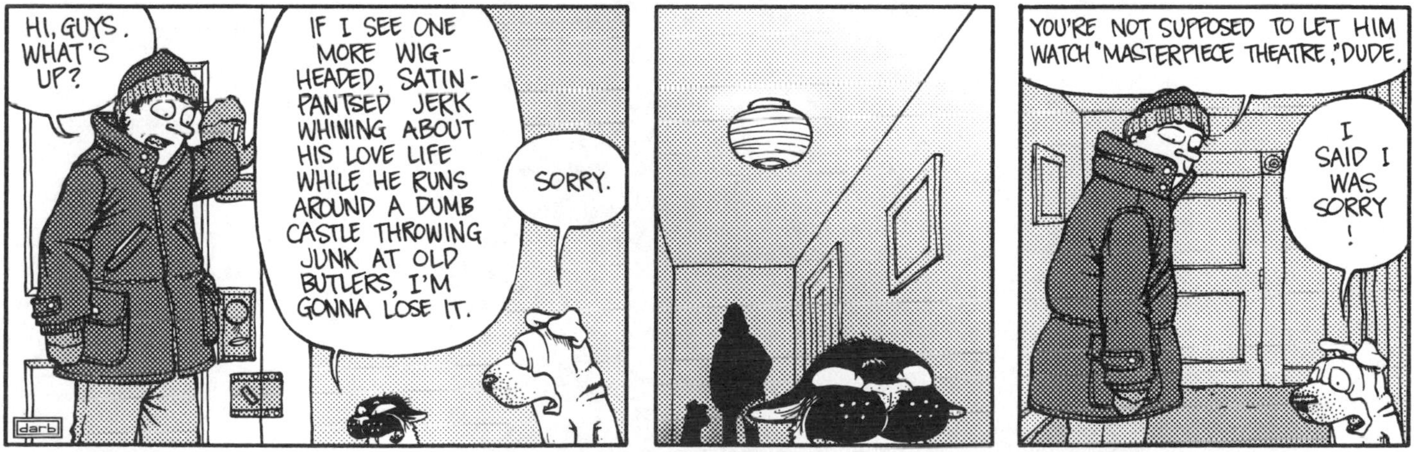
HI, GUYS. WHAT'S UP?
IF I SEE ONE MORE WIG-HEADED, SATIN-PANTSED JERK WHINING ABOUT HIS LOVE LIFE WHILE HE RUNS AROUND A DUMB CASTLE THROWING JUNK AT OLD BUTLERS, I'M GONNA LOSE IT.
SORRY.
darb
YOU'RE NOT SUPPOSED TO LET HIM WATCH "MASTERPIECE THEATRE," DUDE.
I SAID I WAS SORRY!

WHAT UP, PUP?
I FINALLY CONFRONTED BUCKY ABOUT SCRATCHING A HOLE IN MY OLD BEANBAG.
GOOD FOR YOU. HOW DID IT GO?
USA RUGBY
I'M NOT SURE. I SAID WHAT I WANTED TO SAY, BUT HE GOT KIND OF, UM... I GUESS YOU COULD CALL IT "DEFENSIVE."
darb
WELL I HOPE YOU AT LEAST GOT SOME "CLOSURE" AFTER THAT.
UM, NO... BUT I PUT A BOO-BOO STRIP ON IT.
C.S. LEWIS

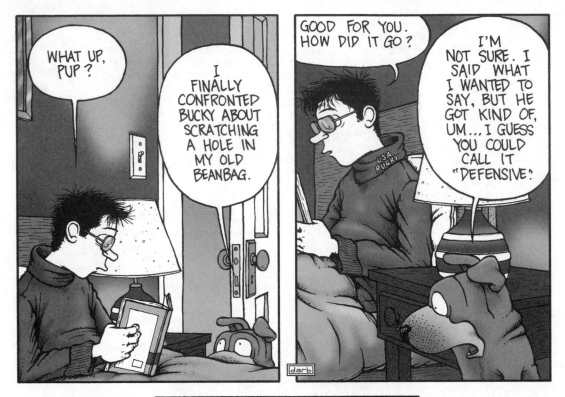

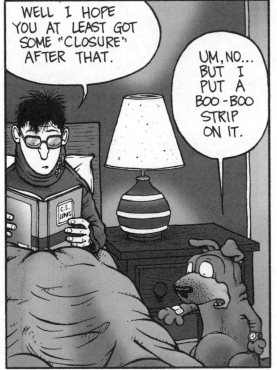

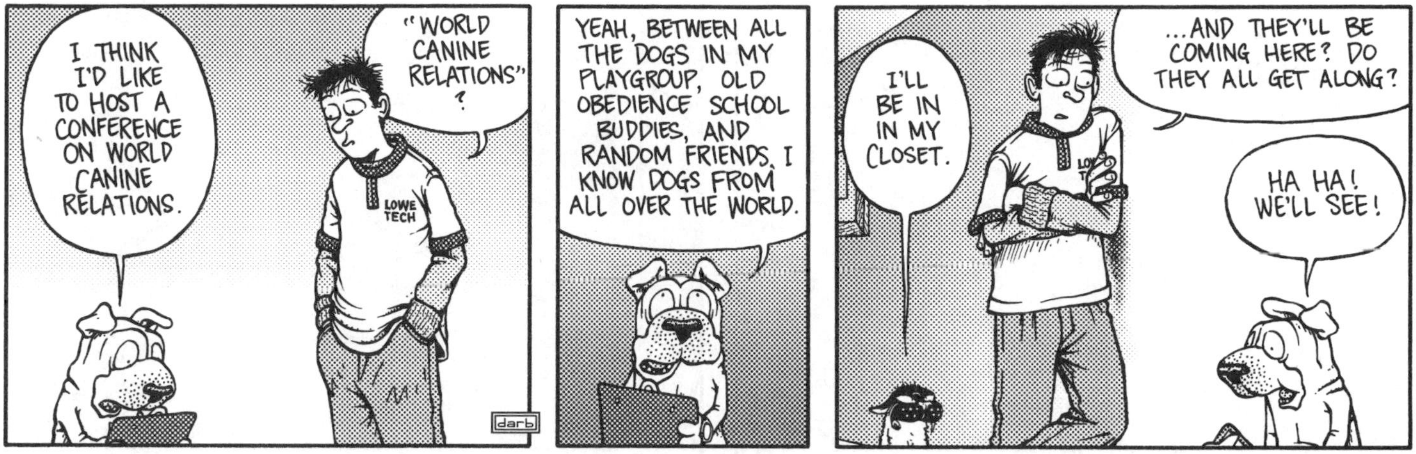
I THINK I'D LIKE TO HOST A CONFERENCE ON WORLD CANINE RELATIONS.
"WORLD CANINE RELATIONS"?
YEAH, BETWEEN ALL THE DOGS IN MY PLAYGROUP, OLD OBEDIENCE SCHOOL BUDDIES, AND RANDOM FRIENDS, I KNOW DOGS FROM ALL OVER THE WORLD.
I'LL BE IN IN MY CLOSET.
...AND THEY'LL BE COMING HERE? DO THEY ALL GET ALONG?
HA HA! WE'LL SEE!
LOWE TECH
darb

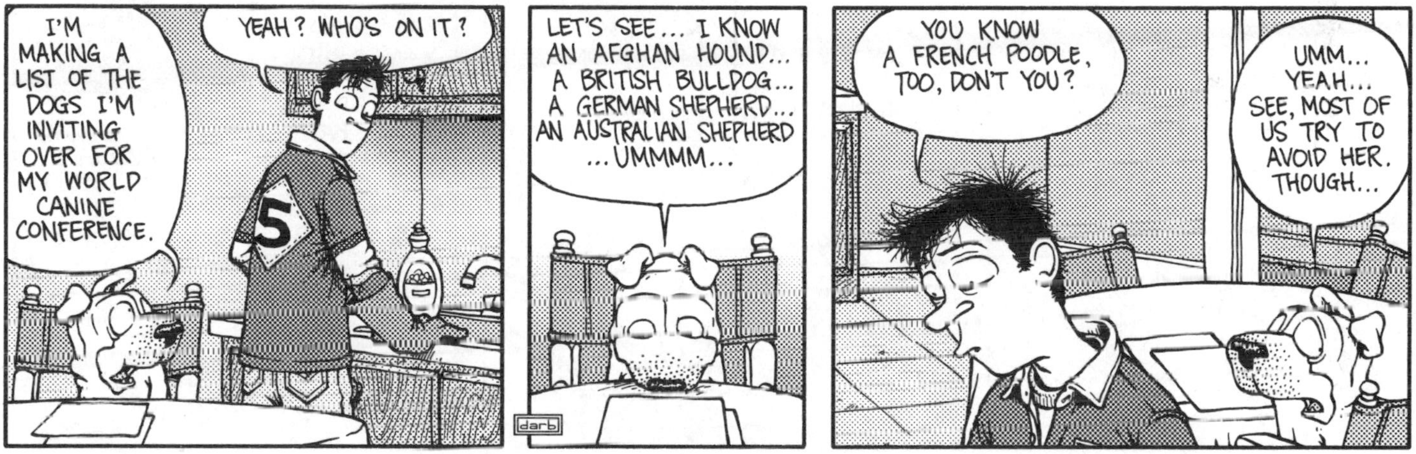
I'M MAKING A LIST OF THE DOGS I'M INVITING OVER FOR MY WORLD CANINE CONFERENCE.
YEAH? WHO'S ON IT?
LET'S SEE... I KNOW AN AFGHAN HOUND... A BRITISH BULLDOG... A GERMAN SHEPHERD... AN AUSTRALIAN SHEPHERD ...UMMMM...
YOU KNOW A FRENCH POODLE, TOO, DON'T YOU?
UMM... YEAH... SEE, MOST OF US TRY TO AVOID HER. THOUGH...
darb

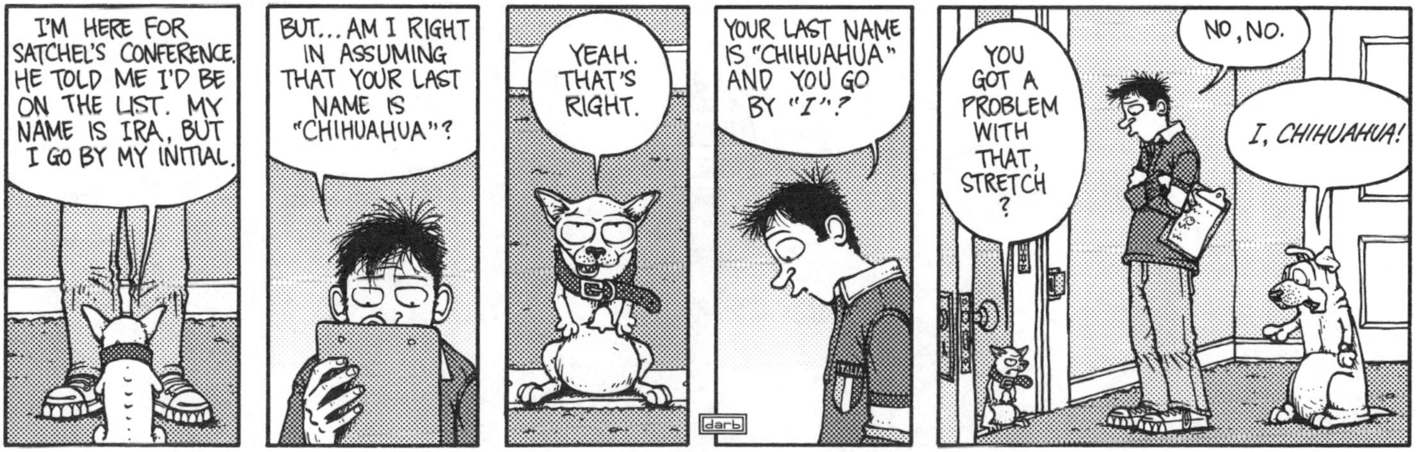
I'M HERE FOR SATCHEL'S CONFERENCE. HE TOLD ME I'D BE ON THE LIST. MY NAME IS IRA, BUT I GO BY MY INITIAL.
BUT... AM I RIGHT IN ASSUMING THAT YOUR LAST NAME IS "CHIHUAHUA"?
YEAH. THAT'S RIGHT.
YOUR LAST NAME IS "CHIHUAHUA" AND YOU GO BY "I"?
YOU GOT A PROBLEM WITH THAT, STRETCH?
NO, NO.
I, CHIHUAHUA!
darb

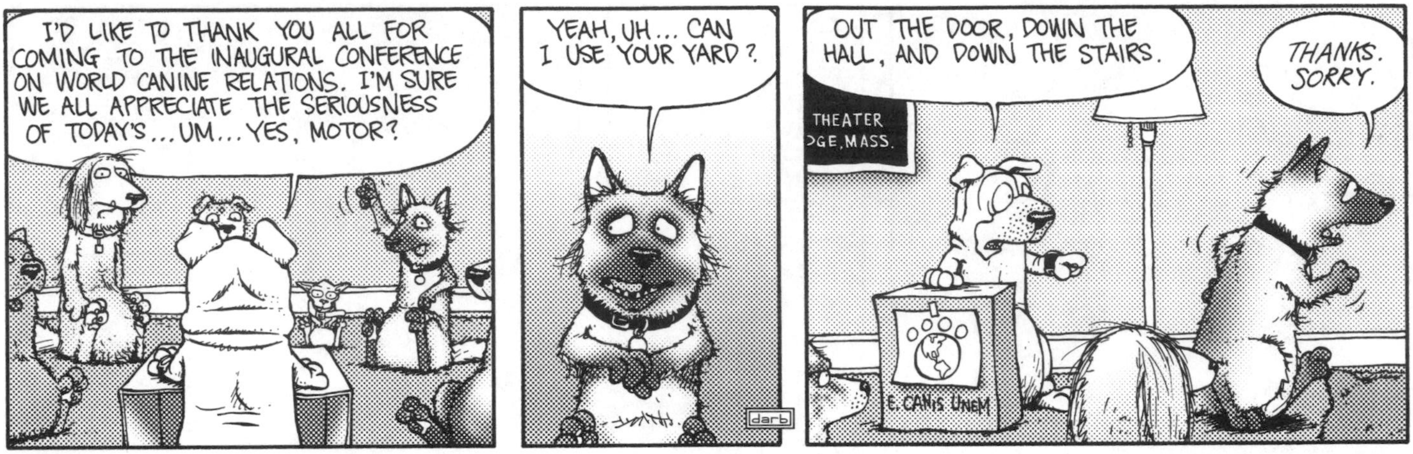
I'D LIKE TO THANK YOU ALL FOR COMING TO THE INAUGURAL CONFERENCE ON WORLD CANINE RELATIONS. I'M SURE WE ALL APPRECIATE THE SERIOUSNESS OF TODAY'S... UM... YES, MOTOR?
YEAH, UH... CAN I USE YOUR YARD?
OUT THE DOOR, DOWN THE HALL, AND DOWN THE STAIRS.
THANKS. SORRY.
THEATER
E. CANIS UNEM
darb

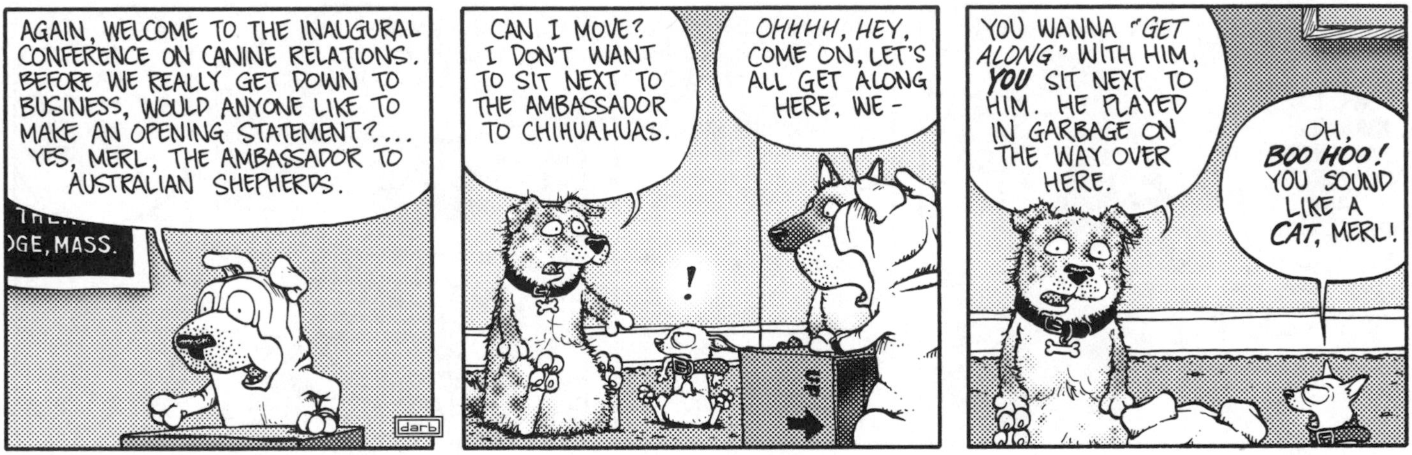
AGAIN, WELCOME TO THE INAUGURAL CONFERENCE ON CANINE RELATIONS. BEFORE WE REALLY GET DOWN TO BUSINESS, WOULD ANYONE LIKE TO MAKE AN OPENING STATEMENT?.... YES, MERL, THE AMBASSADOR TO AUSTRALIAN SHEPHERDS.
darb
CAN I MOVE? I DON'T WANT TO SIT NEXT TO THE AMBASSADOR TO CHIHUAHUAS.
!
OHHHH, HEY, COME ON, LET'S ALL GET ALONG HERE, WE -
YOU WANNA "GET ALONG" WITH HIM, YOU SIT NEXT TO HIM. HE PLAYED IN GARBAGE ON THE WAY OVER HERE.
OH, BOO HOO! YOU SOUND LIKE A CAT, MERL!

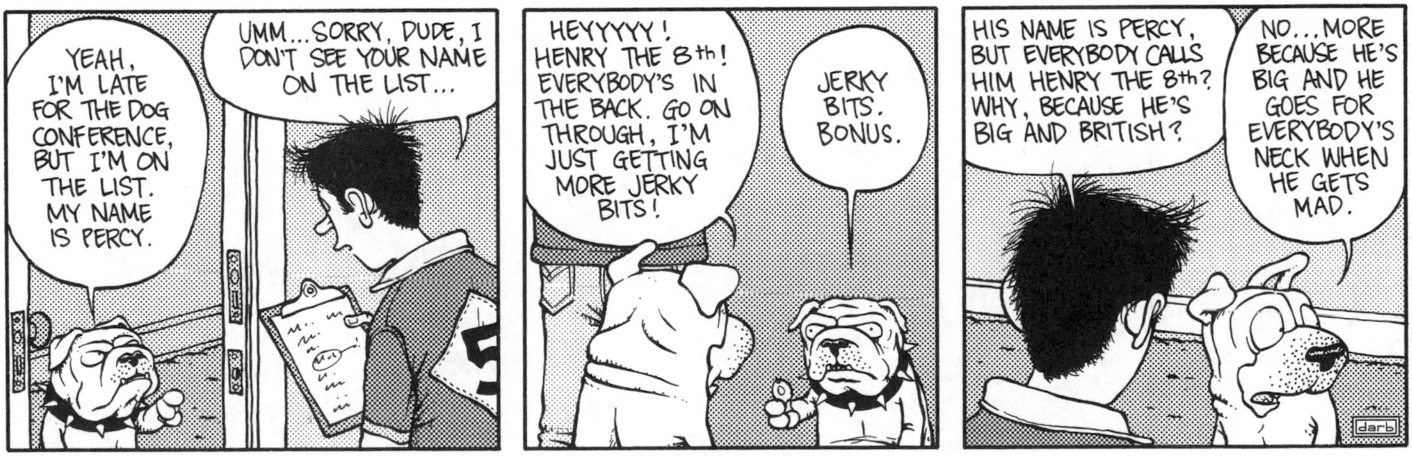
YEAH, I'M LATE FOR THE DOG CONFERENCE, BUT I'M ON THE LIST. MY NAME IS PERCY.
UMM... SORRY, DUDE, I DON'T SEE YOUR NAME ON THE LIST...
HEYYYYY! HENRY THE 8th! EVERYBODY'S IN THE BACK. GO ON THROUGH, I'M JUST GETTING MORE JERKY BITS!
JERKY BITS. BONUS.
HIS NAME IS PERCY, BUT EVERYBODY CALLS HIM HENRY THE 8th? WHY, BECAUSE HE'S BIG AND BRITISH?
NO... MORE BECAUSE HE'S BIG AND HE GOES FOR EVERYBODY'S NECK WHEN HE GETS MAD.
darb

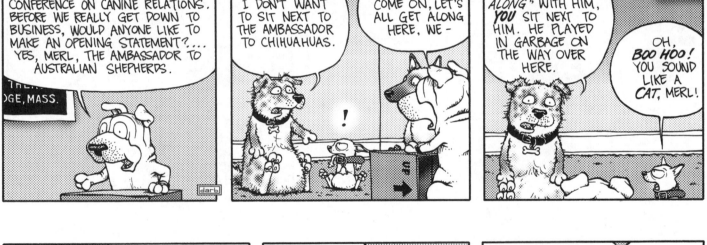

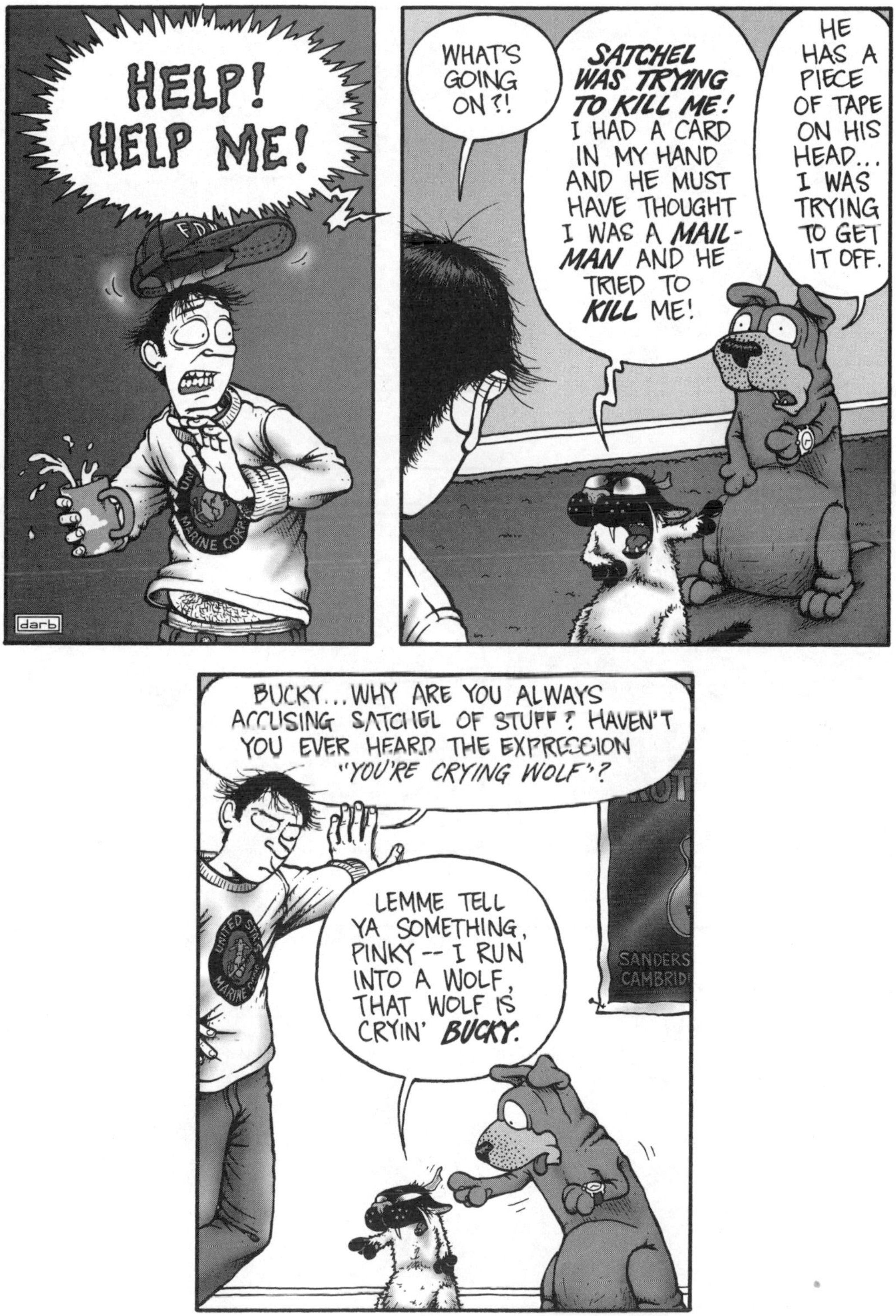
HELP! HELP ME!
darb
WHAT'S GOING ON?!
SATCHEL WAS TRYING TO KILL ME! I HAD A CARD IN MY HAND AND HE MUST HAVE THOUGHT I WAS A MAIL-MAN AND HE TRIED TO KILL ME!
HE HAS A PIECE OF TAPE ON HIS HEAD... I WAS TRYING TO GET IT OFF.
BUCKY...WHY ARE YOU ALWAYS ACCUSING SATCHEL OF STUFF? HAVEN'T YOU EVER HEARD THE EXPRESSION "YOU'RE CRYING WOLF"?
LEMME TELL YA SOMETHING, PINKY -- I RUN INTO A WOLF, THAT WOLF IS CRYIN' BUCKY.

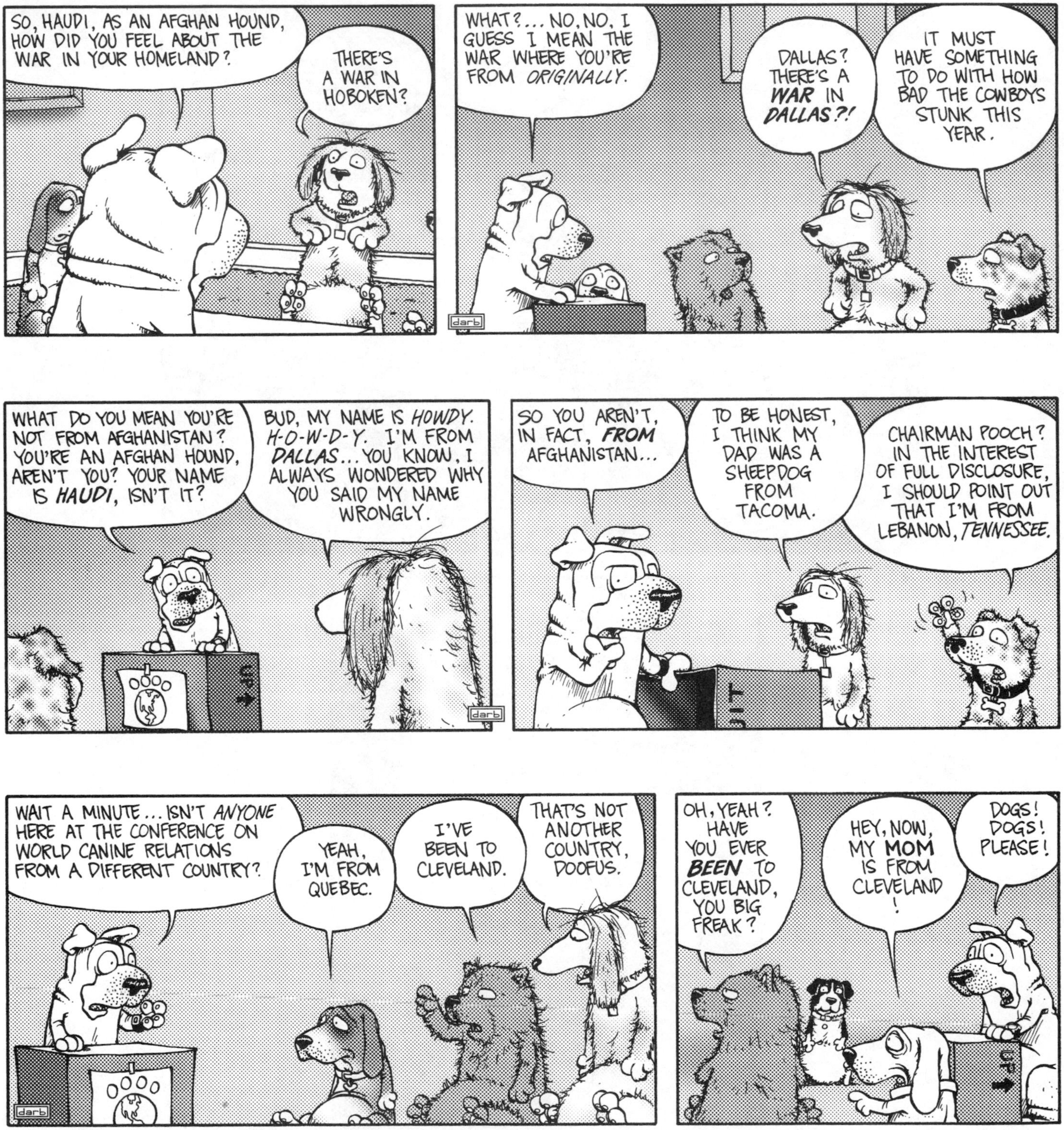
SO, HAUDI, AS AN AFGHAN HOUND, HOW DID YOU FEEL ABOUT THE WAR IN YOUR HOMELAND?
THERE'S A WAR IN HOBOKEN?
WHAT?... NO, NO, I GUESS I MEAN THE WAR WHERE YOU'RE FROM *ORIGINALLY*.
DALLAS? THERE'S A ***WAR*** IN ***DALLAS?!***
IT MUST HAVE SOMETHING TO DO WITH HOW BAD THE COWBOYS STUNK THIS YEAR.
WHAT DO YOU MEAN YOU'RE NOT FROM AFGHANISTAN? YOU'RE AN AFGHAN HOUND, AREN'T YOU? YOUR NAME IS ***HAUDI***, ISN'T IT?
BUD, MY NAME IS *HOWDY*. *H-O-W-D-Y*. I'M FROM ***DALLAS***... YOU KNOW, I ALWAYS WONDERED WHY YOU SAID MY NAME WRONGLY.
SO YOU AREN'T, IN FACT, ***FROM*** AFGHANISTAN...
TO BE HONEST, I THINK MY DAD WAS A SHEEPDOG FROM TACOMA.
CHAIRMAN POOCH? IN THE INTEREST OF FULL DISCLOSURE, I SHOULD POINT OUT THAT I'M FROM LEBANON, *TENNESSEE*.
WAIT A MINUTE... ISN'T *ANYONE* HERE AT THE CONFERENCE ON WORLD CANINE RELATIONS FROM A DIFFERENT COUNTRY?
YEAH, I'M FROM QUEBEC.
I'VE BEEN TO CLEVELAND.
THAT'S NOT ANOTHER COUNTRY, DOOFUS.
OH, YEAH? HAVE YOU EVER ***BEEN*** TO CLEVELAND, YOU BIG FREAK?
HEY, NOW, MY **MOM** IS FROM CLEVELAND!
DOGS! DOGS! PLEASE!

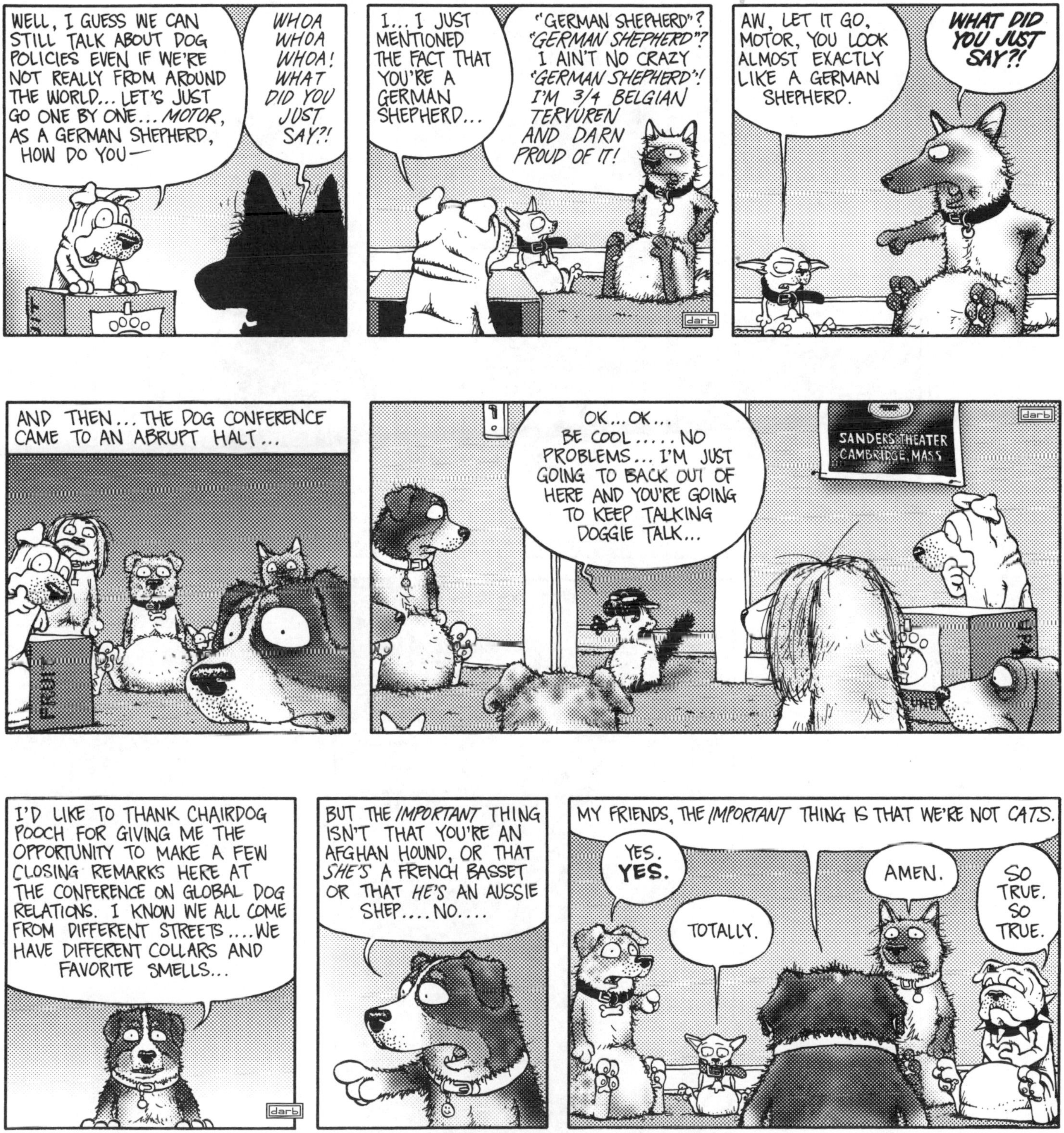

WELL, I GUESS WE CAN STILL TALK ABOUT DOG POLICIES EVEN IF WE'RE NOT REALLY FROM AROUND THE WORLD... LET'S JUST GO ONE BY ONE... *MOTOR*, AS A GERMAN SHEPHERD, HOW DO YOU—
WHOA WHOA WHOA! WHAT DID YOU JUST SAY?!
I... I JUST MENTIONED THE FACT THAT YOU'RE A GERMAN SHEPHERD...
"GERMAN SHEPHERD"? *"GERMAN SHEPHERD"*? I AIN'T NO CRAZY *"GERMAN SHEPHERD"*! *I'M 3/4 BELGIAN TERVUREN AND DARN PROUD OF IT!*
darb
AW, LET IT GO, MOTOR, YOU LOOK ALMOST EXACTLY LIKE A GERMAN SHEPHERD.
WHAT DID YOU JUST SAY?!
AND THEN... THE DOG CONFERENCE CAME TO AN ABRUPT HALT...
FRUIT
OK...OK... BE COOL..... NO PROBLEMS... I'M JUST GOING TO BACK OUT OF HERE AND YOU'RE GOING TO KEEP TALKING DOGGIE TALK...
SANDERS THEATER CAMBRIDGE, MASS
darb
I'D LIKE TO THANK CHAIRDOG POOCH FOR GIVING ME THE OPPORTUNITY TO MAKE A FEW CLOSING REMARKS HERE AT THE CONFERENCE ON GLOBAL DOG RELATIONS. I KNOW WE ALL COME FROM DIFFERENT STREETS....WE HAVE DIFFERENT COLLARS AND FAVORITE SMELLS...
darb
BUT THE *IMPORTANT* THING ISN'T THAT YOU'RE AN AFGHAN HOUND, OR THAT *SHE'S* A FRENCH BASSET OR THAT *HE'S* AN AUSSIE SHEP.... NO....
MY FRIENDS, THE *IMPORTANT* THING IS THAT WE'RE NOT *CATS*.
YES. **YES.**
TOTALLY.
AMEN.
SO TRUE. SO TRUE.

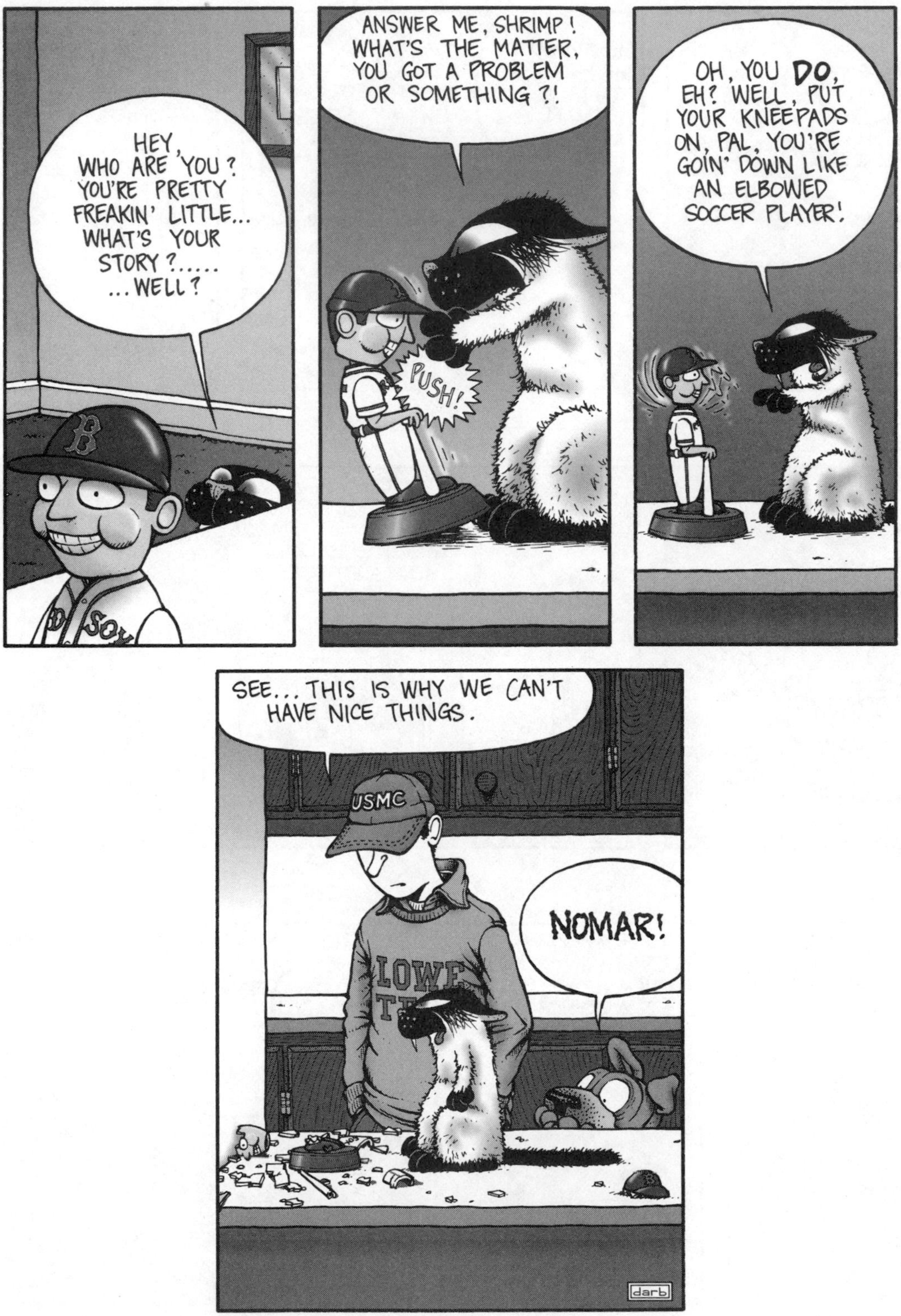
HEY, WHO ARE YOU? YOU'RE PRETTY FREAKIN' LITTLE... WHAT'S YOUR STORY?...... ...WELL?
ANSWER ME, SHRIMP! WHAT'S THE MATTER, YOU GOT A PROBLEM OR SOMETHING?!
PUSH!
OH, YOU DO, EH? WELL, PUT YOUR KNEEPADS ON, PAL, YOU'RE GOIN' DOWN LIKE AN ELBOWED SOCCER PLAYER!
SEE... THIS IS WHY WE CAN'T HAVE NICE THINGS.
NOMAR!
darb

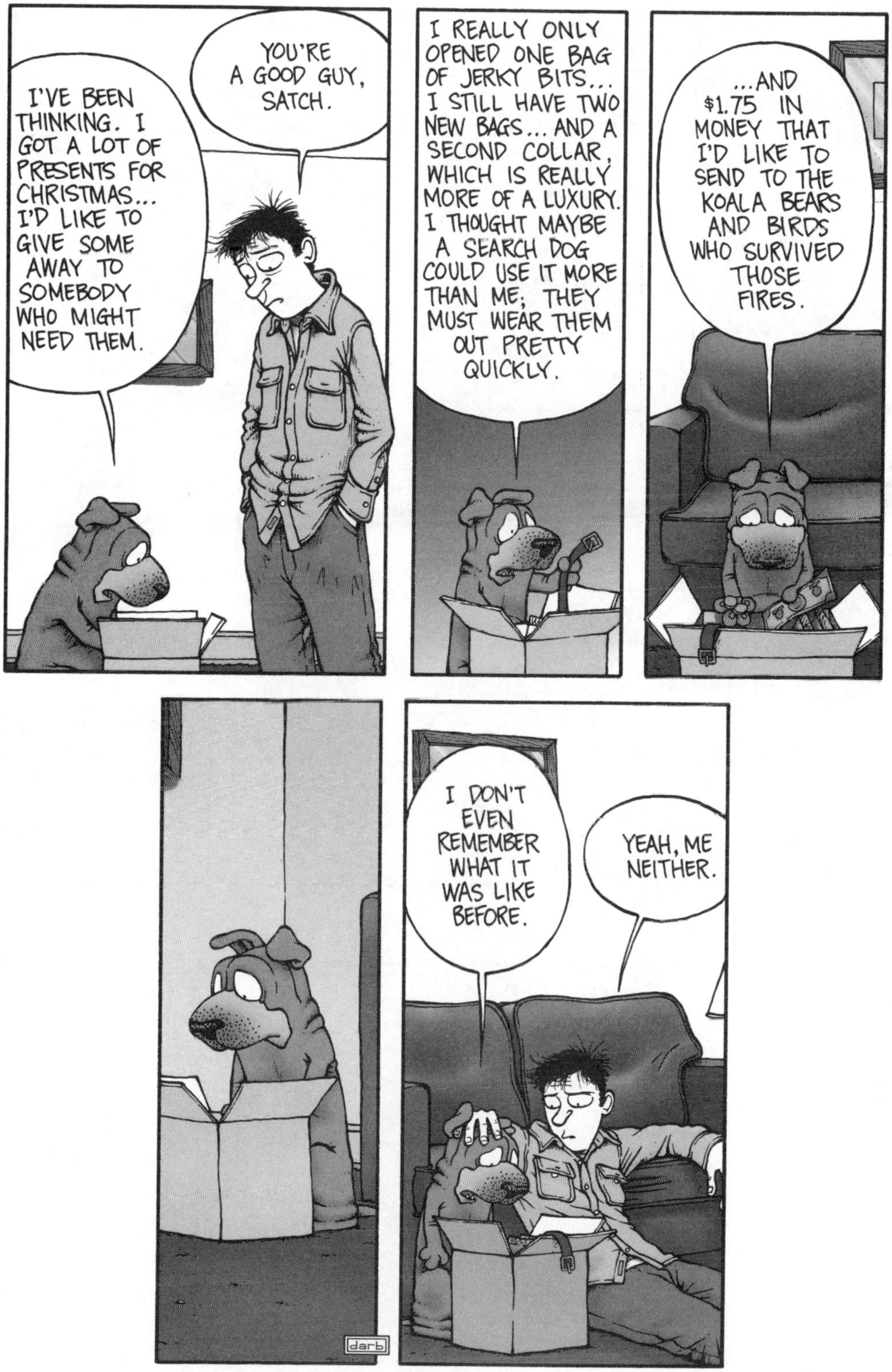
I'VE BEEN THINKING. I GOT A LOT OF PRESENTS FOR CHRISTMAS... I'D LIKE TO GIVE SOME AWAY TO SOMEBODY WHO MIGHT NEED THEM.
YOU'RE A GOOD GUY, SATCH.
I REALLY ONLY OPENED ONE BAG OF JERKY BITS... I STILL HAVE TWO NEW BAGS... AND A SECOND COLLAR, WHICH IS REALLY MORE OF A LUXURY. I THOUGHT MAYBE A SEARCH DOG COULD USE IT MORE THAN ME; THEY MUST WEAR THEM OUT PRETTY QUICKLY.
...AND $1.75 IN MONEY THAT I'D LIKE TO SEND TO THE KOALA BEARS AND BIRDS WHO SURVIVED THOSE FIRES.
darb
I DON'T EVEN REMEMBER WHAT IT WAS LIKE BEFORE.
YEAH, ME NEITHER.

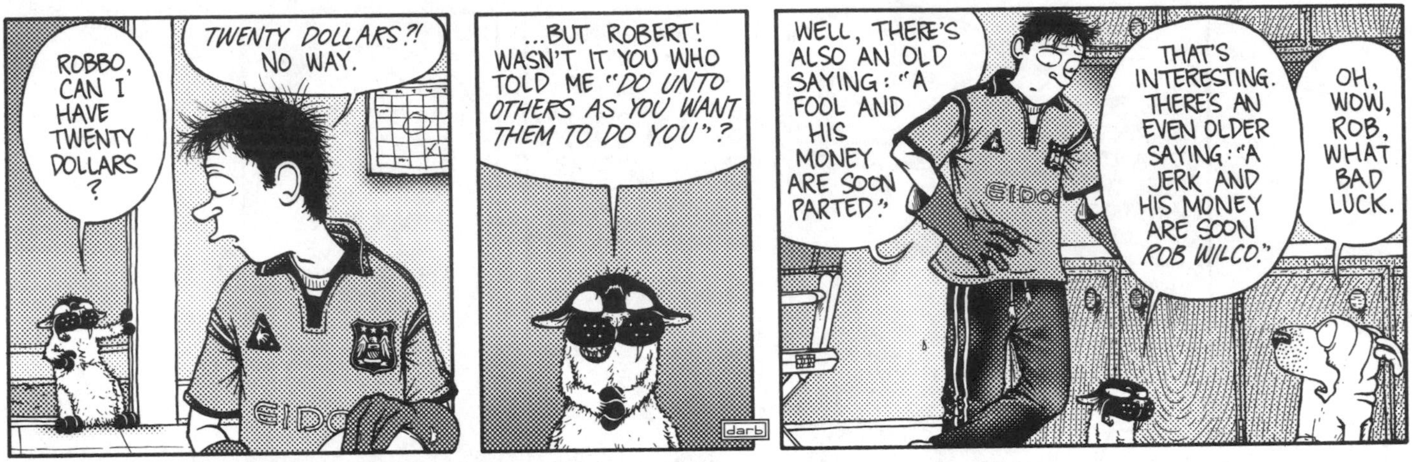
ROBBO, CAN I HAVE TWENTY DOLLARS?
TWENTY DOLLARS?! NO WAY.
...BUT ROBERT! WASN'T IT YOU WHO TOLD ME "DO UNTO OTHERS AS YOU WANT THEM TO DO YOU"?
darb
WELL, THERE'S ALSO AN OLD SAYING: "A FOOL AND HIS MONEY ARE SOON PARTED."
THAT'S INTERESTING. THERE'S AN EVEN OLDER SAYING: "A JERK AND HIS MONEY ARE SOON ROB WILCO."
OH, WOW, ROB, WHAT BAD LUCK.

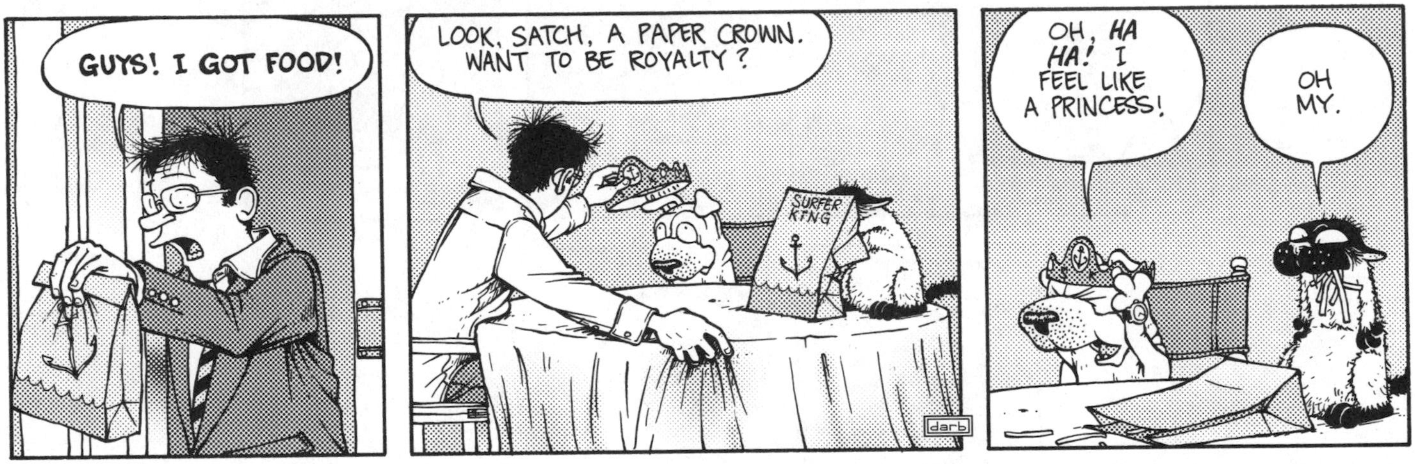
GUYS! I GOT FOOD!
LOOK, SATCH, A PAPER CROWN. WANT TO BE ROYALTY?
SURFER KING
darb
OH, HA HA! I FEEL LIKE A PRINCESS!
OH MY.

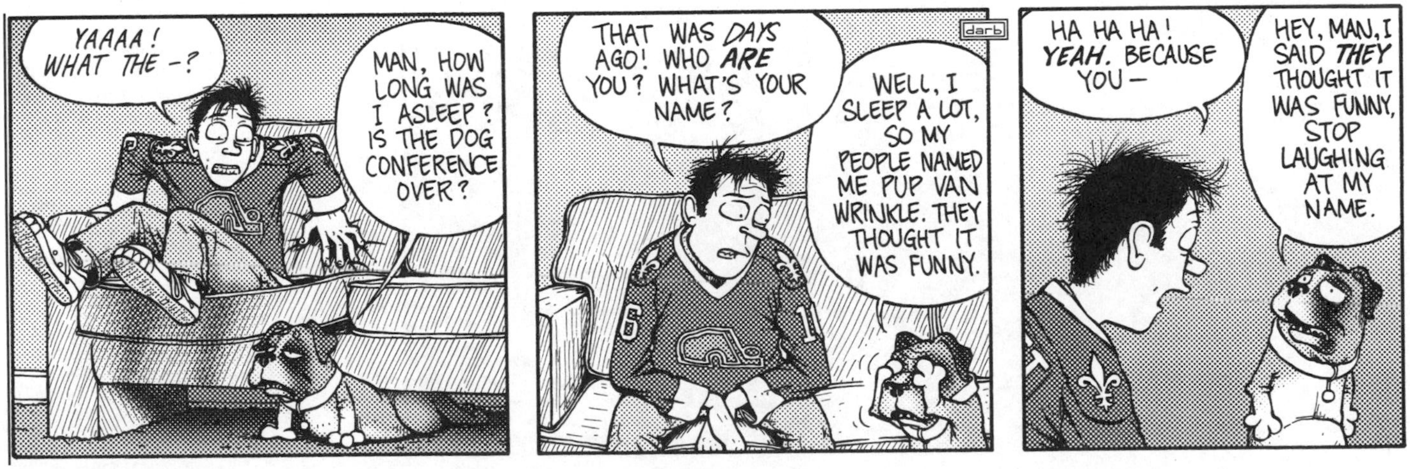
YAAAA! WHAT THE -?
MAN, HOW LONG WAS I ASLEEP? IS THE DOG CONFERENCE OVER?
darb
THAT WAS DAYS AGO! WHO ARE YOU? WHAT'S YOUR NAME?
WELL, I SLEEP A LOT, SO MY PEOPLE NAMED ME PUP VAN WRINKLE. THEY THOUGHT IT WAS FUNNY.
HA HA HA! YEAH. BECAUSE YOU —
HEY, MAN, I SAID THEY THOUGHT IT WAS FUNNY. STOP LAUGHING AT MY NAME.

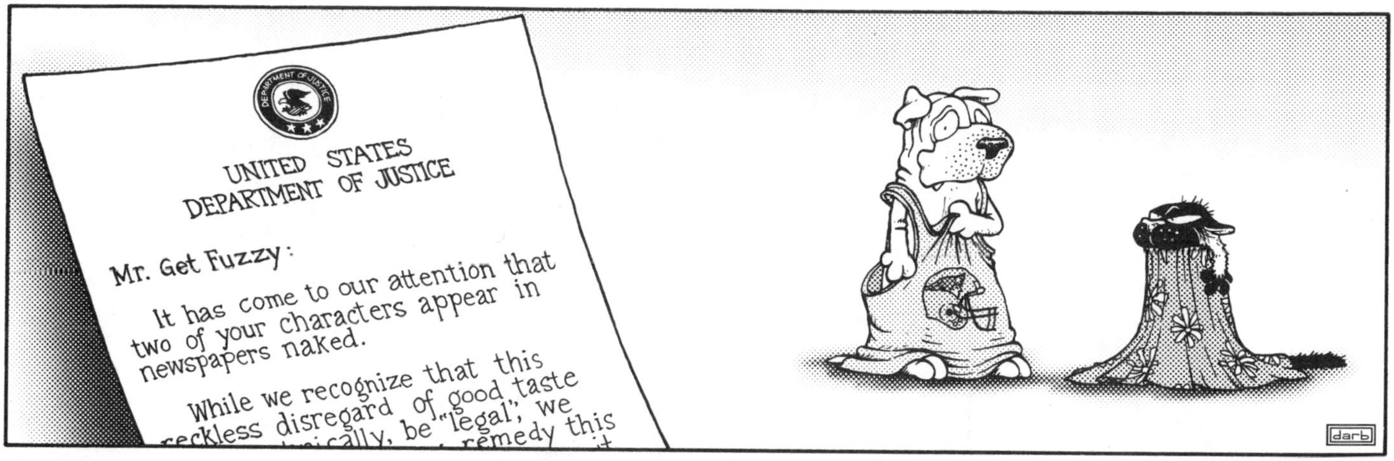
UNITED STATES
DEPARTMENT OF JUSTICE
Mr. Get Fuzzy:
It has come to our attention that two of your characters appear in newspapers naked.
While we recognize that this
reckless disregard of good taste

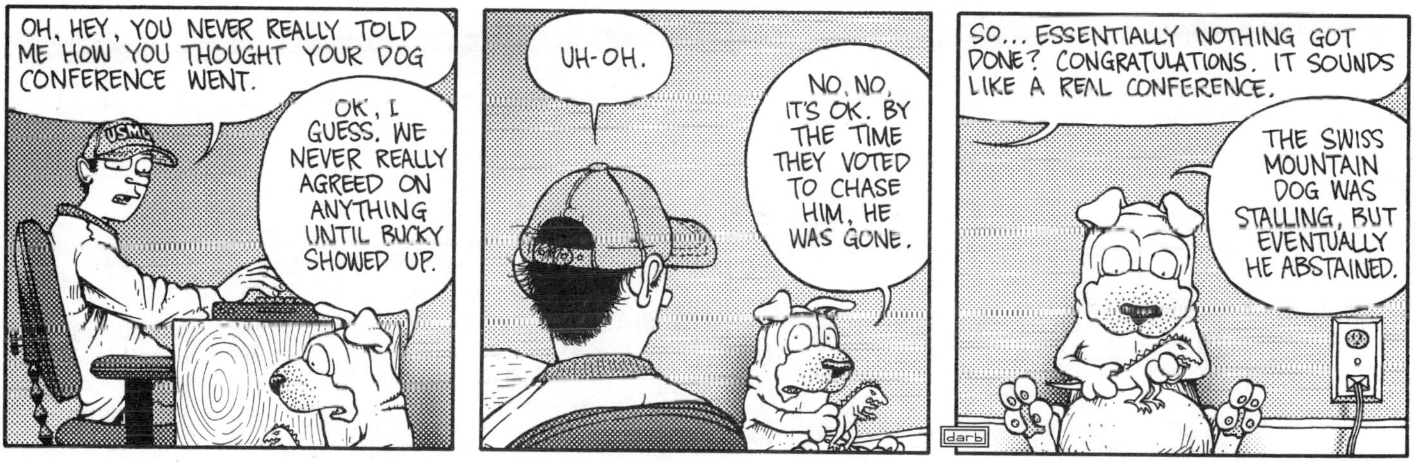
OH, HEY, YOU NEVER REALLY TOLD ME HOW YOU THOUGHT YOUR DOG CONFERENCE WENT.
OK, I GUESS. WE NEVER REALLY AGREED ON ANYTHING UNTIL BUCKY SHOWED UP.
UH-OH.
NO, NO, IT'S OK. BY THE TIME THEY VOTED TO CHASE HIM, HE WAS GONE.
SO... ESSENTIALLY NOTHING GOT DONE? CONGRATULATIONS. IT SOUNDS LIKE A REAL CONFERENCE.
THE SWISS MOUNTAIN DOG WAS STALLING, BUT EVENTUALLY HE ABSTAINED.

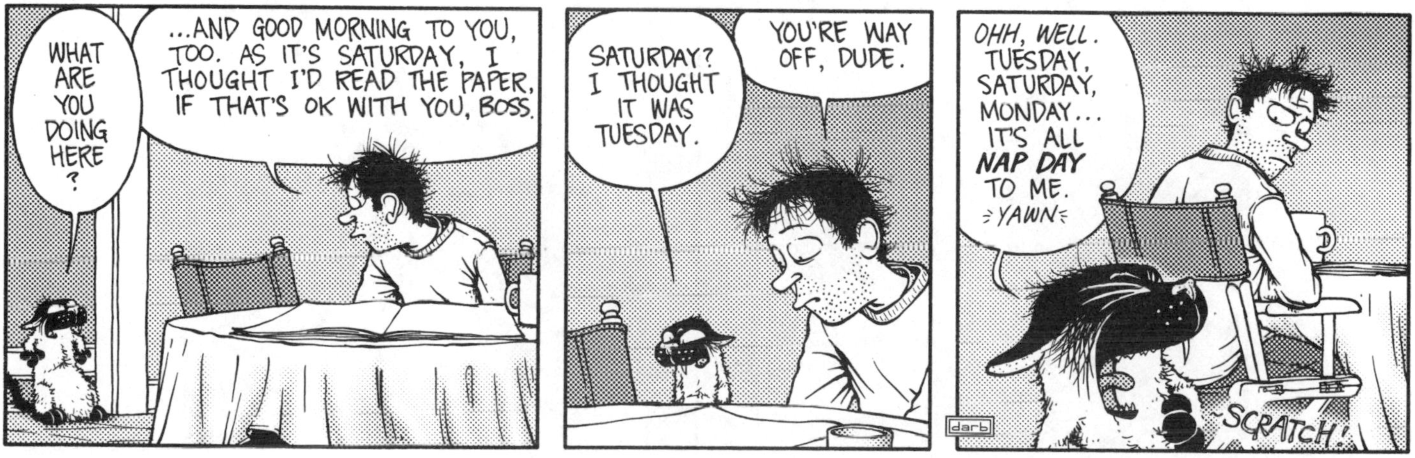
WHAT ARE YOU DOING HERE?
...AND GOOD MORNING TO YOU, TOO. AS IT'S SATURDAY, I THOUGHT I'D READ THE PAPER, IF THAT'S OK WITH YOU, BOSS.
SATURDAY? I THOUGHT IT WAS TUESDAY.
YOU'RE WAY OFF, DUDE.
OHH, WELL. TUESDAY, SATURDAY, MONDAY... IT'S ALL **NAP DAY** TO ME.
YAWN
SCRATCH!

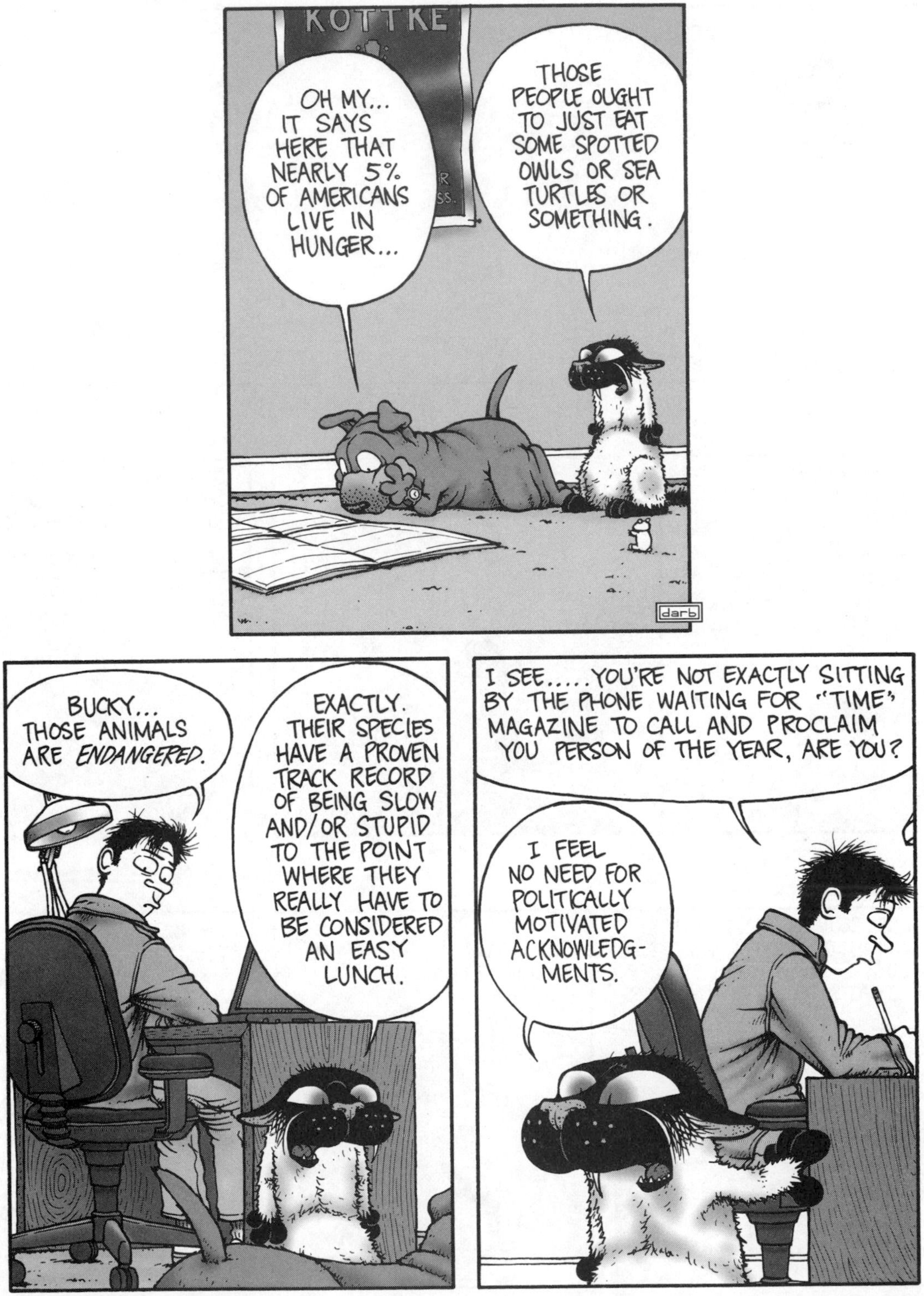
KOTTKE
OH MY... IT SAYS HERE THAT NEARLY 5% OF AMERICANS LIVE IN HUNGER...
THOSE PEOPLE OUGHT TO JUST EAT SOME SPOTTED OWLS OR SEA TURTLES OR SOMETHING.
darb
BUCKY... THOSE ANIMALS ARE *ENDANGERED.*
EXACTLY. THEIR SPECIES HAVE A PROVEN TRACK RECORD OF BEING SLOW AND/OR STUPID TO THE POINT WHERE THEY REALLY HAVE TO BE CONSIDERED AN EASY LUNCH.
I SEE..... YOU'RE NOT EXACTLY SITTING BY THE PHONE WAITING FOR "TIME" MAGAZINE TO CALL AND PROCLAIM YOU PERSON OF THE YEAR, ARE YOU?
I FEEL NO NEED FOR POLITICALLY MOTIVATED ACKNOWLEDG-MENTS.

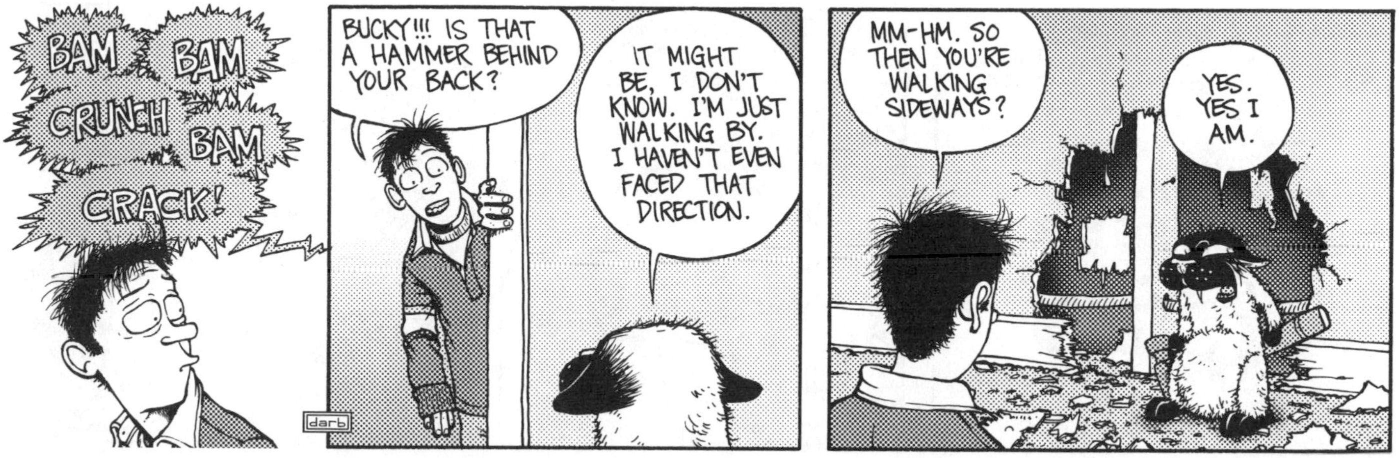
BAM
BAM
CRUNCH
BAM
CRACK!
BUCKY!!! IS THAT A HAMMER BEHIND YOUR BACK?
IT MIGHT BE, I DON'T KNOW. I'M JUST WALKING BY. I HAVEN'T EVEN FACED THAT DIRECTION.
MM-HM. SO THEN YOU'RE WALKING SIDEWAYS?
YES. YES I AM.

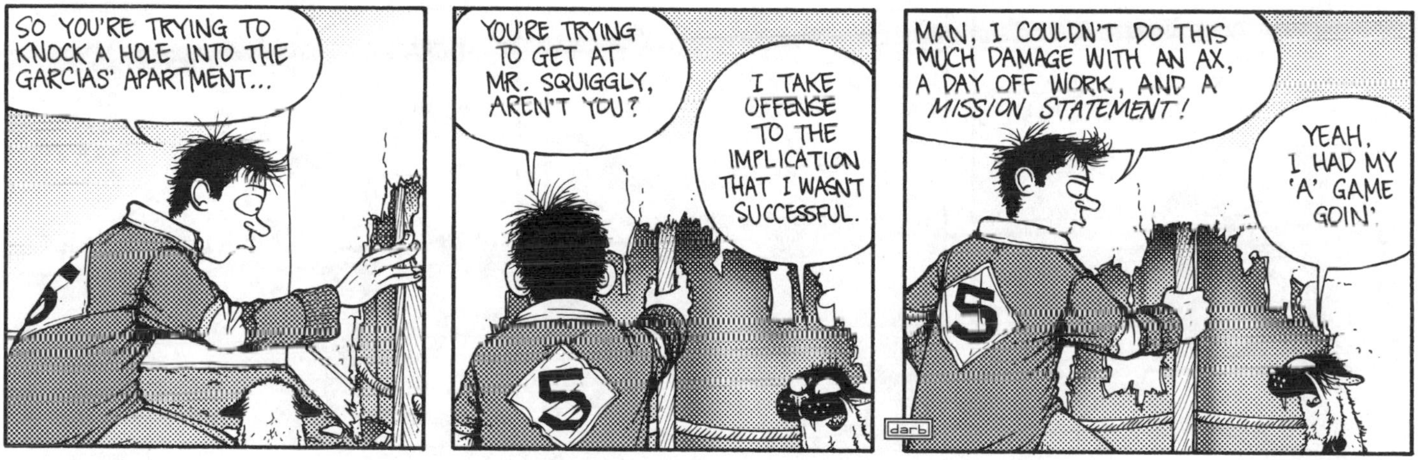
SO YOU'RE TRYING TO KNOCK A HOLE INTO THE GARCIAS' APARTMENT...
YOU'RE TRYING TO GET AT MR. SQUIGGLY, AREN'T YOU?
I TAKE OFFENSE TO THE IMPLICATION THAT I WASN'T SUCCESSFUL.
MAN, I COULDN'T DO THIS MUCH DAMAGE WITH AN AX, A DAY OFF WORK, AND A *MISSION STATEMENT*!
YEAH, I HAD MY 'A' GAME GOIN'.

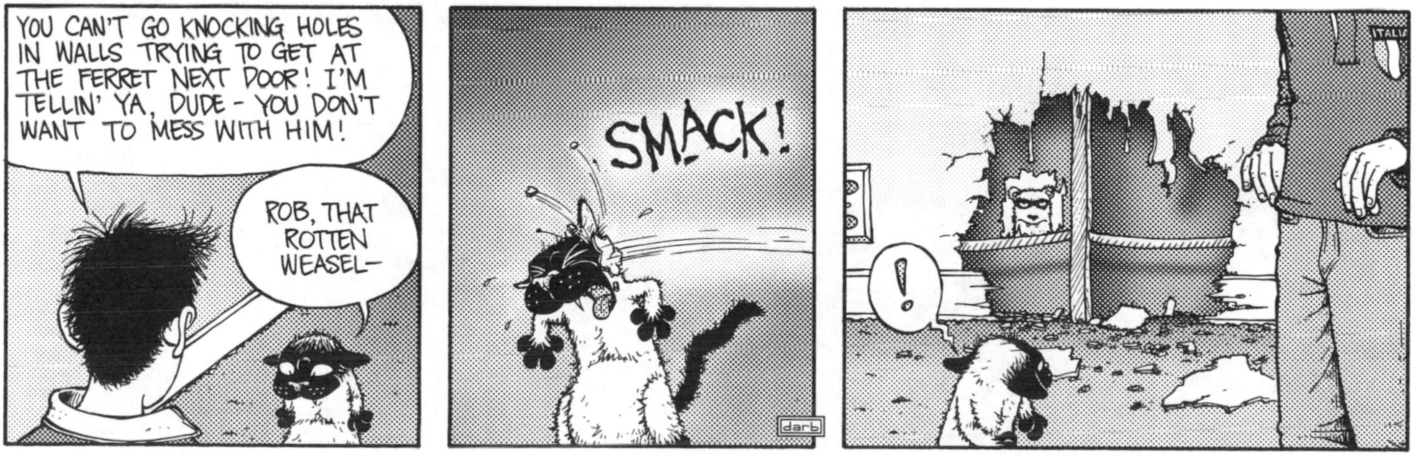
YOU CAN'T GO KNOCKING HOLES IN WALLS TRYING TO GET AT THE FERRET NEXT DOOR! I'M TELLIN' YA, DUDE - YOU DON'T WANT TO MESS WITH HIM!
ROB, THAT ROTTEN WEASEL-
SMACK!
!

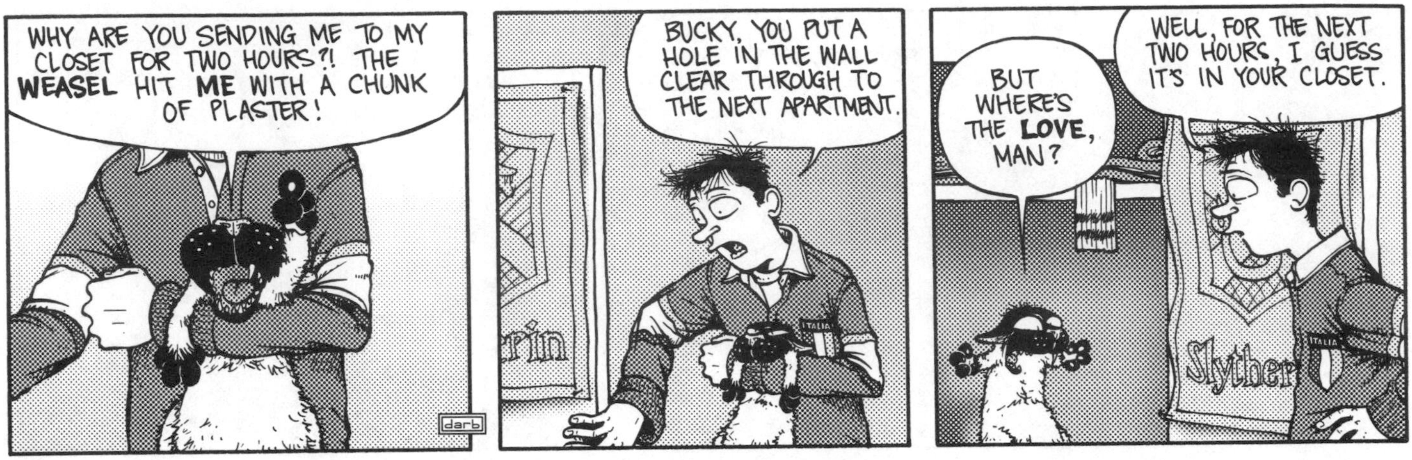
WHY ARE YOU SENDING ME TO MY CLOSET FOR TWO HOURS?! THE **WEASEL** HIT **ME** WITH A CHUNK OF PLASTER!
BUCKY, YOU PUT A HOLE IN THE WALL CLEAR THROUGH TO THE NEXT APARTMENT.
BUT WHERE'S THE **LOVE**, MAN?
WELL, FOR THE NEXT TWO HOURS, I GUESS IT'S IN YOUR CLOSET.

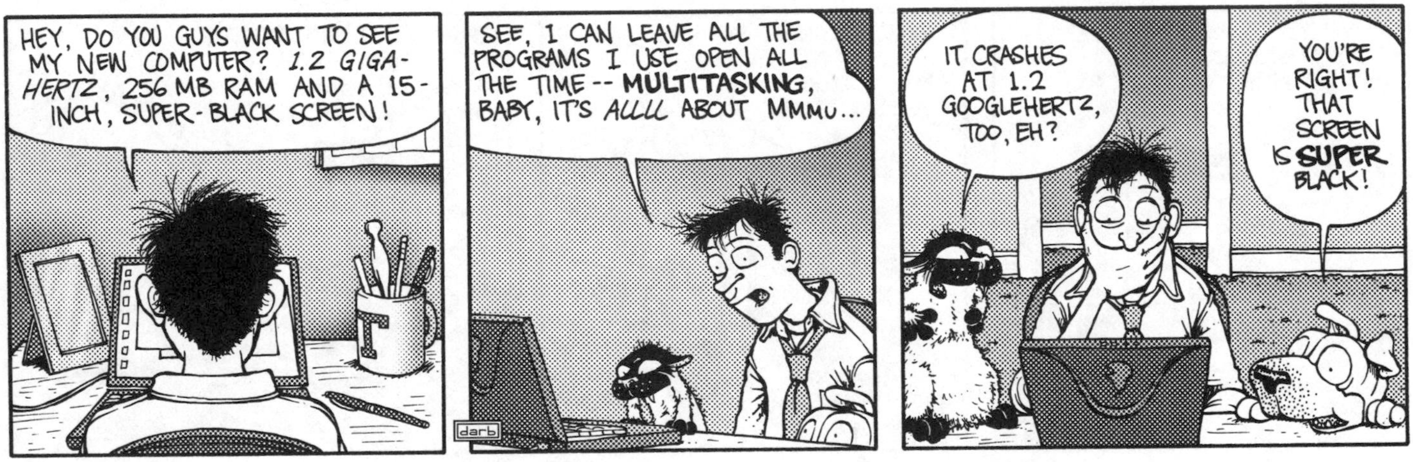
HEY, DO YOU GUYS WANT TO SEE MY NEW COMPUTER? *1.2 GIGA-HERTZ*, 256 MB RAM AND A 15-INCH, SUPER-BLACK SCREEN!
SEE, I CAN LEAVE ALL THE PROGRAMS I USE OPEN ALL THE TIME -- **MULTITASKING**, BABY, IT'S *ALLLL* ABOUT MMMU...
IT CRASHES AT 1.2 GOOGLEHERTZ, TOO, EH?
YOU'RE RIGHT! THAT SCREEN IS **SUPER** BLACK!

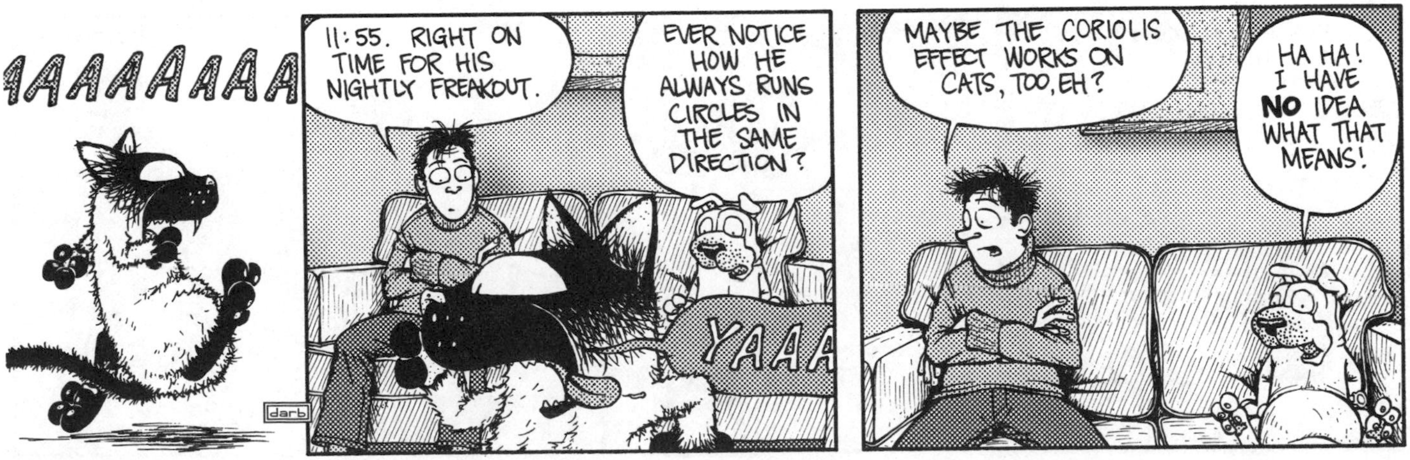
AAAAAAAA
11:55. RIGHT ON TIME FOR HIS NIGHTLY FREAKOUT.
EVER NOTICE HOW HE ALWAYS RUNS CIRCLES IN THE SAME DIRECTION?
YAAA
MAYBE THE CORIOLIS EFFECT WORKS ON CATS, TOO, EH?
HA HA! I HAVE **NO** IDEA WHAT THAT MEANS!

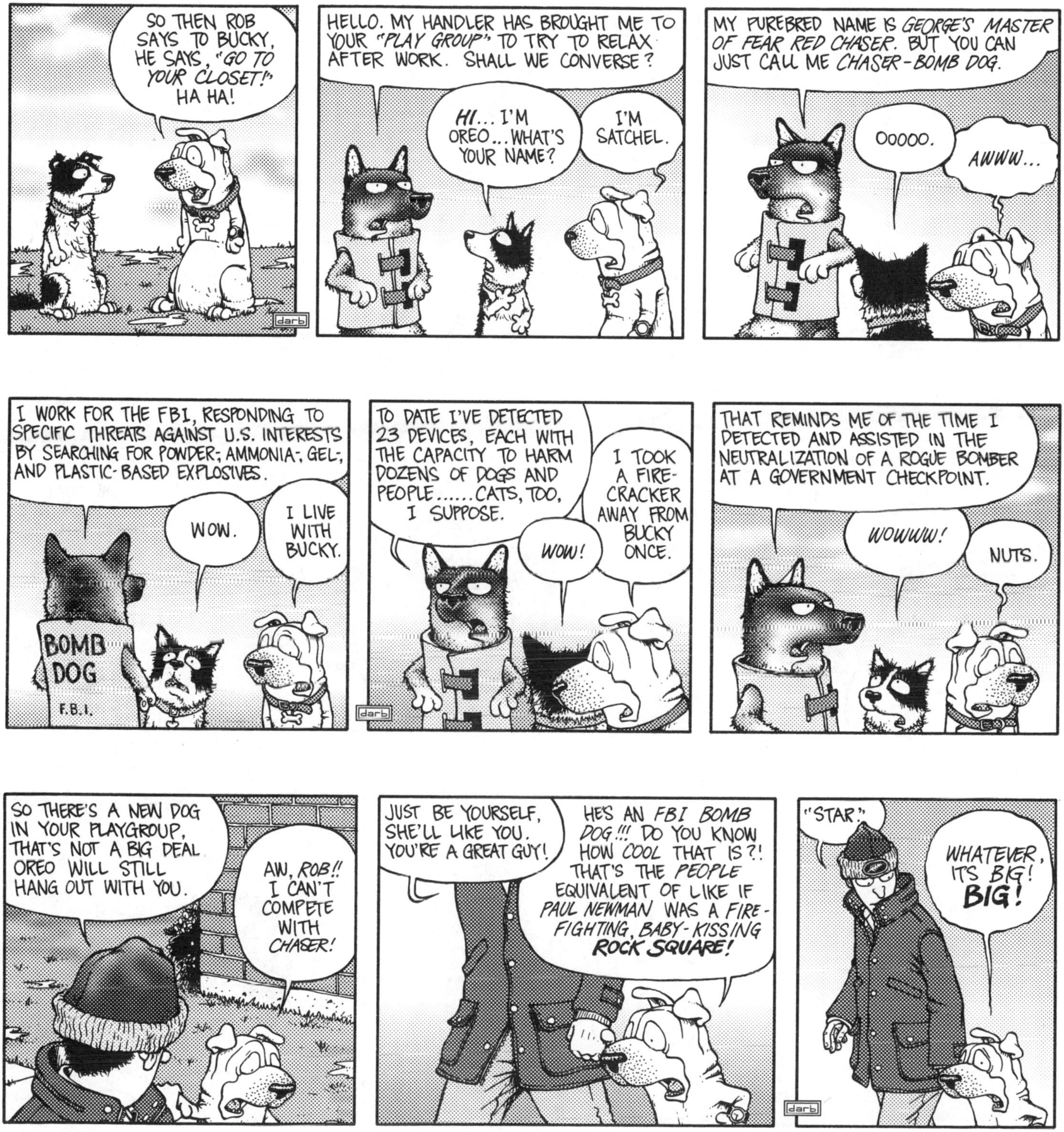
SO THEN ROB SAYS TO BUCKY, HE SAYS, "GO TO YOUR CLOSET!" HA HA!
darb
HELLO. MY HANDLER HAS BROUGHT ME TO YOUR "PLAY GROUP" TO TRY TO RELAX AFTER WORK. SHALL WE CONVERSE?
HI... I'M OREO... WHAT'S YOUR NAME?
I'M SATCHEL.
MY PUREBRED NAME IS GEORGE'S MASTER OF FEAR RED CHASER. BUT YOU CAN JUST CALL ME CHASER-BOMB DOG.
OOOOO.
AWWW...
I WORK FOR THE FBI, RESPONDING TO SPECIFIC THREATS AGAINST U.S. INTERESTS BY SEARCHING FOR POWDER-, AMMONIA-, GEL-, AND PLASTIC-BASED EXPLOSIVES.
WOW.
I LIVE WITH BUCKY.
BOMB DOG
F.B.I.
TO DATE I'VE DETECTED 23 DEVICES, EACH WITH THE CAPACITY TO HARM DOZENS OF DOGS AND PEOPLE...... CATS, TOO, I SUPPOSE.
WOW!
I TOOK A FIRE-CRACKER AWAY FROM BUCKY ONCE.
darb
THAT REMINDS ME OF THE TIME I DETECTED AND ASSISTED IN THE NEUTRALIZATION OF A ROGUE BOMBER AT A GOVERNMENT CHECKPOINT.
WOWWW!
NUTS.
SO THERE'S A NEW DOG IN YOUR PLAYGROUP, THAT'S NOT A BIG DEAL OREO WILL STILL HANG OUT WITH YOU.
AW, ROB!! I CAN'T COMPETE WITH CHASER!
JUST BE YOURSELF, SHE'LL LIKE YOU. YOU'RE A GREAT GUY!
HE'S AN FBI BOMB DOG!!! DO YOU KNOW HOW COOL THAT IS?! THAT'S THE PEOPLE EQUIVALENT OF LIKE IF PAUL NEWMAN WAS A FIRE-FIGHTING, BABY-KISSING ROCK STAR!
"SQUARE."
WHATEVER, IT'S BIG! BIG!
darb

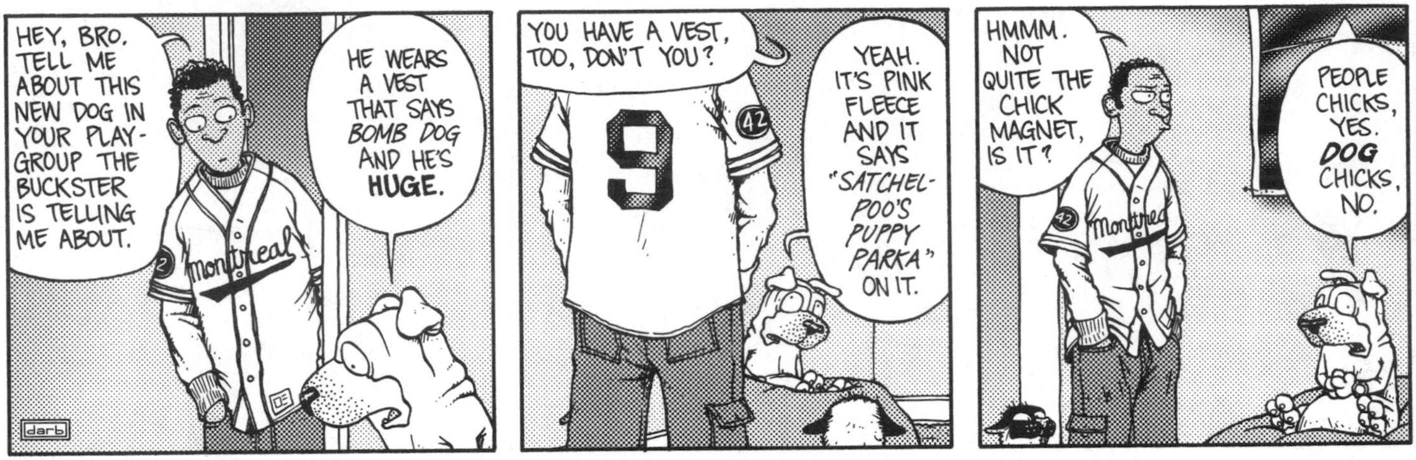
HEY, BRO. TELL ME ABOUT THIS NEW DOG IN YOUR PLAY-GROUP THE BUCKSTER IS TELLING ME ABOUT.
HE WEARS A VEST THAT SAYS *BOMB DOG* AND HE'S **HUGE**.
YOU HAVE A VEST, TOO, DON'T YOU?
YEAH. IT'S PINK FLEECE AND IT SAYS *"SATCHEL-POO'S PUPPY PARKA"* ON IT.
HMMM. NOT QUITE THE CHICK MAGNET, IS IT?
PEOPLE CHICKS, YES. ***DOG*** CHICKS, NO.

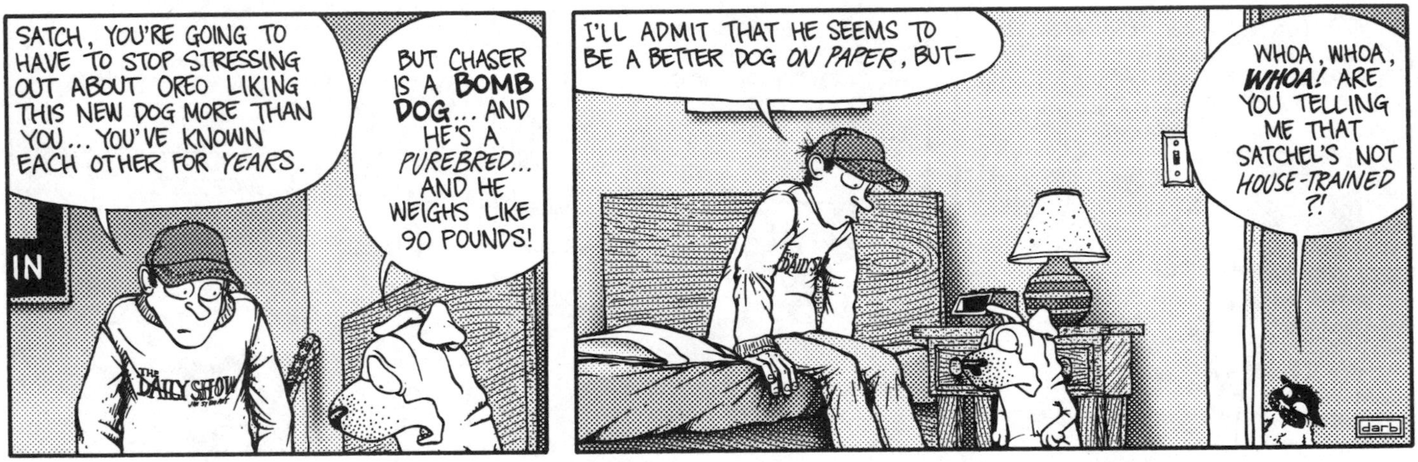
SATCH, YOU'RE GOING TO HAVE TO STOP STRESSING OUT ABOUT OREO LIKING THIS NEW DOG MORE THAN YOU... YOU'VE KNOWN EACH OTHER FOR *YEARS*.
BUT CHASER IS A **BOMB DOG**... AND HE'S A *PUREBRED*... AND HE WEIGHS LIKE 90 POUNDS!
I'LL ADMIT THAT HE SEEMS TO BE A BETTER DOG *ON PAPER*, BUT—
WHOA, WHOA, ***WHOA!*** ARE YOU TELLING ME THAT SATCHEL'S NOT *HOUSE-TRAINED* ?!

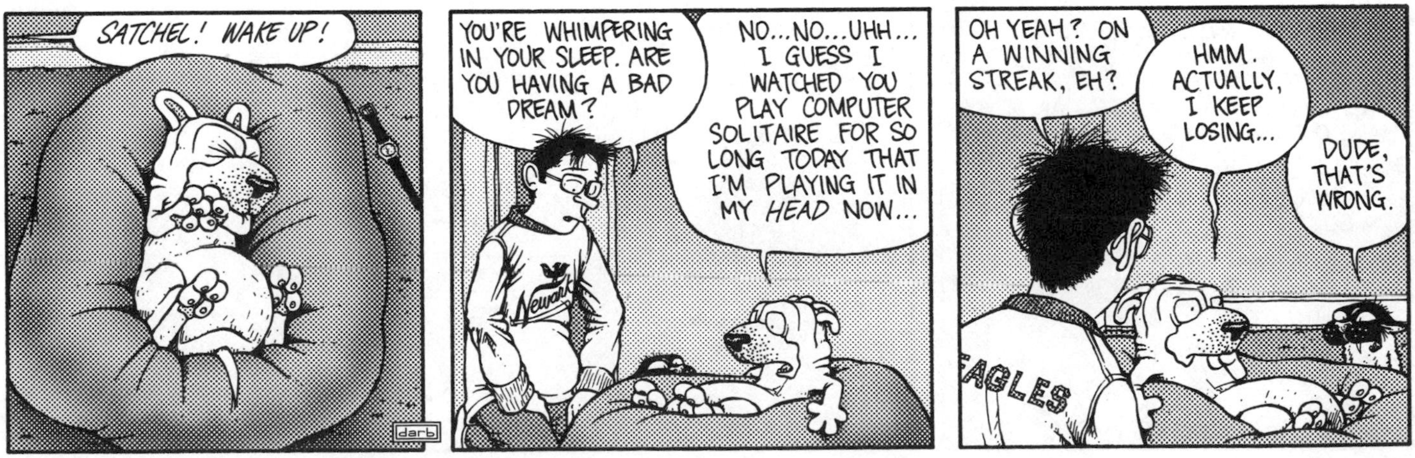
SATCHEL! WAKE UP!
YOU'RE WHIMPERING IN YOUR SLEEP. ARE YOU HAVING A BAD DREAM?
NO...NO...UHH... I GUESS I WATCHED YOU PLAY COMPUTER SOLITAIRE FOR SO LONG TODAY THAT I'M PLAYING IT IN MY *HEAD* NOW...
OH YEAH? ON A WINNING STREAK, EH?
HMM. ACTUALLY, I KEEP LOSING...
DUDE, THAT'S WRONG.

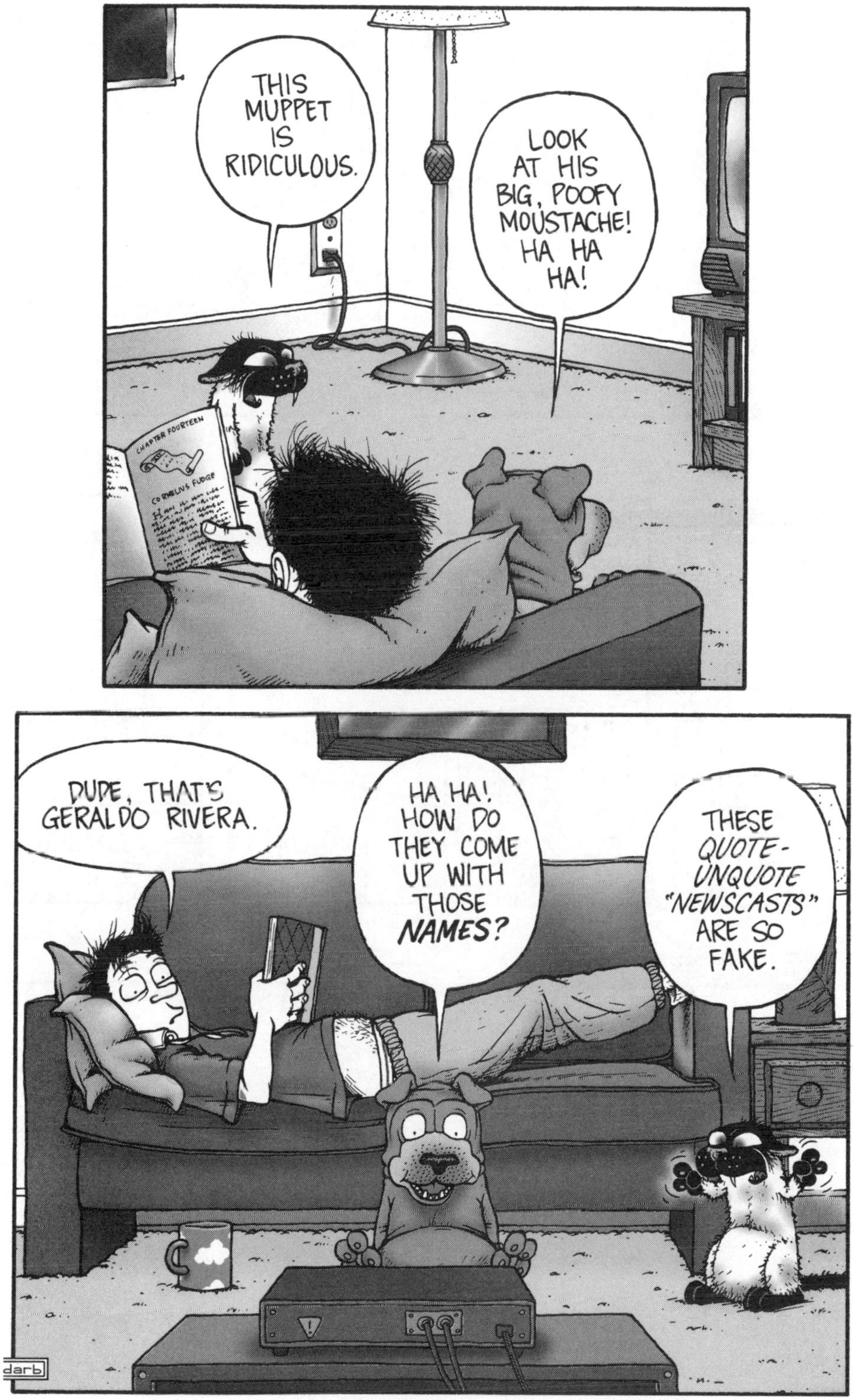
THIS MUPPET IS RIDICULOUS.
LOOK AT HIS BIG, POOFY MOUSTACHE! HA HA HA!
CHAPTER FOURTEEN
CORNELIUS FUDGE
DUDE, THAT'S GERALDO RIVERA.
HA HA! HOW DO THEY COME UP WITH THOSE *NAMES?*
THESE *QUOTE-UNQUOTE "NEWSCASTS"* ARE SO FAKE.
darb

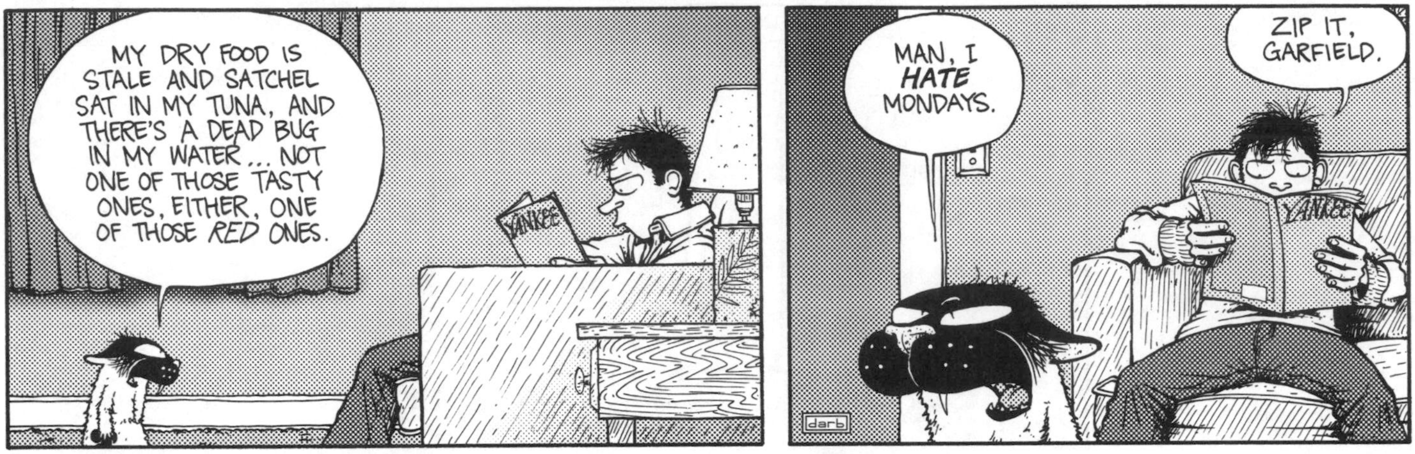
MY DRY FOOD IS STALE AND SATCHEL SAT IN MY TUNA, AND THERE'S A DEAD BUG IN MY WATER... NOT ONE OF THOSE TASTY ONES, EITHER, ONE OF THOSE *RED* ONES.
YANKEE
MAN, I **HATE** MONDAYS.
ZIP IT, GARFIELD.
YANKEE
darb

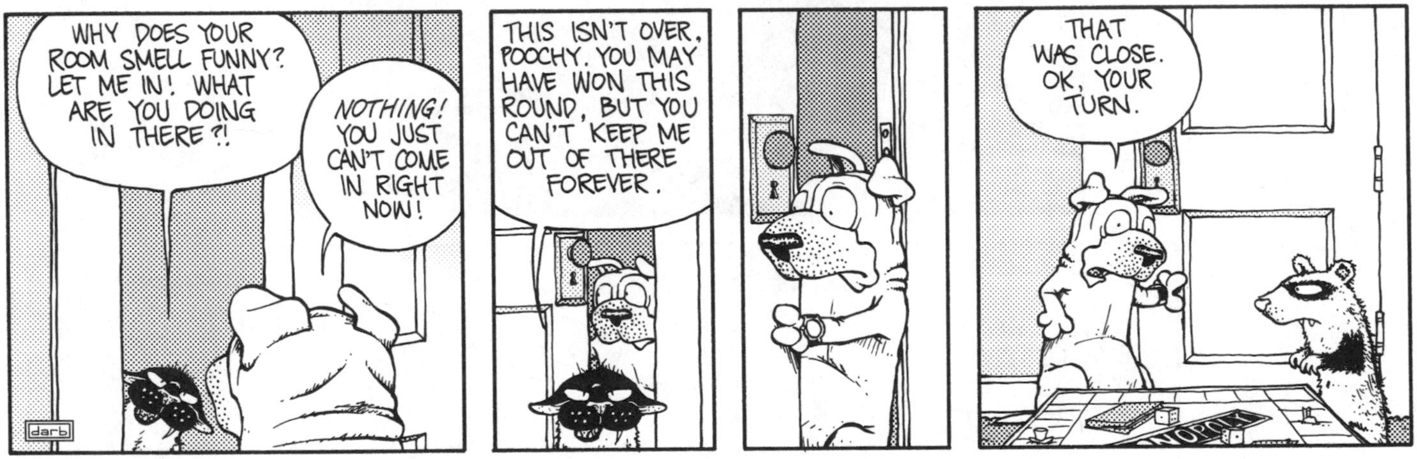
WHY DOES YOUR ROOM SMELL FUNNY? LET ME IN! WHAT ARE YOU DOING IN THERE?!
NOTHING! YOU JUST CAN'T COME IN RIGHT NOW!
darb
THIS ISN'T OVER, POOCHY. YOU MAY HAVE WON THIS ROUND, BUT YOU CAN'T KEEP ME OUT OF THERE FOREVER.
THAT WAS CLOSE. OK, YOUR TURN.

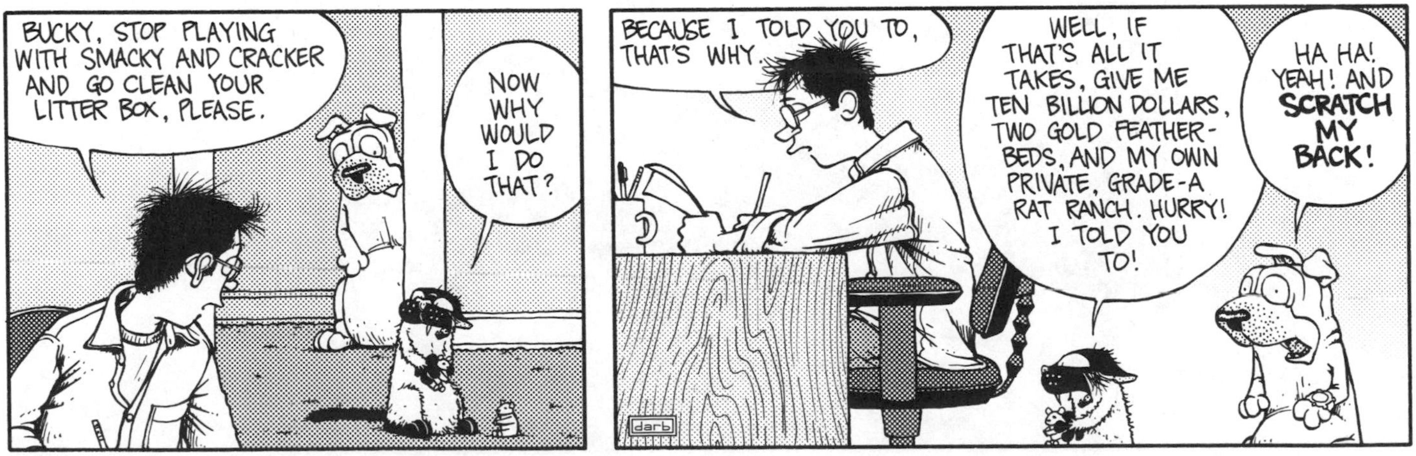
BUCKY, STOP PLAYING WITH SMACKY AND CRACKER AND GO CLEAN YOUR LITTER BOX, PLEASE.
NOW WHY WOULD I DO THAT?
BECAUSE I TOLD YOU TO, THAT'S WHY.
WELL, IF THAT'S ALL IT TAKES, GIVE ME TEN BILLION DOLLARS, TWO GOLD FEATHER-BEDS, AND MY OWN PRIVATE, GRADE-A RAT RANCH. HURRY! I TOLD YOU TO!
HA HA! YEAH! AND **SCRATCH MY BACK!**
darb

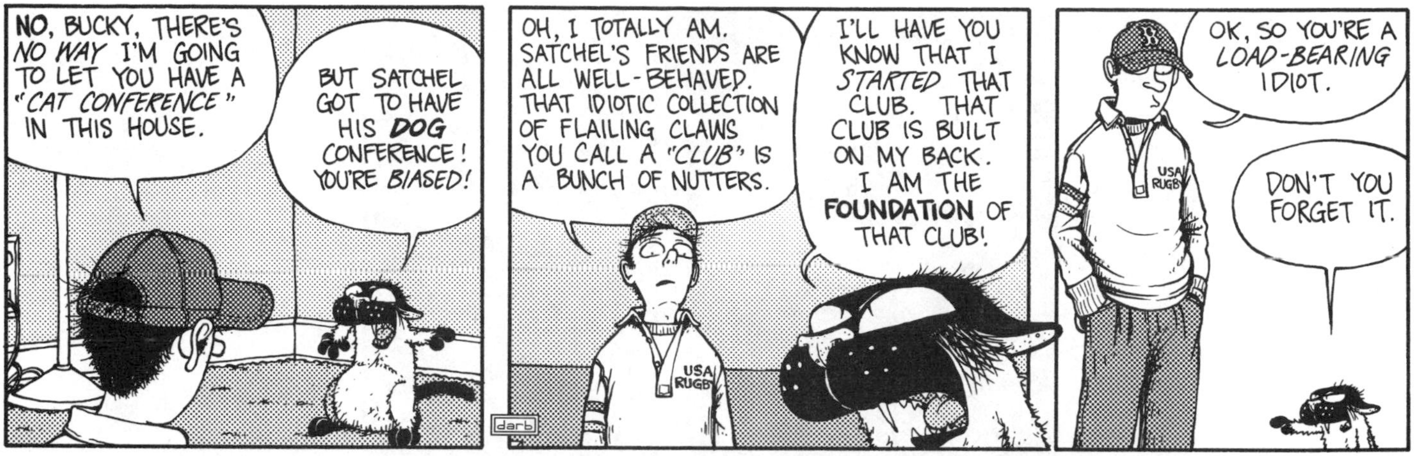
NO, BUCKY, THERE'S NO WAY I'M GOING TO LET YOU HAVE A "CAT CONFERENCE" IN THIS HOUSE.
BUT SATCHEL GOT TO HAVE HIS DOG CONFERENCE! YOU'RE BIASED!
OH, I TOTALLY AM. SATCHEL'S FRIENDS ARE ALL WELL-BEHAVED. THAT IDIOTIC COLLECTION OF FLAILING CLAWS YOU CALL A "CLUB" IS A BUNCH OF NUTTERS.
I'LL HAVE YOU KNOW THAT I STARTED THAT CLUB. THAT CLUB IS BUILT ON MY BACK. I AM THE FOUNDATION OF THAT CLUB!
USA RUGBY
OK, SO YOU'RE A LOAD-BEARING IDIOT.
DON'T YOU FORGET IT.

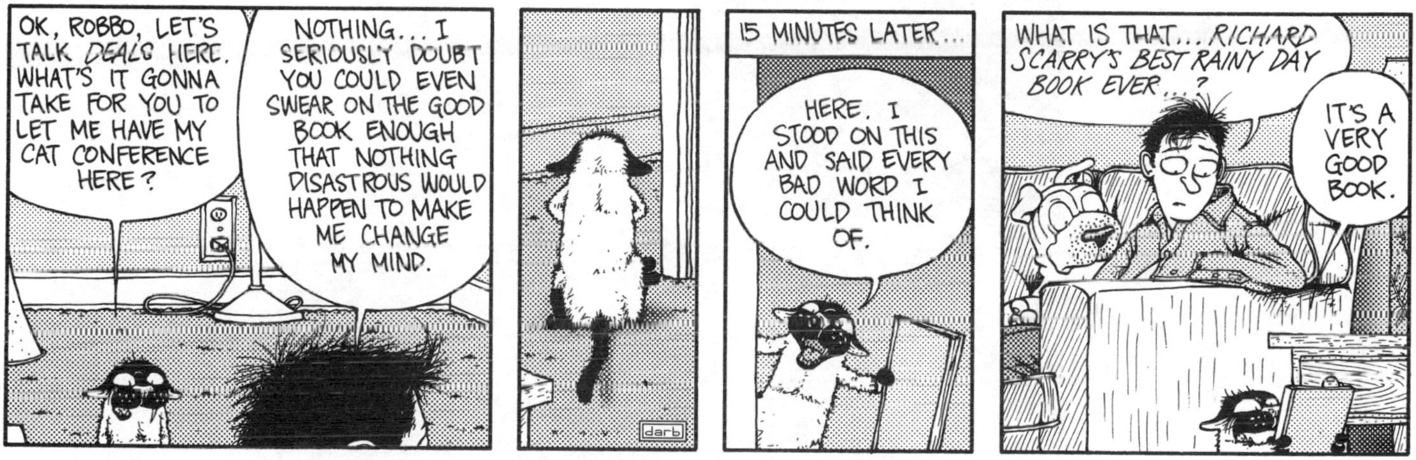
OK, ROBBO, LET'S TALK DEALS HERE. WHAT'S IT GONNA TAKE FOR YOU TO LET ME HAVE MY CAT CONFERENCE HERE?
NOTHING... I SERIOUSLY DOUBT YOU COULD EVEN SWEAR ON THE GOOD BOOK ENOUGH THAT NOTHING DISASTROUS WOULD HAPPEN TO MAKE ME CHANGE MY MIND.
15 MINUTES LATER...
HERE. I STOOD ON THIS AND SAID EVERY BAD WORD I COULD THINK OF.
WHAT IS THAT... RICHARD SCARRY'S BEST RAINY DAY BOOK EVER...?
IT'S A VERY GOOD BOOK.

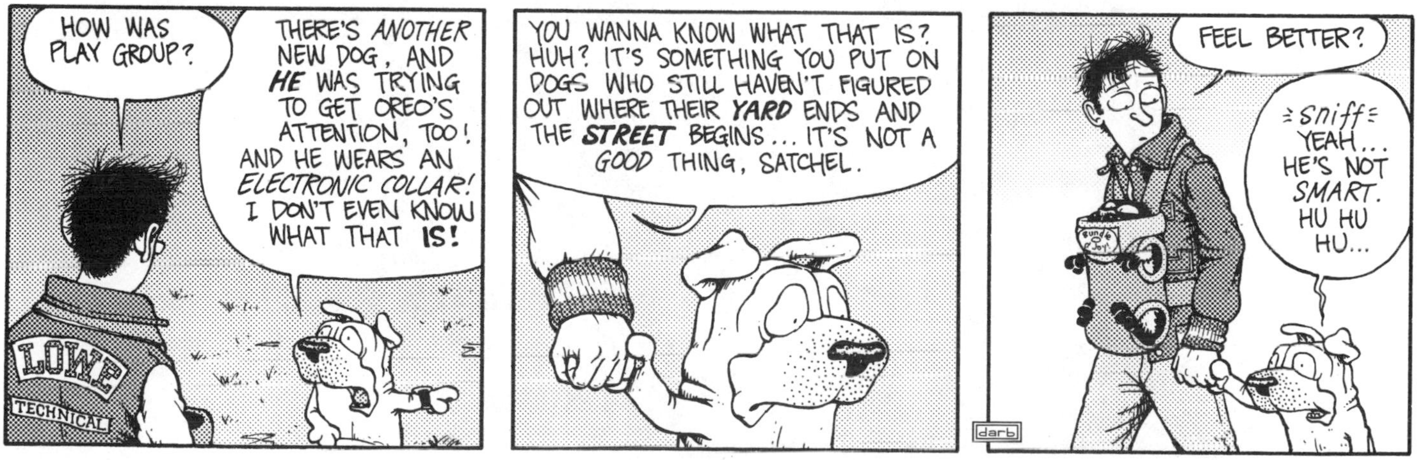
HOW WAS PLAY GROUP?
THERE'S ANOTHER NEW DOG, AND HE WAS TRYING TO GET OREO'S ATTENTION, TOO! AND HE WEARS AN ELECTRONIC COLLAR! I DON'T EVEN KNOW WHAT THAT IS!
LOWE TECHNICAL
YOU WANNA KNOW WHAT THAT IS? HUH? IT'S SOMETHING YOU PUT ON DOGS WHO STILL HAVEN'T FIGURED OUT WHERE THEIR YARD ENDS AND THE STREET BEGINS... IT'S NOT A GOOD THING, SATCHEL.
FEEL BETTER?
sniff YEAH... HE'S NOT SMART. HU HU HU...

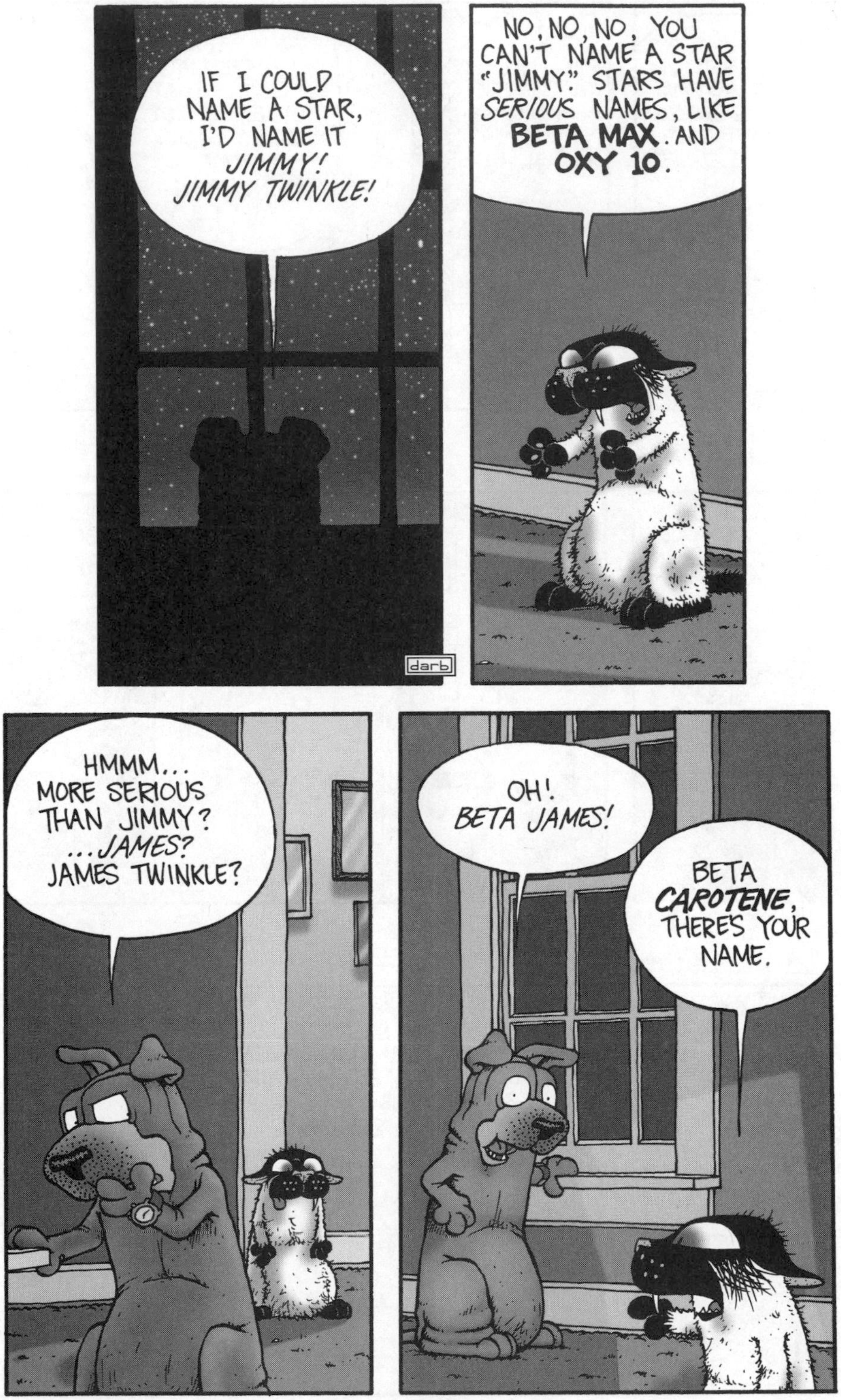
IF I COULD NAME A STAR, I'D NAME IT JIMMY! JIMMY TWINKLE!
darb
NO, NO, NO, YOU CAN'T NAME A STAR "JIMMY." STARS HAVE SERIOUS NAMES, LIKE BETA MAX. AND OXY 10.
HMMM... MORE SERIOUS THAN JIMMY? ...JAMES? JAMES TWINKLE?
OH! BETA JAMES!
BETA CAROTENE, THERE'S YOUR NAME.

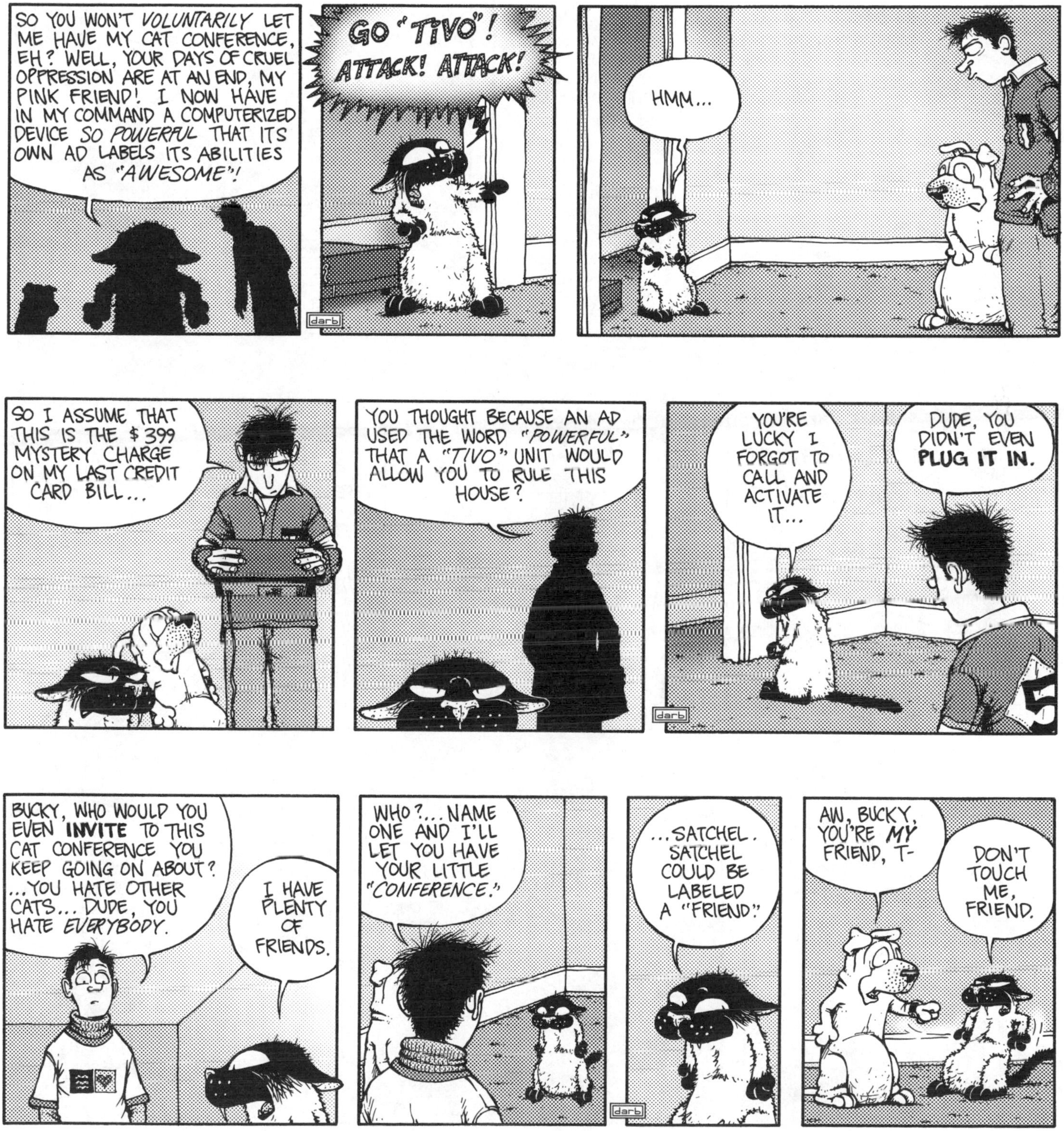
SO YOU WON'T VOLUNTARILY LET ME HAVE MY CAT CONFERENCE, EH? WELL, YOUR DAYS OF CRUEL OPPRESSION ARE AT AN END, MY PINK FRIEND! I NOW HAVE IN MY COMMAND A COMPUTERIZED DEVICE SO POWERFUL THAT ITS OWN AD LABELS ITS ABILITIES AS "AWESOME"!
GO "TIVO"! ATTACK! ATTACK!
HMM...
SO I ASSUME THAT THIS IS THE $399 MYSTERY CHARGE ON MY LAST CREDIT CARD BILL...
YOU THOUGHT BECAUSE AN AD USED THE WORD "POWERFUL" THAT A "TIVO" UNIT WOULD ALLOW YOU TO RULE THIS HOUSE?
YOU'RE LUCKY I FORGOT TO CALL AND ACTIVATE IT...
DUDE, YOU DIDN'T EVEN PLUG IT IN.
BUCKY, WHO WOULD YOU EVEN INVITE TO THIS CAT CONFERENCE YOU KEEP GOING ON ABOUT? ...YOU HATE OTHER CATS... DUDE, YOU HATE EVERYBODY.
I HAVE PLENTY OF FRIENDS.
WHO?... NAME ONE AND I'LL LET YOU HAVE YOUR LITTLE "CONFERENCE."
...SATCHEL. SATCHEL COULD BE LABELED A "FRIEND."
AW, BUCKY, YOU'RE MY FRIEND, T-
DON'T TOUCH ME, FRIEND.

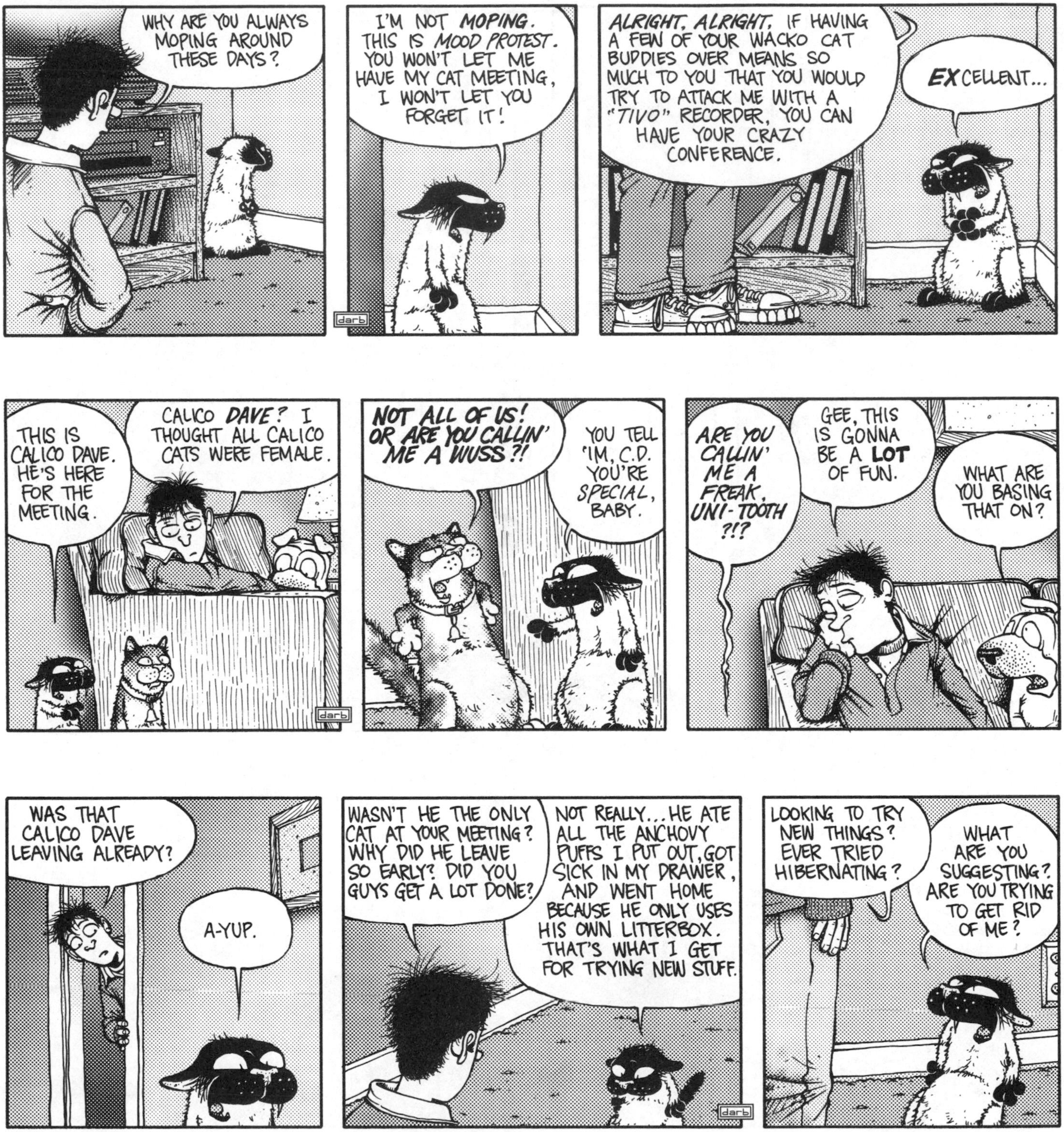

WHY ARE YOU ALWAYS MOPING AROUND THESE DAYS?
I'M NOT **MOPING**. THIS IS *MOOD PROTEST*. YOU WON'T LET ME HAVE MY CAT MEETING, I WON'T LET YOU FORGET IT!
darb
ALRIGHT, ALRIGHT, IF HAVING A FEW OF YOUR WACKO CAT BUDDIES OVER MEANS SO MUCH TO YOU THAT YOU WOULD TRY TO ATTACK ME WITH A "*TIVO*" RECORDER, YOU CAN HAVE YOUR CRAZY CONFERENCE.
EXCELLENT...
THIS IS CALICO DAVE. HE'S HERE FOR THE MEETING.
CALICO **DAVE**? I THOUGHT ALL CALICO CATS WERE FEMALE.
darb
NOT ALL OF US! OR ARE YOU CALLIN' ME A WUSS?!
YOU TELL 'IM, C.D. YOU'RE *SPECIAL*, BABY.
ARE YOU CALLIN' ME A FREAK, UNI-TOOTH ?!?
GEE, THIS IS GONNA BE A **LOT** OF FUN.
WHAT ARE YOU BASING THAT ON?
WAS THAT CALICO DAVE LEAVING ALREADY?
A-YUP.
WASN'T HE THE ONLY CAT AT YOUR MEETING? WHY DID HE LEAVE SO EARLY? DID YOU GUYS GET A LOT DONE?
NOT REALLY... HE ATE ALL THE ANCHOVY PUFFS I PUT OUT, GOT SICK IN MY DRAWER, AND WENT HOME BECAUSE HE ONLY USES HIS OWN LITTERBOX. THAT'S WHAT I GET FOR TRYING NEW STUFF.
darb
LOOKING TO TRY NEW THINGS? EVER TRIED HIBERNATING?
WHAT ARE YOU SUGGESTING? ARE YOU TRYING TO GET RID OF ME?

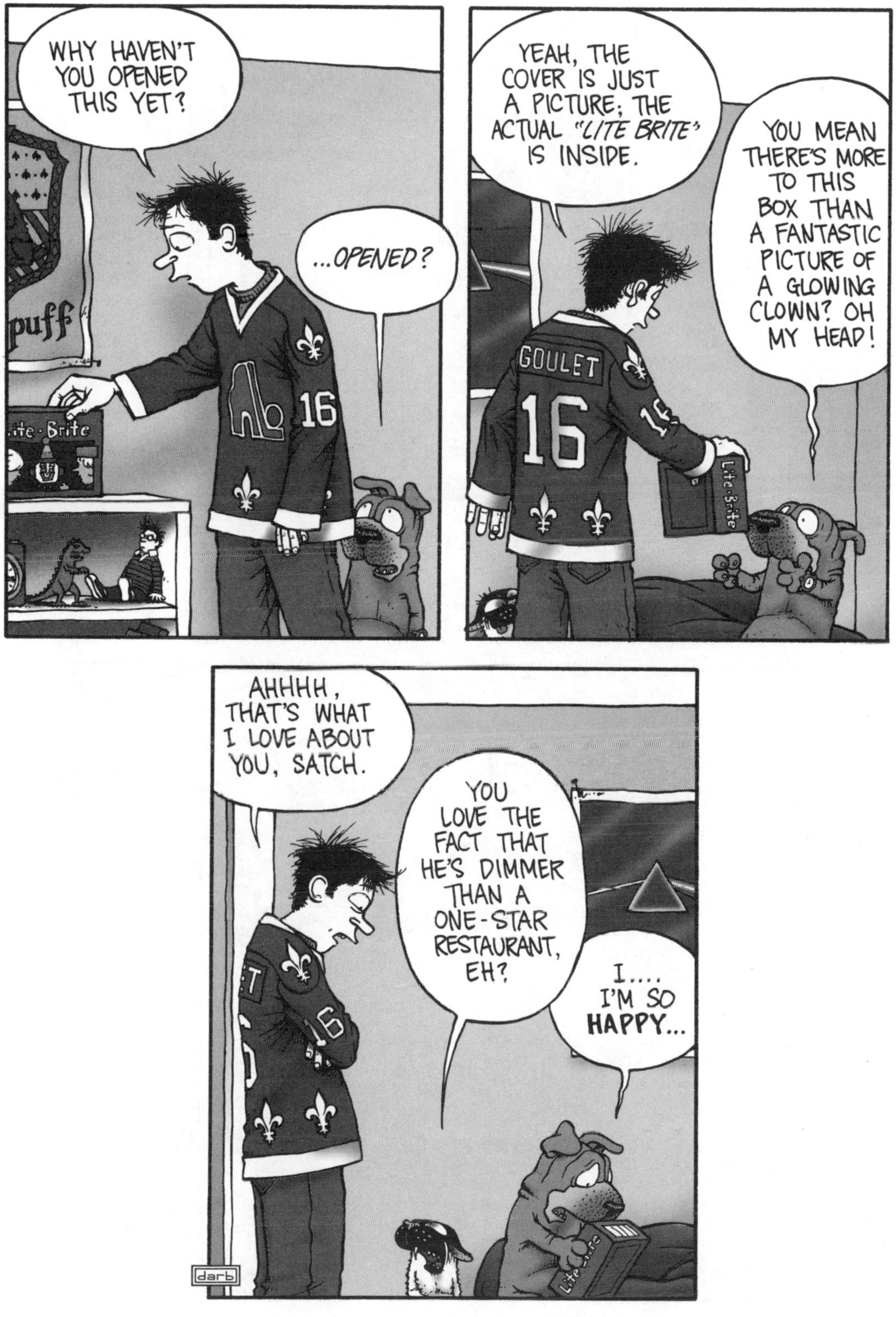
WHY HAVEN'T YOU OPENED THIS YET?
...OPENED?
YEAH, THE COVER IS JUST A PICTURE; THE ACTUAL "LITE BRITE" IS INSIDE.
YOU MEAN THERE'S MORE TO THIS BOX THAN A FANTASTIC PICTURE OF A GLOWING CLOWN? OH MY HEAD!
GOULET
16
Lite-Brite
AHHHH, THAT'S WHAT I LOVE ABOUT YOU, SATCH.
YOU LOVE THE FACT THAT HE'S DIMMER THAN A ONE-STAR RESTAURANT, EH?
I.... I'M SO **HAPPY**...
darb

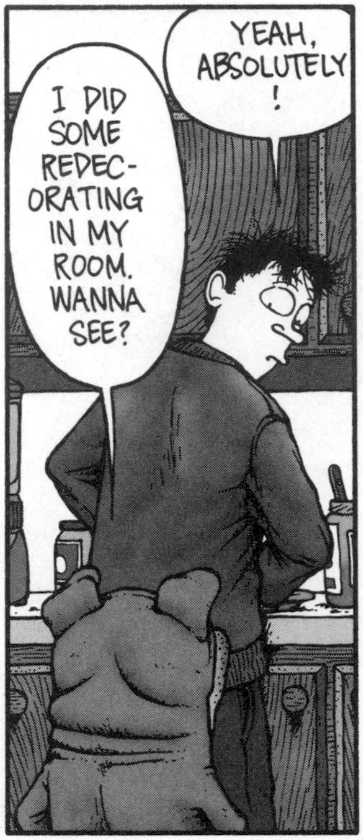
I DID SOME REDEC-ORATING IN MY ROOM. WANNA SEE?
YEAH, ABSOLUTELY!

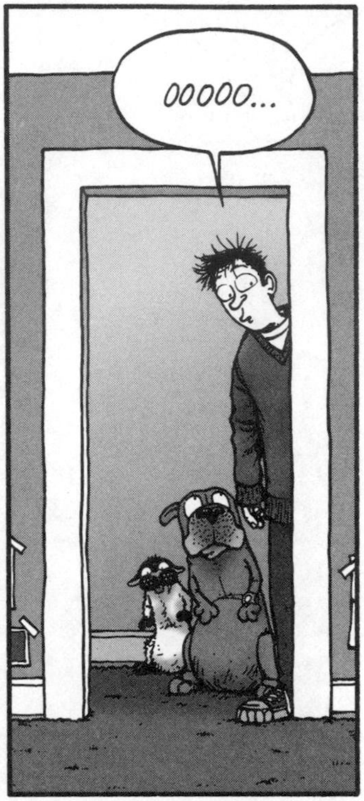
OOOOO...

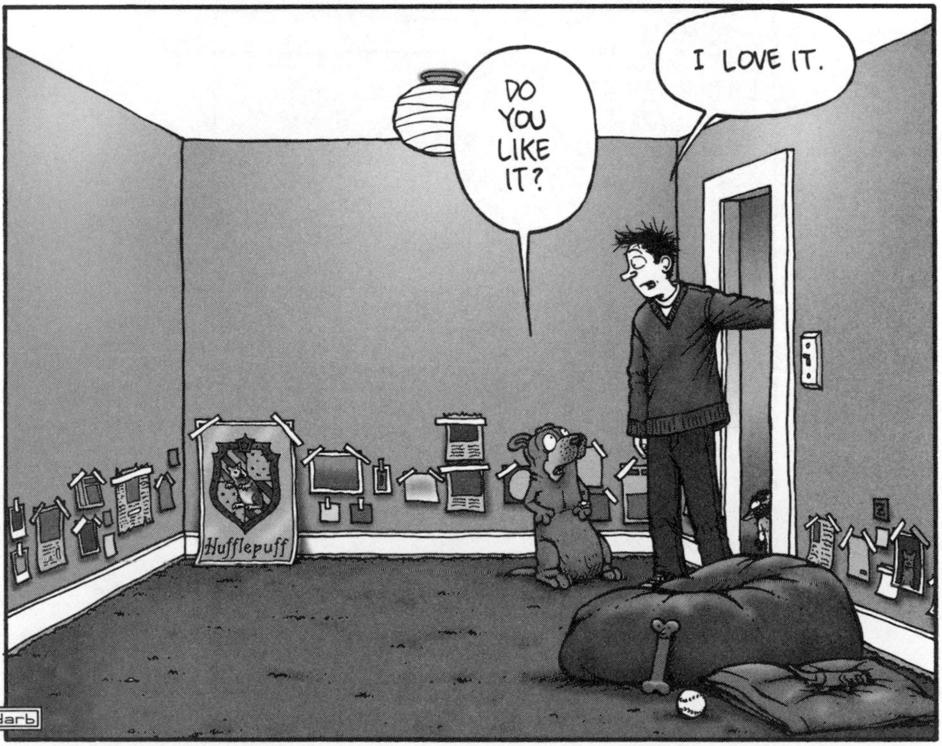
DO YOU LIKE IT?
I LOVE IT.
Hufflepuff
darb

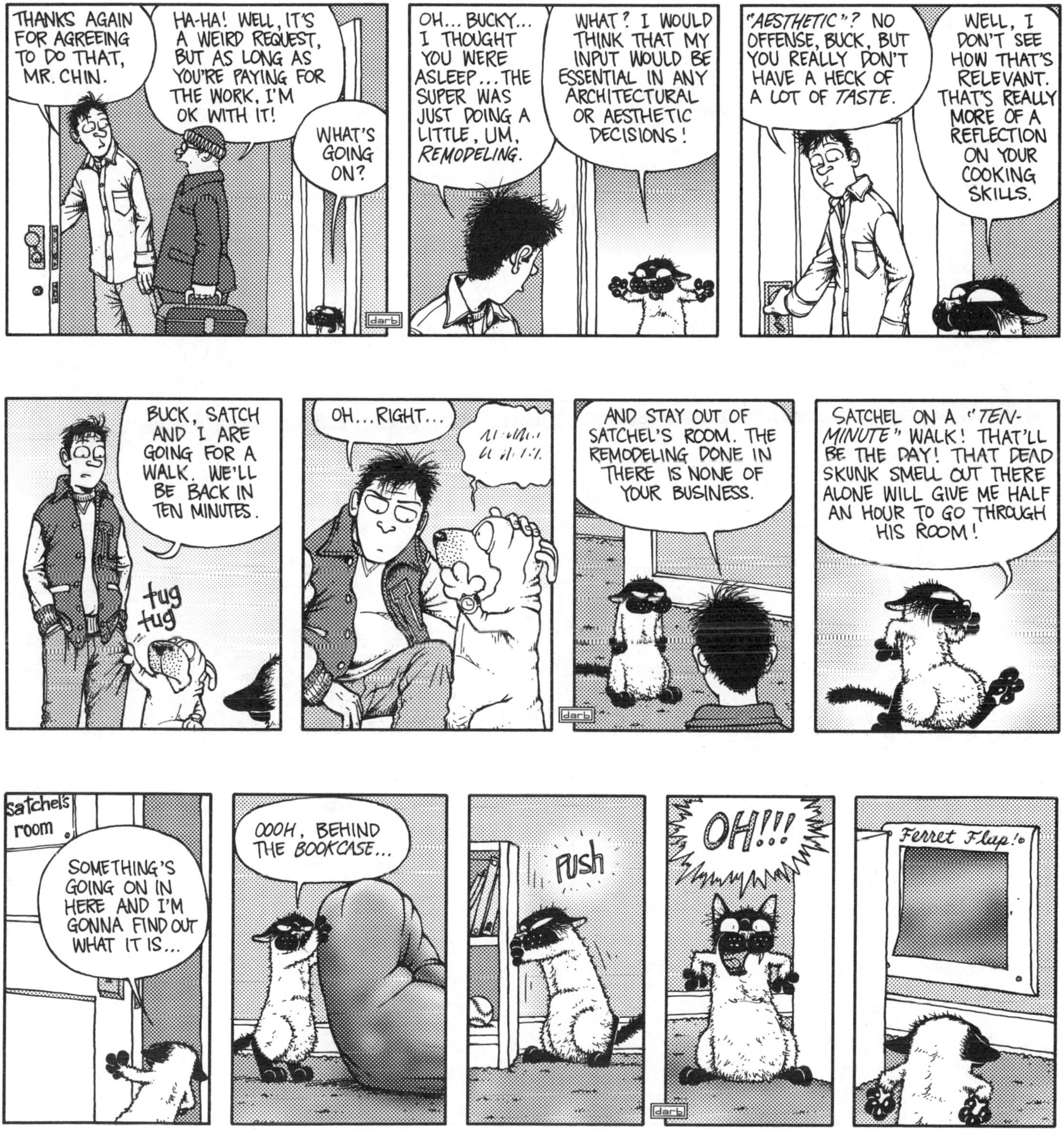
THANKS AGAIN FOR AGREEING TO DO THAT, MR. CHIN.
HA-HA! WELL, IT'S A WEIRD REQUEST, BUT AS LONG AS YOU'RE PAYING FOR THE WORK, I'M OK WITH IT!
WHAT'S GOING ON?
OH... BUCKY... I THOUGHT YOU WERE ASLEEP... THE SUPER WAS JUST DOING A LITTLE, UM, REMODELING.
WHAT? I WOULD THINK THAT MY INPUT WOULD BE ESSENTIAL IN ANY ARCHITECTURAL OR AESTHETIC DECISIONS!
"AESTHETIC"? NO OFFENSE, BUCK, BUT YOU REALLY DON'T HAVE A HECK OF A LOT OF TASTE.
WELL, I DON'T SEE HOW THAT'S RELEVANT. THAT'S REALLY MORE OF A REFLECTION ON YOUR COOKING SKILLS.
BUCK, SATCH AND I ARE GOING FOR A WALK. WE'LL BE BACK IN TEN MINUTES.
tug tug
OH... RIGHT...
AND STAY OUT OF SATCHEL'S ROOM. THE REMODELING DONE IN THERE IS NONE OF YOUR BUSINESS.
SATCHEL ON A "TEN-MINUTE" WALK! THAT'LL BE THE DAY! THAT DEAD SKUNK SMELL OUT THERE ALONE WILL GIVE ME HALF AN HOUR TO GO THROUGH HIS ROOM!
satchel's room
SOMETHING'S GOING ON IN HERE AND I'M GONNA FIND OUT WHAT IT IS...
OOOH, BEHIND THE BOOKCASE...
PUSH
OH!!!
Ferret Flap!

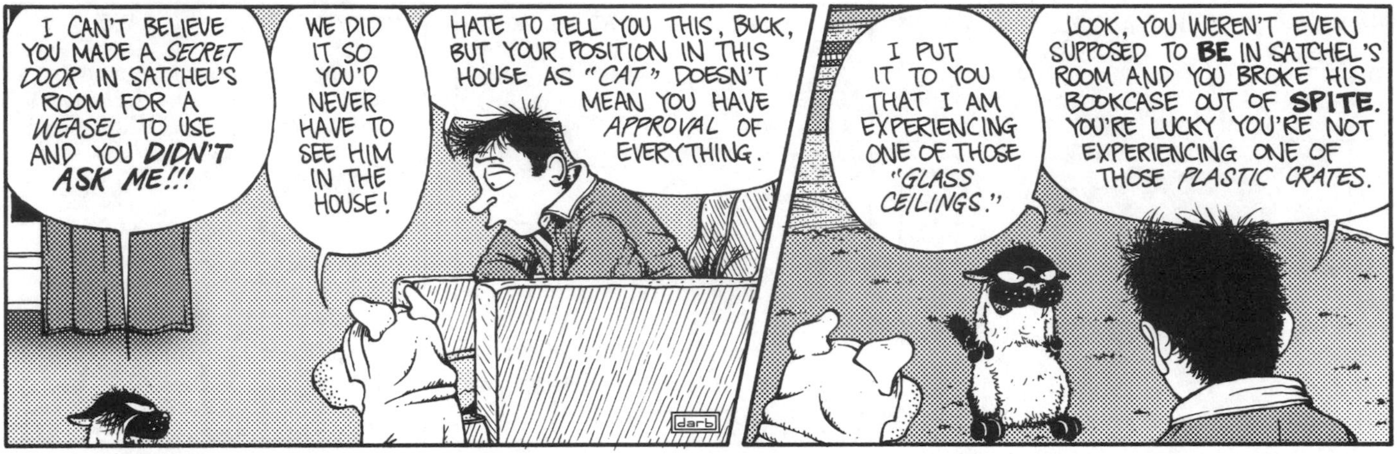
I CAN'T BELIEVE YOU MADE A *SECRET DOOR* IN SATCHEL'S ROOM FOR A *WEASEL* TO USE AND YOU ***DIDN'T ASK ME!!!***
WE DID IT SO YOU'D NEVER HAVE TO SEE HIM IN THE HOUSE!
HATE TO TELL YOU THIS, BUCK, BUT YOUR POSITION IN THIS HOUSE AS *"CAT"* DOESN'T MEAN YOU HAVE *APPROVAL* OF EVERYTHING.
I PUT IT TO YOU THAT I AM EXPERIENCING ONE OF THOSE *"GLASS CEILINGS."*
LOOK, YOU WEREN'T EVEN SUPPOSED TO **BE** IN SATCHEL'S ROOM AND YOU BROKE HIS BOOKCASE OUT OF **SPITE**. YOU'RE LUCKY YOU'RE NOT EXPERIENCING ONE OF THOSE *PLASTIC CRATES*.

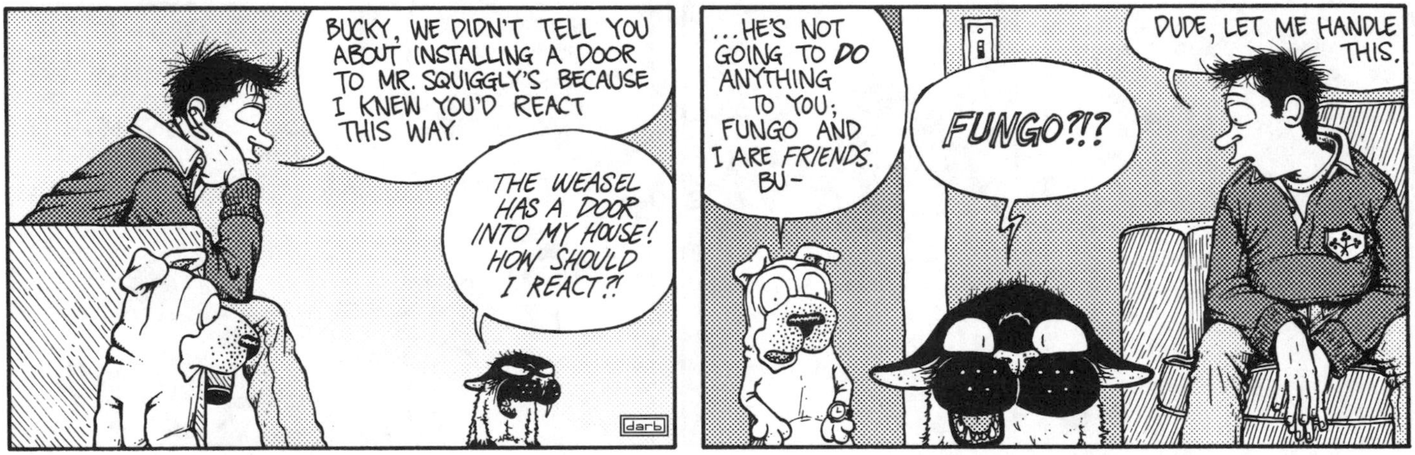
BUCKY, WE DIDN'T TELL YOU ABOUT INSTALLING A DOOR TO MR. SQUIGGLY'S BECAUSE I KNEW YOU'D REACT THIS WAY.
THE WEASEL HAS A DOOR INTO MY HOUSE! HOW SHOULD I REACT?!
...HE'S NOT GOING TO ***DO*** ANYTHING TO YOU; FUNGO AND I ARE *FRIENDS*. BU–
FUNGO?!?
DUDE, LET ME HANDLE THIS.

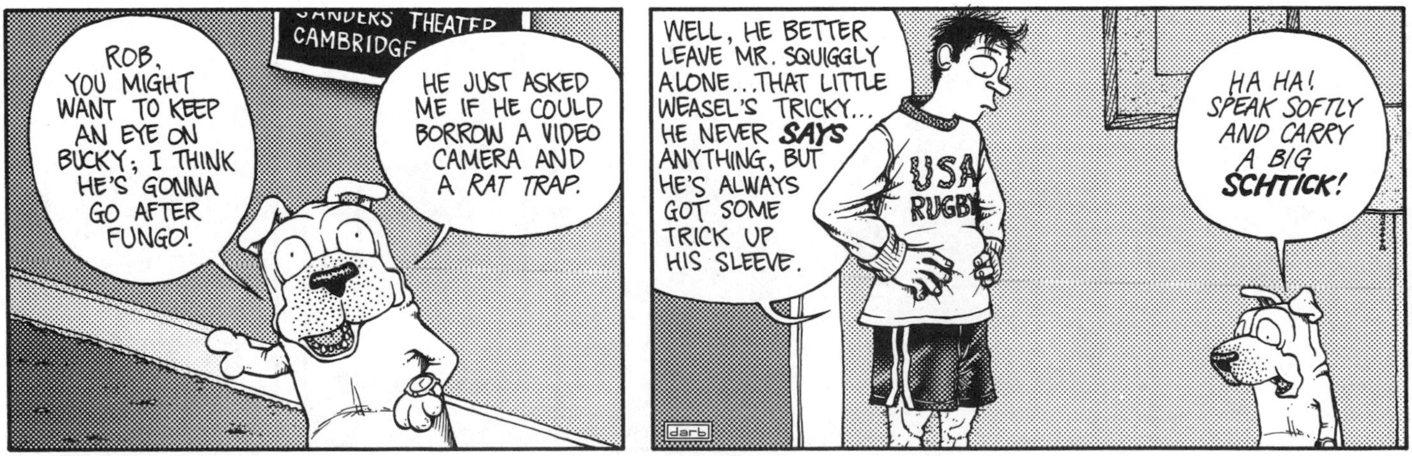
SANDERS' THEATER
CAMBRIDGE
ROB, YOU MIGHT WANT TO KEEP AN EYE ON BUCKY; I THINK HE'S GONNA GO AFTER FUNGO!
HE JUST ASKED ME IF HE COULD BORROW A VIDEO CAMERA AND A *RAT TRAP.*
WELL, HE BETTER LEAVE MR. SQUIGGLY ALONE...THAT LITTLE WEASEL'S TRICKY... HE NEVER ***SAYS*** ANYTHING, BUT HE'S ALWAYS GOT SOME TRICK UP HIS SLEEVE.
USA RUGBY
HA HA! SPEAK SOFTLY AND CARRY A BIG ***SCHTICK!***

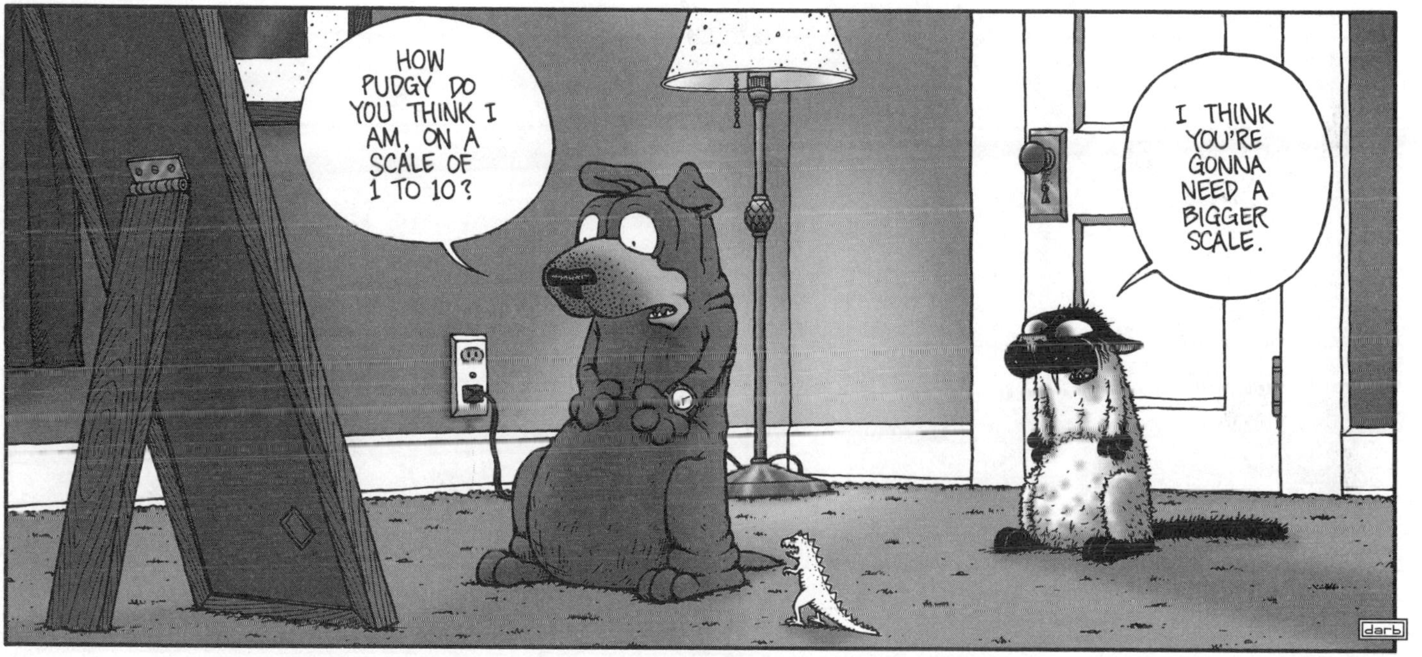
HOW PUDGY DO YOU THINK I AM, ON A SCALE OF 1 TO 10?
I THINK YOU'RE GONNA NEED A BIGGER SCALE.
darb

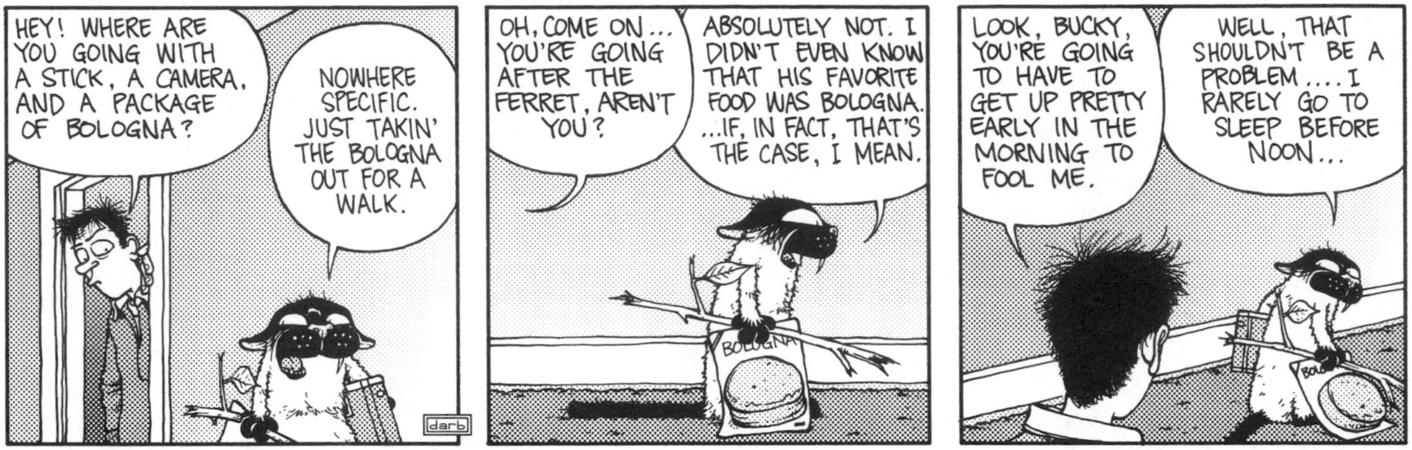
HEY! WHERE ARE YOU GOING WITH A STICK, A CAMERA, AND A PACKAGE OF BOLOGNA?
NOWHERE SPECIFIC. JUST TAKIN' THE BOLOGNA OUT FOR A WALK.
OH, COME ON... YOU'RE GOING AFTER THE FERRET, AREN'T YOU?
ABSOLUTELY NOT. I DIDN'T EVEN KNOW THAT HIS FAVORITE FOOD WAS BOLOGNA. ...IF, IN FACT, THAT'S THE CASE, I MEAN.
LOOK, BUCKY, YOU'RE GOING TO HAVE TO GET UP PRETTY EARLY IN THE MORNING TO FOOL ME.
WELL, THAT SHOULDN'T BE A PROBLEM.... I RARELY GO TO SLEEP BEFORE NOON...
BOLOGNA
darb

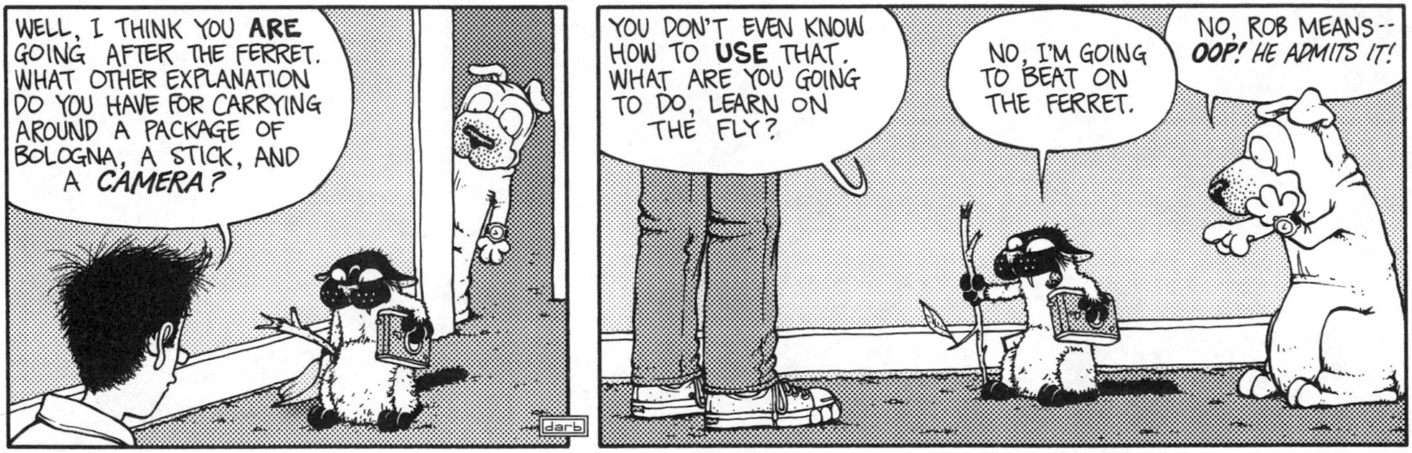
WELL, I THINK YOU **ARE** GOING AFTER THE FERRET. WHAT OTHER EXPLANATION DO YOU HAVE FOR CARRYING AROUND A PACKAGE OF BOLOGNA, A STICK, AND A ***CAMERA?***
darb
YOU DON'T EVEN KNOW HOW TO **USE** THAT. WHAT ARE YOU GOING TO DO, LEARN ON THE FLY?
NO, I'M GOING TO BEAT ON THE FERRET.
NO, ROB MEANS-- ***OOP!*** *HE ADMITS IT!*

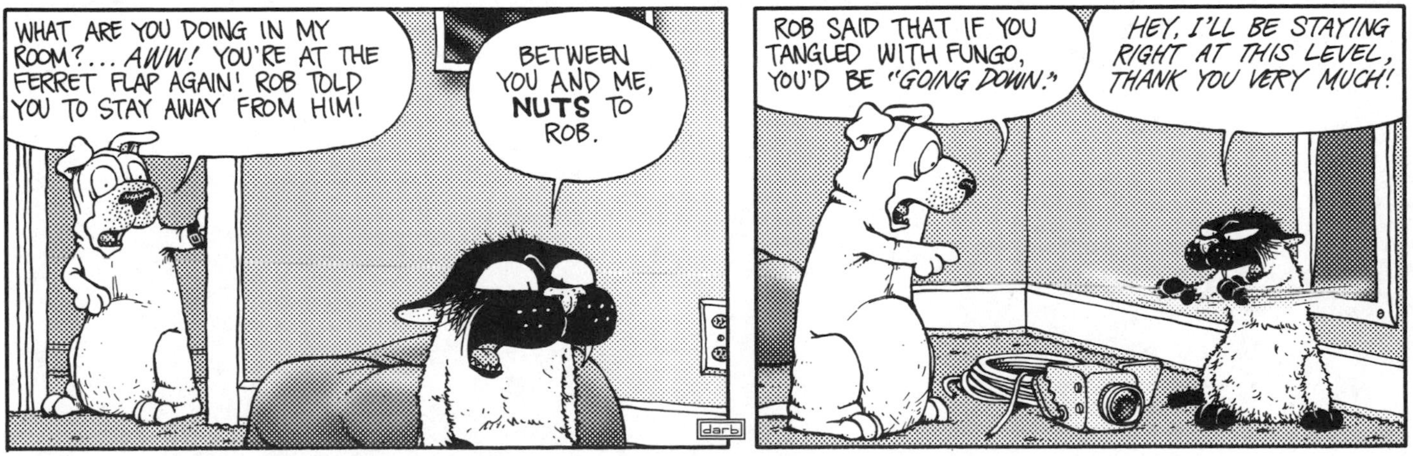
WHAT ARE YOU DOING IN MY ROOM?... *AWW!* YOU'RE AT THE FERRET FLAP AGAIN! ROB TOLD YOU TO STAY AWAY FROM HIM!
BETWEEN YOU AND ME, **NUTS** TO ROB.
darb
ROB SAID THAT IF YOU TANGLED WITH FUNGO, YOU'D BE *"GOING DOWN."*
HEY, I'LL BE STAYING RIGHT AT THIS LEVEL, THANK YOU VERY MUCH!

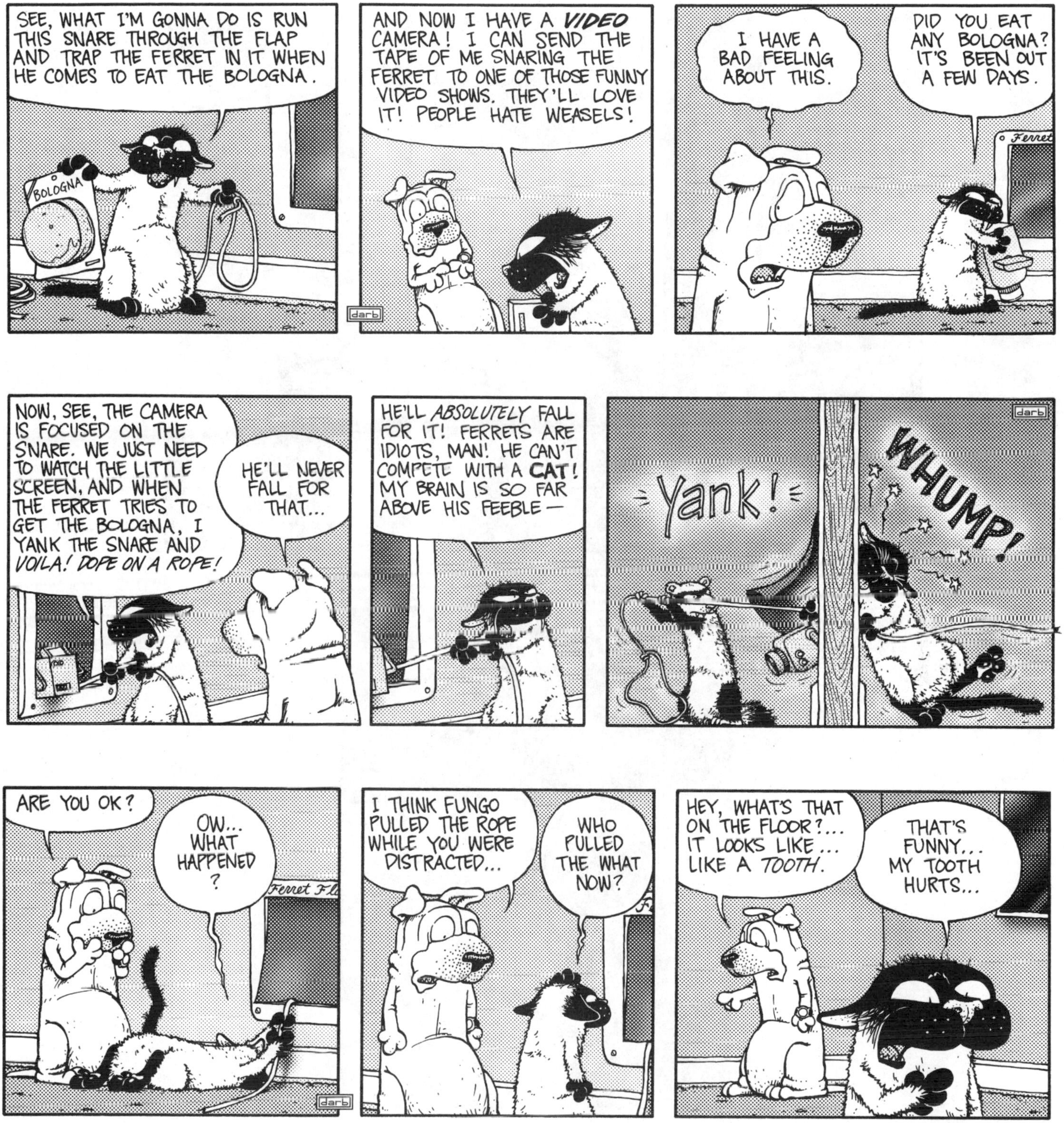
SEE, WHAT I'M GONNA DO IS RUN THIS SNARE THROUGH THE FLAP AND TRAP THE FERRET IN IT WHEN HE COMES TO EAT THE BOLOGNA.
BOLOGNA
darb
AND NOW I HAVE A *VIDEO* CAMERA! I CAN SEND THE TAPE OF ME SNARING THE FERRET TO ONE OF THOSE FUNNY VIDEO SHOWS. THEY'LL LOVE IT! PEOPLE HATE WEASELS!
I HAVE A BAD FEELING ABOUT THIS.
DID YOU EAT ANY BOLOGNA? IT'S BEEN OUT A FEW DAYS.
Ferret
NOW, SEE, THE CAMERA IS FOCUSED ON THE SNARE. WE JUST NEED TO WATCH THE LITTLE SCREEN, AND WHEN THE FERRET TRIES TO GET THE BOLOGNA, I YANK THE SNARE AND *VOILA! DOPE ON A ROPE!*
HE'LL NEVER FALL FOR THAT...
HE'LL *ABSOLUTELY* FALL FOR IT! FERRETS ARE IDIOTS, MAN! HE CAN'T COMPETE WITH A **CAT**! MY BRAIN IS SO FAR ABOVE HIS FEEBLE—
darb
Yank!
WHUMP!
ARE YOU OK?
OW... WHAT HAPPENED?
Ferret Fl
darb
I THINK FUNGO PULLED THE ROPE WHILE YOU WERE DISTRACTED...
WHO PULLED THE WHAT NOW?
HEY, WHAT'S THAT ON THE FLOOR?... IT LOOKS LIKE... LIKE A *TOOTH*.
THAT'S FUNNY... MY TOOTH HURTS...

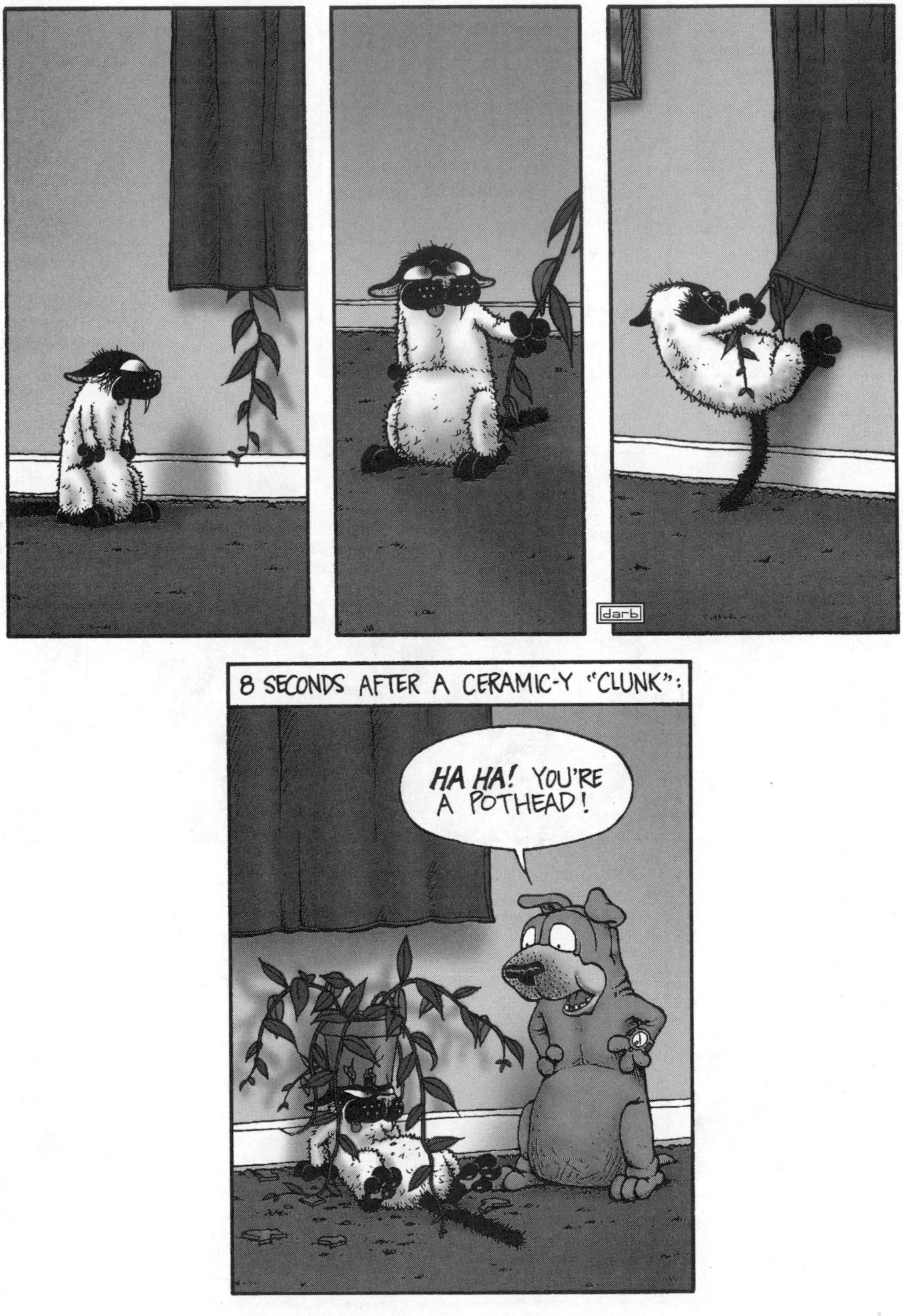
darb
8 SECONDS AFTER A CERAMIC-Y "CLUNK":
HA HA! YOU'RE A POTHEAD!

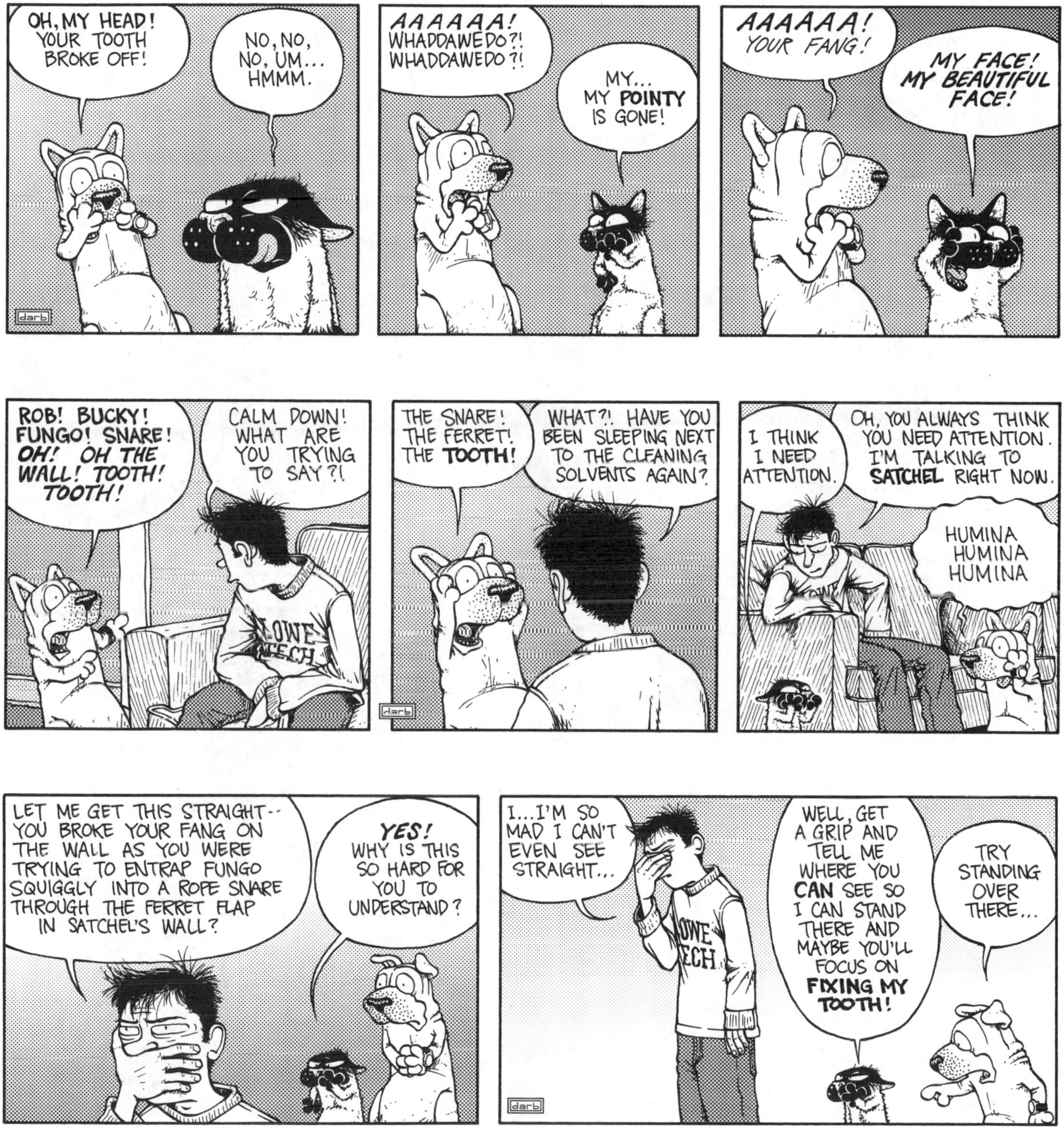
OH, MY HEAD! YOUR TOOTH BROKE OFF!
NO, NO, NO, UM... HMMM.
darb
AAAAAA! WHADDAWEDO?! WHADDAWEDO?!
MY... MY POINTY IS GONE!
AAAAAA! YOUR FANG!
MY FACE! MY BEAUTIFUL FACE!
ROB! BUCKY! FUNGO! SNARE! OH! OH THE WALL! TOOTH! TOOTH!
CALM DOWN! WHAT ARE YOU TRYING TO SAY?!
LOWE TECH
darb
THE SNARE! THE FERRET! THE TOOTH!
WHAT?! HAVE YOU BEEN SLEEPING NEXT TO THE CLEANING SOLVENTS AGAIN?
I THINK I NEED ATTENTION.
OH, YOU ALWAYS THINK YOU NEED ATTENTION. I'M TALKING TO SATCHEL RIGHT NOW.
HUMINA HUMINA HUMINA
LET ME GET THIS STRAIGHT-- YOU BROKE YOUR FANG ON THE WALL AS YOU WERE TRYING TO ENTRAP FUNGO SQUIGGLY INTO A ROPE SNARE THROUGH THE FERRET FLAP IN SATCHEL'S WALL?
YES! WHY IS THIS SO HARD FOR YOU TO UNDERSTAND?
I...I'M SO MAD I CAN'T EVEN SEE STRAIGHT...
WELL, GET A GRIP AND TELL ME WHERE YOU CAN SEE SO I CAN STAND THERE AND MAYBE YOU'LL FOCUS ON FIXING MY TOOTH!
TRY STANDING OVER THERE...
LOWE TECH
darb

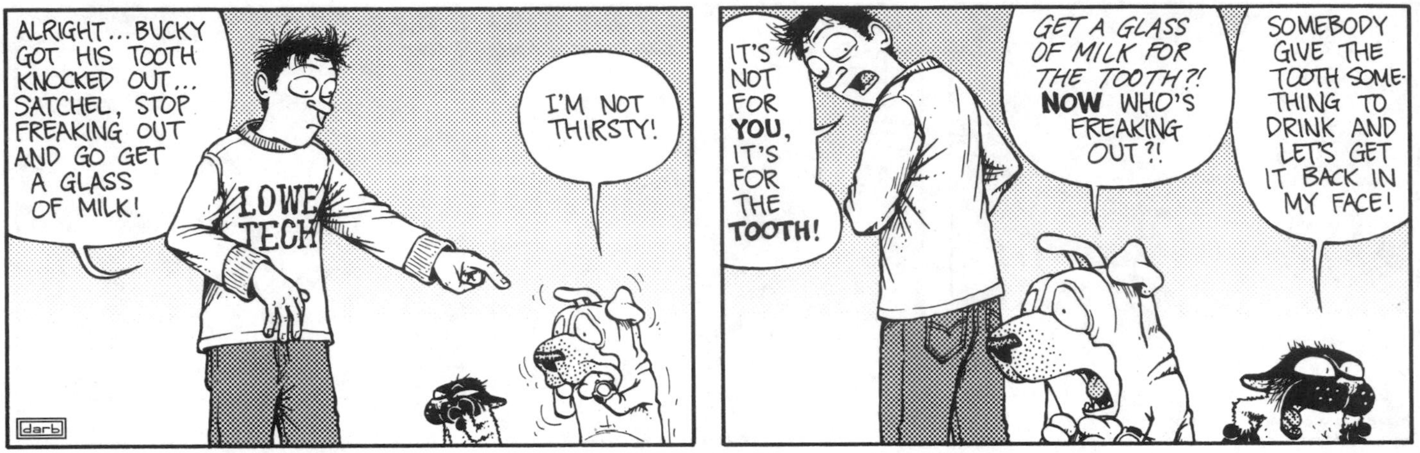
ALRIGHT... BUCKY GOT HIS TOOTH KNOCKED OUT... SATCHEL, STOP FREAKING OUT AND GO GET A GLASS OF MILK!
I'M NOT THIRSTY!
LOWE TECH
IT'S NOT FOR **YOU**, IT'S FOR THE **TOOTH**!
GET A GLASS OF MILK FOR THE TOOTH?! **NOW** WHO'S FREAKING OUT?!
SOMEBODY GIVE THE TOOTH SOMETHING TO DRINK AND LET'S GET IT BACK IN MY FACE!
darb

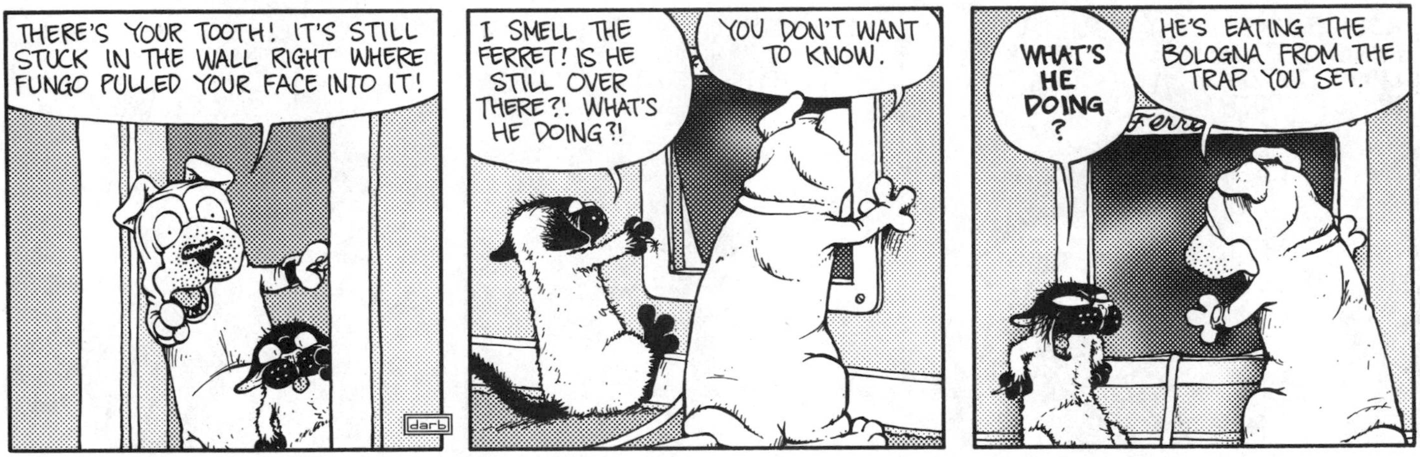
THERE'S YOUR TOOTH! IT'S STILL STUCK IN THE WALL RIGHT WHERE FUNGO PULLED YOUR FACE INTO IT!
I SMELL THE FERRET! IS HE STILL OVER THERE?! WHAT'S HE DOING?!
YOU DON'T WANT TO KNOW.
WHAT'S HE DOING?
HE'S EATING THE BOLOGNA FROM THE TRAP YOU SET.
darb

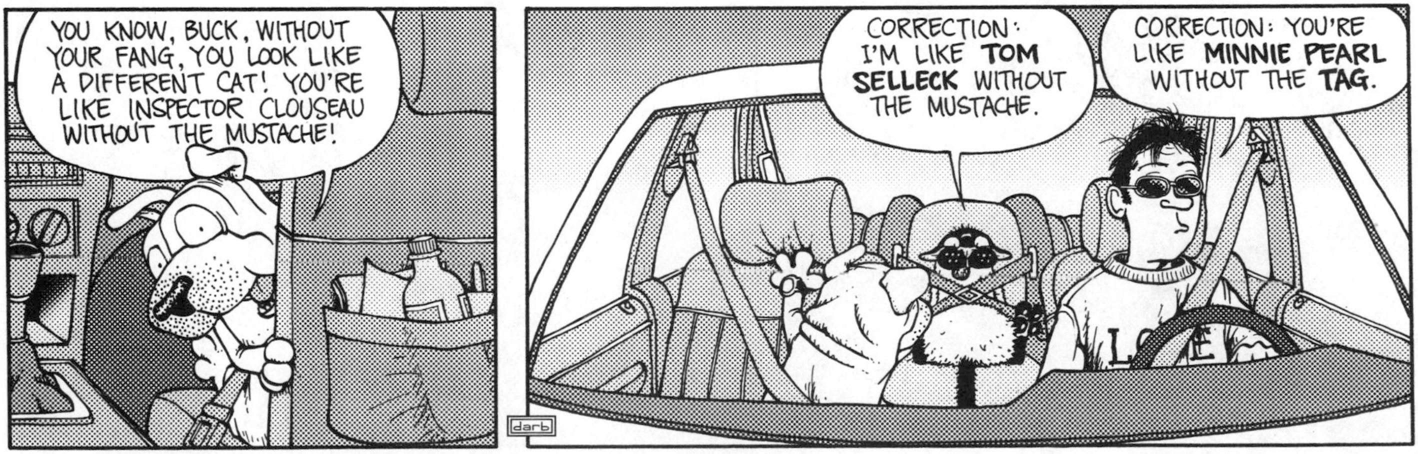
YOU KNOW, BUCK, WITHOUT YOUR FANG, YOU LOOK LIKE A DIFFERENT CAT! YOU'RE LIKE INSPECTOR CLOUSEAU WITHOUT THE MUSTACHE!
CORRECTION: I'M LIKE **TOM SELLECK** WITHOUT THE MUSTACHE.
CORRECTION: YOU'RE LIKE **MINNIE PEARL** WITHOUT THE **TAG**.
darb

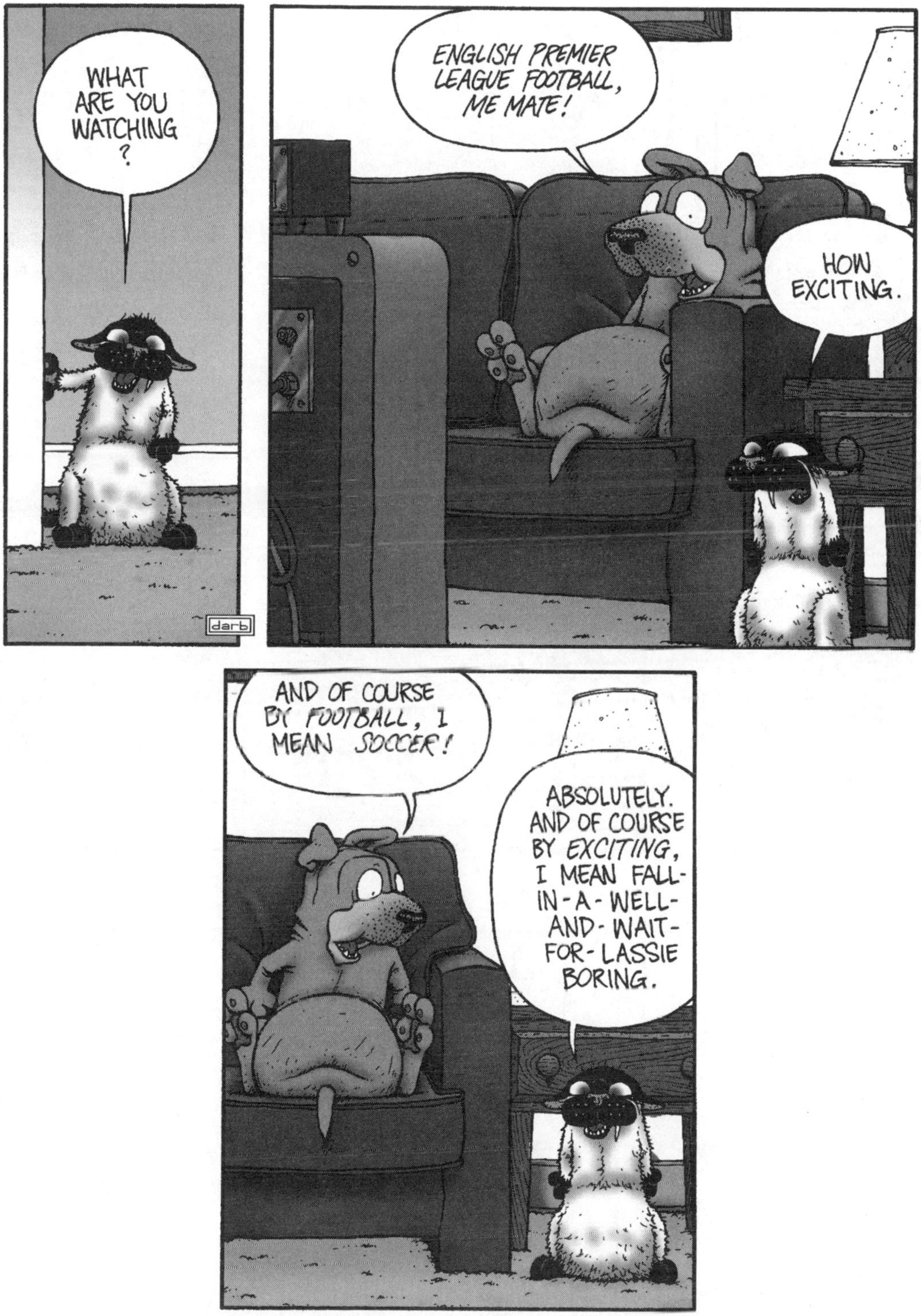
WHAT ARE YOU WATCHING ?
ENGLISH PREMIER LEAGUE FOOTBALL, ME MATE!
HOW EXCITING.
AND OF COURSE BY FOOTBALL, I MEAN SOCCER!
ABSOLUTELY. AND OF COURSE BY EXCITING, I MEAN FALL-IN-A-WELL-AND-WAIT-FOR-LASSIE BORING.

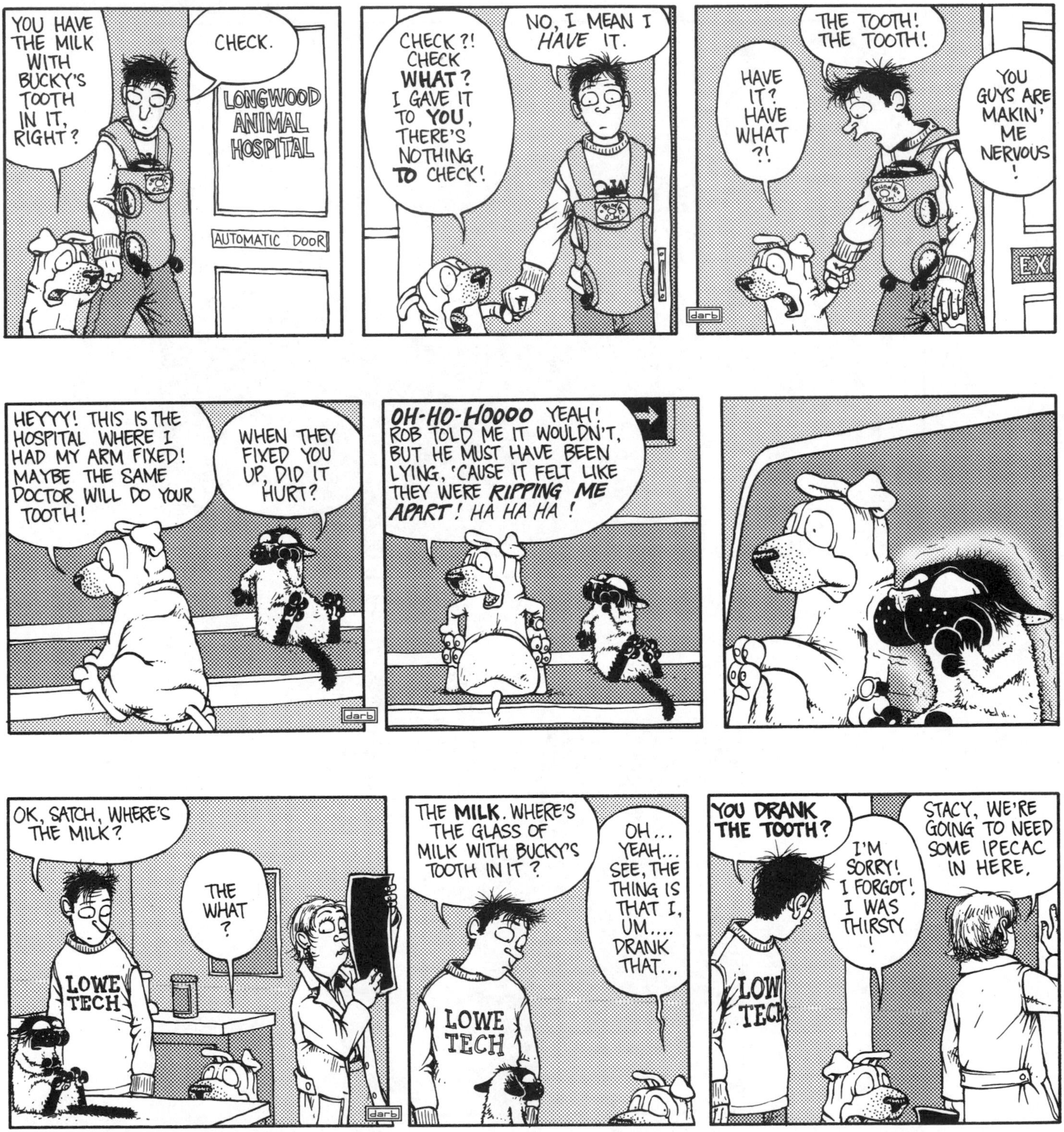

YOU HAVE THE MILK WITH BUCKY'S TOOTH IN IT, RIGHT?
CHECK.
LONGWOOD ANIMAL HOSPITAL
AUTOMATIC DOOR
CHECK?! CHECK WHAT? I GAVE IT TO YOU, THERE'S NOTHING TO CHECK!
NO, I MEAN I HAVE IT.
HAVE IT? HAVE WHAT?!
THE TOOTH! THE TOOTH!
YOU GUYS ARE MAKIN' ME NERVOUS!
HEYYY! THIS IS THE HOSPITAL WHERE I HAD MY ARM FIXED! MAYBE THE SAME DOCTOR WILL DO YOUR TOOTH!
WHEN THEY FIXED YOU UP, DID IT HURT?
OH-HO-HOOOO YEAH! ROB TOLD ME IT WOULDN'T, BUT HE MUST HAVE BEEN LYING, 'CAUSE IT FELT LIKE THEY WERE RIPPING ME APART! HA HA HA!
OK, SATCH, WHERE'S THE MILK?
THE WHAT?
LOWE TECH
THE MILK. WHERE'S THE GLASS OF MILK WITH BUCKY'S TOOTH IN IT?
OH... YEAH... SEE, THE THING IS THAT I, UM.... DRANK THAT...
LOWE TECH
YOU DRANK THE TOOTH?
I'M SORRY! I FORGOT! I WAS THIRSTY!
STACY, WE'RE GOING TO NEED SOME IPECAC IN HERE.

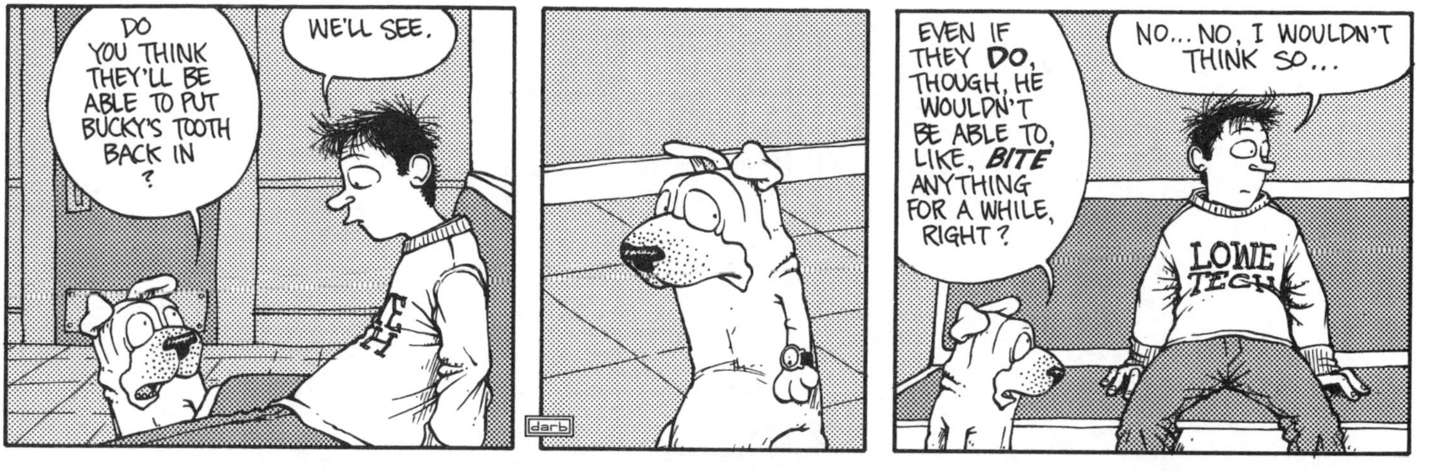
DO YOU THINK THEY'LL BE ABLE TO PUT BUCKY'S TOOTH BACK IN ?
WE'LL SEE.
EVEN IF THEY **DO**, THOUGH, HE WOULDN'T BE ABLE TO, LIKE, ***BITE*** ANYTHING FOR A WHILE, RIGHT ?
NO... NO, I WOULDN'T THINK SO...

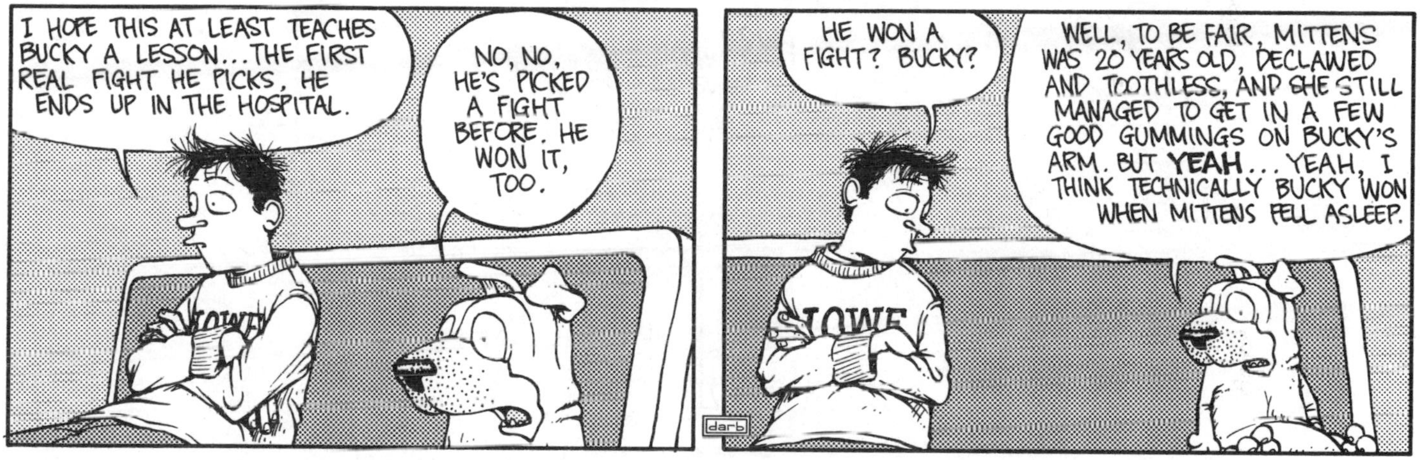
I HOPE THIS AT LEAST TEACHES BUCKY A LESSON... THE FIRST REAL FIGHT HE PICKS, HE ENDS UP IN THE HOSPITAL.
NO, NO, HE'S PICKED A FIGHT BEFORE. HE WON IT, TOO.
HE WON A FIGHT? BUCKY?
WELL, TO BE FAIR, MITTENS WAS 20 YEARS OLD, DECLAWED AND TOOTHLESS, AND SHE STILL MANAGED TO GET IN A FEW GOOD GUMMINGS ON BUCKY'S ARM. BUT **YEAH**... YEAH, I THINK TECHNICALLY BUCKY WON WHEN MITTENS FELL ASLEEP.

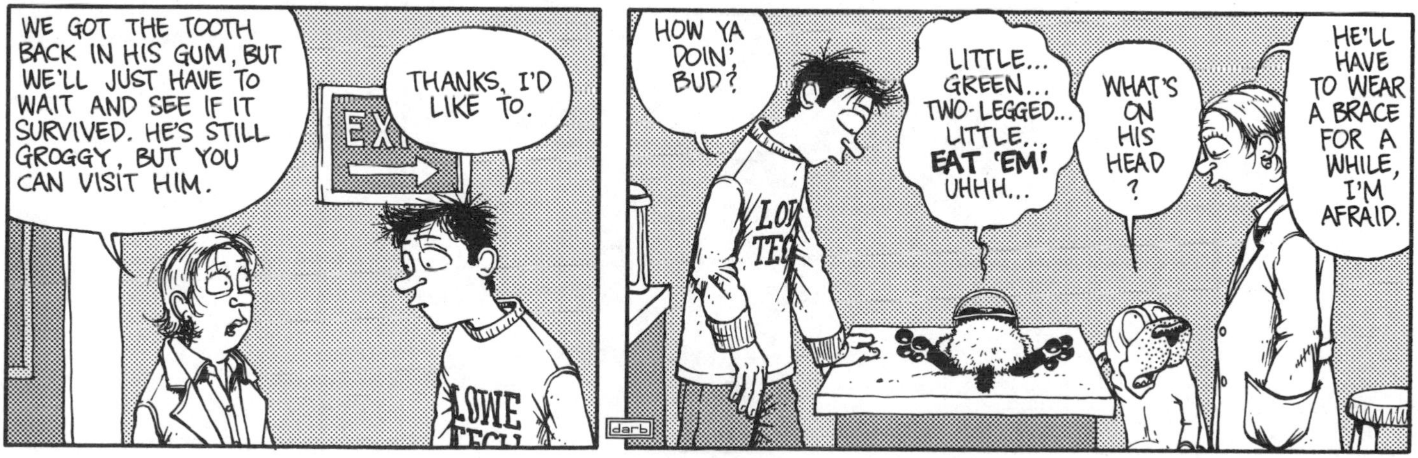
WE GOT THE TOOTH BACK IN HIS GUM, BUT WE'LL JUST HAVE TO WAIT AND SEE IF IT SURVIVED. HE'S STILL GROGGY, BUT YOU CAN VISIT HIM.
THANKS, I'D LIKE TO.
HOW YA DOIN', BUD?
LITTLE... GREEN... TWO-LEGGED... LITTLE... **EAT 'EM!** UHHH...
WHAT'S ON HIS HEAD ?
HE'LL HAVE TO WEAR A BRACE FOR A WHILE, I'M AFRAID.

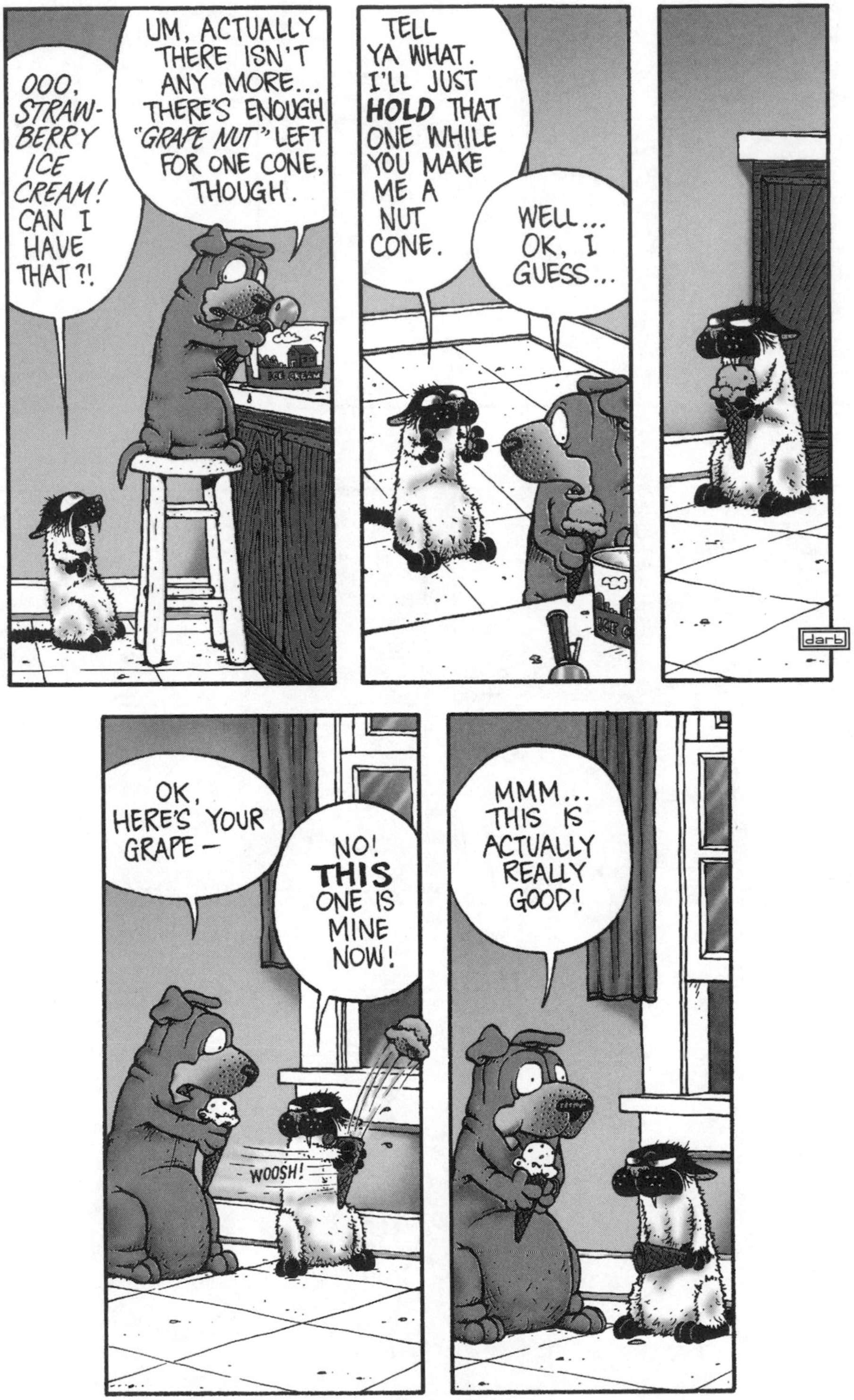
OOO, STRAWBERRY ICE CREAM! CAN I HAVE THAT?!
UM, ACTUALLY THERE ISN'T ANY MORE... THERE'S ENOUGH "GRAPE NUT" LEFT FOR ONE CONE, THOUGH.
ICE CREAM
TELL YA WHAT. I'LL JUST HOLD THAT ONE WHILE YOU MAKE ME A NUT CONE.
WELL... OK, I GUESS...
darb
OK, HERE'S YOUR GRAPE–
NO! THIS ONE IS MINE NOW!
WOOSH!
MMM... THIS IS ACTUALLY REALLY GOOD!

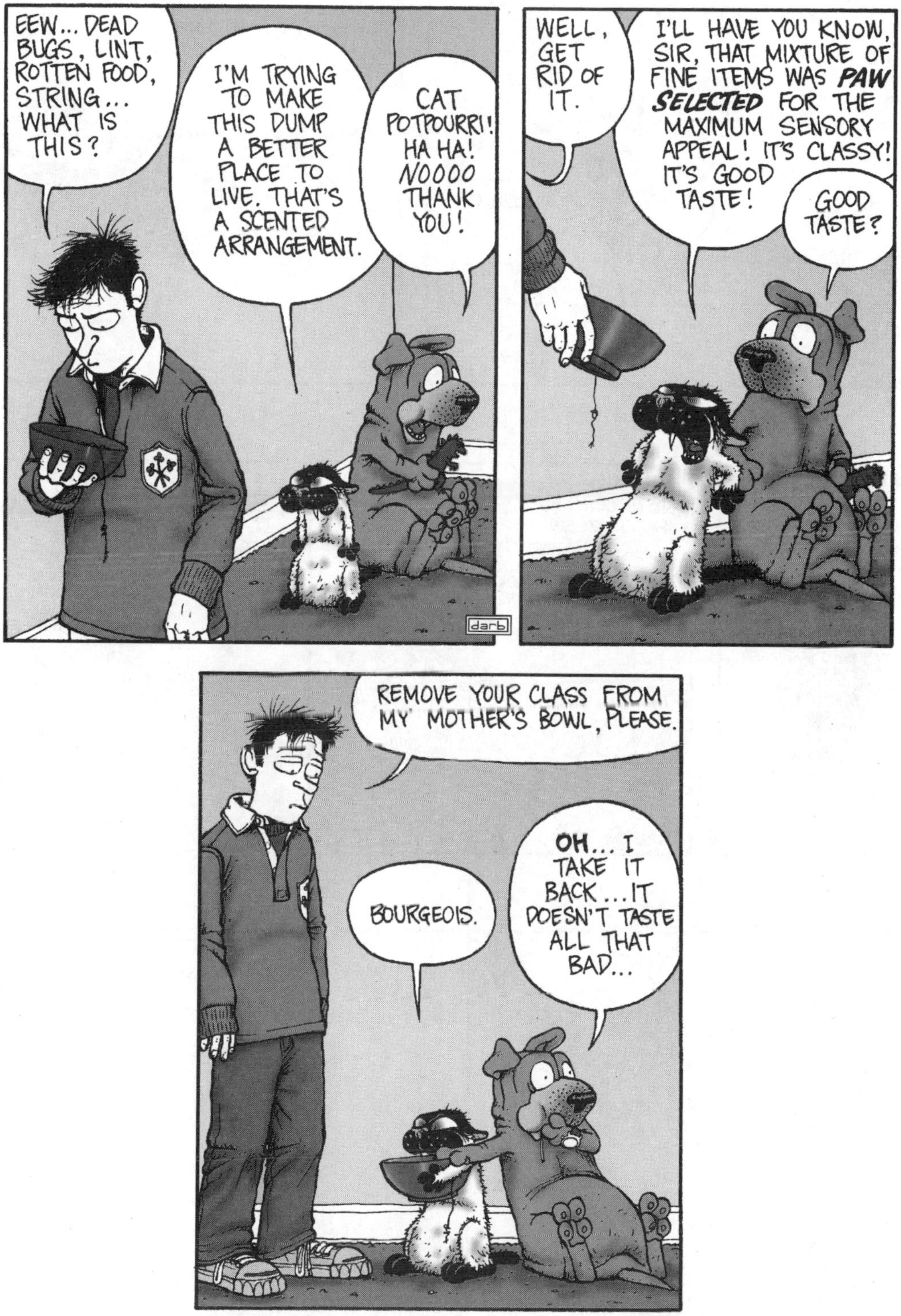
EEW... DEAD BUGS, LINT, ROTTEN FOOD, STRING... WHAT IS THIS?
I'M TRYING TO MAKE THIS DUMP A BETTER PLACE TO LIVE. THAT'S A SCENTED ARRANGEMENT.
CAT POTPOURRI! HA HA! NOOOO THANK YOU!
darb
WELL, GET RID OF IT.
I'LL HAVE YOU KNOW, SIR, THAT MIXTURE OF FINE ITEMS WAS **PAW SELECTED** FOR THE MAXIMUM SENSORY APPEAL! IT'S CLASSY! IT'S GOOD TASTE!
GOOD TASTE?
REMOVE YOUR CLASS FROM MY MOTHER'S BOWL, PLEASE.
BOURGEOIS.
OH... I TAKE IT BACK... IT DOESN'T TASTE ALL THAT BAD...

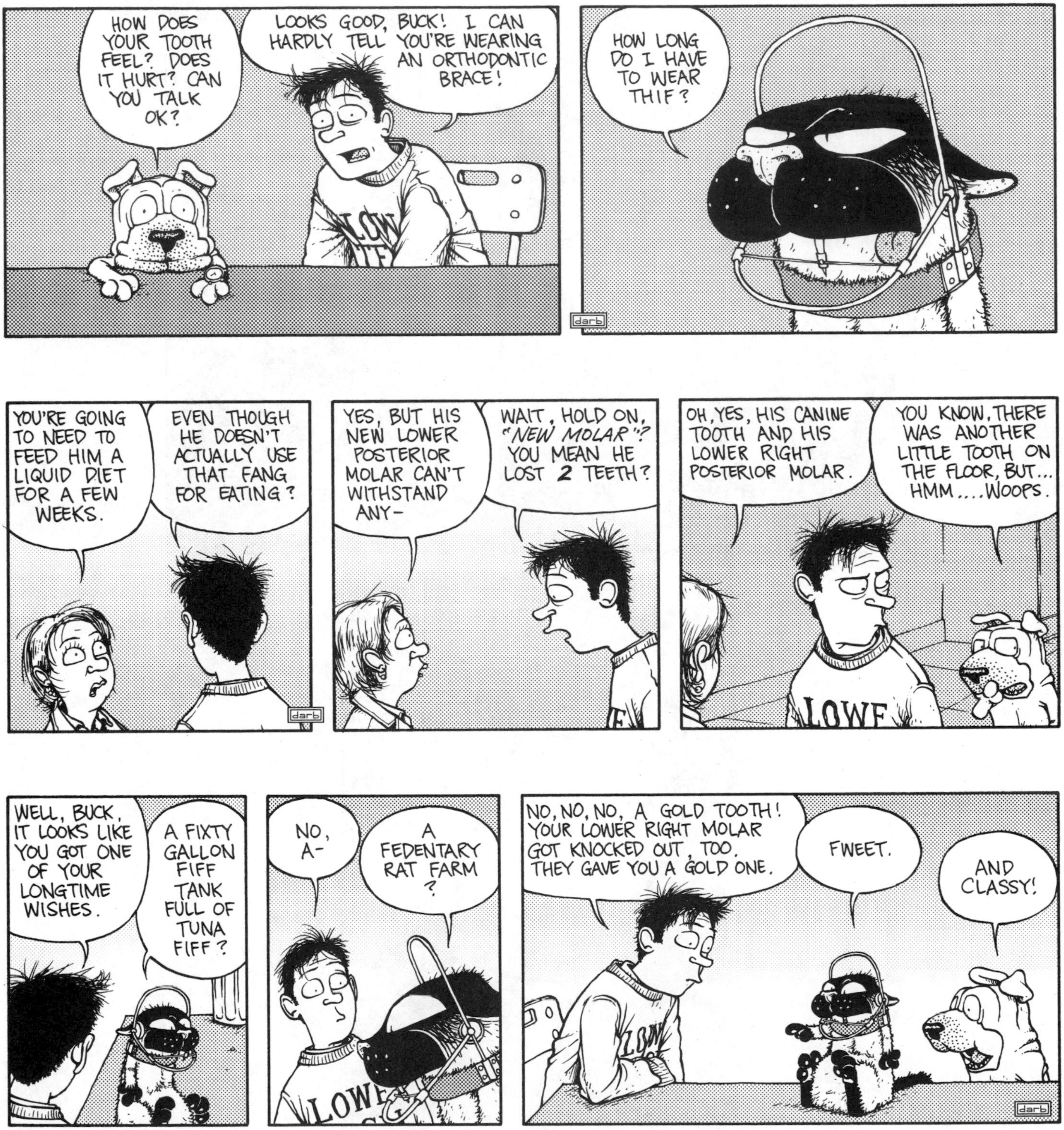
HOW DOES YOUR TOOTH FEEL? DOES IT HURT? CAN YOU TALK OK?
LOOKS GOOD, BUCK! I CAN HARDLY TELL YOU'RE WEARING AN ORTHODONTIC BRACE!
HOW LONG DO I HAVE TO WEAR THIF?
darb
YOU'RE GOING TO NEED TO FEED HIM A LIQUID DIET FOR A FEW WEEKS.
EVEN THOUGH HE DOESN'T ACTUALLY USE THAT FANG FOR EATING?
darb
YES, BUT HIS NEW LOWER POSTERIOR MOLAR CAN'T WITHSTAND ANY-
WAIT, HOLD ON, "NEW MOLAR"? YOU MEAN HE LOST 2 TEETH?
OH, YES, HIS CANINE TOOTH AND HIS LOWER RIGHT POSTERIOR MOLAR.
YOU KNOW, THERE WAS ANOTHER LITTLE TOOTH ON THE FLOOR, BUT... HMM.... WOOPS.
WELL, BUCK, IT LOOKS LIKE YOU GOT ONE OF YOUR LONGTIME WISHES.
A FIXTY GALLON FIFF TANK FULL OF TUNA FIFF?
NO, A-
A FEDENTARY RAT FARM?
NO, NO, NO, A GOLD TOOTH! YOUR LOWER RIGHT MOLAR GOT KNOCKED OUT, TOO. THEY GAVE YOU A GOLD ONE.
FWEET.
AND CLASSY!
darb

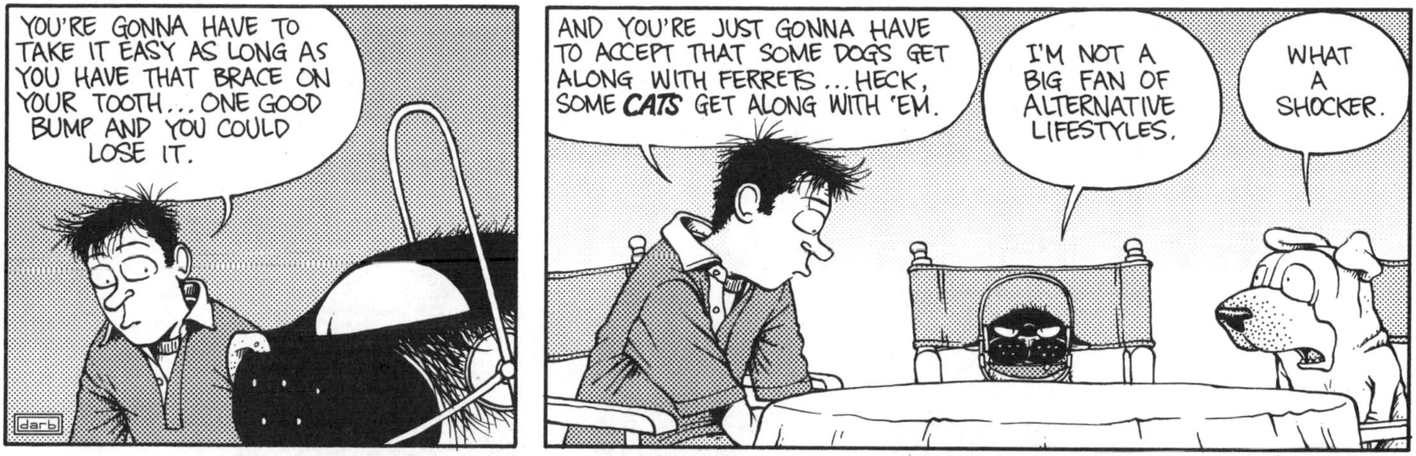
YOU'RE GONNA HAVE TO TAKE IT EASY AS LONG AS YOU HAVE THAT BRACE ON YOUR TOOTH... ONE GOOD BUMP AND YOU COULD LOSE IT.
AND YOU'RE JUST GONNA HAVE TO ACCEPT THAT SOME DOGS GET ALONG WITH FERRETS... HECK, SOME CATS GET ALONG WITH 'EM.
I'M NOT A BIG FAN OF ALTERNATIVE LIFESTYLES.
WHAT A SHOCKER.

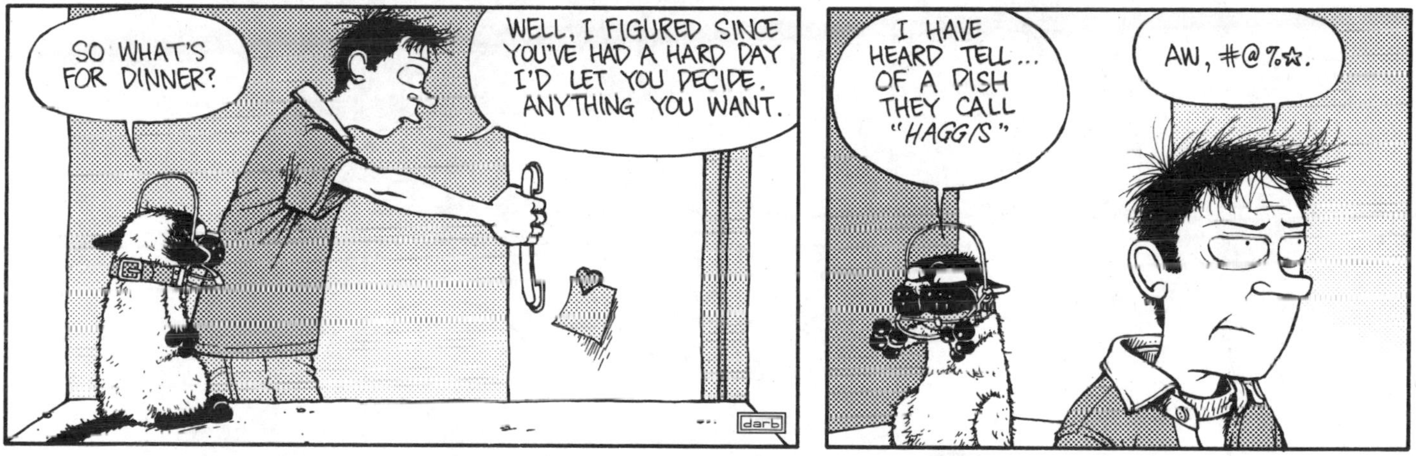
SO WHAT'S FOR DINNER?
WELL, I FIGURED SINCE YOU'VE HAD A HARD DAY I'D LET YOU DECIDE. ANYTHING YOU WANT.
I HAVE HEARD TELL... OF A DISH THEY CALL "HAGGIS"
AW, #@%☆.

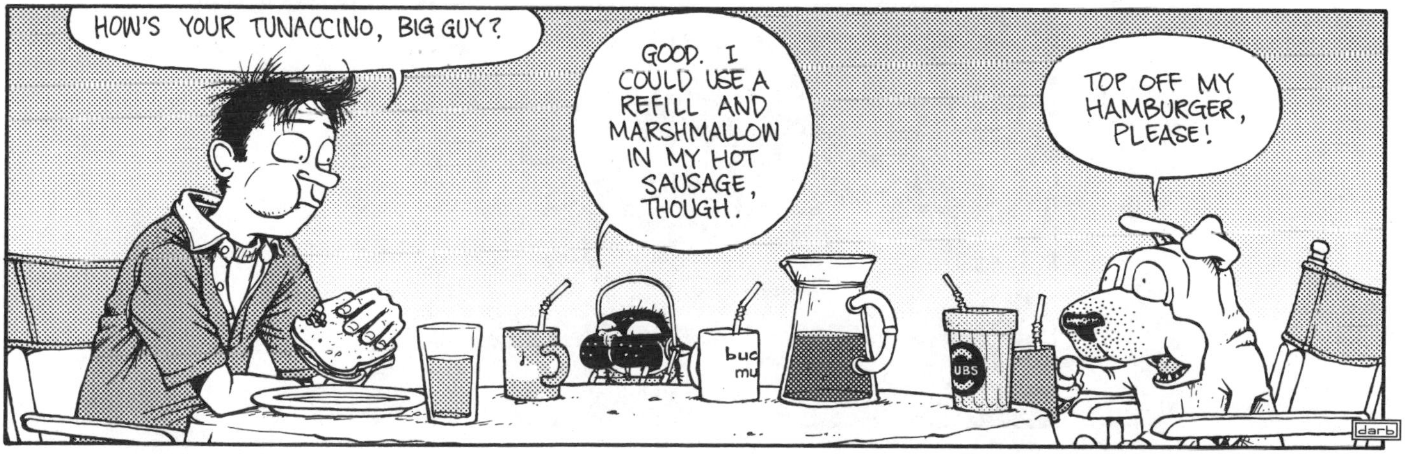
HOW'S YOUR TUNACCINO, BIG GUY?
GOOD. I COULD USE A REFILL AND MARSHMALLOW IN MY HOT SAUSAGE, THOUGH.
TOP OFF MY HAMBURGER, PLEASE!

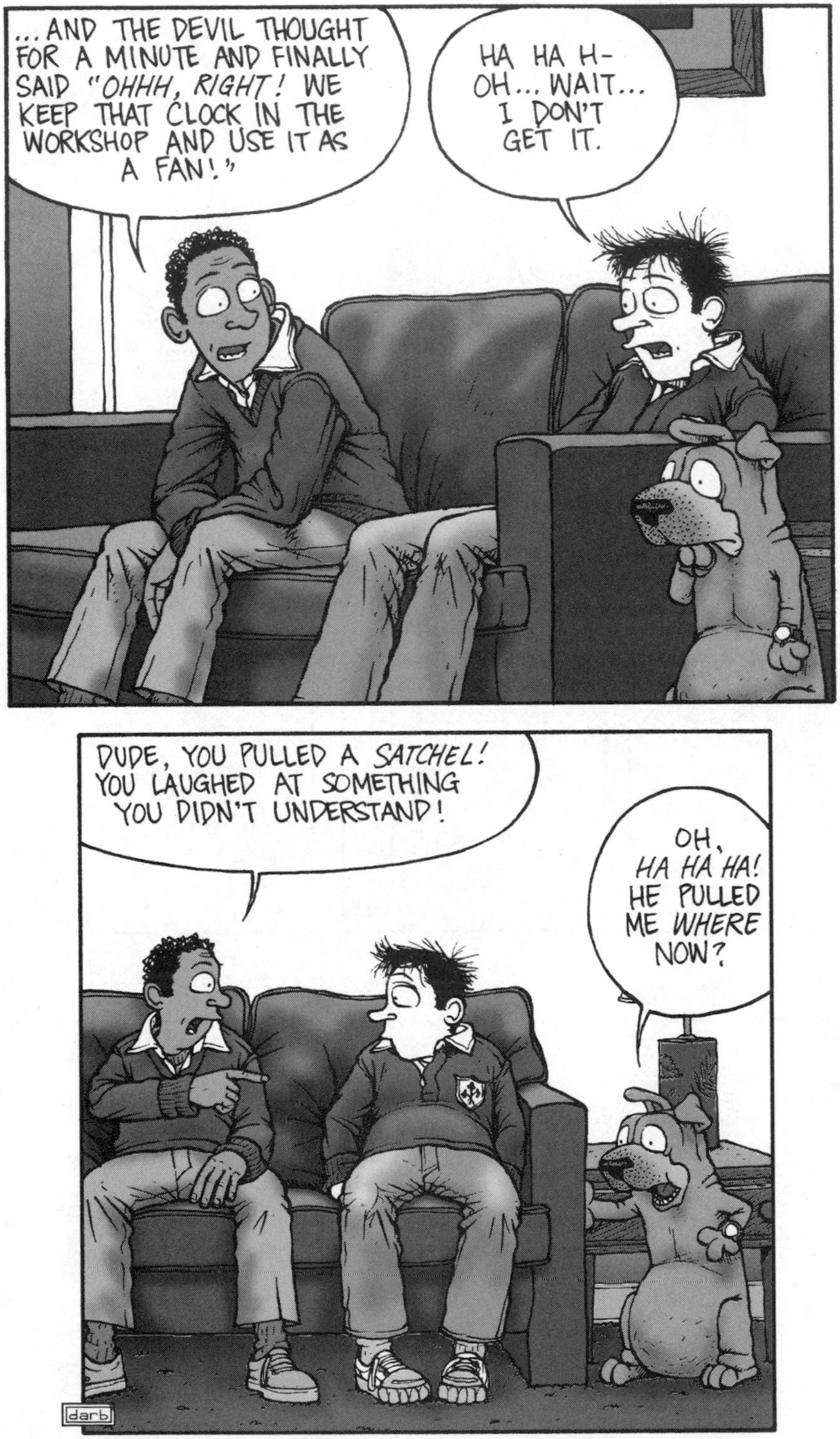
...AND THE DEVIL THOUGHT FOR A MINUTE AND FINALLY SAID "OHHH, RIGHT! WE KEEP THAT CLOCK IN THE WORKSHOP AND USE IT AS A FAN!"
HA HA H- OH... WAIT... I DON'T GET IT.
DUDE, YOU PULLED A SATCHEL! YOU LAUGHED AT SOMETHING YOU DIDN'T UNDERSTAND!
OH, HA HA HA! HE PULLED ME WHERE NOW?
darb

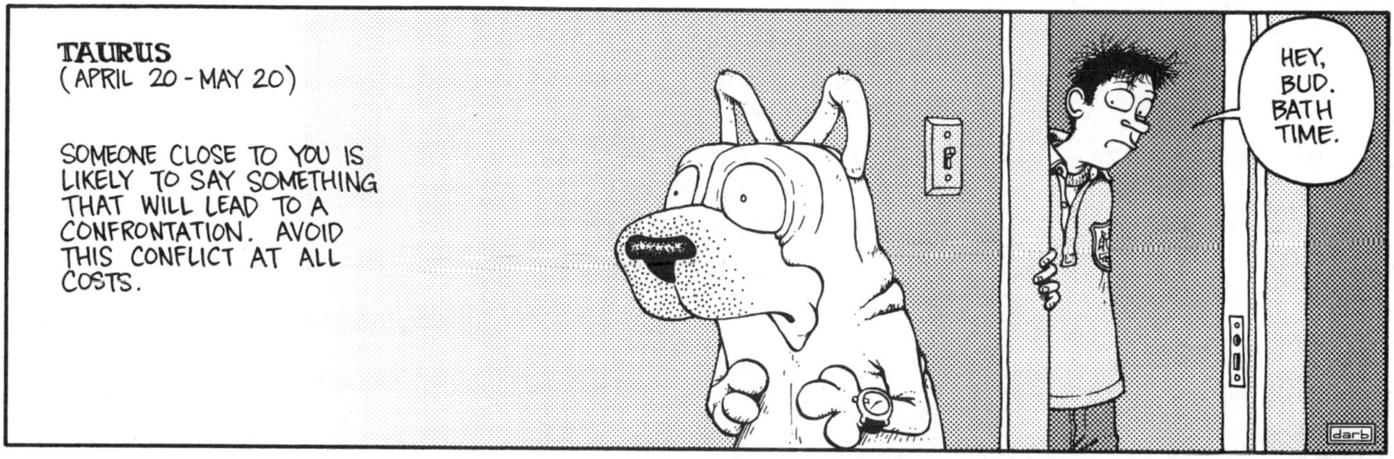
TAURUS
(APRIL 20 - MAY 20)
SOMEONE CLOSE TO YOU IS LIKELY TO SAY SOMETHING THAT WILL LEAD TO A CONFRONTATION. AVOID THIS CONFLICT AT ALL COSTS.
HEY, BUD. BATH TIME.

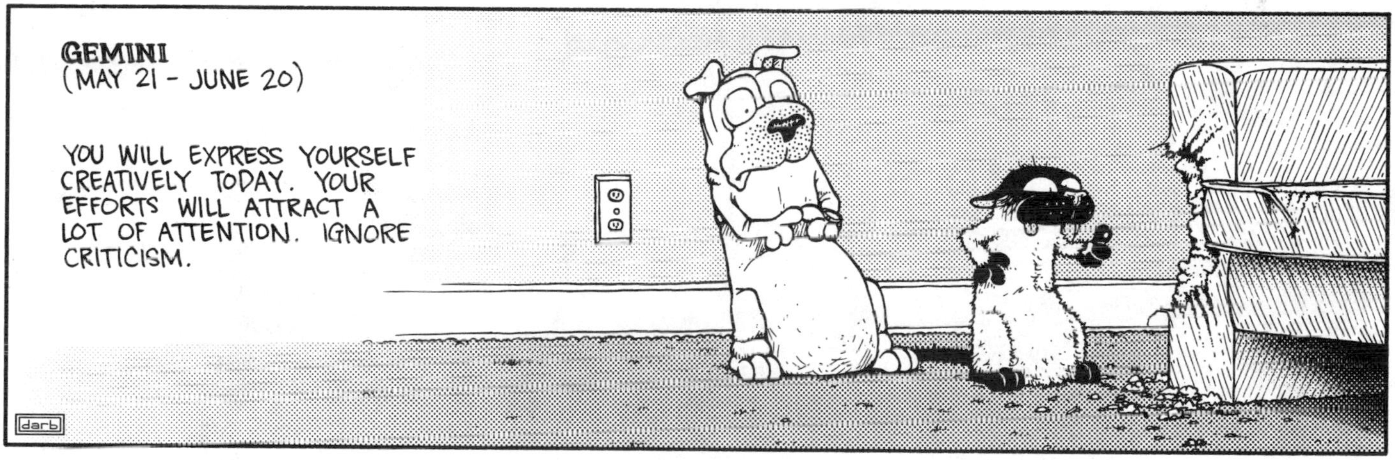
GEMINI
(MAY 21 - JUNE 20)
YOU WILL EXPRESS YOURSELF CREATIVELY TODAY. YOUR EFFORTS WILL ATTRACT A LOT OF ATTENTION. IGNORE CRITICISM.

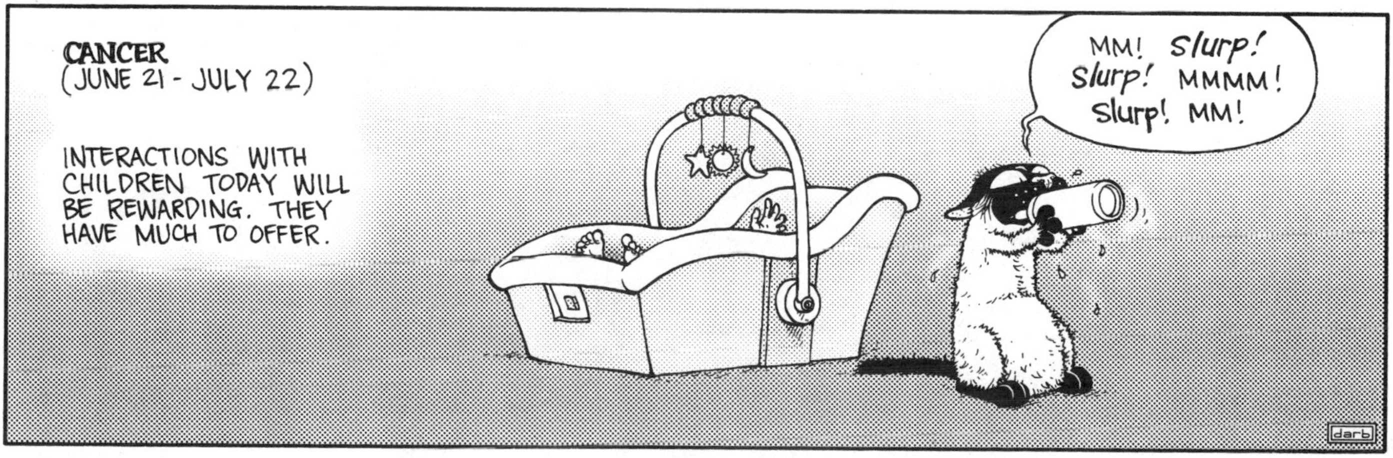
CANCER
(JUNE 21 - JULY 22)
INTERACTIONS WITH CHILDREN TODAY WILL BE REWARDING. THEY HAVE MUCH TO OFFER.
MM! slurp! slurp! MMMM! slurp! MM!

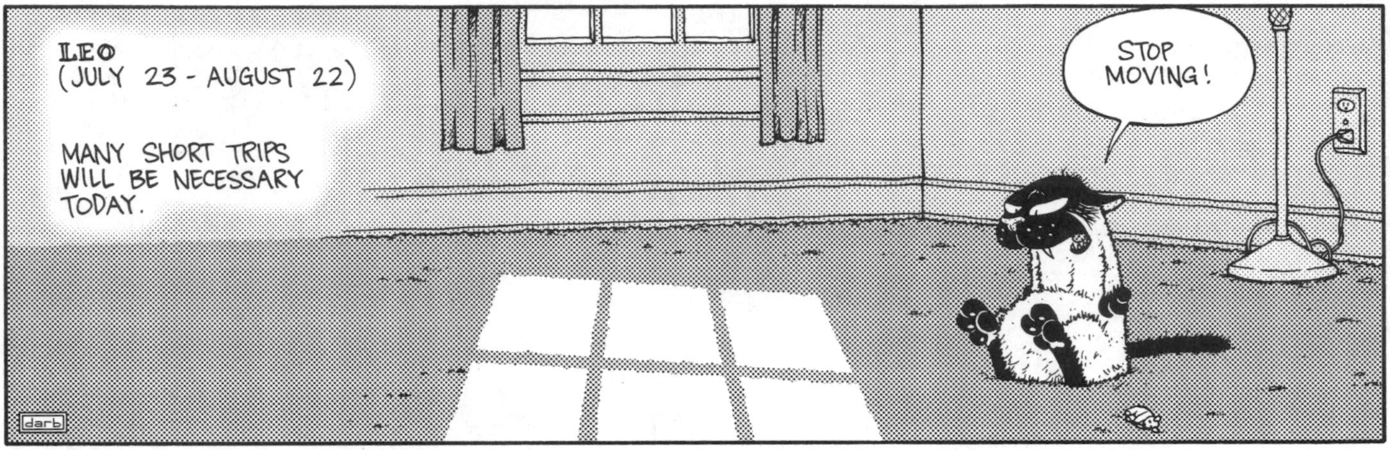
LEO
(JULY 23 - AUGUST 22)
MANY SHORT TRIPS WILL BE NECESSARY TODAY.
STOP MOVING!
darb

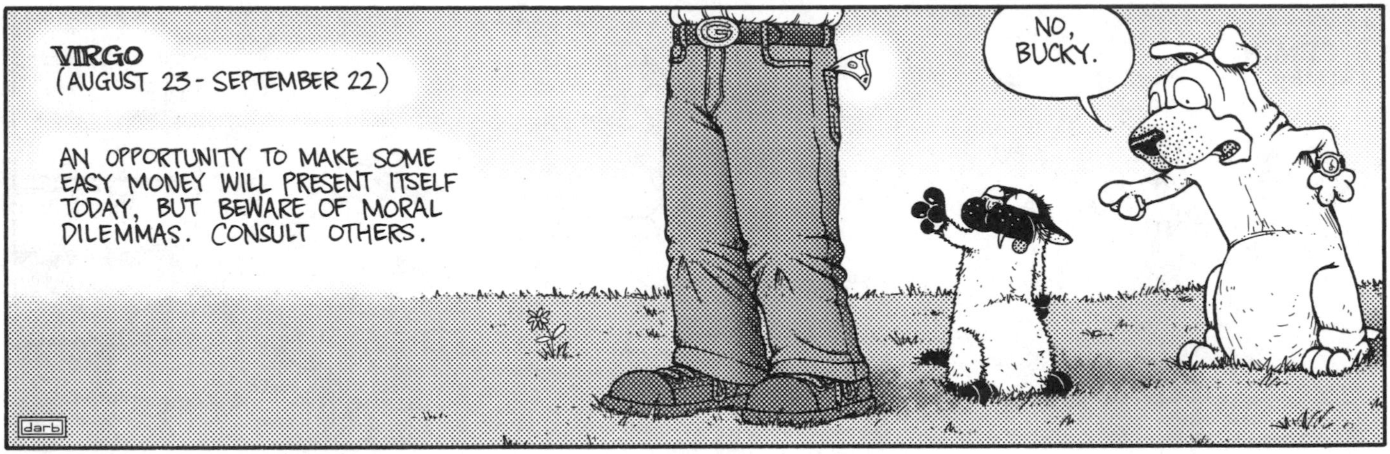
VIRGO
(AUGUST 23 - SEPTEMBER 22)
AN OPPORTUNITY TO MAKE SOME EASY MONEY WILL PRESENT ITSELF TODAY, BUT BEWARE OF MORAL DILEMMAS. CONSULT OTHERS.
NO, BUCKY.
darb

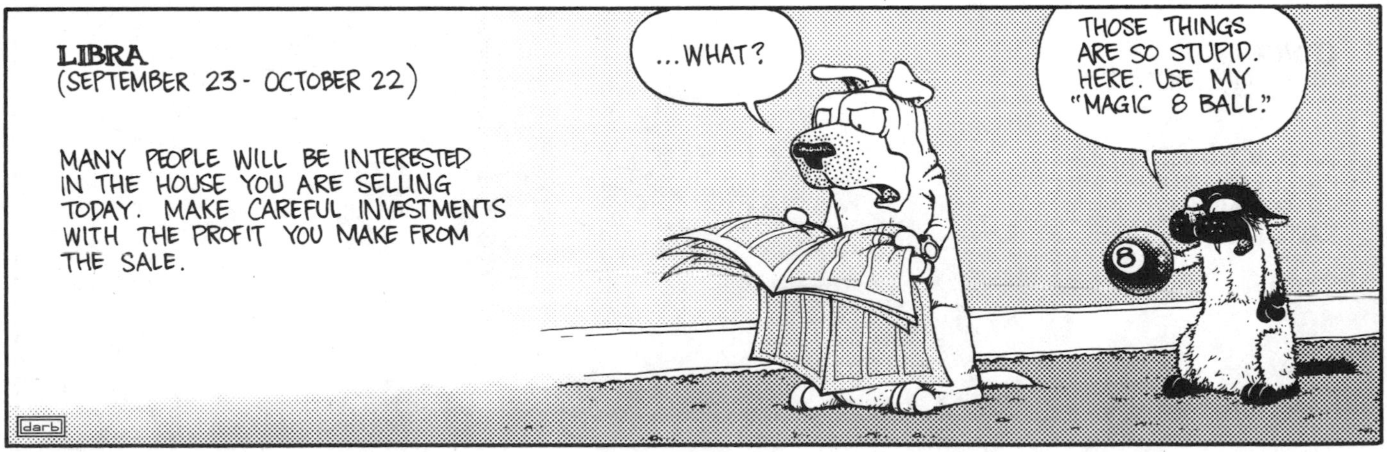
LIBRA
(SEPTEMBER 23 - OCTOBER 22)
MANY PEOPLE WILL BE INTERESTED IN THE HOUSE YOU ARE SELLING TODAY. MAKE CAREFUL INVESTMENTS WITH THE PROFIT YOU MAKE FROM THE SALE.
...WHAT?
THOSE THINGS ARE SO STUPID. HERE. USE MY "MAGIC 8 BALL."
darb

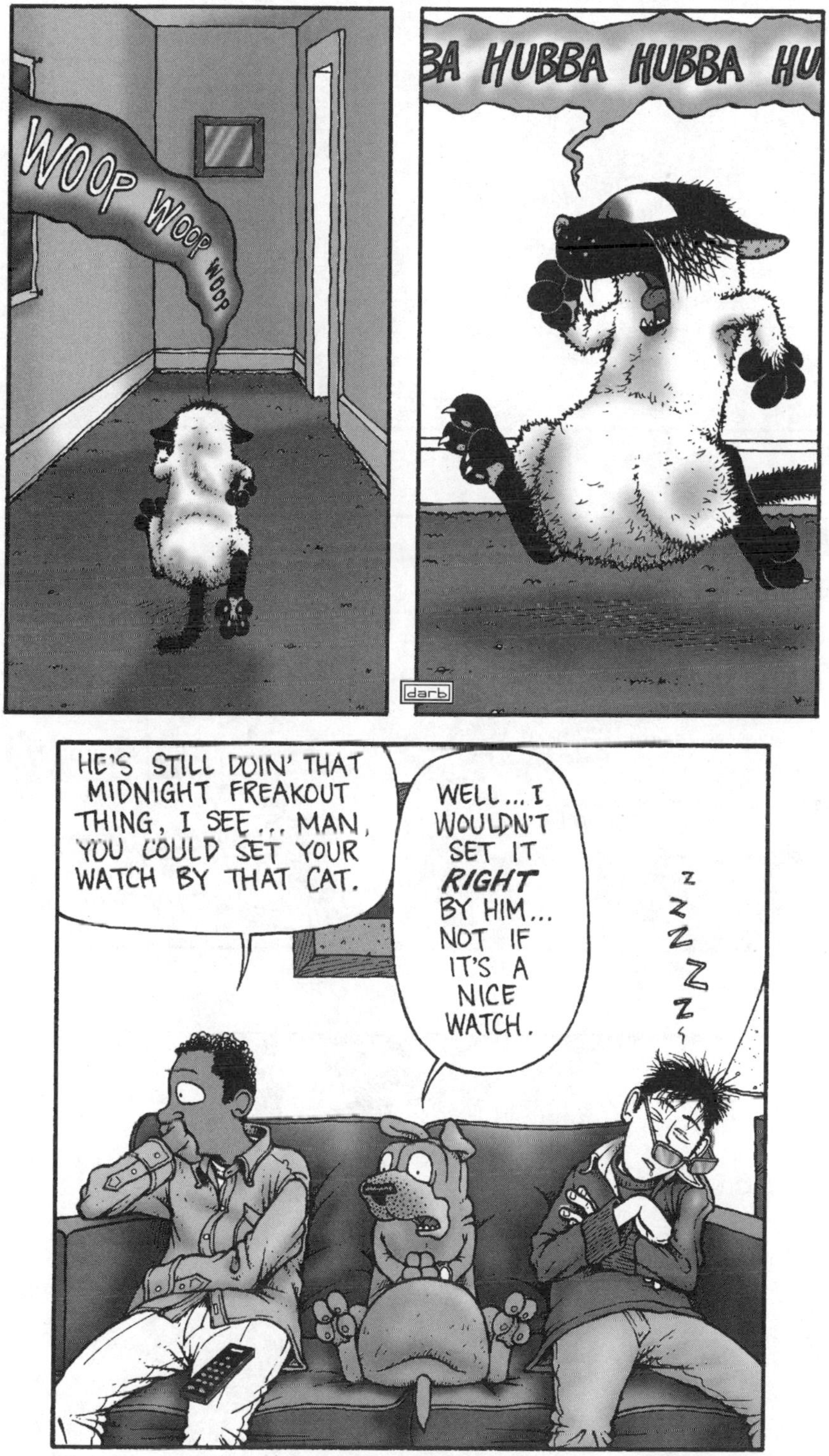
WOOP WOOP WOOP WOOP
BA HUBBA HUBBA HU
darb
HE'S STILL DOIN' THAT MIDNIGHT FREAKOUT THING, I SEE... MAN, YOU COULD SET YOUR WATCH BY THAT CAT.
WELL... I WOULDN'T SET IT **RIGHT** BY HIM... NOT IF IT'S A NICE WATCH.
Z Z Z Z Z

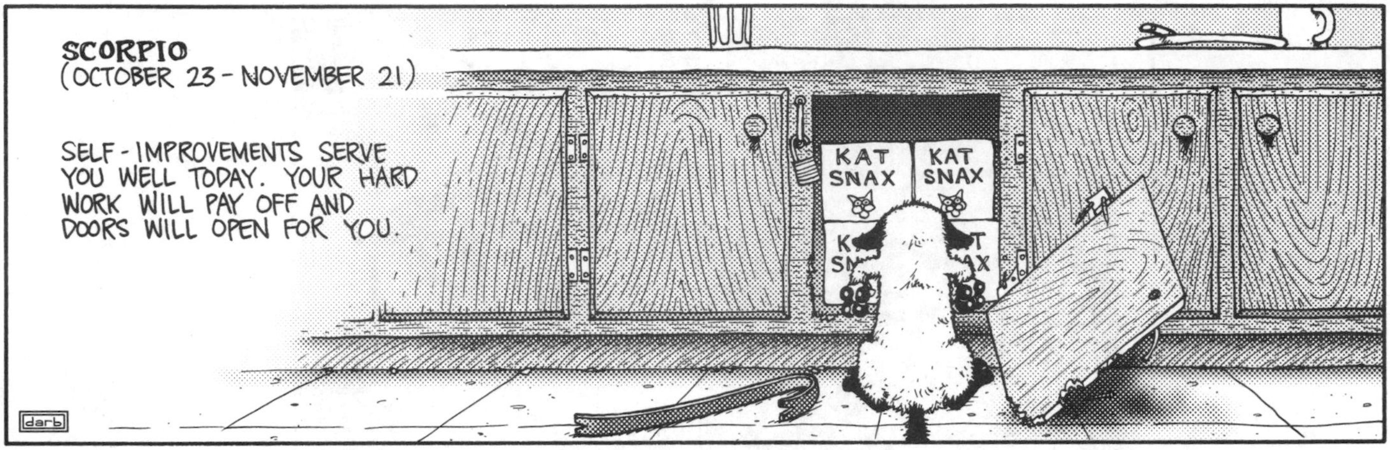
SCORPIO
(OCTOBER 23 - NOVEMBER 21)
SELF-IMPROVEMENTS SERVE YOU WELL TODAY. YOUR HARD WORK WILL PAY OFF AND DOORS WILL OPEN FOR YOU.
KAT SNAX
KAT SNAX

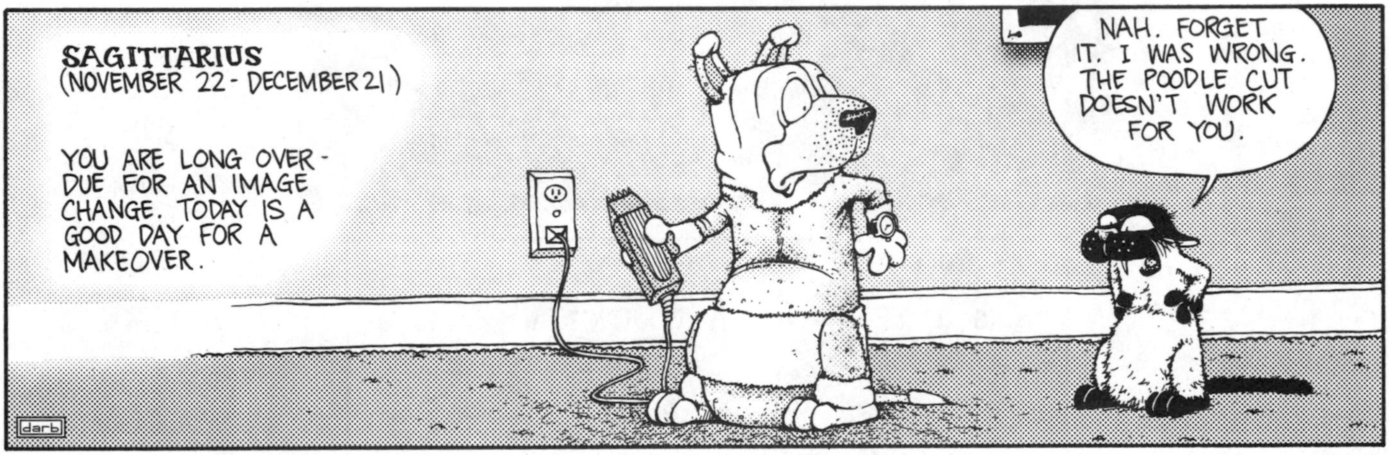
SAGITTARIUS
(NOVEMBER 22 - DECEMBER 21)
YOU ARE LONG OVER-DUE FOR AN IMAGE CHANGE. TODAY IS A GOOD DAY FOR A MAKEOVER.
NAH. FORGET IT. I WAS WRONG. THE POODLE CUT DOESN'T WORK FOR YOU.

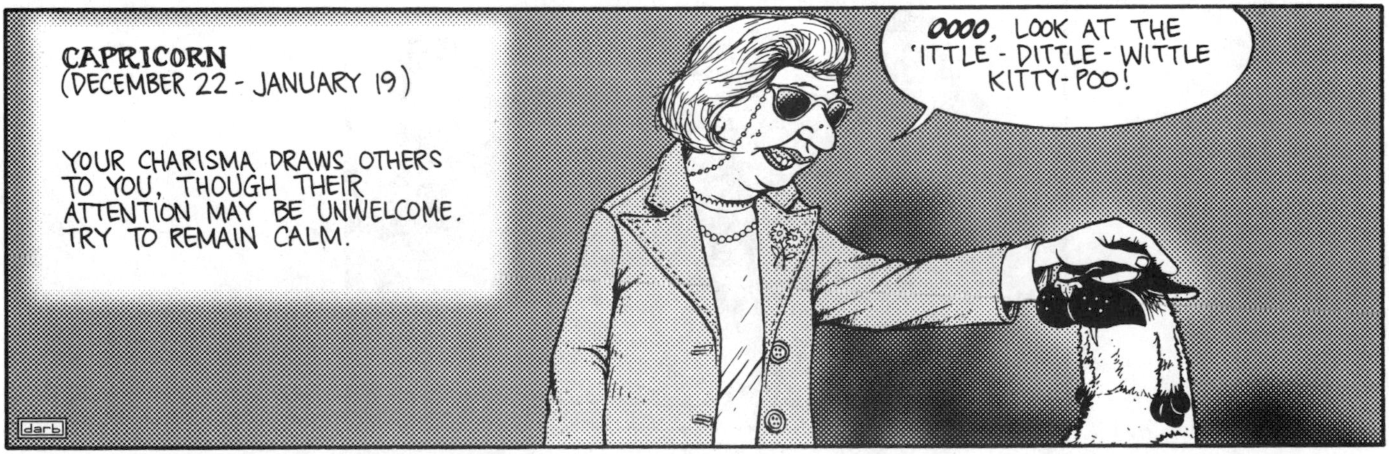
CAPRICORN
(DECEMBER 22 - JANUARY 19)
YOUR CHARISMA DRAWS OTHERS TO YOU, THOUGH THEIR ATTENTION MAY BE UNWELCOME. TRY TO REMAIN CALM.
OOOO, LOOK AT THE 'ITTLE-DITTLE-WITTLE KITTY-POO!

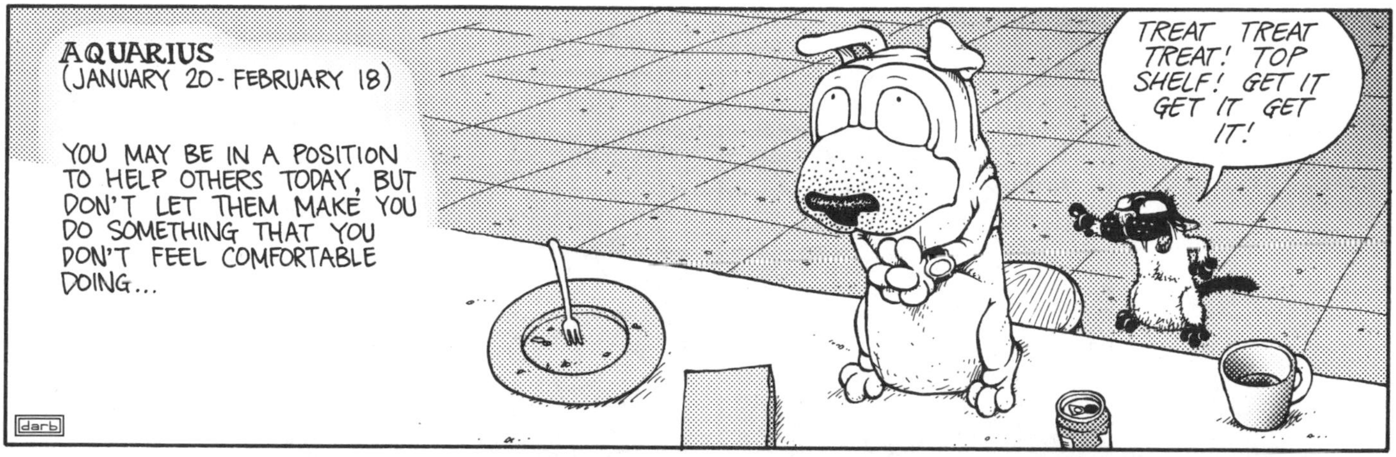
AQUARIUS
(JANUARY 20 - FEBRUARY 18)
YOU MAY BE IN A POSITION TO HELP OTHERS TODAY, BUT DON'T LET THEM MAKE YOU DO SOMETHING THAT YOU DON'T FEEL COMFORTABLE DOING...
TREAT TREAT TREAT! TOP SHELF! GET IT GET IT GET IT!
darb

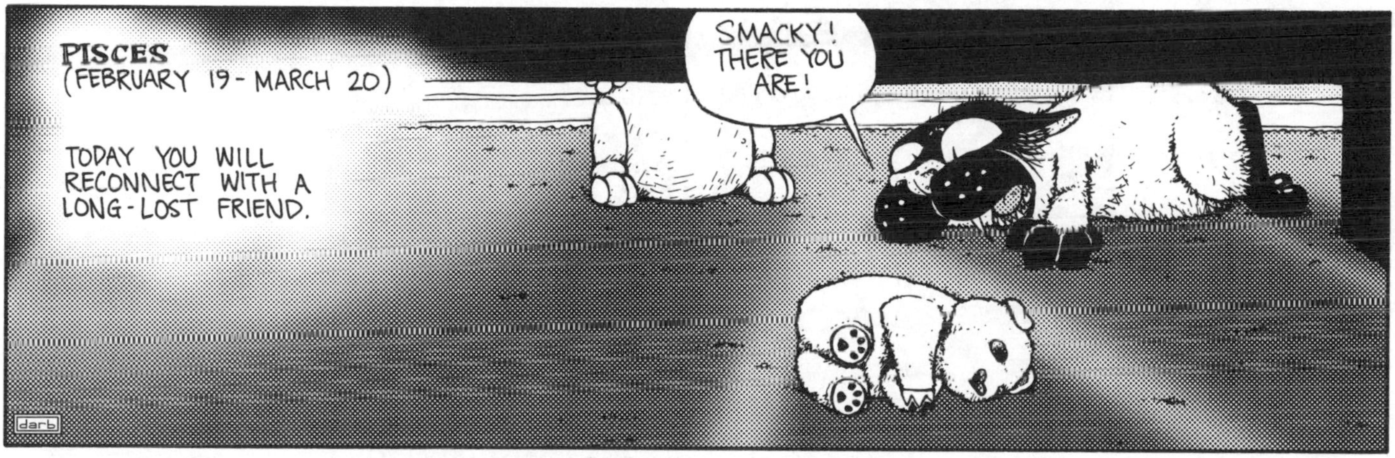
PISCES
(FEBRUARY 19 - MARCH 20)
TODAY YOU WILL RECONNECT WITH A LONG-LOST FRIEND.
SMACKY! THERE YOU ARE!
darb

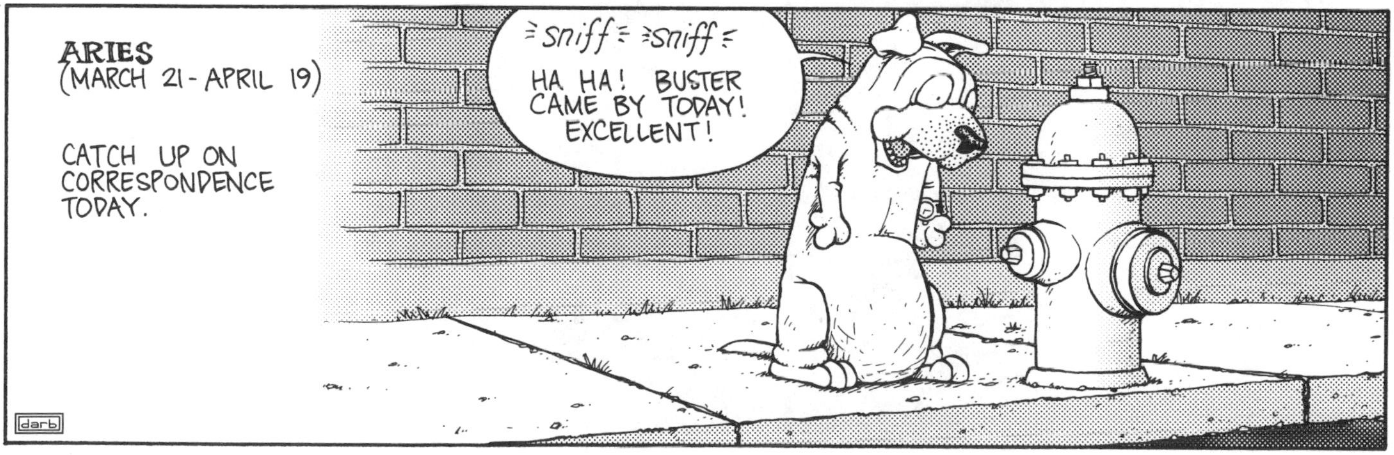
ARIES
(MARCH 21 - APRIL 19)
CATCH UP ON CORRESPONDENCE TODAY.
sniff sniff
HA HA! BUSTER CAME BY TODAY! EXCELLENT!
darb

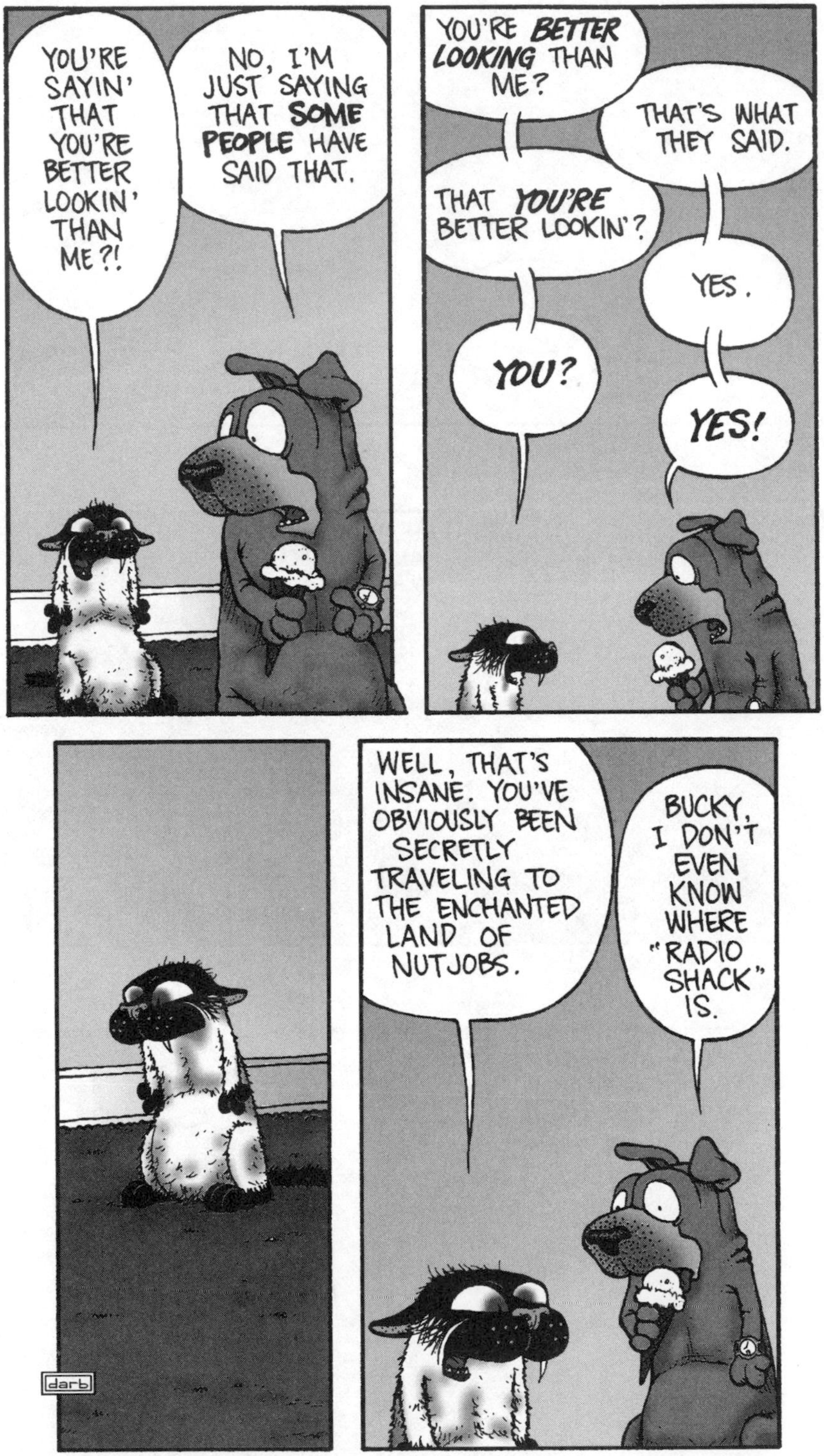
YOU'RE SAYIN' THAT YOU'RE BETTER LOOKIN' THAN ME?!
NO, I'M JUST SAYING THAT **SOME PEOPLE** HAVE SAID THAT.
YOU'RE ***BETTER LOOKING*** THAN ME?
THAT'S WHAT THEY SAID.
THAT ***YOU'RE*** BETTER LOOKIN'?
YES.
YOU?
YES!
WELL, THAT'S INSANE. YOU'VE OBVIOUSLY BEEN SECRETLY TRAVELING TO THE ENCHANTED LAND OF NUTJOBS.
BUCKY, I DON'T EVEN KNOW WHERE "RADIO SHACK" IS.
darb

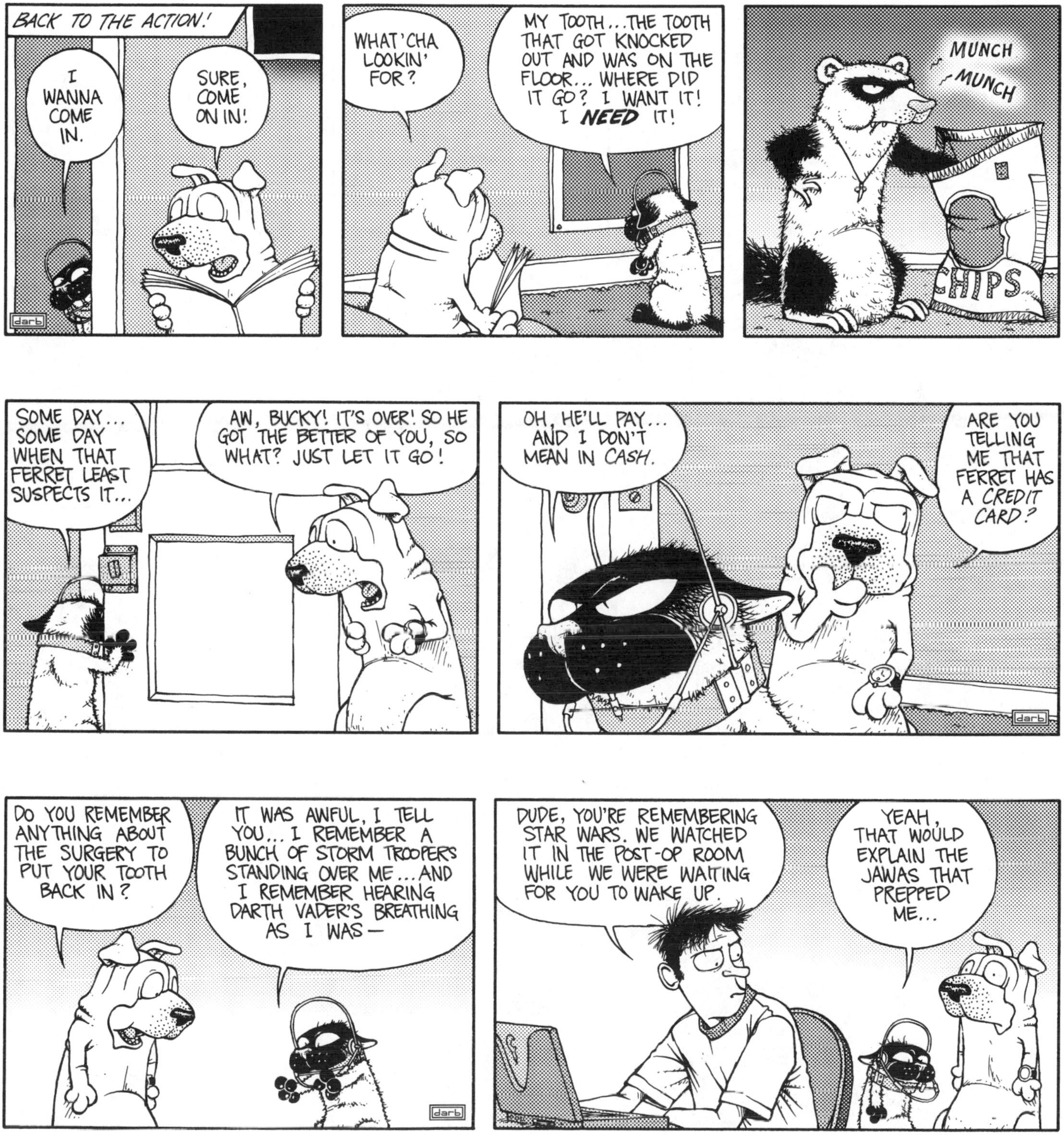
BACK TO THE ACTION!
I WANNA COME IN.
SURE, COME ON IN!
WHAT'CHA LOOKIN' FOR?
MY TOOTH...THE TOOTH THAT GOT KNOCKED OUT AND WAS ON THE FLOOR... WHERE DID IT GO? I WANT IT! I NEED IT!
MUNCH
MUNCH
CHIPS
SOME DAY... SOME DAY WHEN THAT FERRET LEAST SUSPECTS IT...
AW, BUCKY! IT'S OVER! SO HE GOT THE BETTER OF YOU, SO WHAT? JUST LET IT GO!
OH, HE'LL PAY... AND I DON'T MEAN IN CASH.
ARE YOU TELLING ME THAT FERRET HAS A CREDIT CARD?
DO YOU REMEMBER ANYTHING ABOUT THE SURGERY TO PUT YOUR TOOTH BACK IN?
IT WAS AWFUL, I TELL YOU... I REMEMBER A BUNCH OF STORM TROOPERS STANDING OVER ME...AND I REMEMBER HEARING DARTH VADER'S BREATHING AS I WAS—
DUDE, YOU'RE REMEMBERING STAR WARS. WE WATCHED IT IN THE POST-OP ROOM WHILE WE WERE WAITING FOR YOU TO WAKE UP.
YEAH, THAT WOULD EXPLAIN THE JAWAS THAT PREPPED ME...

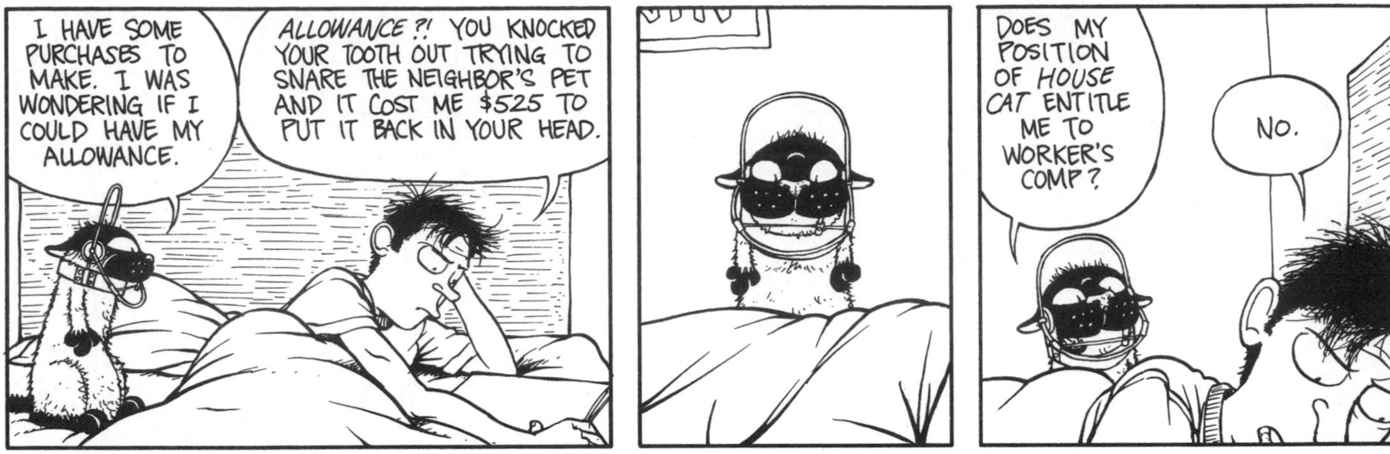
I HAVE SOME PURCHASES TO MAKE. I WAS WONDERING IF I COULD HAVE MY ALLOWANCE.
ALLOWANCE?! YOU KNOCKED YOUR TOOTH OUT TRYING TO SNARE THE NEIGHBOR'S PET AND IT COST ME $525 TO PUT IT BACK IN YOUR HEAD.
DOES MY POSITION OF *HOUSE CAT* ENTITLE ME TO WORKER'S COMP?
NO.

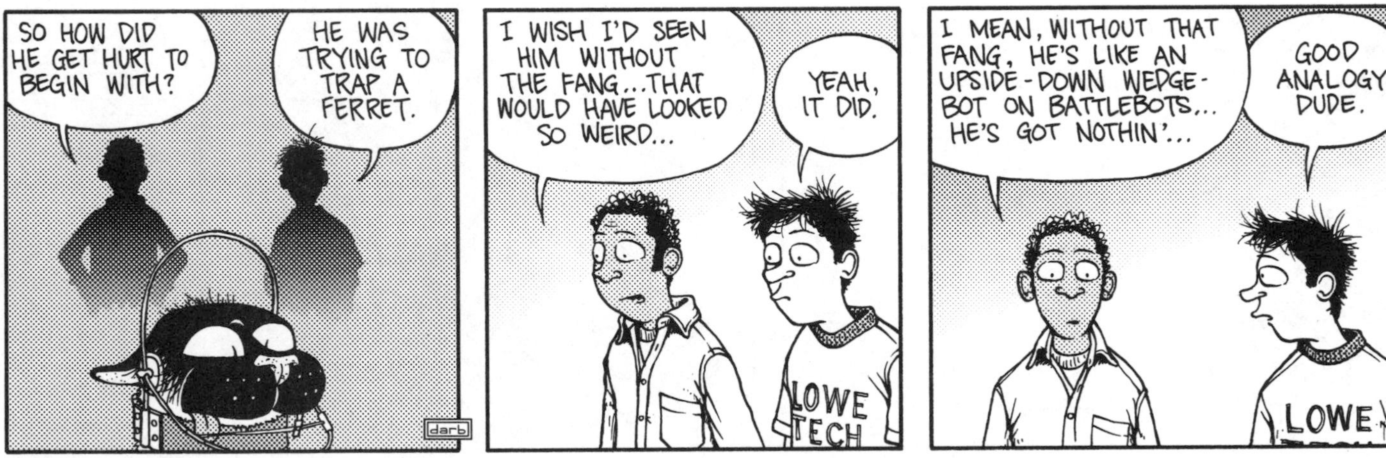
SO HOW DID HE GET HURT TO BEGIN WITH?
HE WAS TRYING TO TRAP A FERRET.
darb
I WISH I'D SEEN HIM WITHOUT THE FANG...THAT WOULD HAVE LOOKED SO WEIRD...
YEAH, IT DID.
LOWE TECH
I MEAN, WITHOUT THAT FANG, HE'S LIKE AN UPSIDE-DOWN WEDGE-BOT ON BATTLEBOTS... HE'S GOT NOTHIN'...
GOOD ANALOGY, DUDE.
LOWE

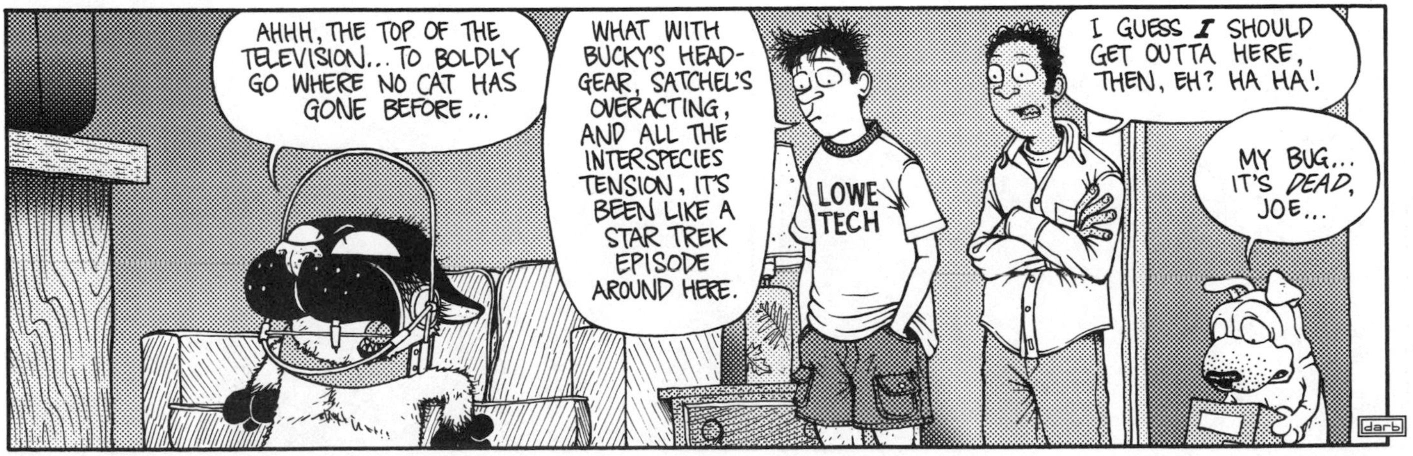
AHHH, THE TOP OF THE TELEVISION... TO BOLDLY GO WHERE NO CAT HAS GONE BEFORE...
WHAT WITH BUCKY'S HEAD-GEAR, SATCHEL'S OVERACTING, AND ALL THE INTERSPECIES TENSION, IT'S BEEN LIKE A STAR TREK EPISODE AROUND HERE.
LOWE TECH
I GUESS **I** SHOULD GET OUTTA HERE, THEN, EH? HA HA!
MY BUG... IT'S *DEAD*, JOE...
darb

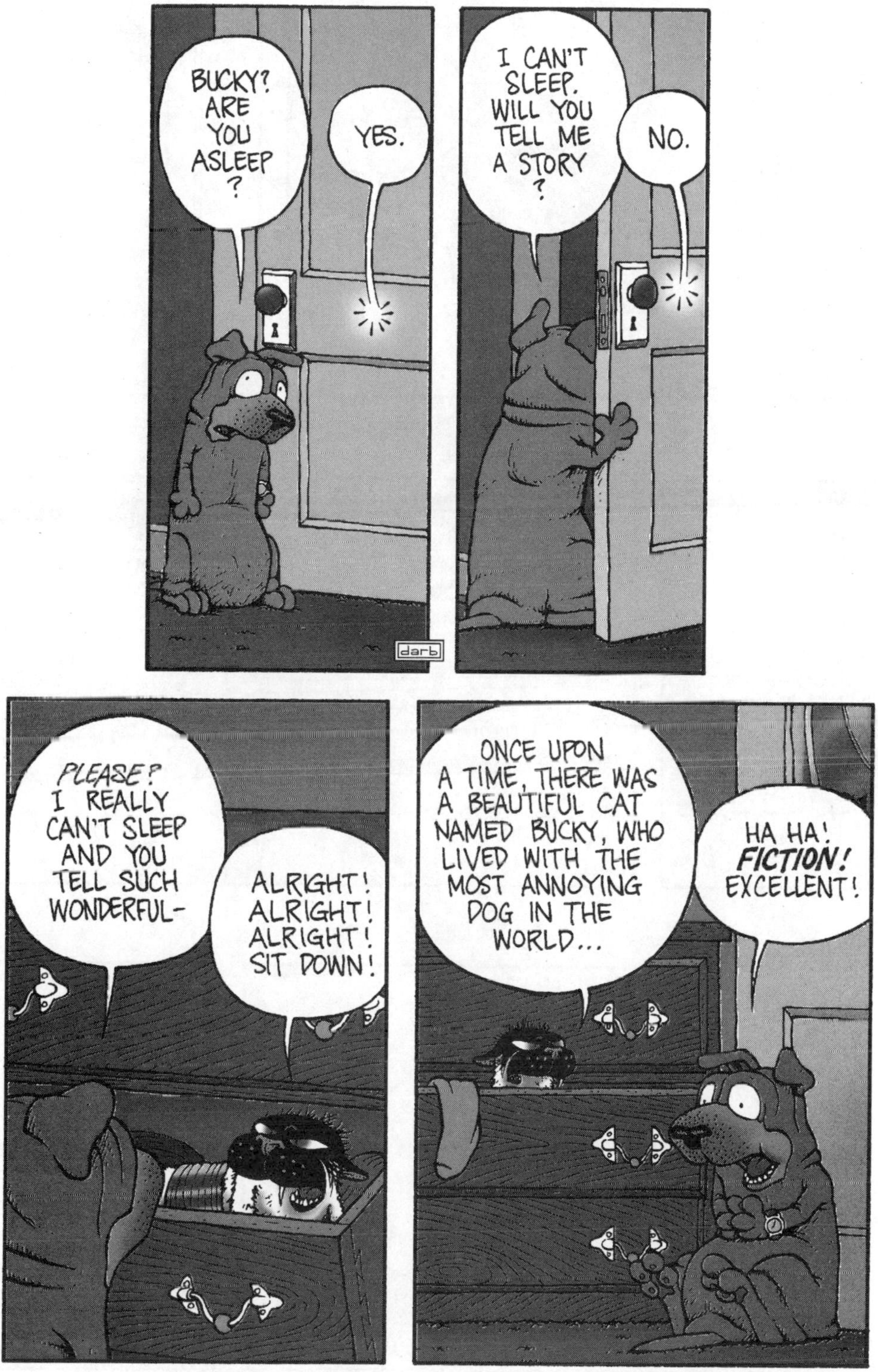
BUCKY? ARE YOU ASLEEP ?
YES.
I CAN'T SLEEP. WILL YOU TELL ME A STORY ?
NO.
PLEASE? I REALLY CAN'T SLEEP AND YOU TELL SUCH WONDERFUL-
ALRIGHT! ALRIGHT! ALRIGHT! SIT DOWN!
ONCE UPON A TIME, THERE WAS A BEAUTIFUL CAT NAMED BUCKY, WHO LIVED WITH THE MOST ANNOYING DOG IN THE WORLD...
HA HA! FICTION! EXCELLENT!
darb

CAN I HELP YOU ?
UHHH...
ARE YOU LOOKING FOR SATCHEL?
NNNNOOO... NO... NO... UHHHH...
4F
MAIL
WAIT- *YEAH.* YEAH. SATCHEL.
SATCHEL, YOU HAVE A VISITOR.
A *VISITOR* ?!
HEYYY, BURGER! LONG TIME NO SMELL!
HOLD ON. LET'S SEE WHO YOUR VISITOR IS...
WELL... AREN'T **YOU** THE VISITOR ?
NO, NO, NO, I'M JUST... OH WAIT, YES. YES, I AM THAT.
AWWW, COOL! A ROBOTIC CAT!
DON'T TOUCH ME.
HE HE HE HE! IT TALKS!
I DON'T LIKE YOU.
WOW, THE PROGRAMMERS SURE GOT "CAT" DOWN! HE HE HE!
SATCHEL!

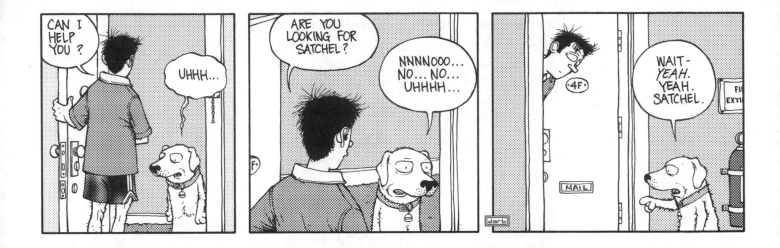

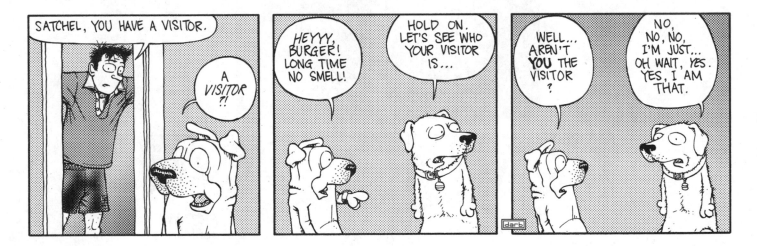

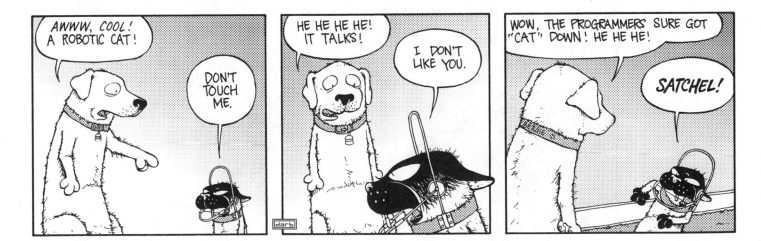

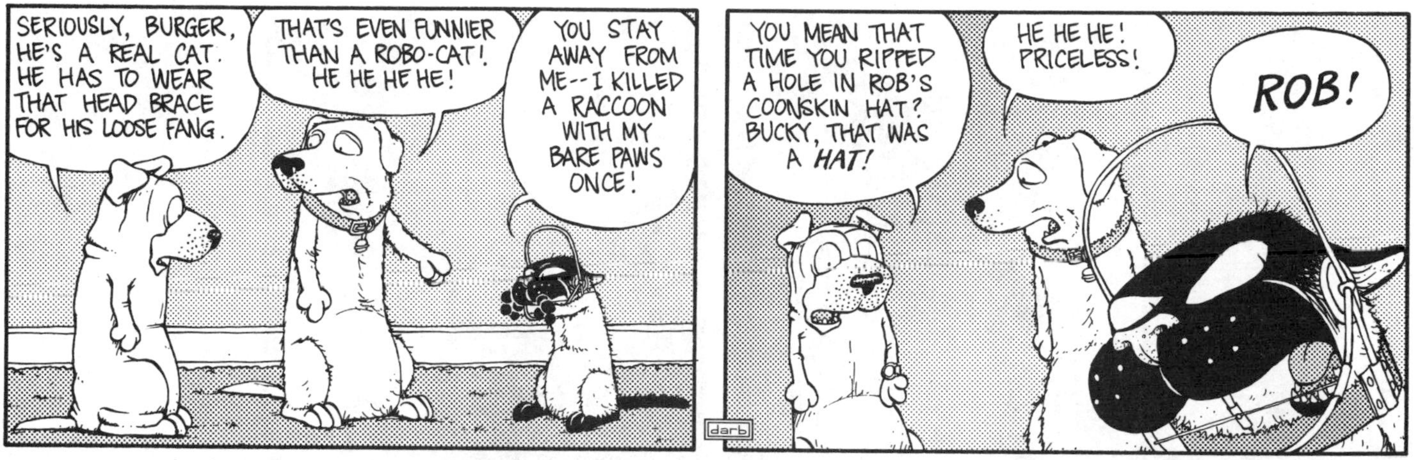
SERIOUSLY, BURGER, HE'S A REAL CAT. HE HAS TO WEAR THAT HEAD BRACE FOR HIS LOOSE FANG.
THAT'S EVEN FUNNIER THAN A ROBO-CAT! HE HE HE HE!
YOU STAY AWAY FROM ME--I KILLED A RACCOON WITH MY BARE PAWS ONCE!
YOU MEAN THAT TIME YOU RIPPED A HOLE IN ROB'S COONSKIN HAT? BUCKY, THAT WAS A *HAT!*
HE HE HE! PRICELESS!
ROB!
darb

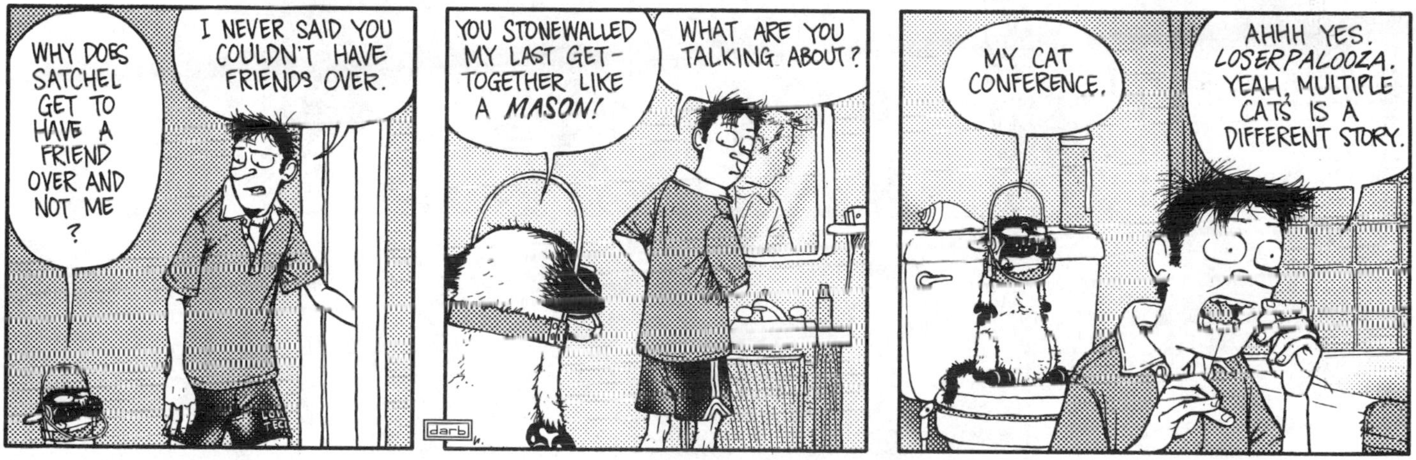
WHY DOES SATCHEL GET TO HAVE A FRIEND OVER AND NOT ME?
I NEVER SAID YOU COULDN'T HAVE FRIENDS OVER.
YOU STONEWALLED MY LAST GET-TOGETHER LIKE A *MASON!*
WHAT ARE YOU TALKING ABOUT?
darb
MY CAT CONFERENCE.
AHHH YES. *LOSERPALOOZA.* YEAH, MULTIPLE CATS IS A DIFFERENT STORY.

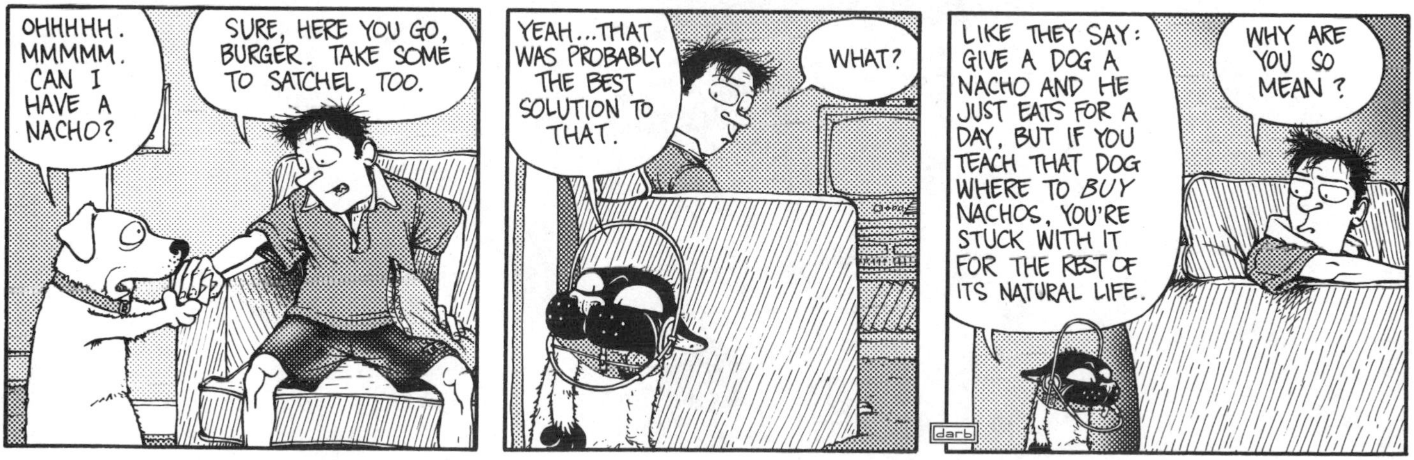
OHHHHH. MMMMM. CAN I HAVE A NACHO?
SURE, HERE YOU GO, BURGER. TAKE SOME TO SATCHEL, TOO.
YEAH...THAT WAS PROBABLY THE BEST SOLUTION TO THAT.
WHAT?
LIKE THEY SAY: GIVE A DOG A NACHO AND HE JUST EATS FOR A DAY, BUT IF YOU TEACH THAT DOG WHERE TO *BUY* NACHOS, YOU'RE STUCK WITH IT FOR THE REST OF ITS NATURAL LIFE.
WHY ARE YOU SO MEAN?
darb

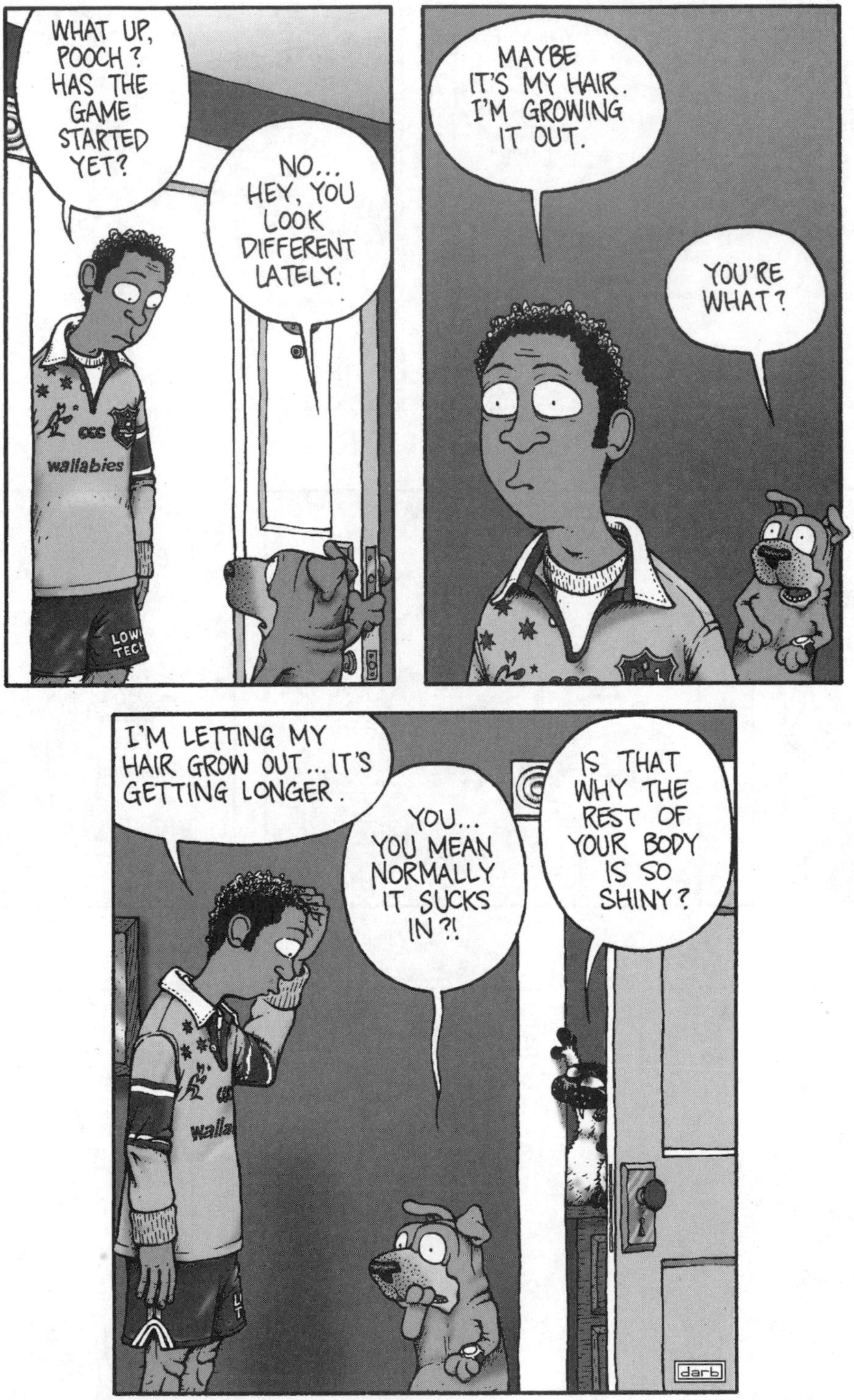
WHAT UP, POOCH? HAS THE GAME STARTED YET?
NO... HEY, YOU LOOK DIFFERENT LATELY.
MAYBE IT'S MY HAIR. I'M GROWING IT OUT.
YOU'RE WHAT?
I'M LETTING MY HAIR GROW OUT... IT'S GETTING LONGER.
YOU... YOU MEAN NORMALLY IT SUCKS IN?!
IS THAT WHY THE REST OF YOUR BODY IS SO SHINY?
darb

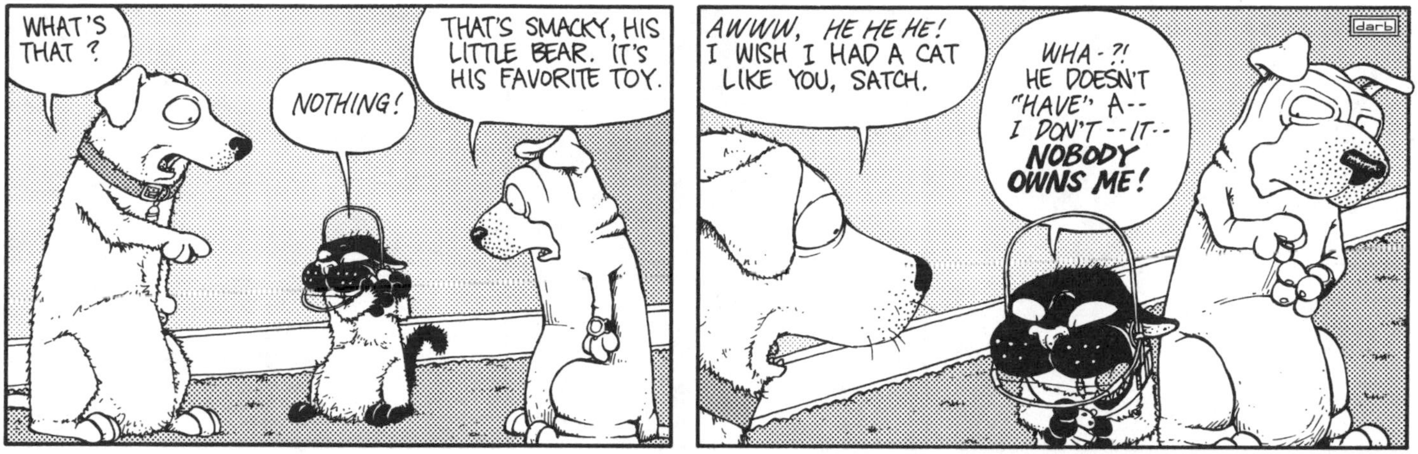
WHAT'S THAT ?
NOTHING!
THAT'S SMACKY, HIS LITTLE BEAR. IT'S HIS FAVORITE TOY.
darb
AWWW, HE HE HE! I WISH I HAD A CAT LIKE YOU, SATCH.
WHA-?! HE DOESN'T "HAVE" A-- I DON'T--IT-- NOBODY OWNS ME!

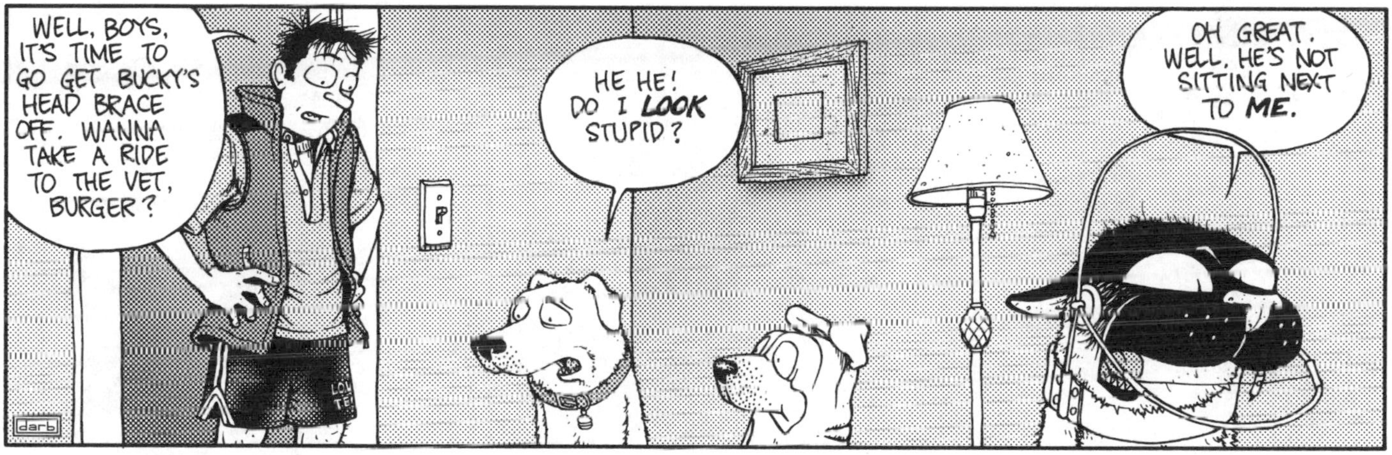
WELL, BOYS, IT'S TIME TO GO GET BUCKY'S HEAD BRACE OFF. WANNA TAKE A RIDE TO THE VET, BURGER?
darb
HE HE! DO I LOOK STUPID?
OH GREAT. WELL, HE'S NOT SITTING NEXT TO ME.

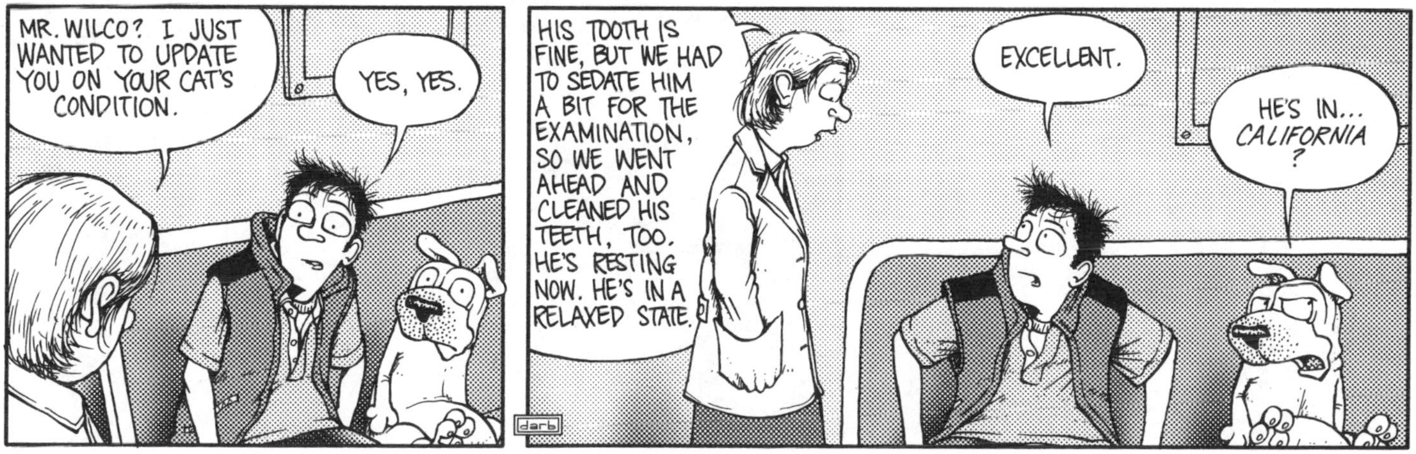
MR. WILCO? I JUST WANTED TO UPDATE YOU ON YOUR CAT'S CONDITION.
YES, YES.
darb
HIS TOOTH IS FINE, BUT WE HAD TO SEDATE HIM A BIT FOR THE EXAMINATION, SO WE WENT AHEAD AND CLEANED HIS TEETH, TOO. HE'S RESTING NOW. HE'S IN A RELAXED STATE.
EXCELLENT.
HE'S IN... CALIFORNIA?

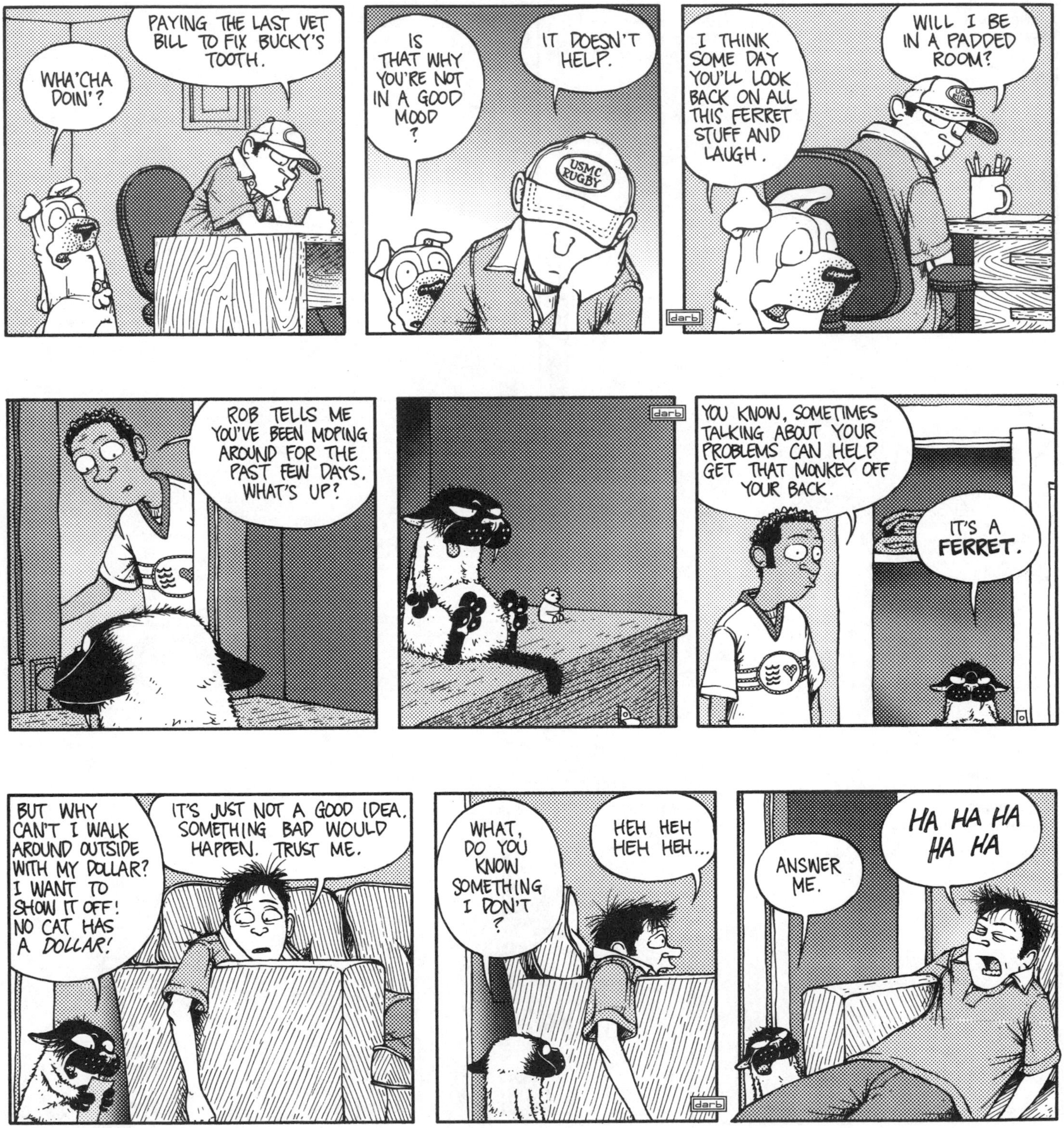
WHA'CHA DOIN'?
PAYING THE LAST VET BILL TO FIX BUCKY'S TOOTH.
IS THAT WHY YOU'RE NOT IN A GOOD MOOD?
IT DOESN'T HELP.
I THINK SOME DAY YOU'LL LOOK BACK ON ALL THIS FERRET STUFF AND LAUGH.
WILL I BE IN A PADDED ROOM?
ROB TELLS ME YOU'VE BEEN MOPING AROUND FOR THE PAST FEW DAYS. WHAT'S UP?
YOU KNOW, SOMETIMES TALKING ABOUT YOUR PROBLEMS CAN HELP GET THAT MONKEY OFF YOUR BACK.
IT'S A **FERRET.**
BUT WHY CAN'T I WALK AROUND OUTSIDE WITH MY DOLLAR? I WANT TO SHOW IT OFF! NO CAT HAS A *DOLLAR!*
IT'S JUST NOT A GOOD IDEA. SOMETHING BAD WOULD HAPPEN. TRUST ME.
WHAT, DO YOU KNOW SOMETHING I DON'T?
HEH HEH HEH HEH...
ANSWER ME.
HA HA HA HA HA

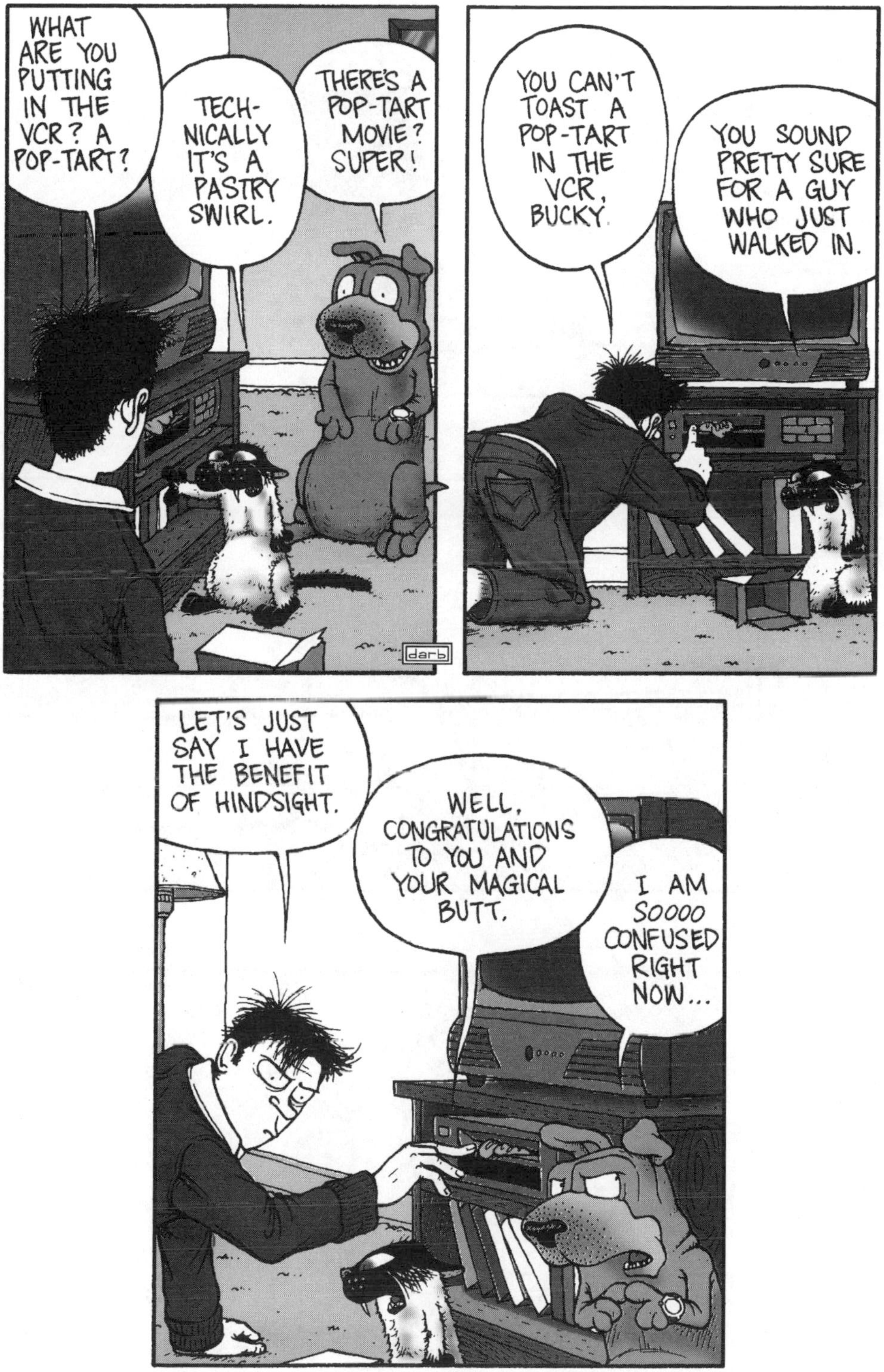
WHAT ARE YOU PUTTING IN THE VCR? A POP-TART?
TECH-NICALLY IT'S A PASTRY SWIRL.
THERE'S A POP-TART MOVIE? SUPER!
darb
YOU CAN'T TOAST A POP-TART IN THE VCR, BUCKY.
YOU SOUND PRETTY SURE FOR A GUY WHO JUST WALKED IN.
LET'S JUST SAY I HAVE THE BENEFIT OF HINDSIGHT.
WELL, CONGRATULATIONS TO YOU AND YOUR MAGICAL BUTT.
I AM SOOOO CONFUSED RIGHT NOW...

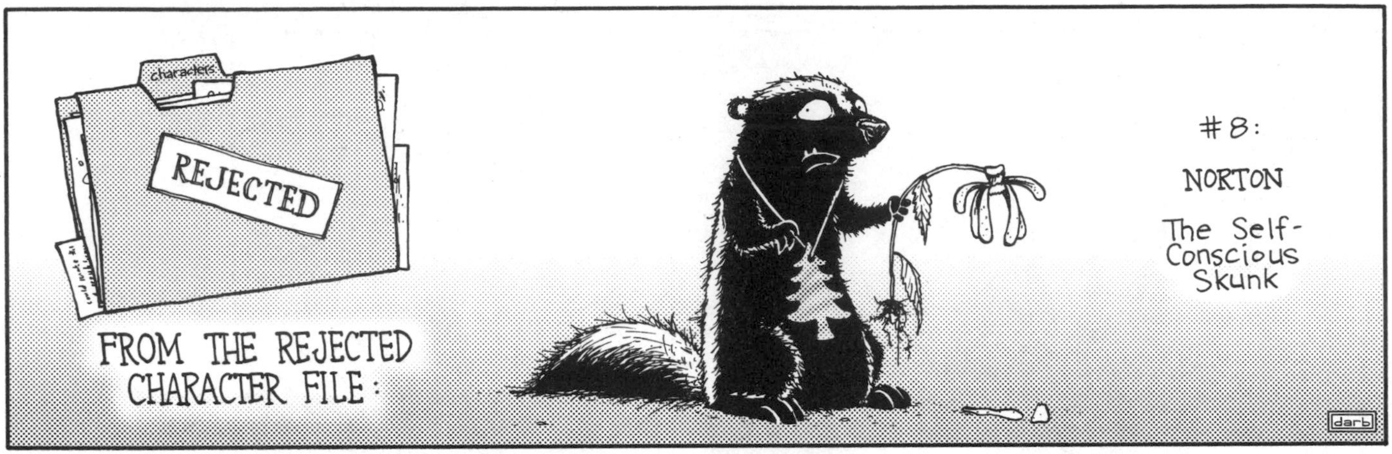
characters
REJECTED
FROM THE REJECTED CHARACTER FILE:
#8:
NORTON
The Self-Conscious Skunk
darb

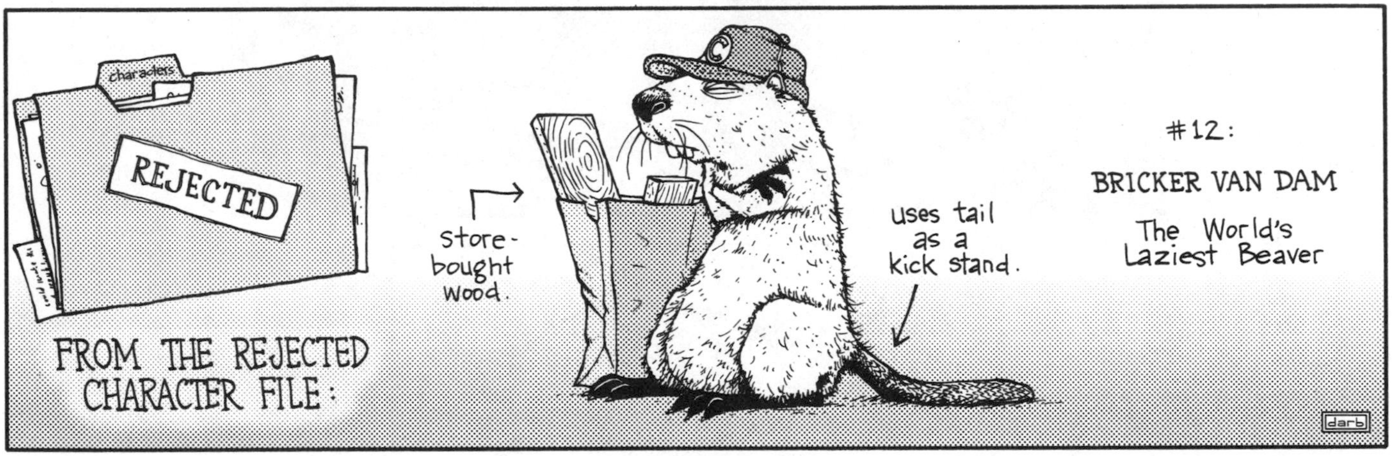
characters
REJECTED
FROM THE REJECTED CHARACTER FILE:
store-bought wood.
uses tail as a kick stand.
#12:
BRICKER VAN DAM
The World's Laziest Beaver
darb

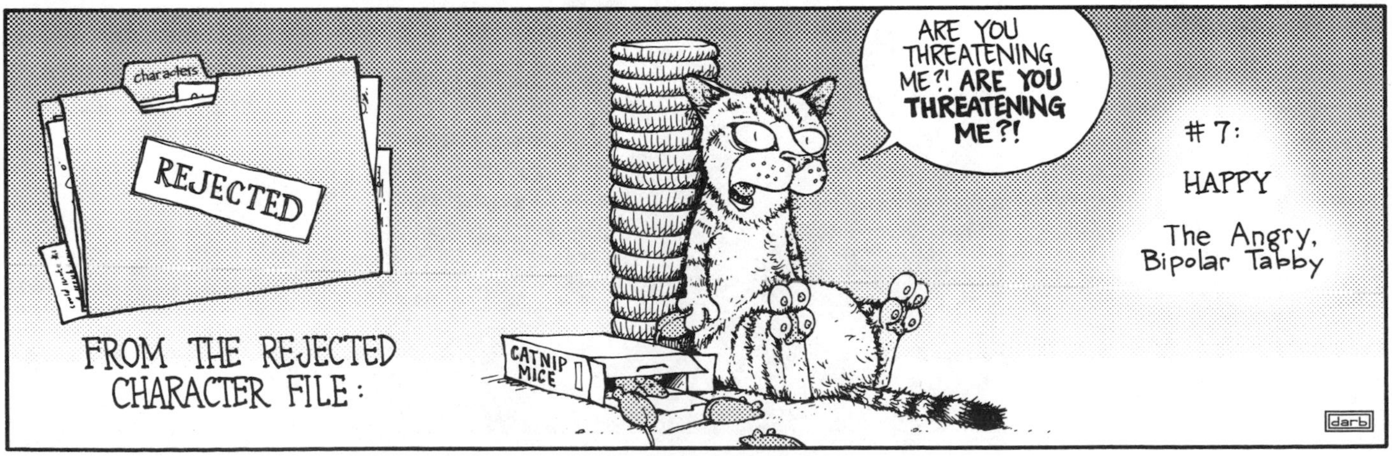
characters
REJECTED
FROM THE REJECTED CHARACTER FILE:
CATNIP MICE
ARE YOU THREATENING ME?! ARE YOU THREATENING ME?!
#7:
HAPPY
The Angry, Bipolar Tabby
darb

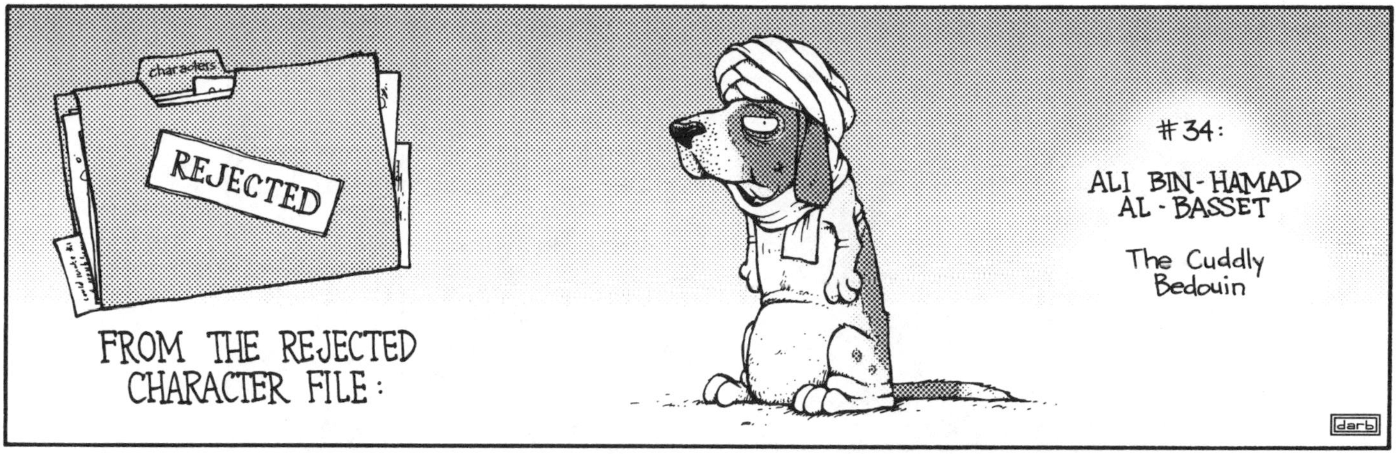
characters
REJECTED
FROM THE REJECTED CHARACTER FILE:
#34:
ALI BIN-HAMAD AL-BASSET
The Cuddly Bedouin
darb

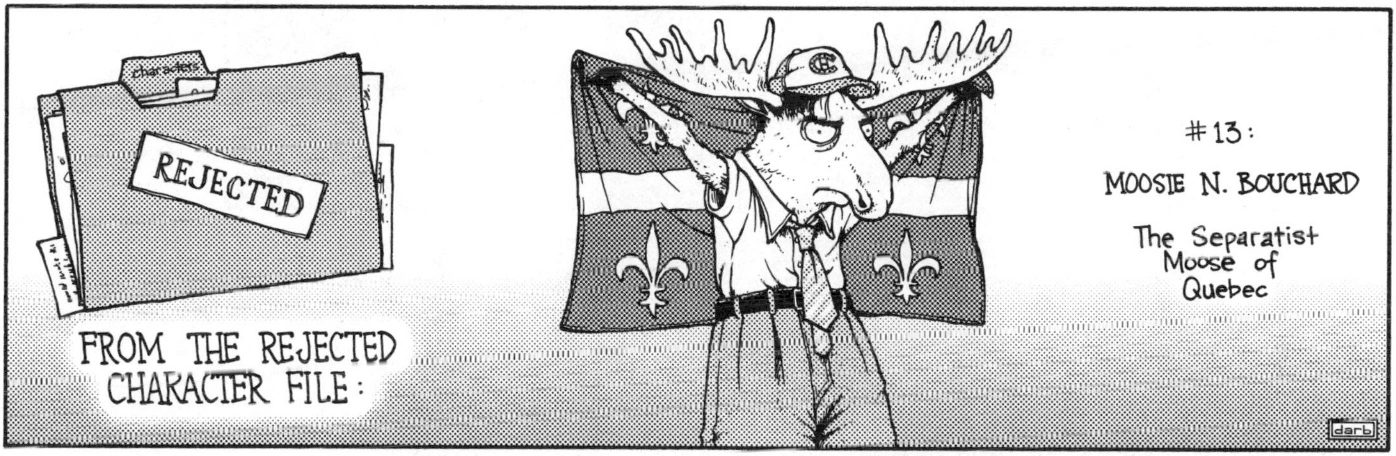
characters
REJECTED
FROM THE REJECTED CHARACTER FILE:
#13:
MOOSIE N. BOUCHARD
The Separatist Moose of Quebec
darb

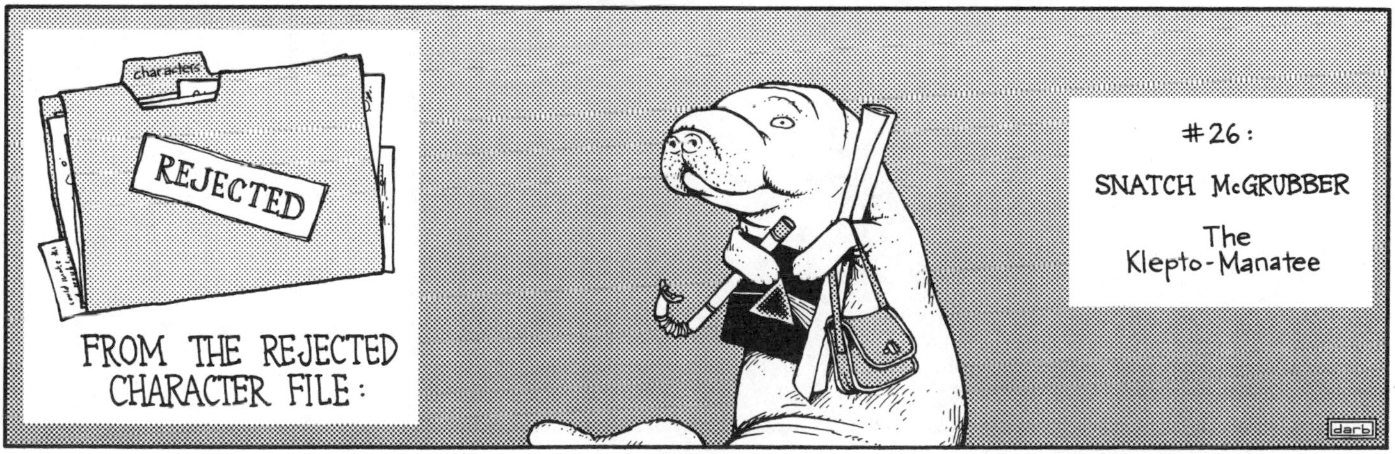
characters
REJECTED
FROM THE REJECTED CHARACTER FILE:
#26:
SNATCH McGRUBBER
The Klepto-Manatee
darb

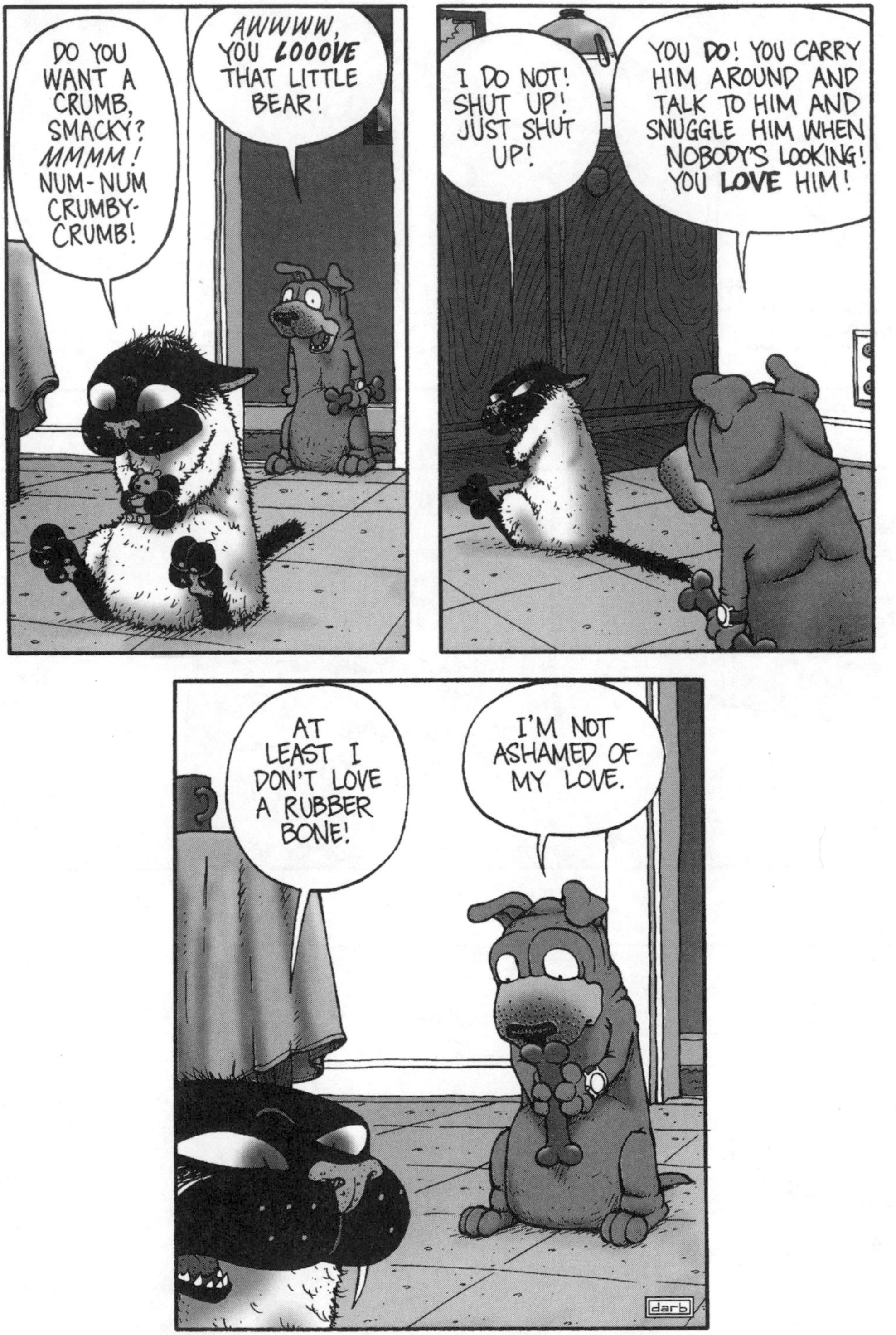
DO YOU WANT A CRUMB, SMACKY? MMMM! NUM-NUM CRUMBY-CRUMB!
AWWWW, YOU LOOOVE THAT LITTLE BEAR!
I DO NOT! SHUT UP! JUST SHUT UP!
YOU DO! YOU CARRY HIM AROUND AND TALK TO HIM AND SNUGGLE HIM WHEN NOBODY'S LOOKING! YOU LOVE HIM!
AT LEAST I DON'T LOVE A RUBBER BONE!
I'M NOT ASHAMED OF MY LOVE.
darb

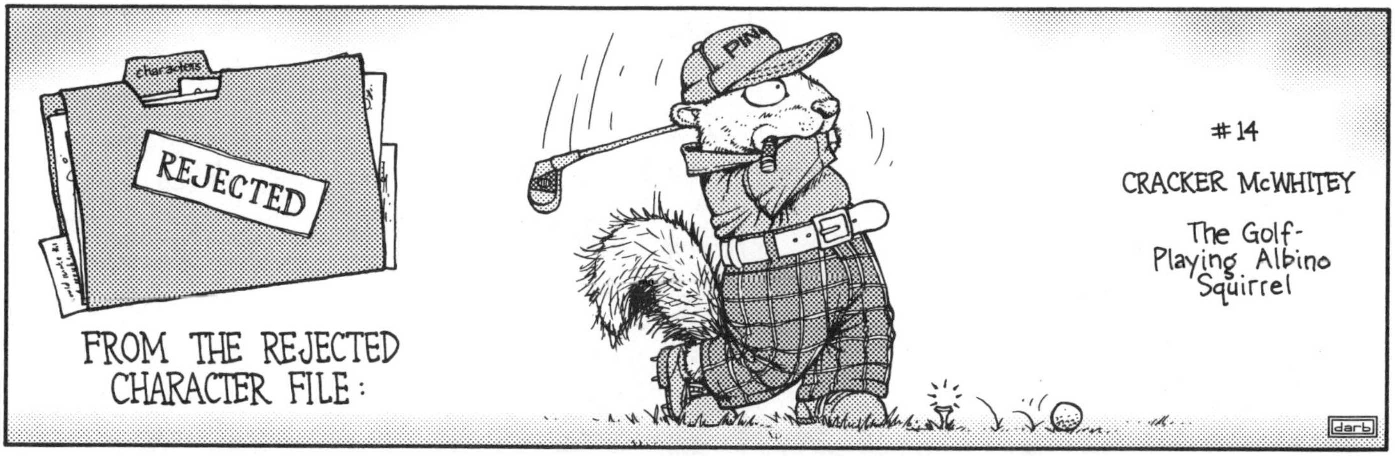
characters
REJECTED
FROM THE REJECTED CHARACTER FILE:
#14
CRACKER McWHITEY
The Golf-Playing Albino Squirrel

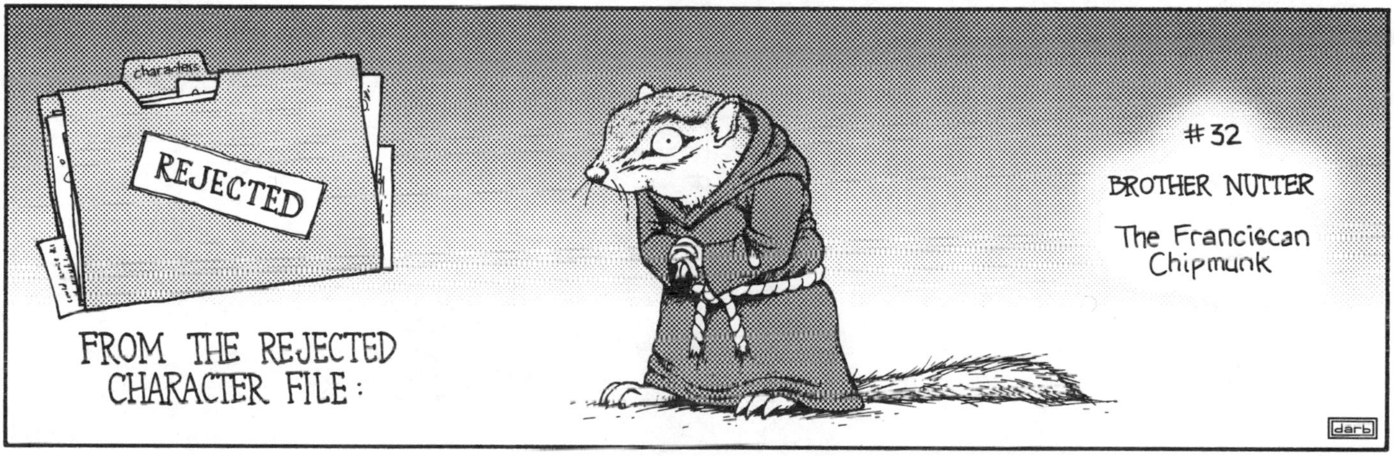
characters
REJECTED
FROM THE REJECTED CHARACTER FILE:
#32
BROTHER NUTTER
The Franciscan Chipmunk

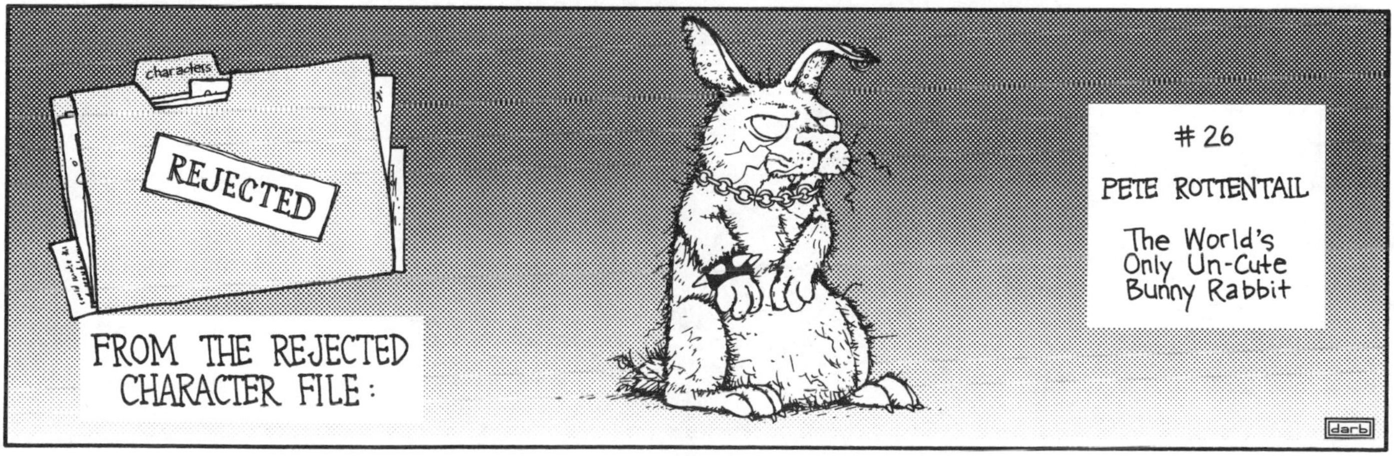
characters
REJECTED
FROM THE REJECTED CHARACTER FILE:
#26
PETE ROTTENTAIL
The World's Only Un-Cute Bunny Rabbit

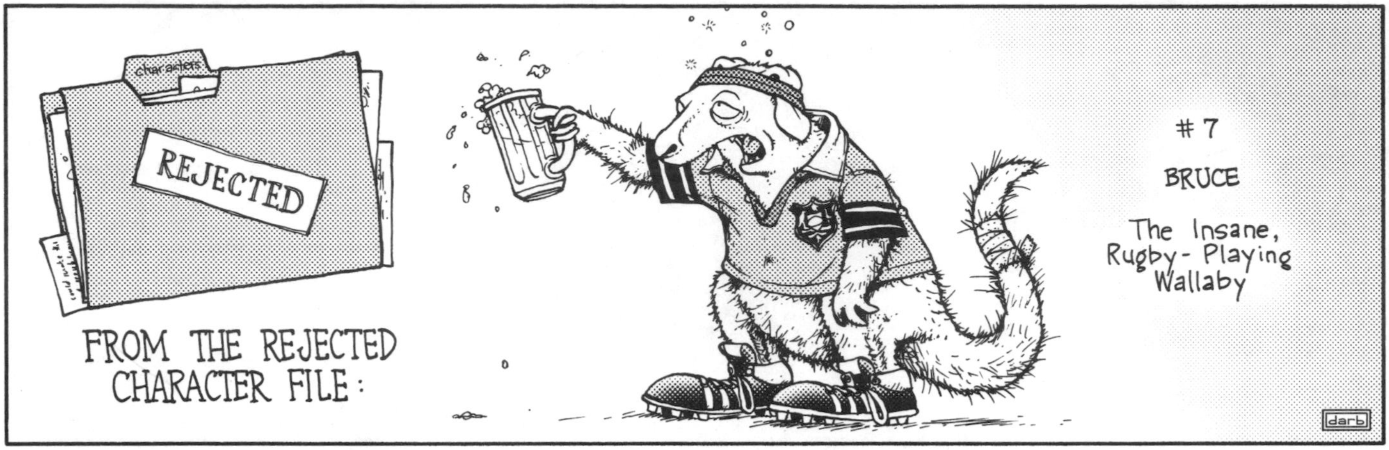
characters
REJECTED
FROM THE REJECTED CHARACTER FILE:
#7
BRUCE
The Insane, Rugby-Playing Wallaby
darb

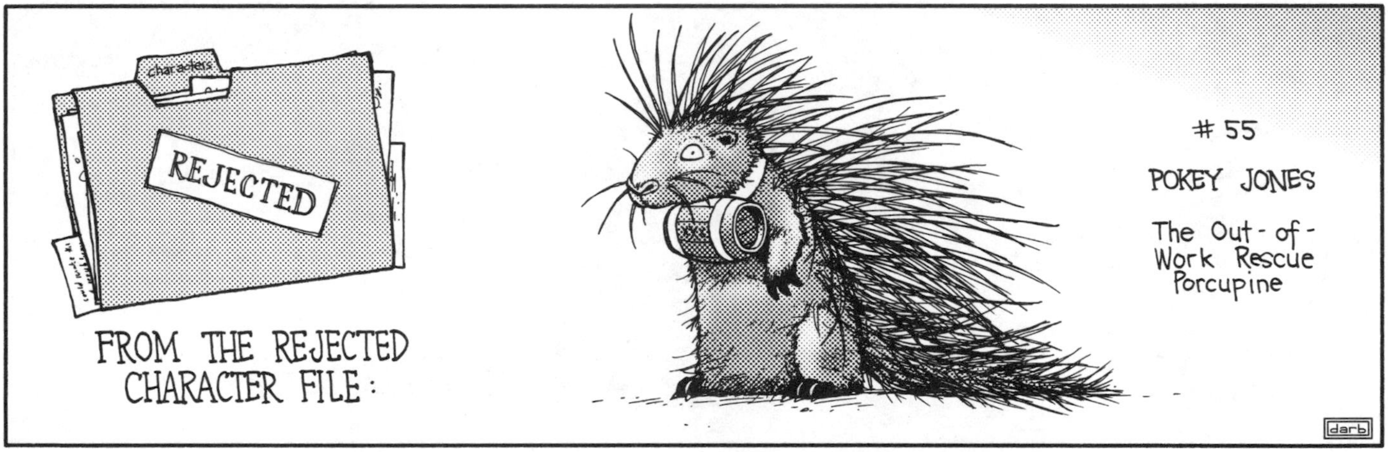
characters
REJECTED
FROM THE REJECTED CHARACTER FILE:
#55
POKEY JONES
The Out-of-Work Rescue Porcupine
darb

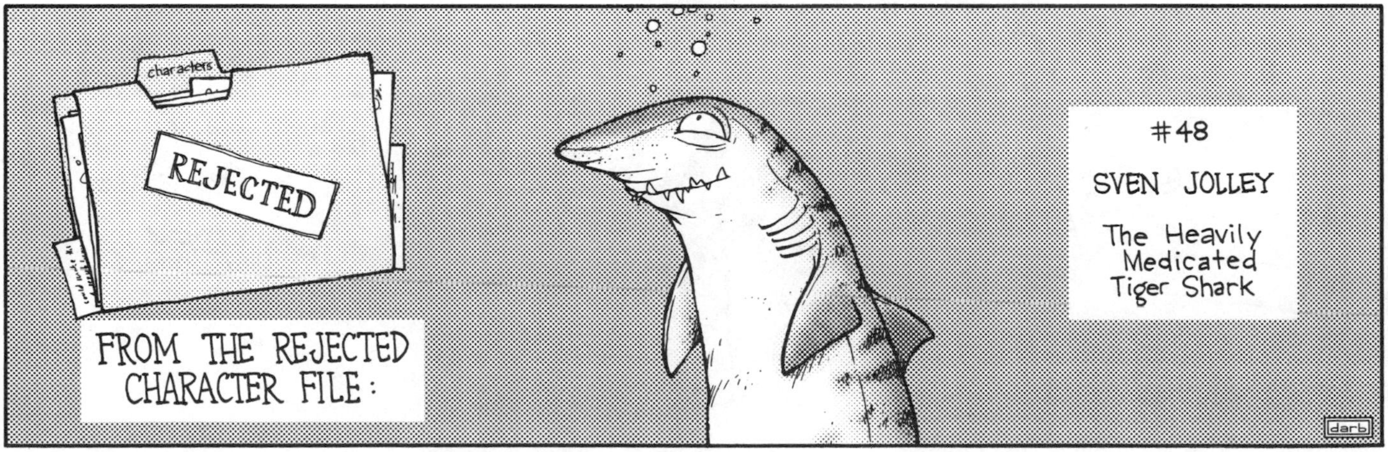
characters
REJECTED
FROM THE REJECTED CHARACTER FILE:
#48
SVEN JOLLEY
The Heavily Medicated Tiger Shark
darb

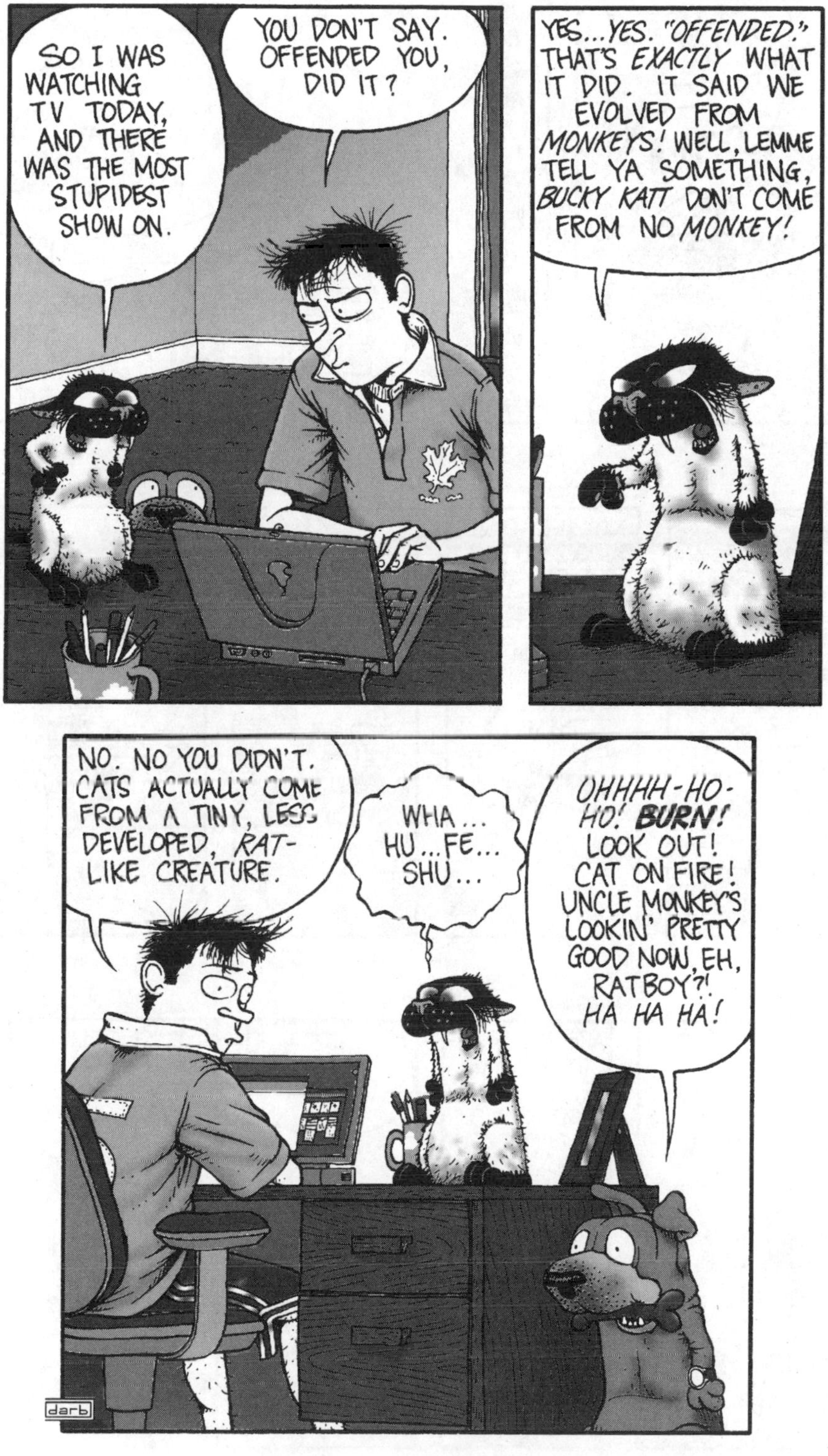
SO I WAS WATCHING TV TODAY, AND THERE WAS THE MOST STUPIDEST SHOW ON.
YOU DON'T SAY. OFFENDED YOU, DID IT?
YES...YES. "OFFENDED." THAT'S EXACTLY WHAT IT DID. IT SAID WE EVOLVED FROM MONKEYS! WELL, LEMME TELL YA SOMETHING, BUCKY KATT DON'T COME FROM NO MONKEY!
NO. NO YOU DIDN'T. CATS ACTUALLY COME FROM A TINY, LESS DEVELOPED, RAT-LIKE CREATURE.
WHA... HU...FE... SHU...
OHHHH-HO-HO! BURN! LOOK OUT! CAT ON FIRE! UNCLE MONKEY'S LOOKIN' PRETTY GOOD NOW, EH, RATBOY?! HA HA HA!
darb

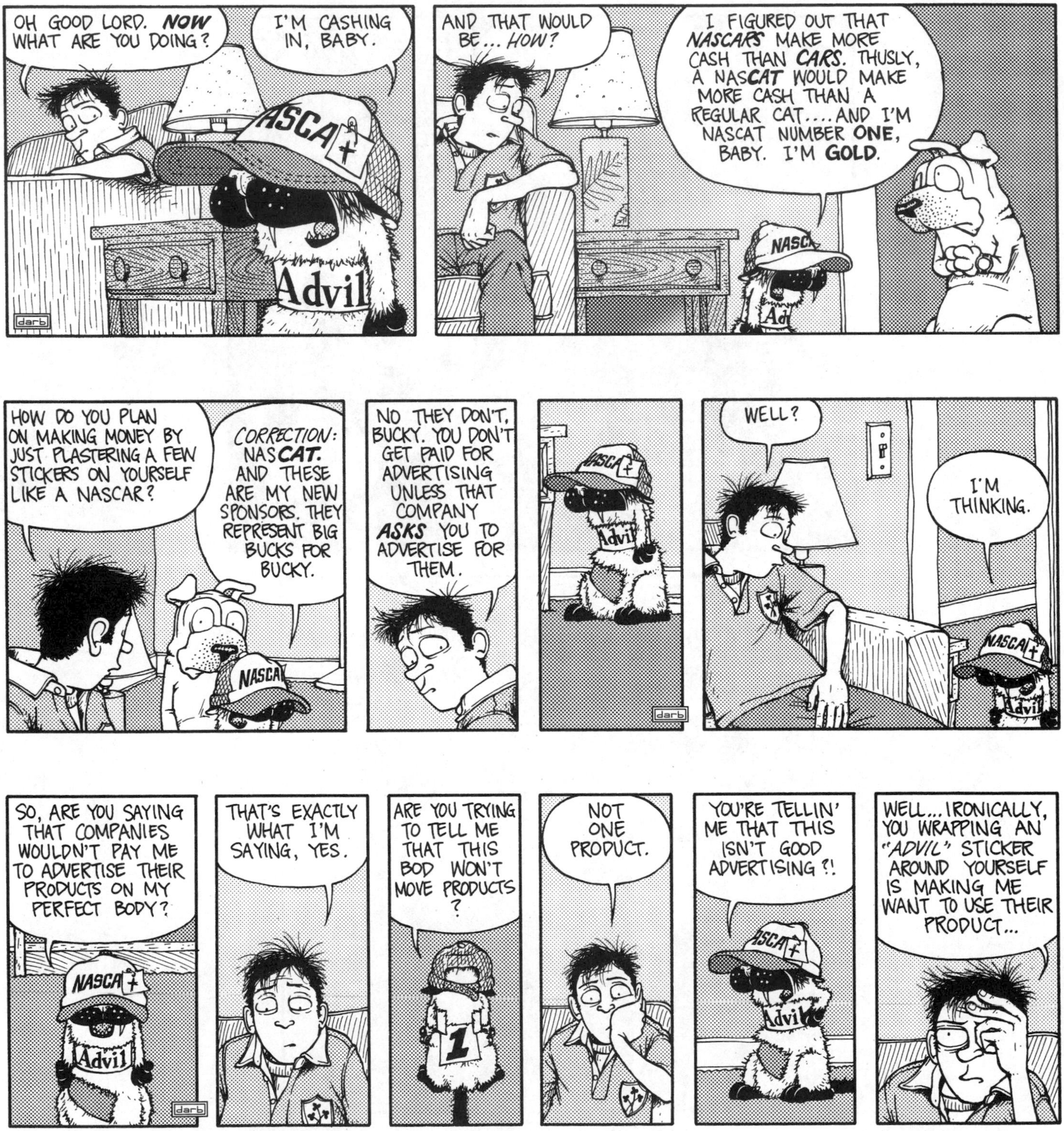
OH GOOD LORD. NOW WHAT ARE YOU DOING?
I'M CASHING IN, BABY.
NASCA
Advil
darb
AND THAT WOULD BE... HOW?
I FIGURED OUT THAT NASCARS MAKE MORE CASH THAN CARS. THUSLY, A NASCAT WOULD MAKE MORE CASH THAN A REGULAR CAT.... AND I'M NASCAT NUMBER ONE, BABY. I'M GOLD.
HOW DO YOU PLAN ON MAKING MONEY BY JUST PLASTERING A FEW STICKERS ON YOURSELF LIKE A NASCAR?
CORRECTION: NASCAT. AND THESE ARE MY NEW SPONSORS. THEY REPRESENT BIG BUCKS FOR BUCKY.
NO THEY DON'T, BUCKY. YOU DON'T GET PAID FOR ADVERTISING UNLESS THAT COMPANY ASKS YOU TO ADVERTISE FOR THEM.
darb
WELL?
I'M THINKING.
SO, ARE YOU SAYING THAT COMPANIES WOULDN'T PAY ME TO ADVERTISE THEIR PRODUCTS ON MY PERFECT BODY?
darb
THAT'S EXACTLY WHAT I'M SAYING, YES.
ARE YOU TRYING TO TELL ME THAT THIS BOD WON'T MOVE PRODUCTS?
NOT ONE PRODUCT.
YOU'RE TELLIN' ME THAT THIS ISN'T GOOD ADVERTISING?!
WELL... IRONICALLY, YOU WRAPPING AN "ADVIL" STICKER AROUND YOURSELF IS MAKING ME WANT TO USE THEIR PRODUCT...

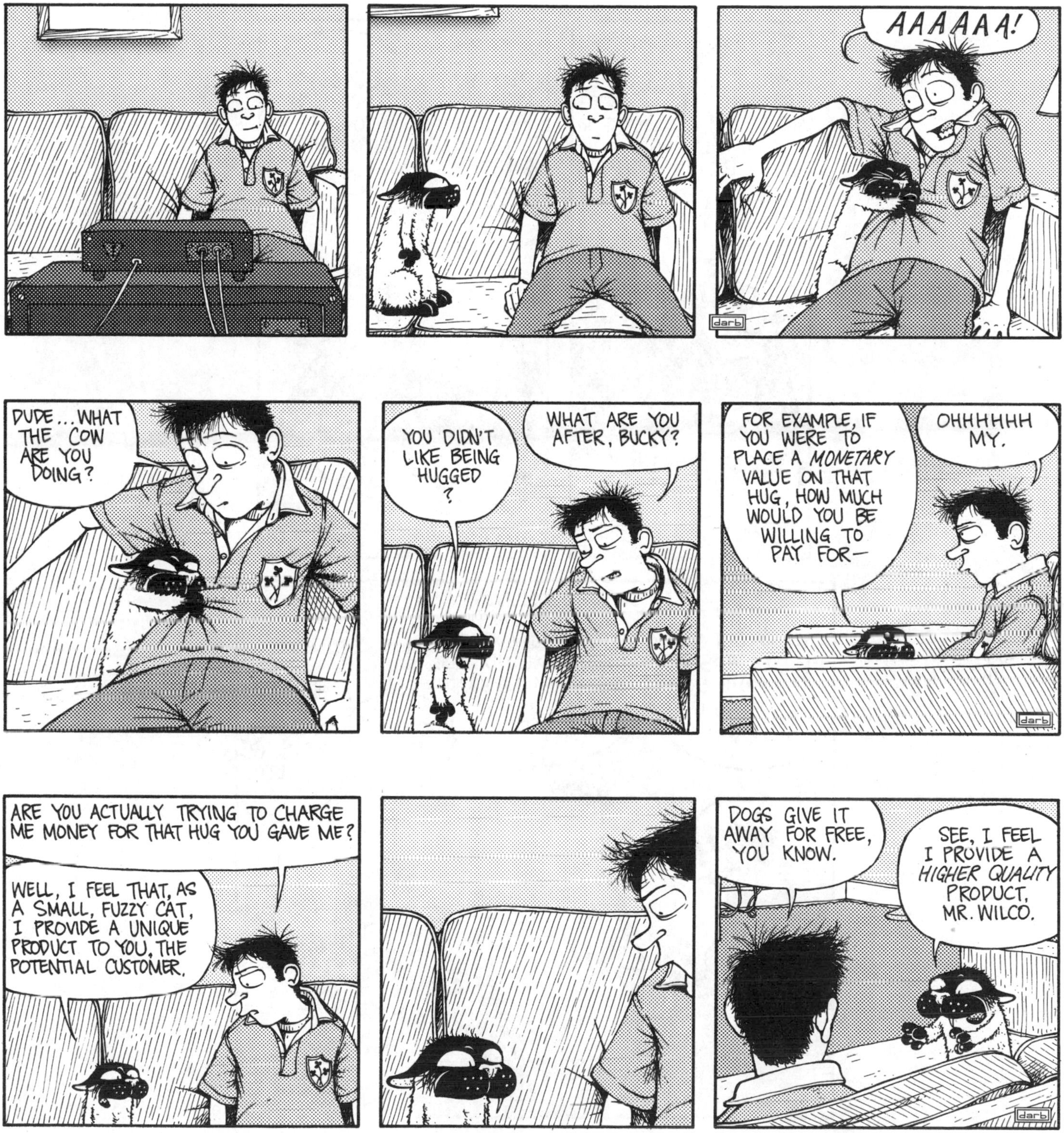

AAAAAA!
darb
DUDE...WHAT THE COW ARE YOU DOING?
WHAT ARE YOU AFTER, BUCKY?
YOU DIDN'T LIKE BEING HUGGED ?
FOR EXAMPLE, IF YOU WERE TO PLACE A *MONETARY* VALUE ON THAT HUG, HOW MUCH WOULD YOU BE WILLING TO PAY FOR—
OHHHHHH MY.
darb
ARE YOU ACTUALLY TRYING TO CHARGE ME MONEY FOR THAT HUG YOU GAVE ME?
WELL, I FEEL THAT, AS A SMALL, FUZZY CAT, I PROVIDE A UNIQUE PRODUCT TO YOU, THE POTENTIAL CUSTOMER.
DOGS GIVE IT AWAY FOR FREE, YOU KNOW.
SEE, I FEEL I PROVIDE A *HIGHER QUALITY* PRODUCT, MR. WILCO.
darb

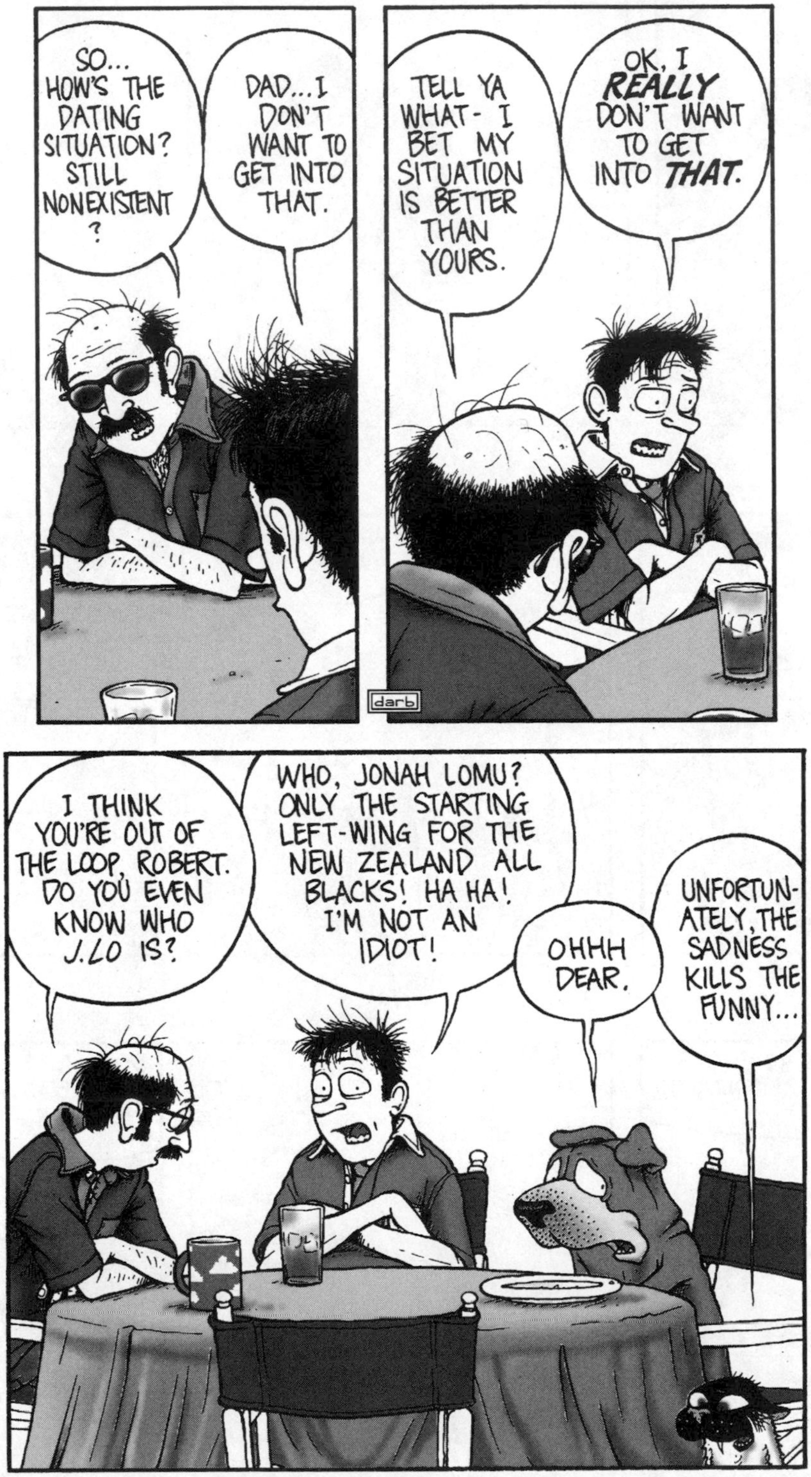
SO... HOW'S THE DATING SITUATION? STILL NONEXISTENT ?
DAD...I DON'T WANT TO GET INTO THAT.
TELL YA WHAT- I BET MY SITUATION IS BETTER THAN YOURS.
OK, I **REALLY** DON'T WANT TO GET INTO **THAT**.
darb
I THINK YOU'RE OUT OF THE LOOP, ROBERT. DO YOU EVEN KNOW WHO J.LO IS?
WHO, JONAH LOMU? ONLY THE STARTING LEFT-WING FOR THE NEW ZEALAND ALL BLACKS! HA HA! I'M NOT AN IDIOT!
OHHH DEAR.
UNFORTUN-ATELY, THE SADNESS KILLS THE FUNNY...

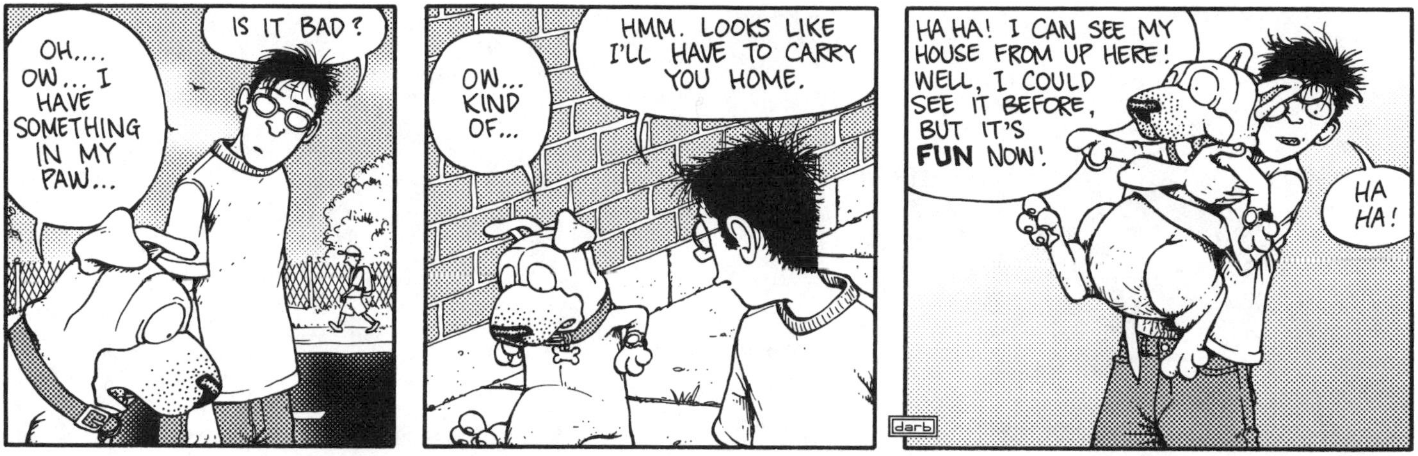
OH,... OW... I HAVE SOMETHING IN MY PAW...
IS IT BAD?
OW... KIND OF...
HMM. LOOKS LIKE I'LL HAVE TO CARRY YOU HOME.
HA HA! I CAN SEE MY HOUSE FROM UP HERE! WELL, I COULD SEE IT BEFORE, BUT IT'S **FUN** NOW!
HA HA!
darb

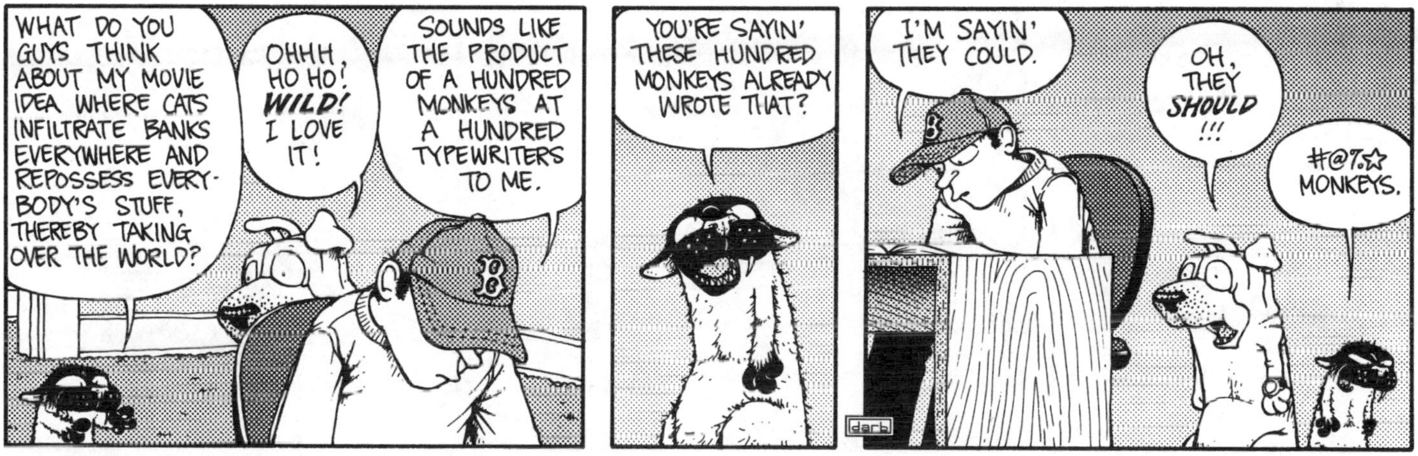
WHAT DO YOU GUYS THINK ABOUT MY MOVIE IDEA WHERE CATS INFILTRATE BANKS EVERYWHERE AND REPOSSESS EVERYBODY'S STUFF, THEREBY TAKING OVER THE WORLD?
OHHH HO HO! ***WILD!*** I LOVE IT!
SOUNDS LIKE THE PRODUCT OF A HUNDRED MONKEYS AT A HUNDRED TYPEWRITERS TO ME.
YOU'RE SAYIN' THESE HUNDRED MONKEYS ALREADY WROTE THAT?
I'M SAYIN' THEY COULD.
OH, THEY ***SHOULD*** !!!
#@%☆ MONKEYS.
darb

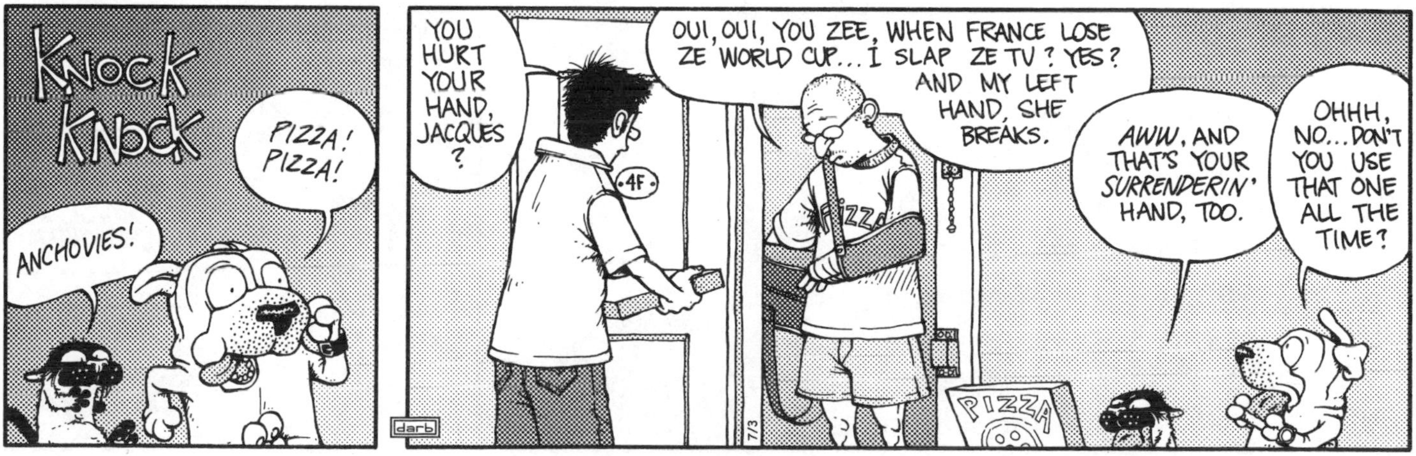
KNOCK KNOCK
PIZZA! PIZZA!
ANCHOVIES!
YOU HURT YOUR HAND, JACQUES?
OUI, OUI, YOU ZEE, WHEN FRANCE LOSE ZE WORLD CUP... I SLAP ZE TV? YES? AND MY LEFT HAND, SHE BREAKS.
AWW, AND THAT'S YOUR *SURRENDERIN'* HAND, TOO.
OHHH, NO... DON'T YOU USE THAT ONE ALL THE TIME?
4F
PIZZA
PIZZA
darb

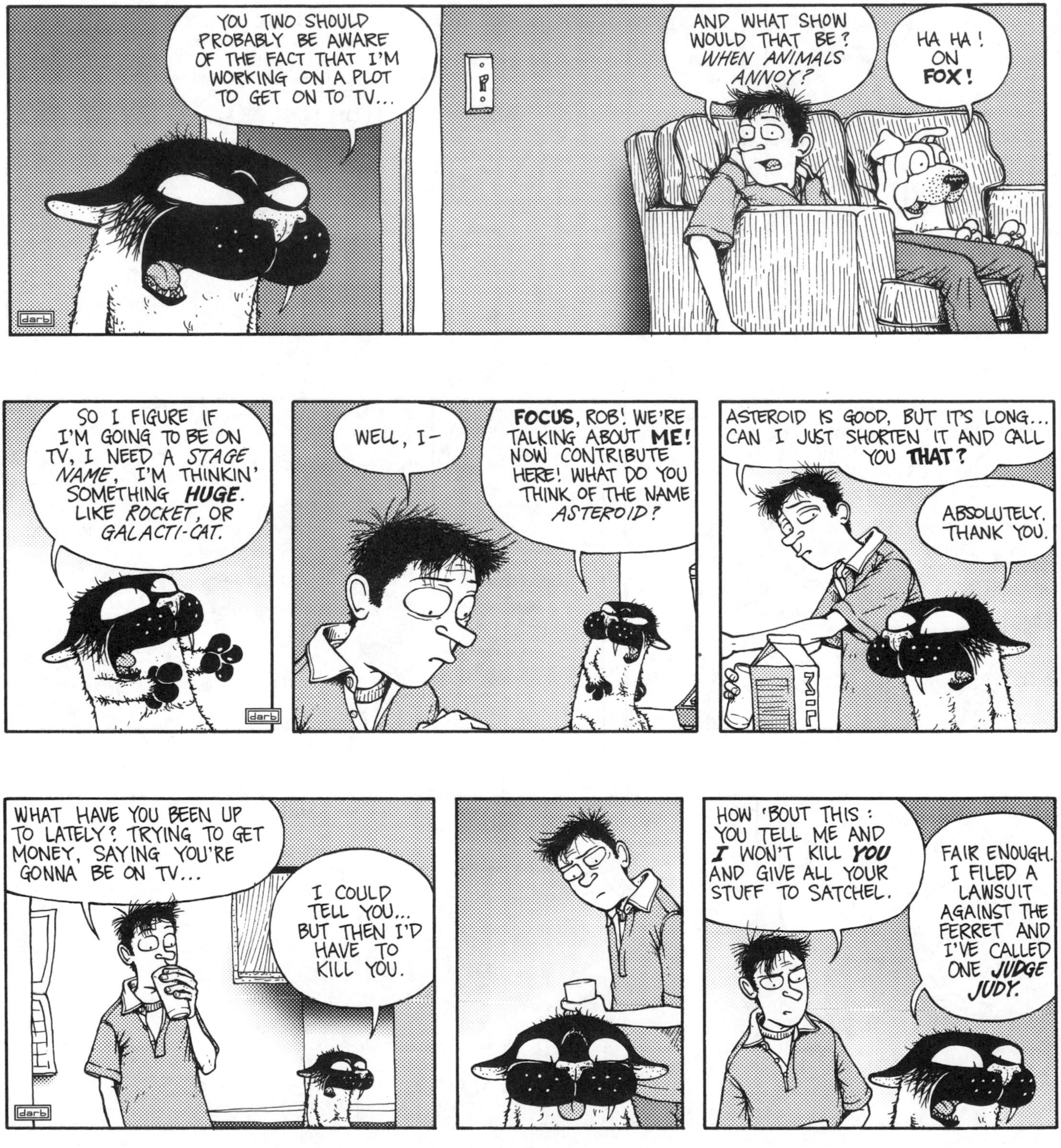
YOU TWO SHOULD PROBABLY BE AWARE OF THE FACT THAT I'M WORKING ON A PLOT TO GET ON TO TV...
AND WHAT SHOW WOULD THAT BE? WHEN ANIMALS ANNOY?
HA HA! ON FOX!
darb
SO I FIGURE IF I'M GOING TO BE ON TV, I NEED A STAGE NAME, I'M THINKIN' SOMETHING HUGE. LIKE ROCKET, OR GALACTI-CAT.
WELL, I-
FOCUS, ROB! WE'RE TALKING ABOUT ME! NOW CONTRIBUTE HERE! WHAT DO YOU THINK OF THE NAME ASTEROID?
ASTEROID IS GOOD, BUT IT'S LONG... CAN I JUST SHORTEN IT AND CALL YOU THAT?
ABSOLUTELY. THANK YOU.
darb
WHAT HAVE YOU BEEN UP TO LATELY? TRYING TO GET MONEY, SAYING YOU'RE GONNA BE ON TV...
I COULD TELL YOU... BUT THEN I'D HAVE TO KILL YOU.
HOW 'BOUT THIS: YOU TELL ME AND I WON'T KILL YOU AND GIVE ALL YOUR STUFF TO SATCHEL.
FAIR ENOUGH. I FILED A LAWSUIT AGAINST THE FERRET AND I'VE CALLED ONE JUDGE JUDY.
darb

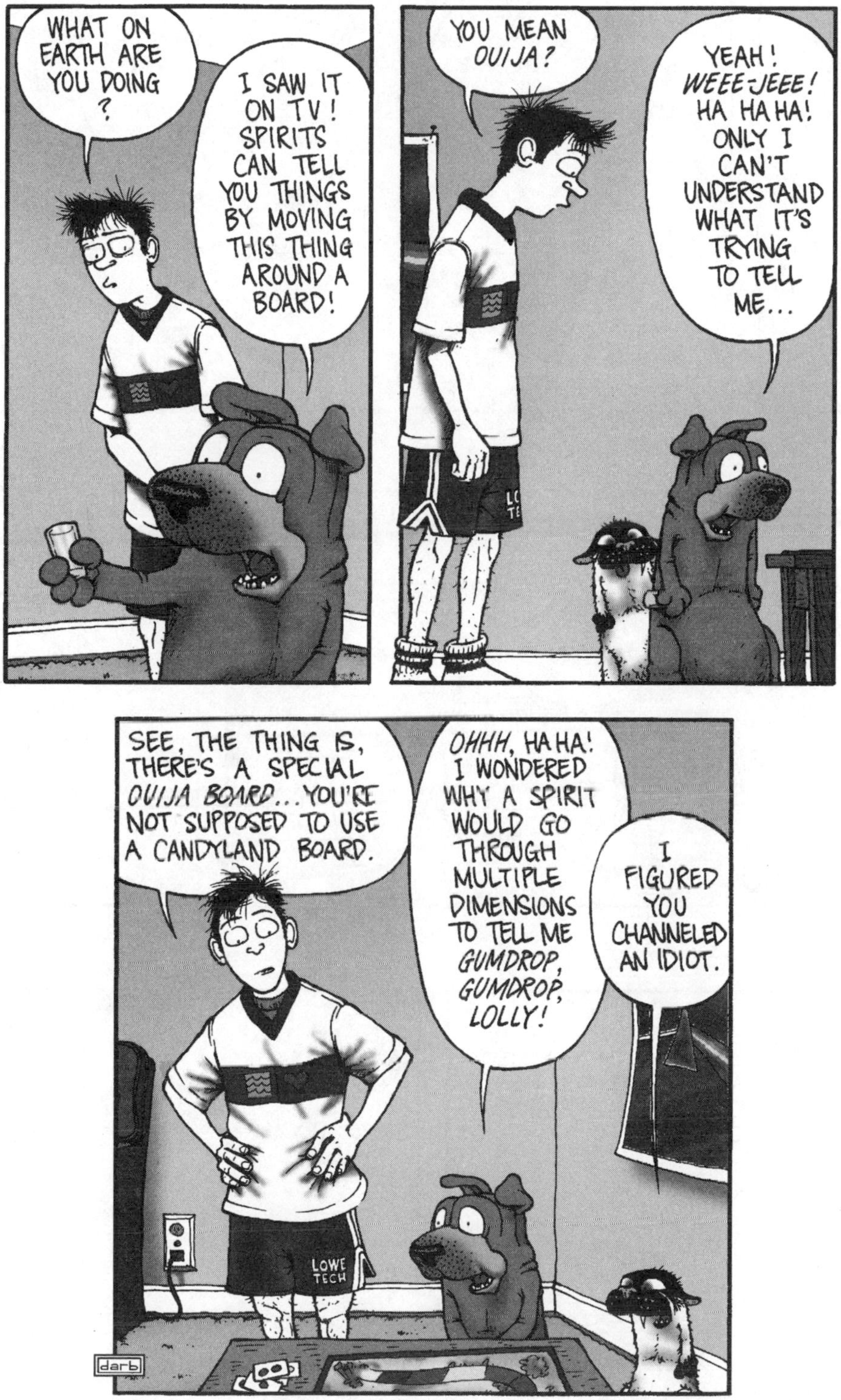
WHAT ON EARTH ARE YOU DOING ?
I SAW IT ON TV! SPIRITS CAN TELL YOU THINGS BY MOVING THIS THING AROUND A BOARD!
YOU MEAN *OUIJA?*
YEAH! *WEEE-JEEE!* HA HA HA! ONLY I CAN'T UNDERSTAND WHAT IT'S TRYING TO TELL ME...
SEE, THE THING IS, THERE'S A SPECIAL *OUIJA BOARD*... YOU'RE NOT SUPPOSED TO USE A CANDYLAND BOARD.
OHHH, HA HA! I WONDERED WHY A SPIRIT WOULD GO THROUGH MULTIPLE DIMENSIONS TO TELL ME *GUMDROP, GUMDROP, LOLLY!*
I FIGURED YOU CHANNELED AN IDIOT.
LOWE TECH
darb

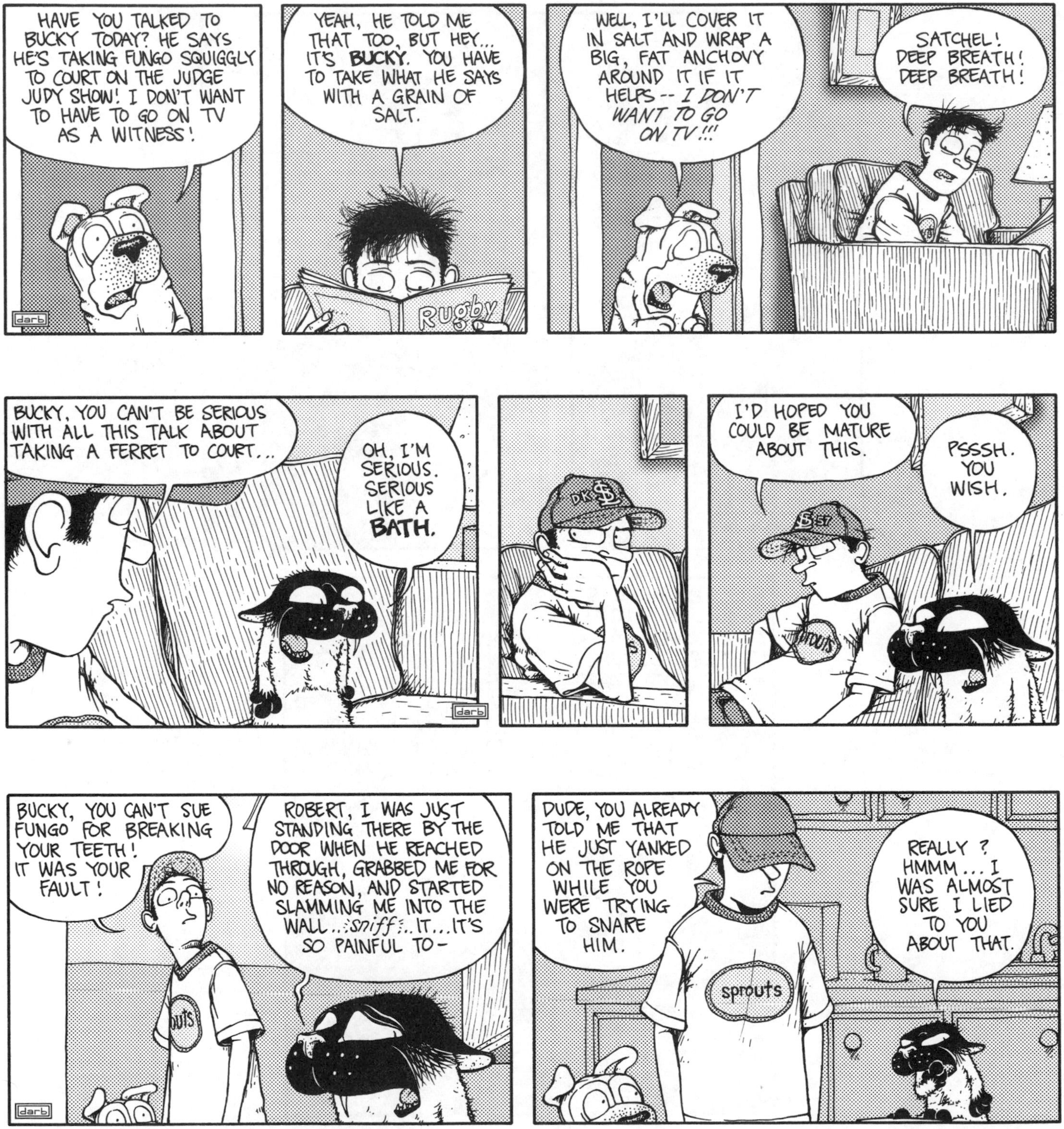

HAVE YOU TALKED TO BUCKY TODAY? HE SAYS HE'S TAKING FUNGO SQUIGGLY TO COURT ON THE JUDGE JUDY SHOW! I DON'T WANT TO HAVE TO GO ON TV AS A WITNESS!
darb
YEAH, HE TOLD ME THAT TOO, BUT HEY... IT'S BUCKY. YOU HAVE TO TAKE WHAT HE SAYS WITH A GRAIN OF SALT.
Rugby
WELL, I'LL COVER IT IN SALT AND WRAP A BIG, FAT ANCHOVY AROUND IT IF IT HELPS -- I DON'T WANT TO GO ON TV!!!
SATCHEL! DEEP BREATH! DEEP BREATH!
BUCKY, YOU CAN'T BE SERIOUS WITH ALL THIS TALK ABOUT TAKING A FERRET TO COURT...
OH, I'M SERIOUS. SERIOUS LIKE A BATH.
darb
I'D HOPED YOU COULD BE MATURE ABOUT THIS.
PSSSH. YOU WISH.
BUCKY, YOU CAN'T SUE FUNGO FOR BREAKING YOUR TEETH! IT WAS YOUR FAULT!
ROBERT, I WAS JUST STANDING THERE BY THE DOOR WHEN HE REACHED THROUGH, GRABBED ME FOR NO REASON, AND STARTED SLAMMING ME INTO THE WALL...sniff...IT...IT'S SO PAINFUL TO-
darb
DUDE, YOU ALREADY TOLD ME THAT HE JUST YANKED ON THE ROPE WHILE YOU WERE TRYING TO SNARE HIM.
sprouts
REALLY? HMMM... I WAS ALMOST SURE I LIED TO YOU ABOUT THAT.

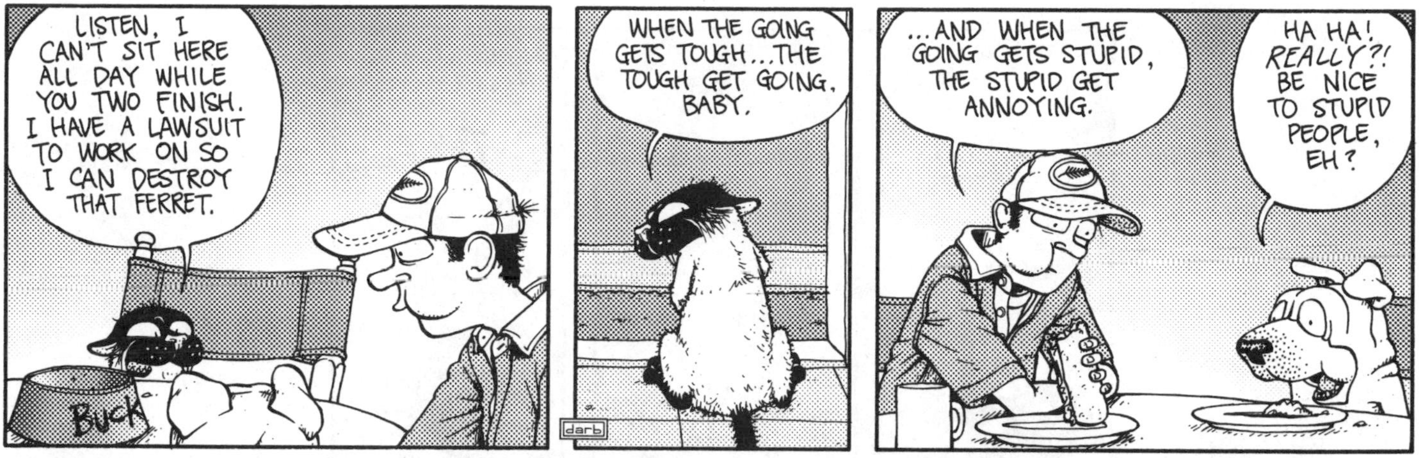
LISTEN, I CAN'T SIT HERE ALL DAY WHILE YOU TWO FINISH. I HAVE A LAWSUIT TO WORK ON SO I CAN DESTROY THAT FERRET.
BUCK
WHEN THE GOING GETS TOUGH...THE TOUGH GET GOING. BABY.
darb
...AND WHEN THE GOING GETS STUPID, THE STUPID GET ANNOYING.
HA HA! *REALLY?!* BE NICE TO STUPID PEOPLE, EH?

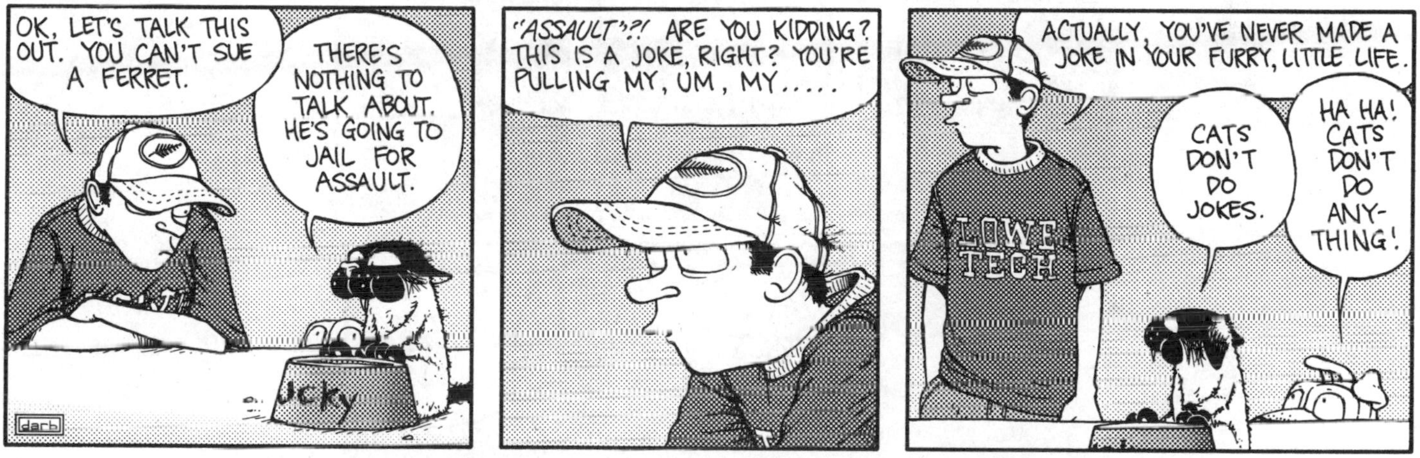
OK, LET'S TALK THIS OUT. YOU CAN'T SUE A FERRET.
THERE'S NOTHING TO TALK ABOUT. HE'S GOING TO JAIL FOR ASSAULT.
UCKY
darb
"ASSAULT"?! ARE YOU KIDDING? THIS IS A JOKE, RIGHT? YOU'RE PULLING MY, UM, MY.....
ACTUALLY, YOU'VE NEVER MADE A JOKE IN YOUR FURRY, LITTLE LIFE.
CATS DON'T DO JOKES.
HA HA! CATS DON'T DO ANY-THING!
LOWE TECH

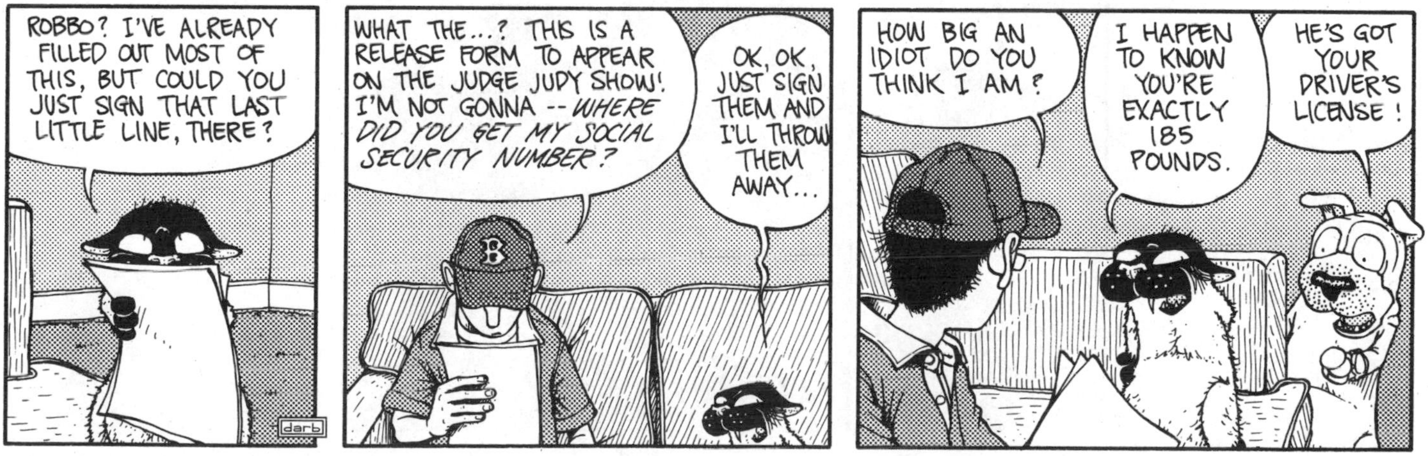
ROBBO? I'VE ALREADY FILLED OUT MOST OF THIS, BUT COULD YOU JUST SIGN THAT LAST LITTLE LINE, THERE?
darb
WHAT THE...? THIS IS A RELEASE FORM TO APPEAR ON THE JUDGE JUDY SHOW! I'M NOT GONNA -- *WHERE DID YOU GET MY SOCIAL SECURITY NUMBER?*
OK, OK, JUST SIGN THEM AND I'LL THROW THEM AWAY...
HOW BIG AN IDIOT DO YOU THINK I AM?
I HAPPEN TO KNOW YOU'RE EXACTLY 185 POUNDS.
HE'S GOT YOUR DRIVER'S LICENSE!

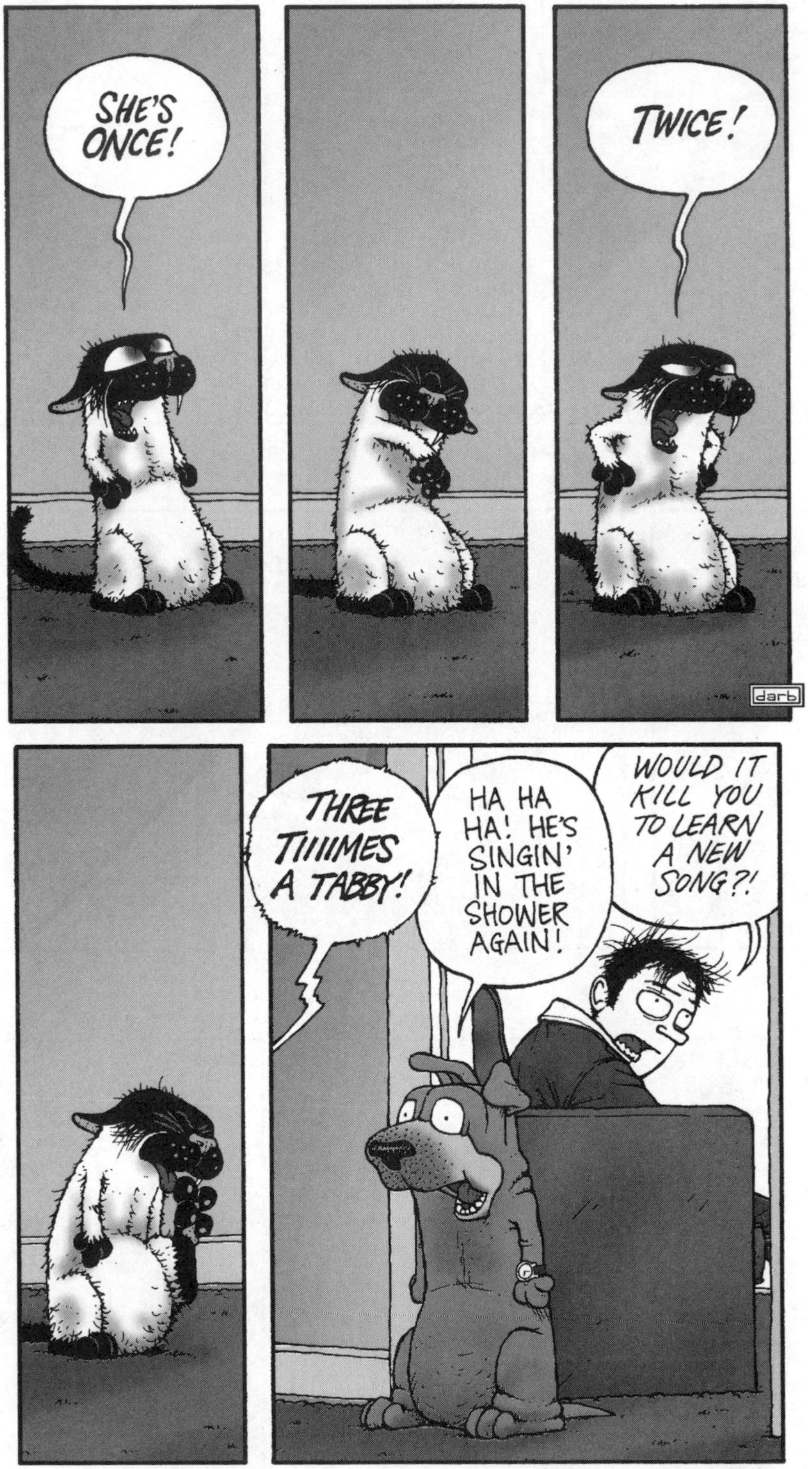
SHE'S ONCE!
TWICE!
darb
THREE TIIIIMES A TABBY!
HA HA HA! HE'S SINGIN' IN THE SHOWER AGAIN!
WOULD IT KILL YOU TO LEARN A NEW SONG?!

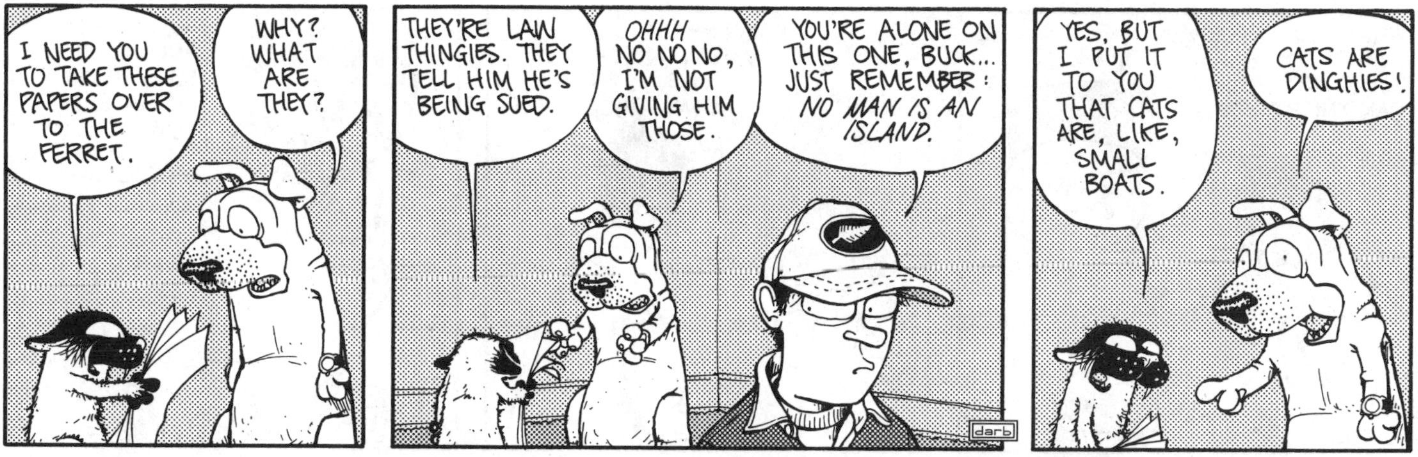
I NEED YOU TO TAKE THESE PAPERS OVER TO THE FERRET.
WHY? WHAT ARE THEY?
THEY'RE LAW THINGIES. THEY TELL HIM HE'S BEING SUED.
OHHH NO NO NO, I'M NOT GIVING HIM THOSE.
YOU'RE ALONE ON THIS ONE, BUCK... JUST REMEMBER: *NO MAN IS AN ISLAND.*
darb
YES, BUT I PUT IT TO YOU THAT CATS ARE, LIKE, SMALL BOATS.
CATS ARE DINGHIES!

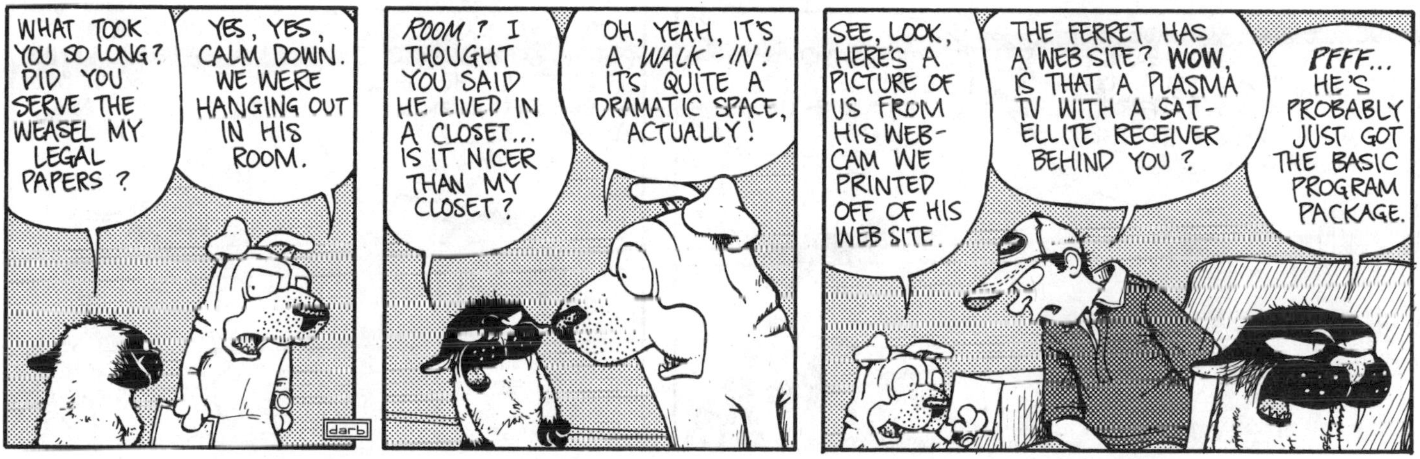
WHAT TOOK YOU SO LONG? DID YOU SERVE THE WEASEL MY LEGAL PAPERS?
YES, YES, CALM DOWN. WE WERE HANGING OUT IN HIS ROOM.
darb
ROOM? I THOUGHT YOU SAID HE LIVED IN A CLOSET... IS IT NICER THAN MY CLOSET?
OH, YEAH, IT'S A *WALK-IN*! IT'S QUITE A DRAMATIC SPACE, ACTUALLY!
SEE, LOOK, HERE'S A PICTURE OF US FROM HIS WEB-CAM WE PRINTED OFF OF HIS WEB SITE.
THE FERRET HAS A WEB SITE? **WOW**, IS THAT A PLASMA TV WITH A SATELLITE RECEIVER BEHIND YOU?
PFFF... HE'S PROBABLY JUST GOT THE BASIC PROGRAM PACKAGE.

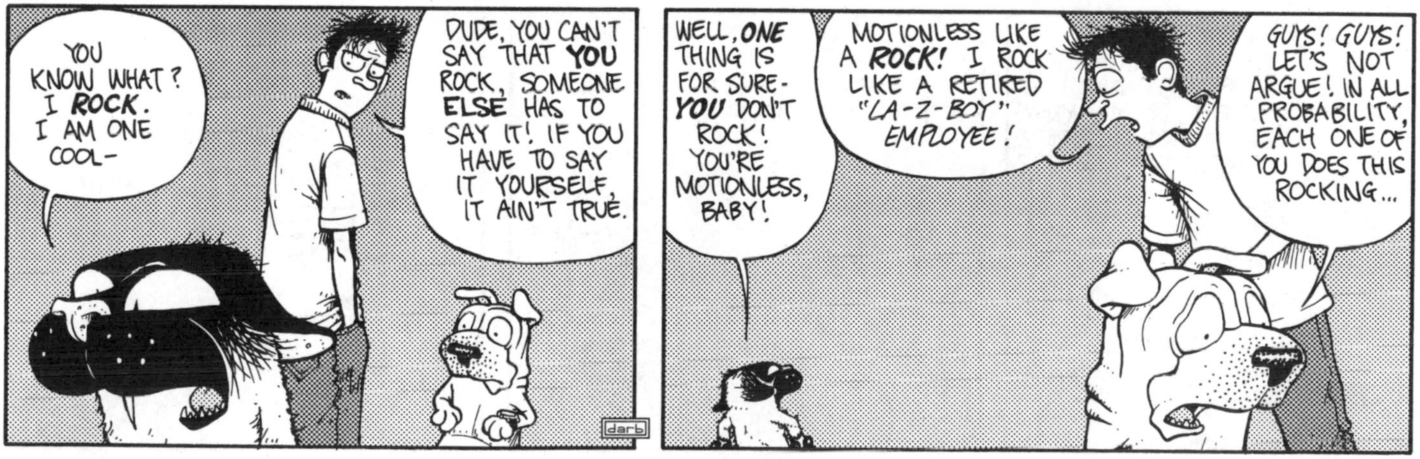
YOU KNOW WHAT? I **ROCK**. I AM ONE COOL-
DUDE, YOU CAN'T SAY THAT **YOU** ROCK, SOMEONE **ELSE** HAS TO SAY IT! IF YOU HAVE TO SAY IT YOURSELF, IT AIN'T TRUE.
darb
WELL, ***ONE*** THING IS FOR SURE- ***YOU*** DON'T ROCK! YOU'RE MOTIONLESS, BABY!
MOTIONLESS LIKE A ***ROCK!*** I ROCK LIKE A RETIRED *"LA-Z-BOY" EMPLOYEE!*
GUYS! GUYS! LET'S NOT ARGUE! IN ALL PROBABILITY, EACH ONE OF YOU DOES THIS ROCKING...

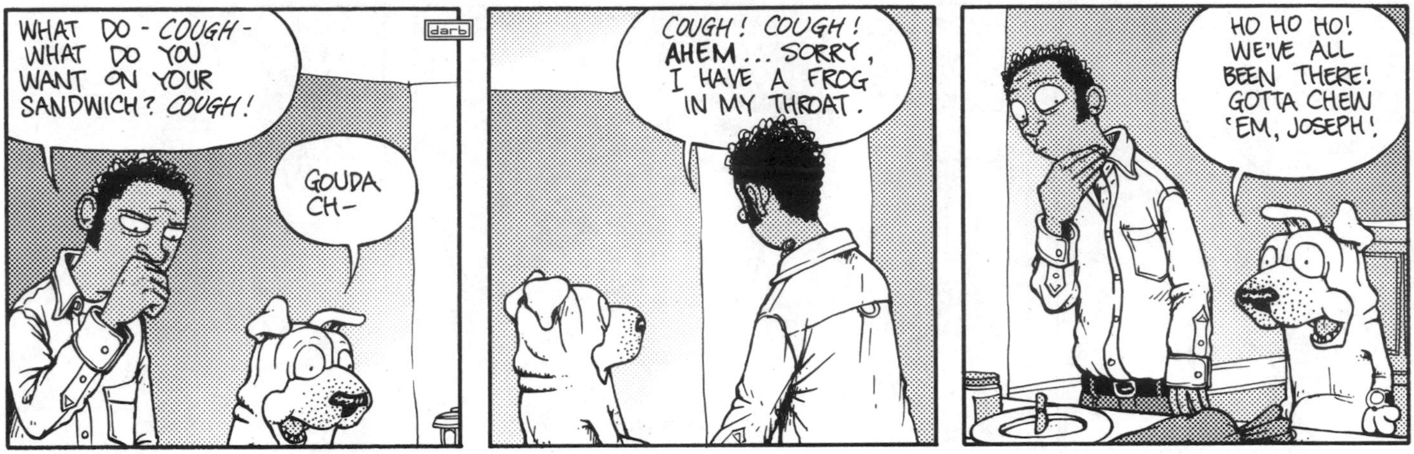
WHAT DO - COUGH - WHAT DO YOU WANT ON YOUR SANDWICH? COUGH!
GOUDA CH-
COUGH! COUGH! AHEM... SORRY, I HAVE A FROG IN MY THROAT.
HO HO HO! WE'VE ALL BEEN THERE! GOTTA CHEW 'EM, JOSEPH!

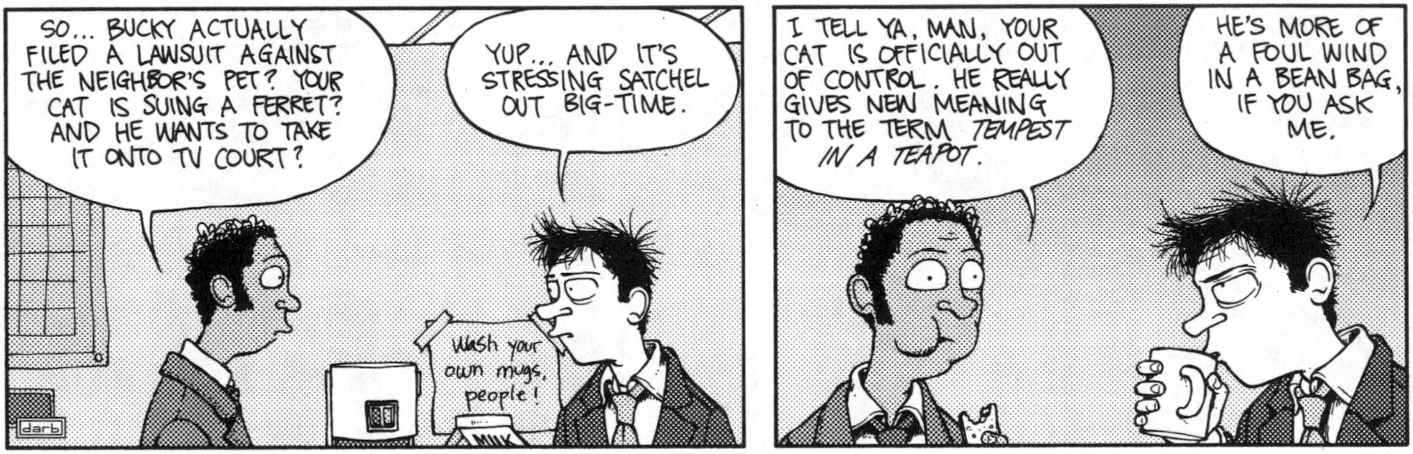
SO... BUCKY ACTUALLY FILED A LAWSUIT AGAINST THE NEIGHBOR'S PET? YOUR CAT IS SUING A FERRET? AND HE WANTS TO TAKE IT ONTO TV COURT?
YUP... AND IT'S STRESSING SATCHEL OUT BIG-TIME.
Wash your own mugs, people!
MILK
I TELL YA, MAN, YOUR CAT IS OFFICIALLY OUT OF CONTROL. HE REALLY GIVES NEW MEANING TO THE TERM TEMPEST IN A TEAPOT.
HE'S MORE OF A FOUL WIND IN A BEAN BAG, IF YOU ASK ME.

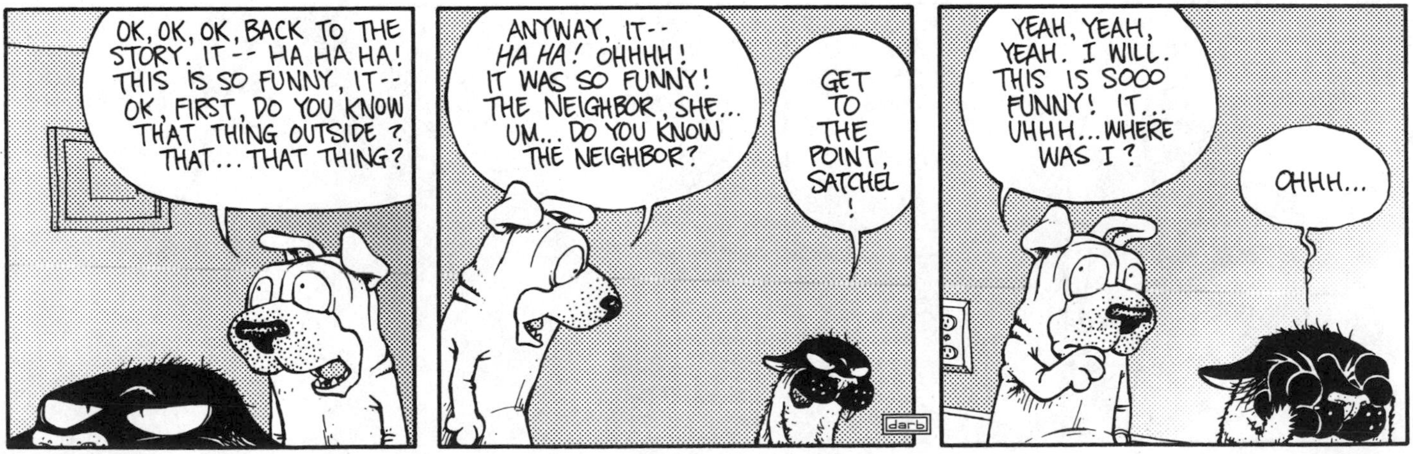
OK, OK, OK, BACK TO THE STORY. IT -- HA HA HA! THIS IS SO FUNNY, IT -- OK, FIRST, DO YOU KNOW THAT THING OUTSIDE? THAT... THAT THING?
ANYWAY, IT -- HA HA! OHHHH! IT WAS SO FUNNY! THE NEIGHBOR, SHE... UM... DO YOU KNOW THE NEIGHBOR?
GET TO THE POINT, SATCHEL!
YEAH, YEAH, YEAH. I WILL. THIS IS SOOO FUNNY! IT... UHHH... WHERE WAS I?
OHHH...

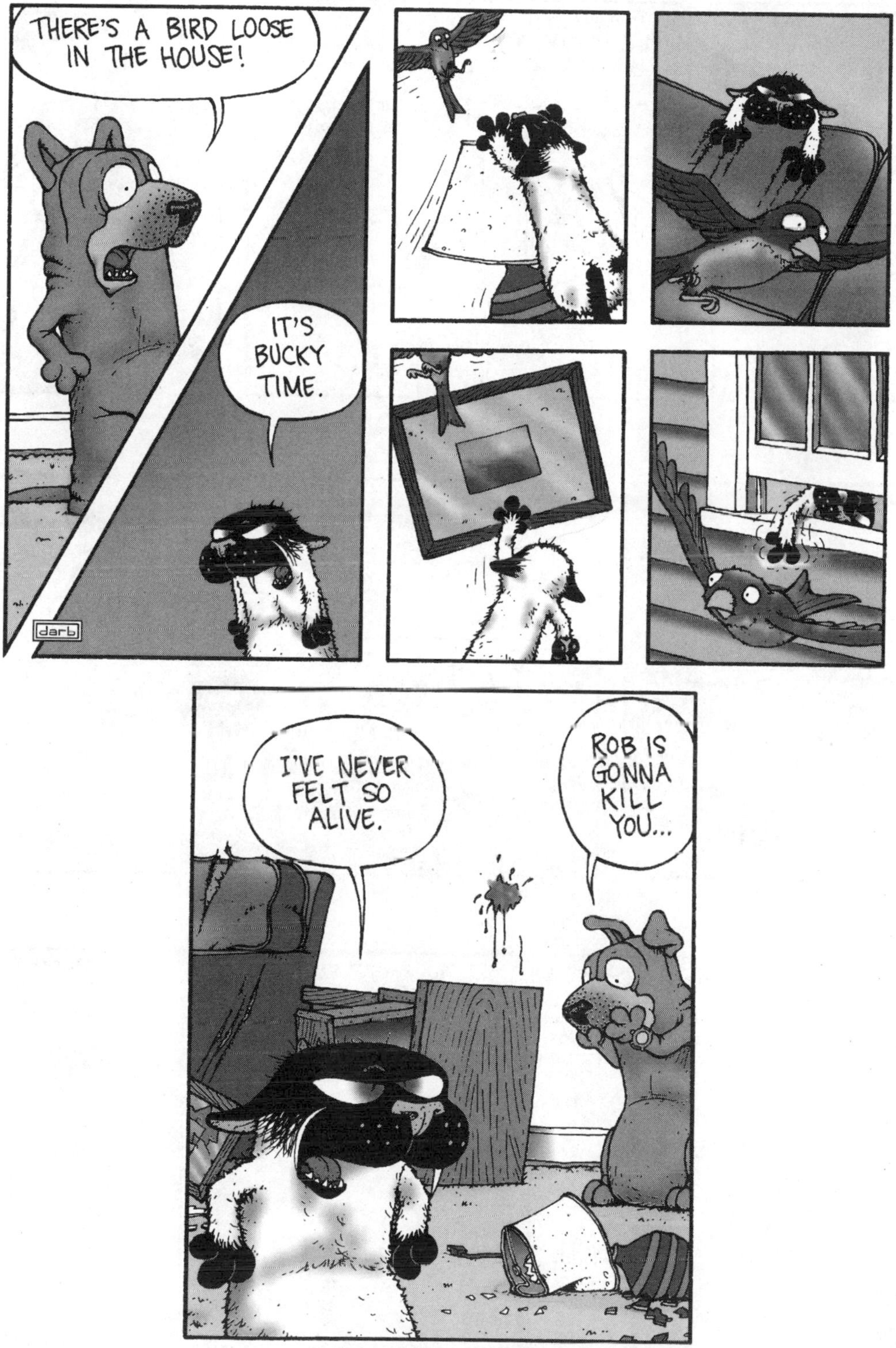
THERE'S A BIRD LOOSE IN THE HOUSE!
IT'S BUCKY TIME.
darb
I'VE NEVER FELT SO ALIVE.
ROB IS GONNA KILL YOU...

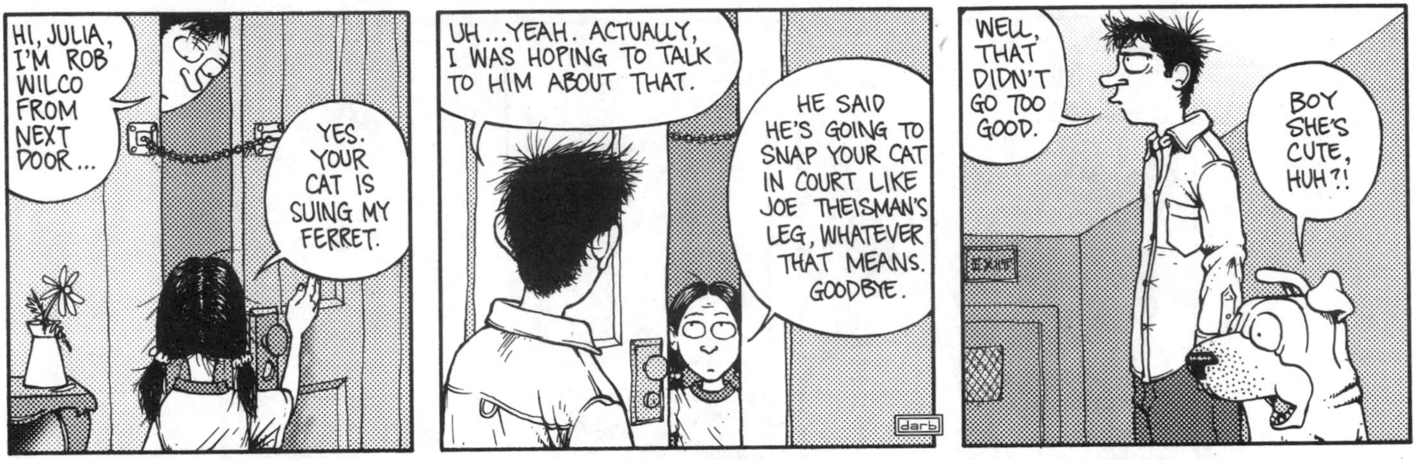
HI, JULIA, I'M ROB WILCO FROM NEXT DOOR...
YES. YOUR CAT IS SUING MY FERRET.
UH...YEAH. ACTUALLY, I WAS HOPING TO TALK TO HIM ABOUT THAT.
HE SAID HE'S GOING TO SNAP YOUR CAT IN COURT LIKE JOE THEISMAN'S LEG, WHATEVER THAT MEANS. GOODBYE.
darb
WELL, THAT DIDN'T GO TOO GOOD.
BOY SHE'S CUTE, HUH?!

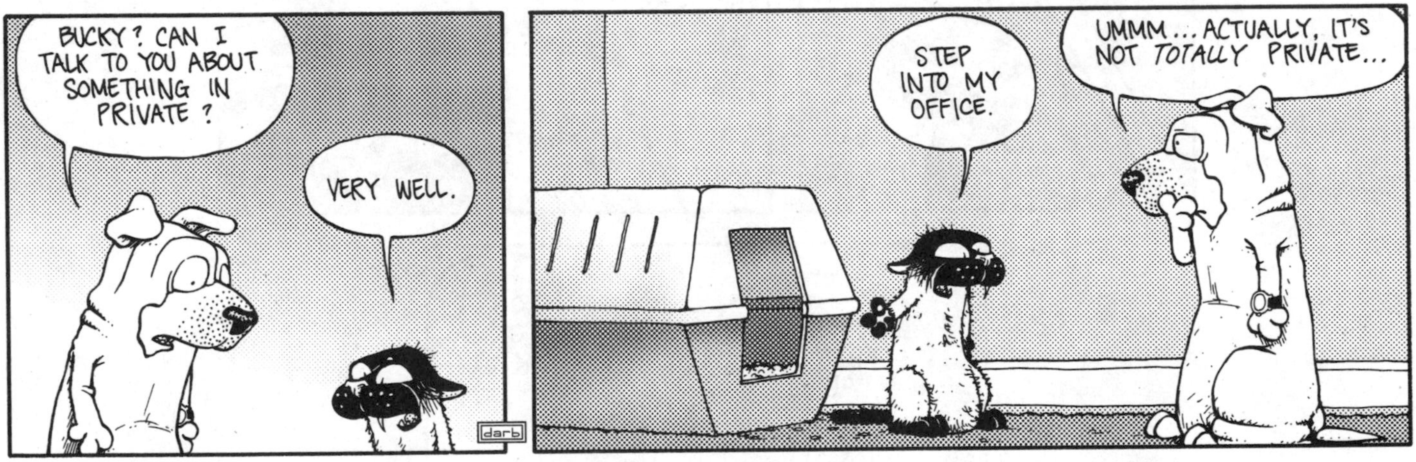
BUCKY? CAN I TALK TO YOU ABOUT SOMETHING IN PRIVATE?
VERY WELL.
darb
STEP INTO MY OFFICE.
UMMM... ACTUALLY, IT'S NOT *TOTALLY* PRIVATE...

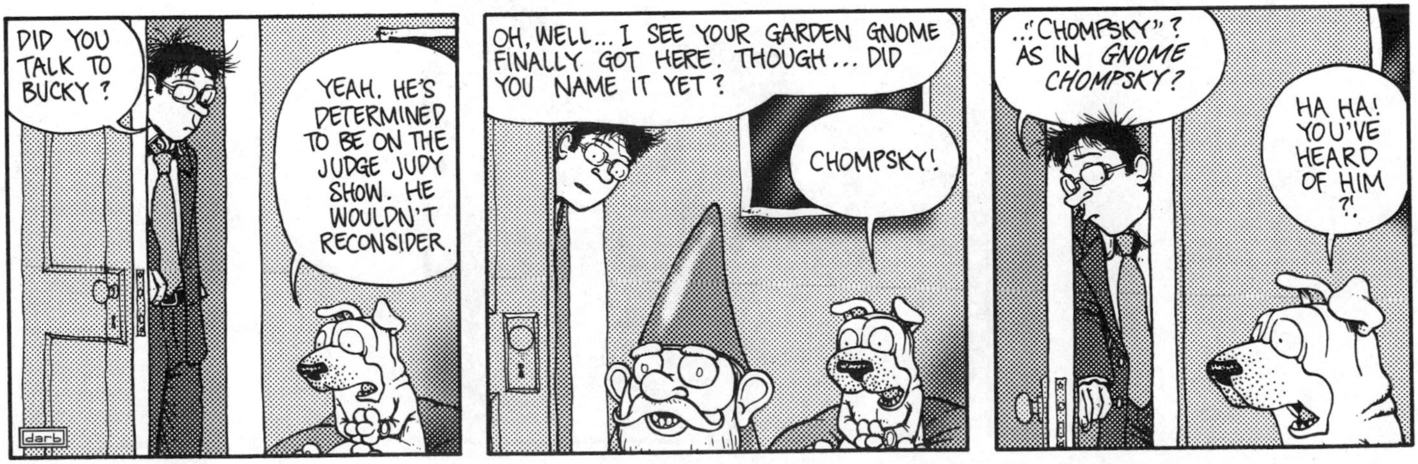
DID YOU TALK TO BUCKY?
YEAH. HE'S DETERMINED TO BE ON THE JUDGE JUDY SHOW. HE WOULDN'T RECONSIDER.
darb
OH, WELL... I SEE YOUR GARDEN GNOME FINALLY GOT HERE. THOUGH... DID YOU NAME IT YET?
CHOMPSKY!
..."CHOMPSKY"? AS IN *GNOME CHOMPSKY*?
HA HA! YOU'VE HEARD OF HIM?!

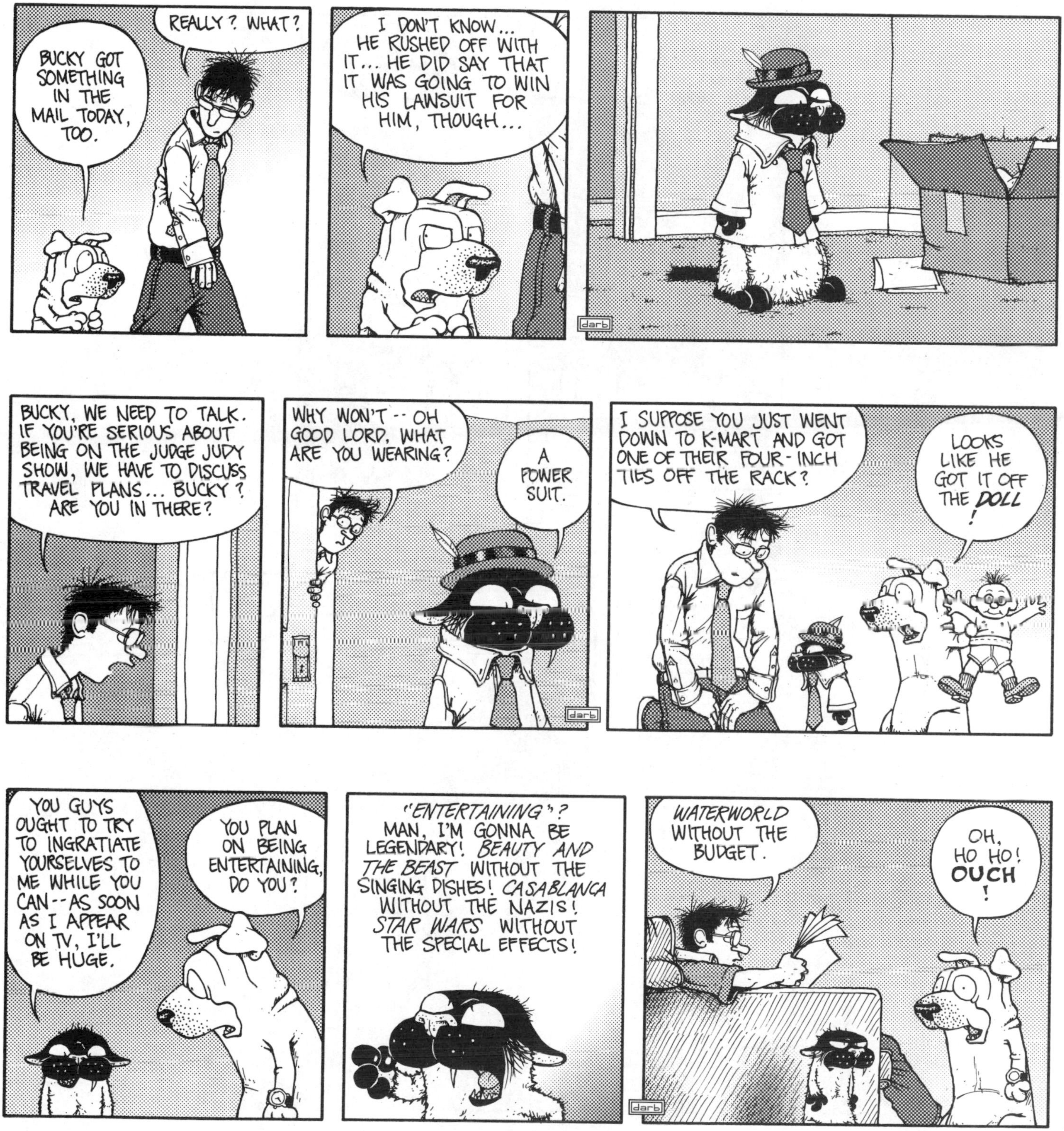
BUCKY GOT SOMETHING IN THE MAIL TODAY, TOO.
REALLY? WHAT?
I DON'T KNOW... HE RUSHED OFF WITH IT... HE DID SAY THAT IT WAS GOING TO WIN HIS LAWSUIT FOR HIM, THOUGH...
darb
BUCKY, WE NEED TO TALK. IF YOU'RE SERIOUS ABOUT BEING ON THE JUDGE JUDY SHOW, WE HAVE TO DISCUSS TRAVEL PLANS... BUCKY? ARE YOU IN THERE?
WHY WON'T -- OH GOOD LORD, WHAT ARE YOU WEARING?
A POWER SUIT.
darb
I SUPPOSE YOU JUST WENT DOWN TO K-MART AND GOT ONE OF THEIR FOUR-INCH TIES OFF THE RACK?
LOOKS LIKE HE GOT IT OFF THE *DOLL*!
YOU GUYS OUGHT TO TRY TO INGRATIATE YOURSELVES TO ME WHILE YOU CAN--AS SOON AS I APPEAR ON TV, I'LL BE HUGE.
YOU PLAN ON BEING ENTERTAINING, DO YOU?
"ENTERTAINING"? MAN, I'M GONNA BE LEGENDARY! *BEAUTY AND THE BEAST* WITHOUT THE SINGING DISHES! *CASABLANCA* WITHOUT THE NAZIS! *STAR WARS* WITHOUT THE SPECIAL EFFECTS!
darb
WATERWORLD WITHOUT THE BUDGET.
OH, HO HO! **OUCH**!

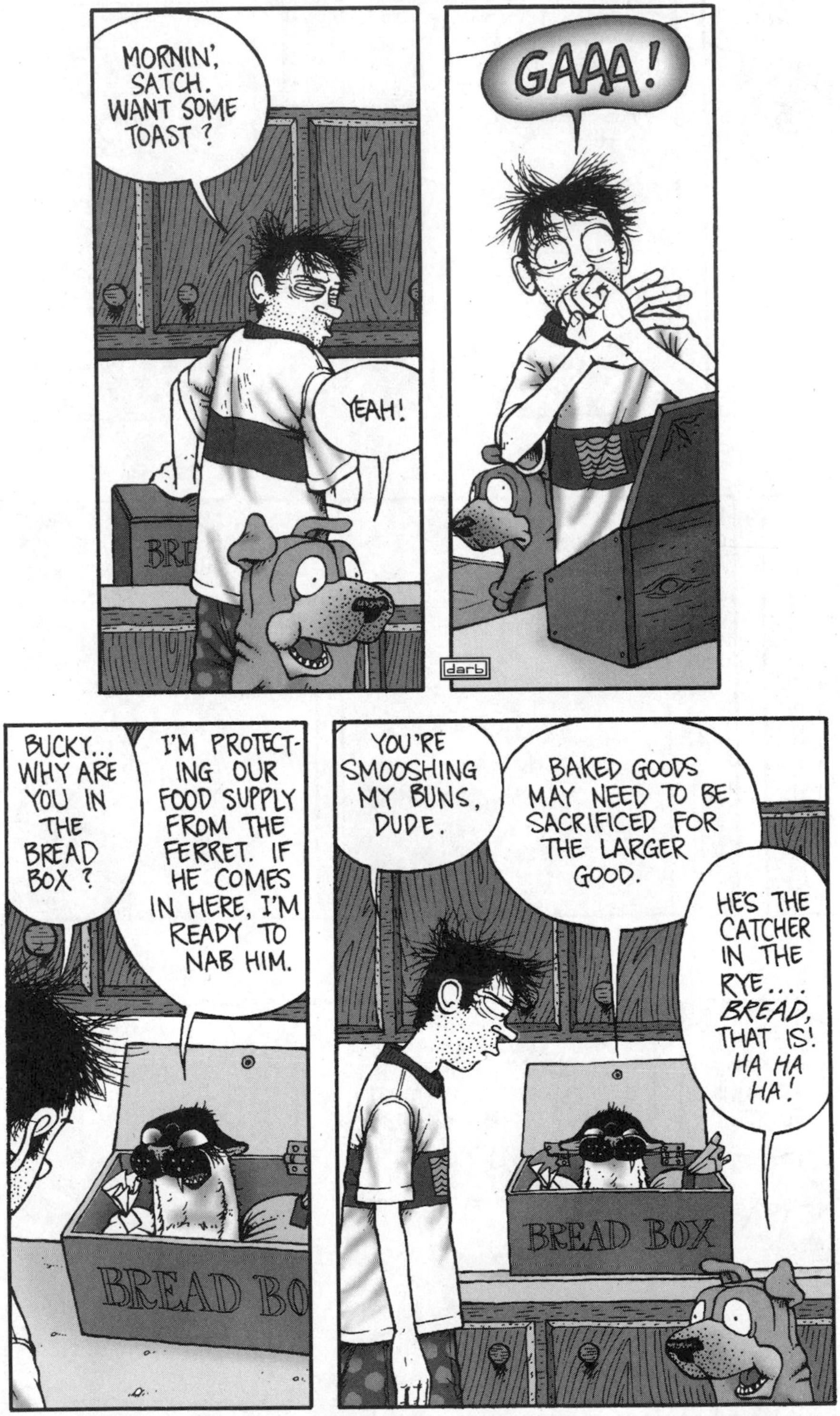
MORNIN', SATCH. WANT SOME TOAST ?
YEAH!
GAAA!
BRE
darb
BUCKY... WHY ARE YOU IN THE BREAD BOX ?
I'M PROTECT-ING OUR FOOD SUPPLY FROM THE FERRET. IF HE COMES IN HERE, I'M READY TO NAB HIM.
BREAD BO
YOU'RE SMOOSHING MY BUNS, DUDE.
BAKED GOODS MAY NEED TO BE SACRIFICED FOR THE LARGER GOOD.
HE'S THE CATCHER IN THE RYE.... *BREAD*, THAT IS! HA HA HA!
BREAD BOX

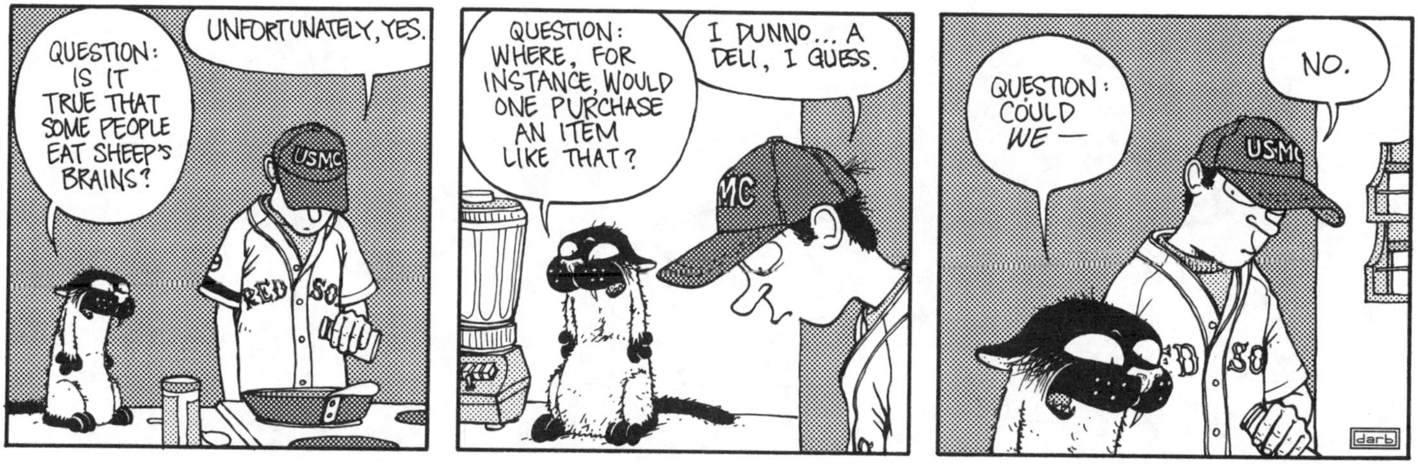
QUESTION: IS IT TRUE THAT SOME PEOPLE EAT SHEEP'S BRAINS?
UNFORTUNATELY, YES.
QUESTION: WHERE, FOR INSTANCE, WOULD ONE PURCHASE AN ITEM LIKE THAT?
I DUNNO... A DELI, I GUESS.
QUESTION: COULD *WE*—
NO.

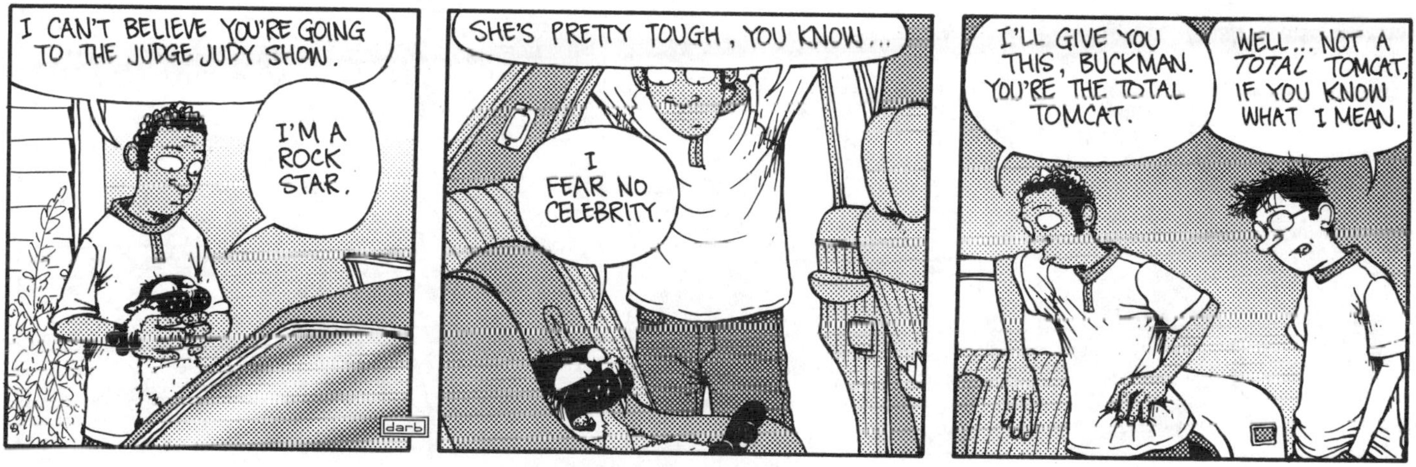
I CAN'T BELIEVE YOU'RE GOING TO THE JUDGE JUDY SHOW.
I'M A ROCK STAR.
SHE'S PRETTY TOUGH, YOU KNOW...
I FEAR NO CELEBRITY.
I'LL GIVE YOU THIS, BUCKMAN. YOU'RE THE TOTAL TOMCAT.
WELL... NOT A *TOTAL* TOMCAT, IF YOU KNOW WHAT I MEAN.

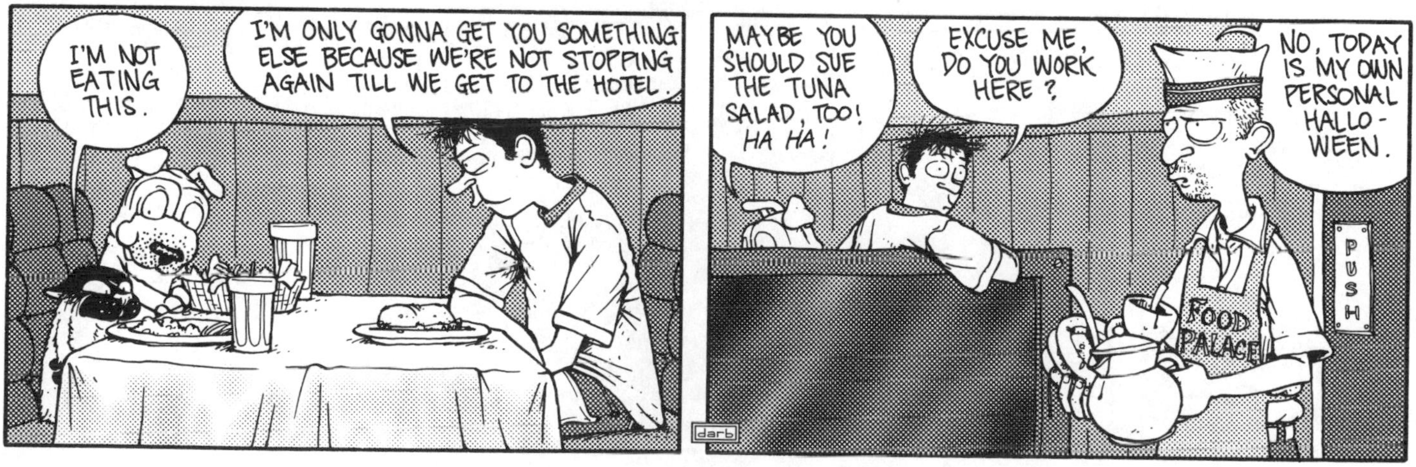
I'M NOT EATING THIS.
I'M ONLY GONNA GET YOU SOMETHING ELSE BECAUSE WE'RE NOT STOPPING AGAIN TILL WE GET TO THE HOTEL.
MAYBE YOU SHOULD SUE THE TUNA SALAD, TOO! *HA HA!*
EXCUSE ME, DO YOU WORK HERE?
NO, TODAY IS MY OWN PERSONAL HALLO-WEEN.
PUSH
FOOD PALACE

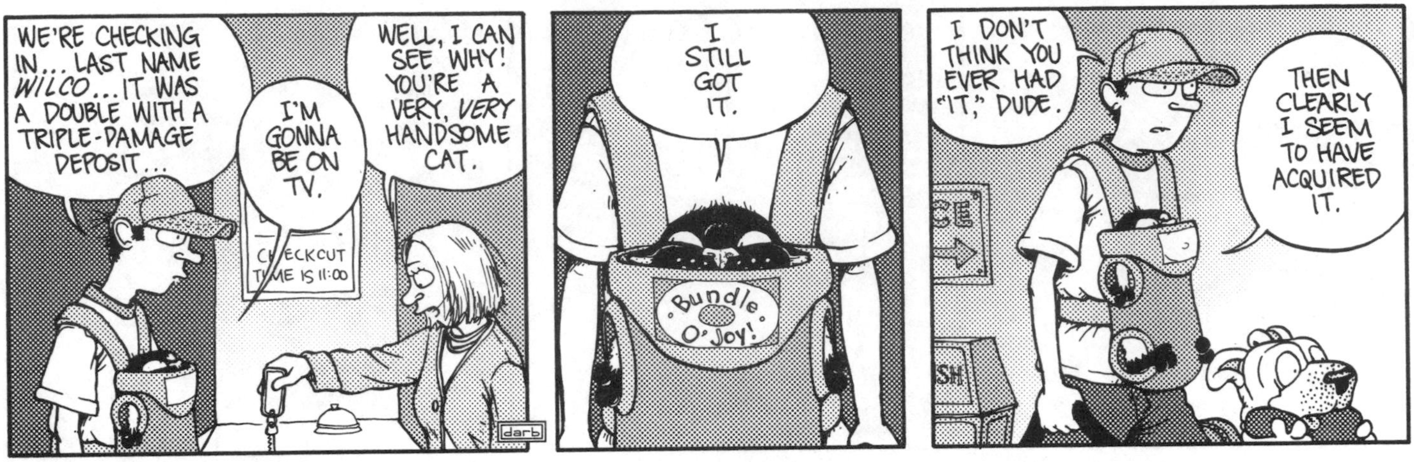
WE'RE CHECKING IN... LAST NAME *WILCO*... IT WAS A DOUBLE WITH A TRIPLE-DAMAGE DEPOSIT...
I'M GONNA BE ON TV.
WELL, I CAN SEE WHY! YOU'RE A VERY, *VERY* HANDSOME CAT.
CHECKOUT TIME IS 11:00
I STILL GOT IT.
Bundle O' Joy!
I DON'T THINK YOU EVER HAD "IT," DUDE.
THEN CLEARLY I SEEM TO HAVE ACQUIRED IT.
darb

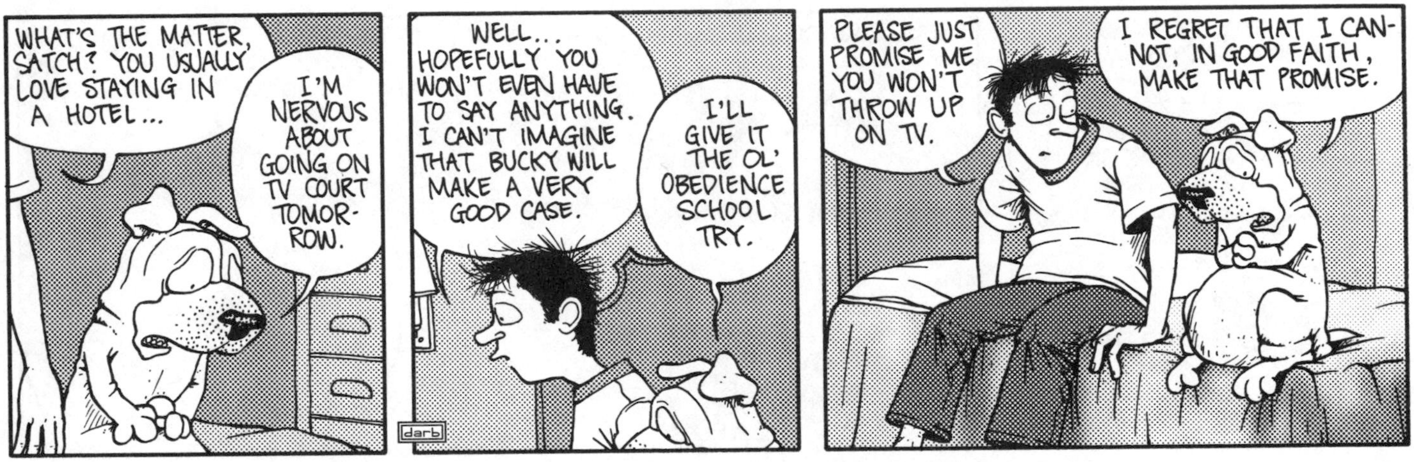
WHAT'S THE MATTER, SATCH? YOU USUALLY LOVE STAYING IN A HOTEL...
I'M NERVOUS ABOUT GOING ON TV COURT TOMOR-ROW.
WELL... HOPEFULLY YOU WON'T EVEN HAVE TO SAY ANYTHING. I CAN'T IMAGINE THAT BUCKY WILL MAKE A VERY GOOD CASE.
I'LL GIVE IT THE OL' OBEDIENCE SCHOOL TRY.
PLEASE JUST PROMISE ME YOU WON'T THROW UP ON TV.
I REGRET THAT I CAN-NOT, IN GOOD FAITH, MAKE THAT PROMISE.
darb

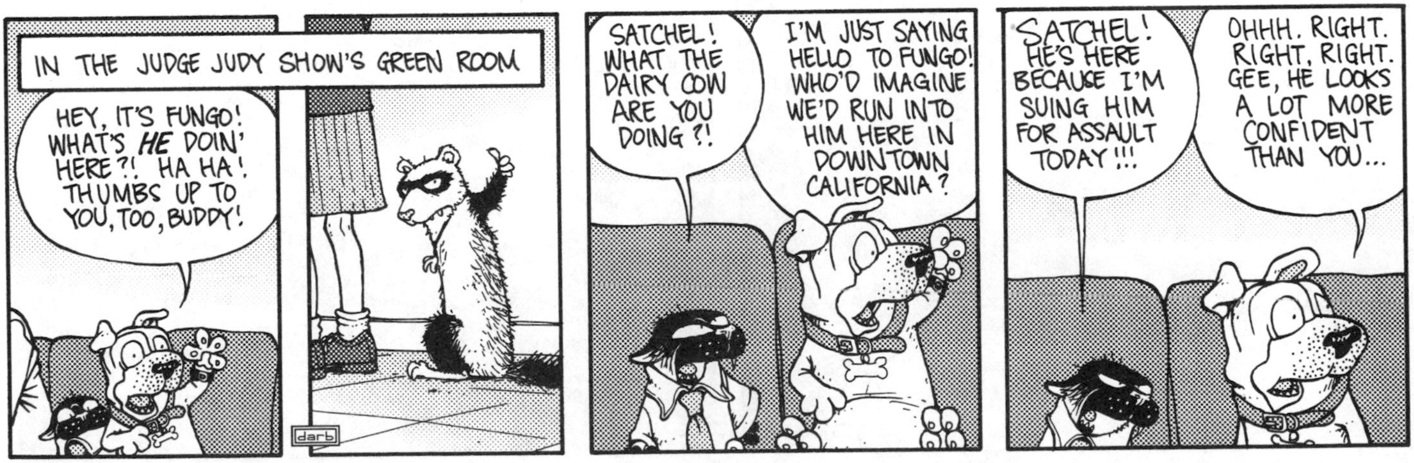
IN THE JUDGE JUDY SHOW'S GREEN ROOM
HEY, IT'S FUNGO! WHAT'S *HE* DOIN' HERE?! HA HA! THUMBS UP TO YOU, TOO, BUDDY!
SATCHEL! WHAT THE DAIRY COW ARE YOU DOING?!
I'M JUST SAYING HELLO TO FUNGO! WHO'D IMAGINE WE'D RUN INTO HIM HERE IN DOWNTOWN CALIFORNIA?
SATCHEL! HE'S HERE BECAUSE I'M SUING HIM FOR ASSAULT TODAY!!!
OHHH. RIGHT. RIGHT, RIGHT. GEE, HE LOOKS A LOT MORE CONFIDENT THAN YOU...
darb

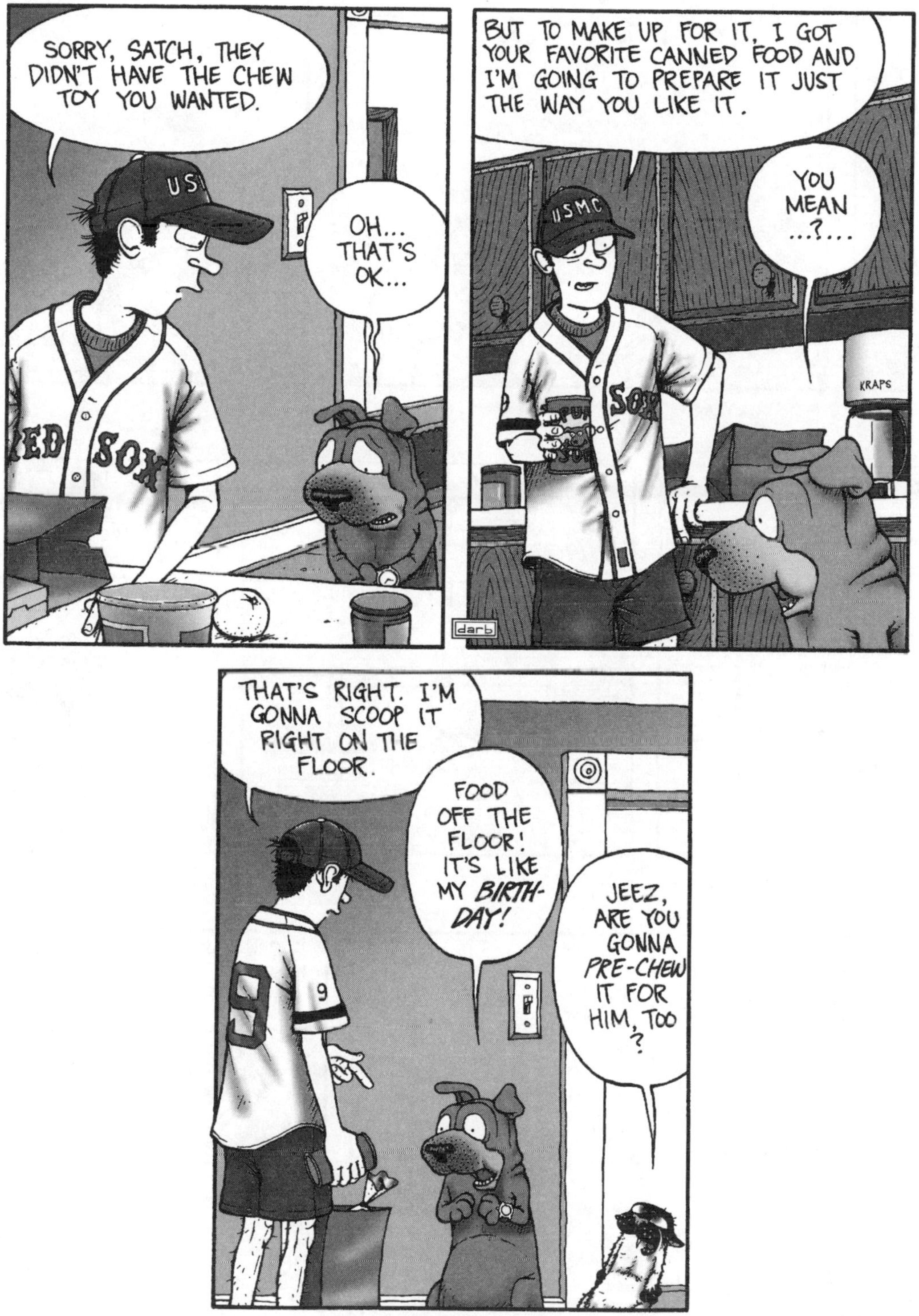
SORRY, SATCH, THEY DIDN'T HAVE THE CHEW TOY YOU WANTED.
OH... THAT'S OK...
BUT TO MAKE UP FOR IT, I GOT YOUR FAVORITE CANNED FOOD AND I'M GOING TO PREPARE IT JUST THE WAY YOU LIKE IT.
YOU MEAN ...?...
USMC
KRAPS
darb
THAT'S RIGHT. I'M GONNA SCOOP IT RIGHT ON THE FLOOR.
FOOD OFF THE FLOOR! IT'S LIKE MY *BIRTH-DAY!*
JEEZ, ARE YOU GONNA *PRE-CHEW* IT FOR HIM, TOO?

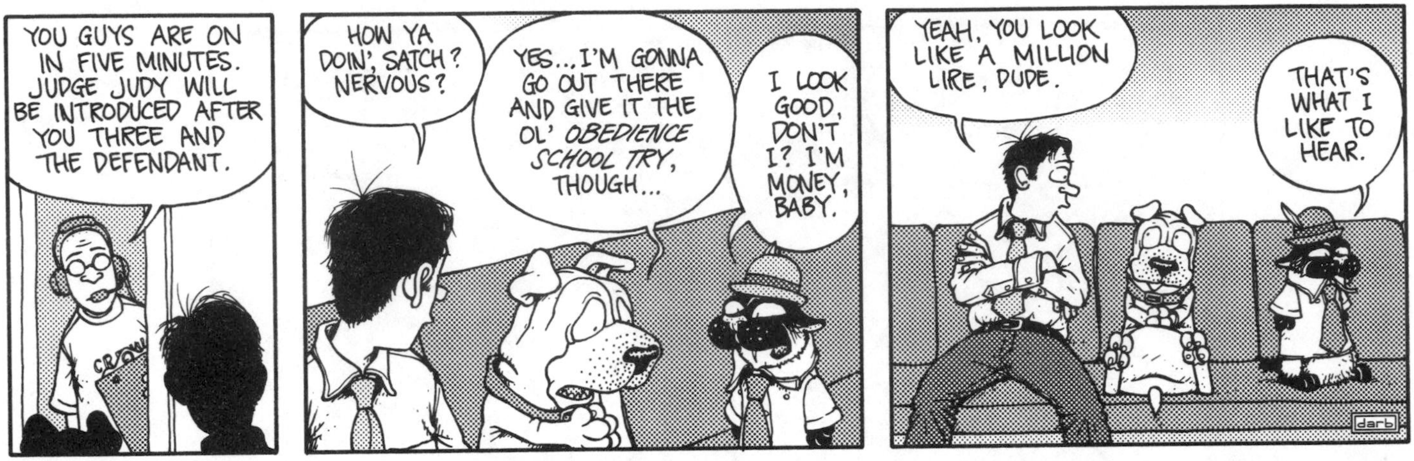
YOU GUYS ARE ON IN FIVE MINUTES. JUDGE JUDY WILL BE INTRODUCED AFTER YOU THREE AND THE DEFENDANT.
HOW YA DOIN', SATCH? NERVOUS?
YES...I'M GONNA GO OUT THERE AND GIVE IT THE OL' *OBEDIENCE SCHOOL TRY*, THOUGH...
I LOOK GOOD, DON'T I? I'M MONEY, BABY.
YEAH, YOU LOOK LIKE A MILLION LIKE, DUDE.
THAT'S WHAT I LIKE TO HEAR.
darb

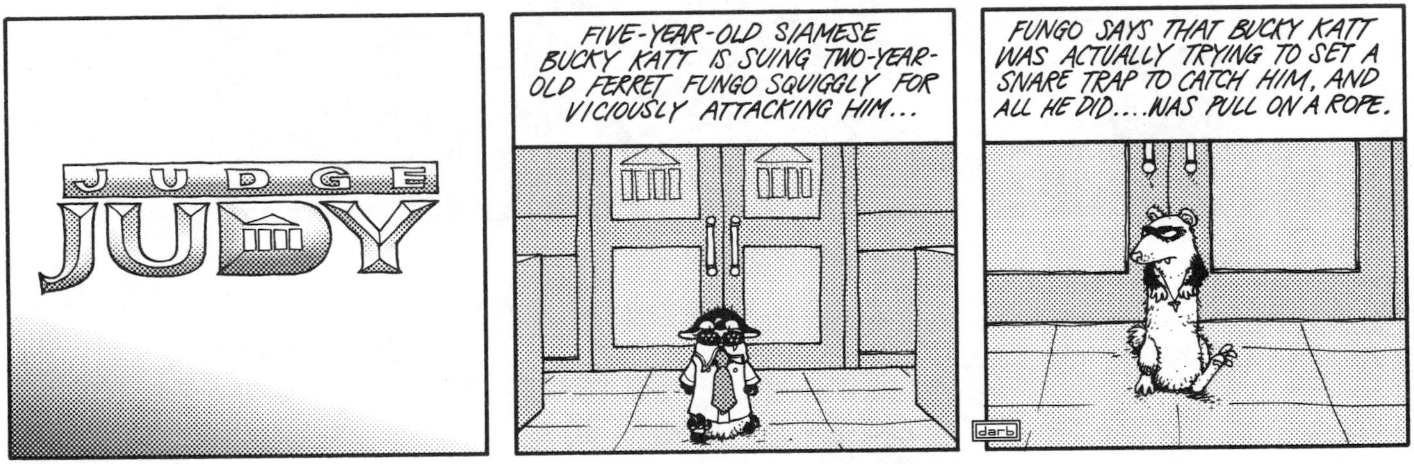
JUDGE JUDY
FIVE-YEAR-OLD SIAMESE BUCKY KATT IS SUING TWO-YEAR-OLD FERRET FUNGO SQUIGGLY FOR VICIOUSLY ATTACKING HIM...
FUNGO SAYS THAT BUCKY KATT WAS ACTUALLY TRYING TO SET A SNARE TRAP TO CATCH HIM, AND ALL HE DID....WAS PULL ON A ROPE.
darb

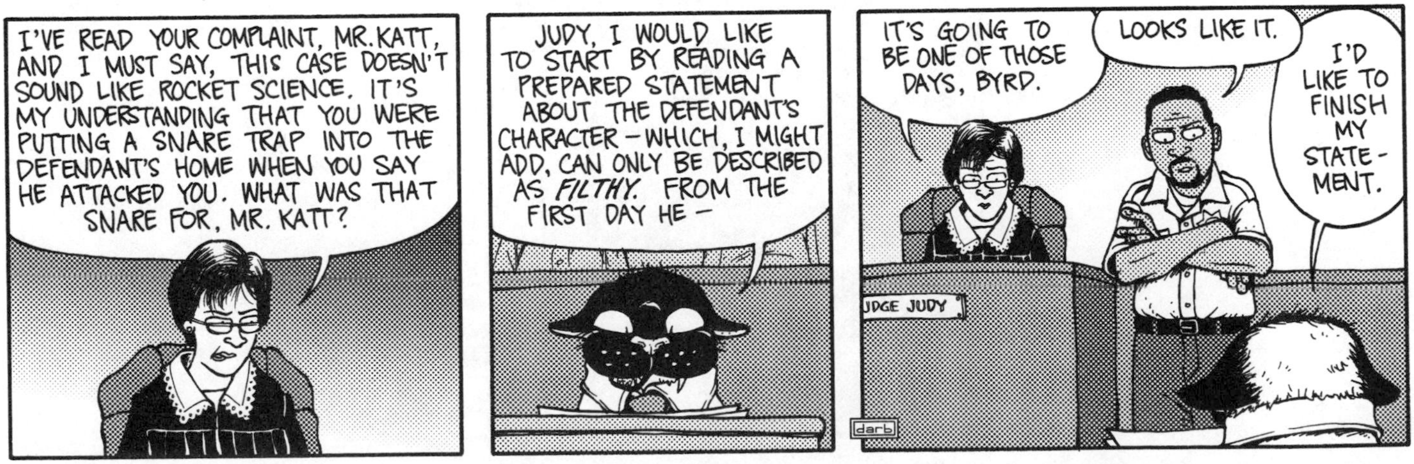
I'VE READ YOUR COMPLAINT, MR. KATT, AND I MUST SAY, THIS CASE DOESN'T SOUND LIKE ROCKET SCIENCE. IT'S MY UNDERSTANDING THAT YOU WERE PUTTING A SNARE TRAP INTO THE DEFENDANT'S HOME WHEN YOU SAY HE ATTACKED YOU. WHAT WAS THAT SNARE FOR, MR. KATT?
JUDY, I WOULD LIKE TO START BY READING A PREPARED STATEMENT ABOUT THE DEFENDANT'S CHARACTER—WHICH, I MIGHT ADD, CAN ONLY BE DESCRIBED AS *FILTHY*. FROM THE FIRST DAY HE—
IT'S GOING TO BE ONE OF THOSE DAYS, BYRD.
LOOKS LIKE IT.
I'D LIKE TO FINISH MY STATE-MENT.
darb

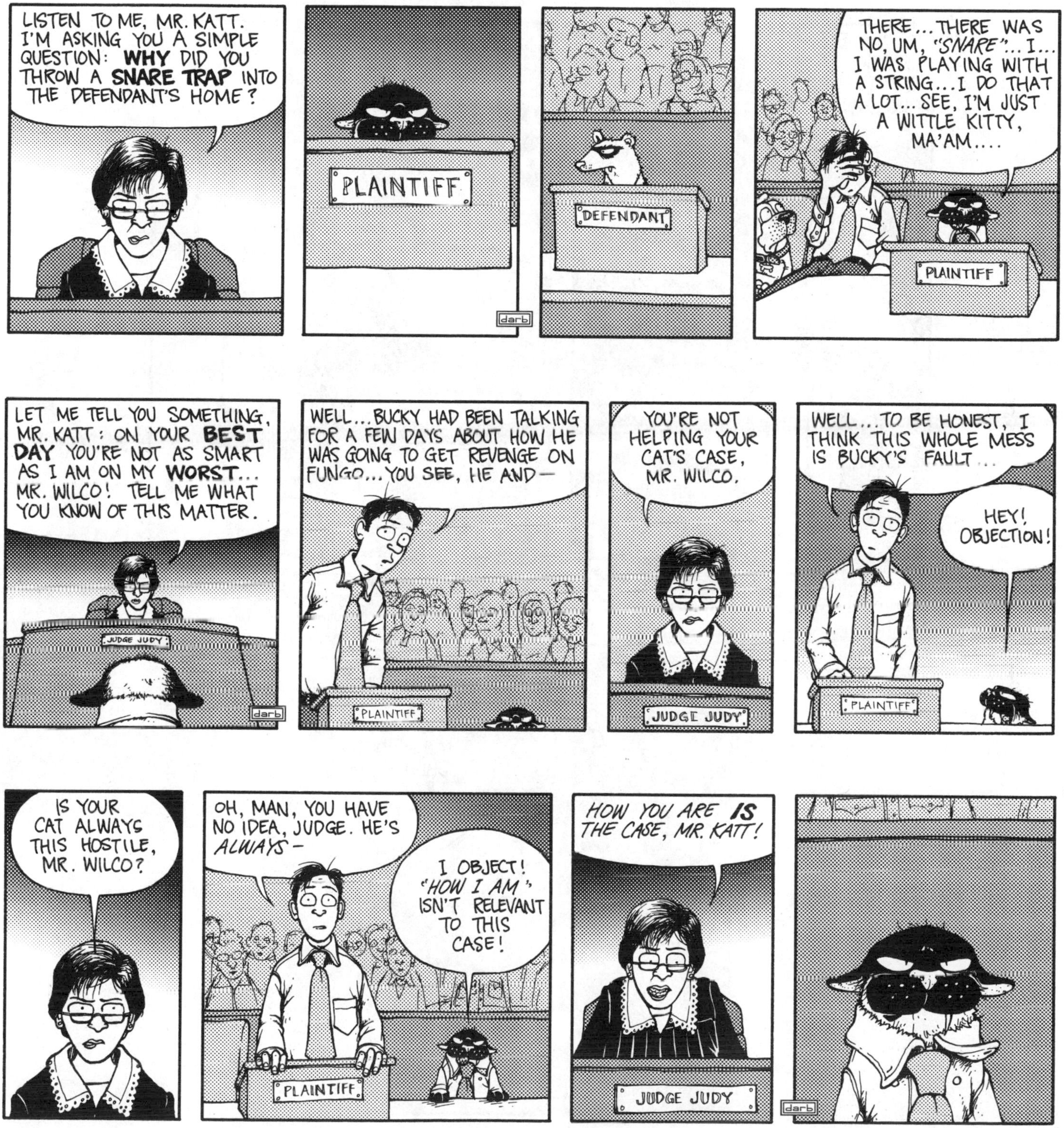
LISTEN TO ME, MR. KATT. I'M ASKING YOU A SIMPLE QUESTION: **WHY** DID YOU THROW A **SNARE TRAP** INTO THE DEFENDANT'S HOME?
PLAINTIFF
DEFENDANT
THERE... THERE WAS NO, UM, "*SNARE*"... I... I WAS PLAYING WITH A STRING... I DO THAT A LOT... SEE, I'M JUST A WITTLE KITTY, MA'AM....
PLAINTIFF
LET ME TELL YOU SOMETHING, MR. KATT: ON YOUR **BEST DAY** YOU'RE NOT AS SMART AS I AM ON MY **WORST**... MR. WILCO! TELL ME WHAT YOU KNOW OF THIS MATTER.
JUDGE JUDY
WELL... BUCKY HAD BEEN TALKING FOR A FEW DAYS ABOUT HOW HE WAS GOING TO GET REVENGE ON FUNGO... YOU SEE, HE AND—
PLAINTIFF
YOU'RE NOT HELPING YOUR CAT'S CASE, MR. WILCO.
JUDGE JUDY
WELL... TO BE HONEST, I THINK THIS WHOLE MESS IS BUCKY'S FAULT...
HEY! OBJECTION!
PLAINTIFF
IS YOUR CAT ALWAYS THIS HOSTILE, MR. WILCO?
OH, MAN, YOU HAVE NO IDEA, JUDGE. HE'S *ALWAYS*—
I OBJECT! "*HOW I AM*" ISN'T RELEVANT TO THIS CASE!
PLAINTIFF
HOW YOU ARE ***IS*** *THE CASE, MR. KATT!*
JUDGE JUDY

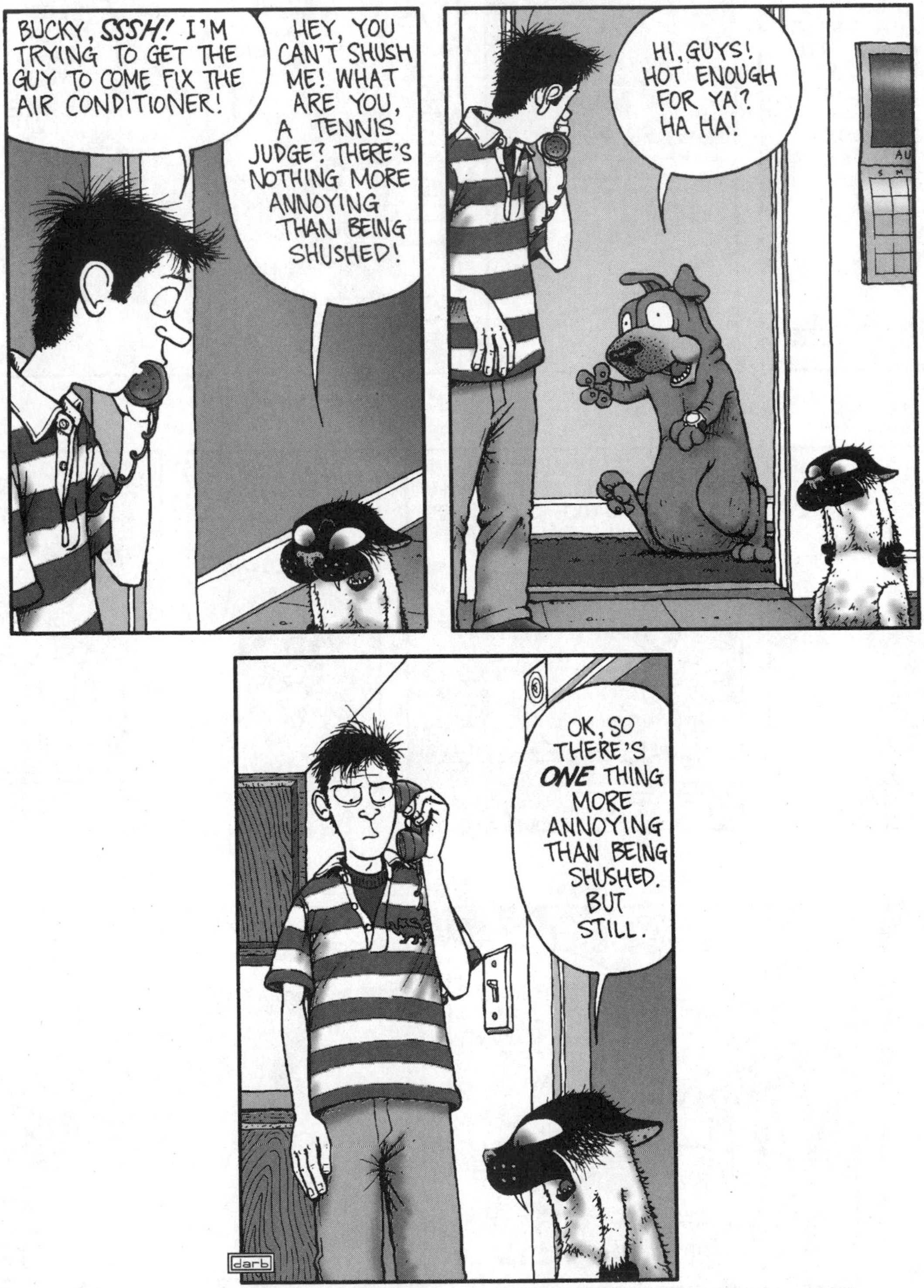
BUCKY, SSSH! I'M TRYING TO GET THE GUY TO COME FIX THE AIR CONDITIONER!
HEY, YOU CAN'T SHUSH ME! WHAT ARE YOU, A TENNIS JUDGE? THERE'S NOTHING MORE ANNOYING THAN BEING SHUSHED!
HI, GUYS! HOT ENOUGH FOR YA? HA HA!
OK, SO THERE'S ONE THING MORE ANNOYING THAN BEING SHUSHED. BUT STILL.
darb

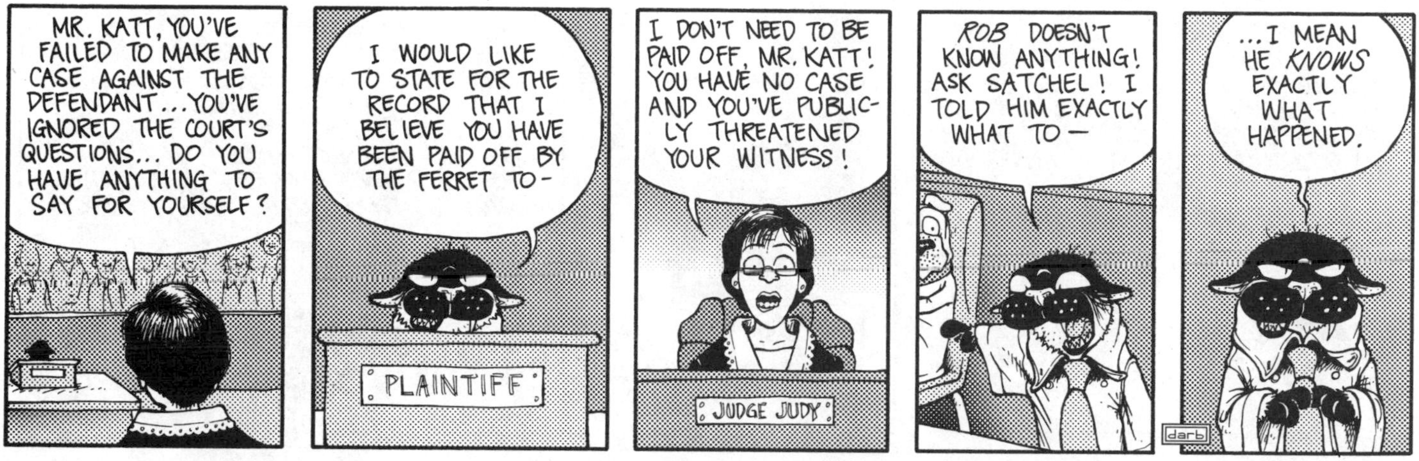
MR. KATT, YOU'VE FAILED TO MAKE ANY CASE AGAINST THE DEFENDANT... YOU'VE IGNORED THE COURT'S QUESTIONS... DO YOU HAVE ANYTHING TO SAY FOR YOURSELF?
I WOULD LIKE TO STATE FOR THE RECORD THAT I BELIEVE YOU HAVE BEEN PAID OFF BY THE FERRET TO-
PLAINTIFF
I DON'T NEED TO BE PAID OFF, MR. KATT! YOU HAVE NO CASE AND YOU'VE PUBLICLY THREATENED YOUR WITNESS!
JUDGE JUDY
ROB DOESN'T KNOW ANYTHING! ASK SATCHEL! I TOLD HIM EXACTLY WHAT TO—
...I MEAN HE *KNOWS* EXACTLY WHAT HAPPENED.
darb

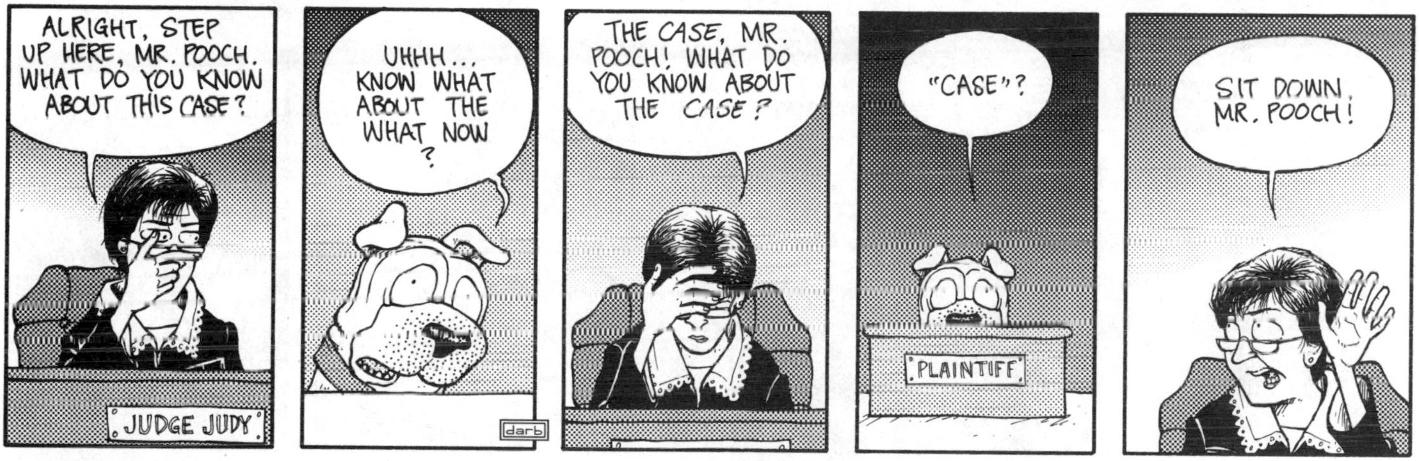
ALRIGHT, STEP UP HERE, MR. POOCH. WHAT DO YOU KNOW ABOUT THIS CASE?
JUDGE JUDY
UHHH... KNOW WHAT ABOUT THE WHAT NOW?
darb
THE *CASE*, MR. POOCH! WHAT DO YOU KNOW ABOUT THE *CASE*?
"CASE"?
PLAINTIFF
SIT DOWN, MR. POOCH!

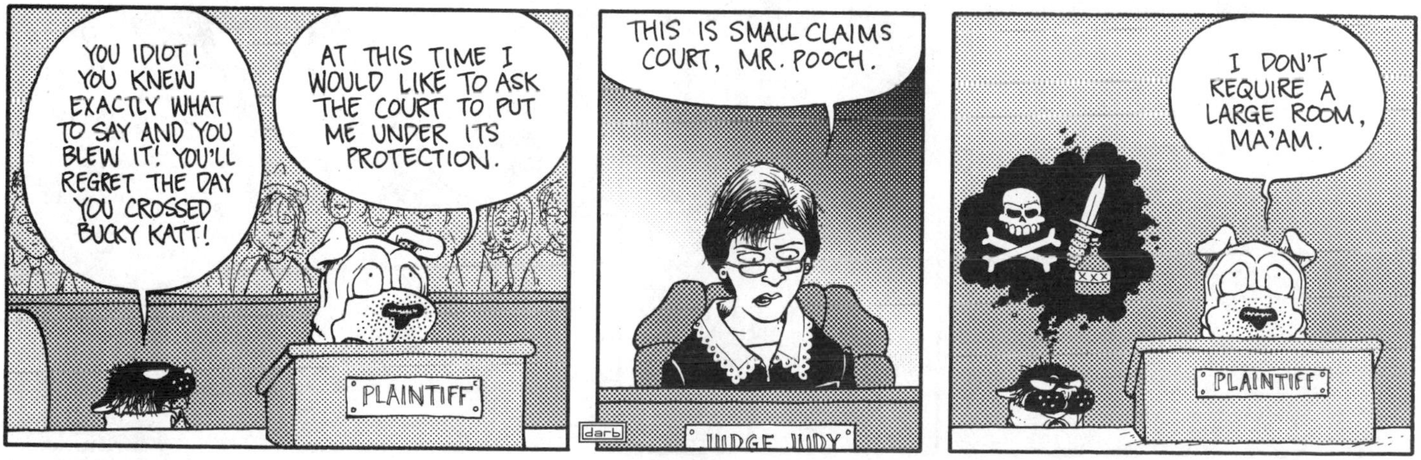
YOU IDIOT! YOU KNEW EXACTLY WHAT TO SAY AND YOU BLEW IT! YOU'LL REGRET THE DAY YOU CROSSED BUCKY KATT!
AT THIS TIME I WOULD LIKE TO ASK THE COURT TO PUT ME UNDER ITS PROTECTION.
PLAINTIFF
darb
THIS IS SMALL CLAIMS COURT, MR. POOCH.
JUDGE JUDY
I DON'T REQUIRE A LARGE ROOM, MA'AM.
PLAINTIFF

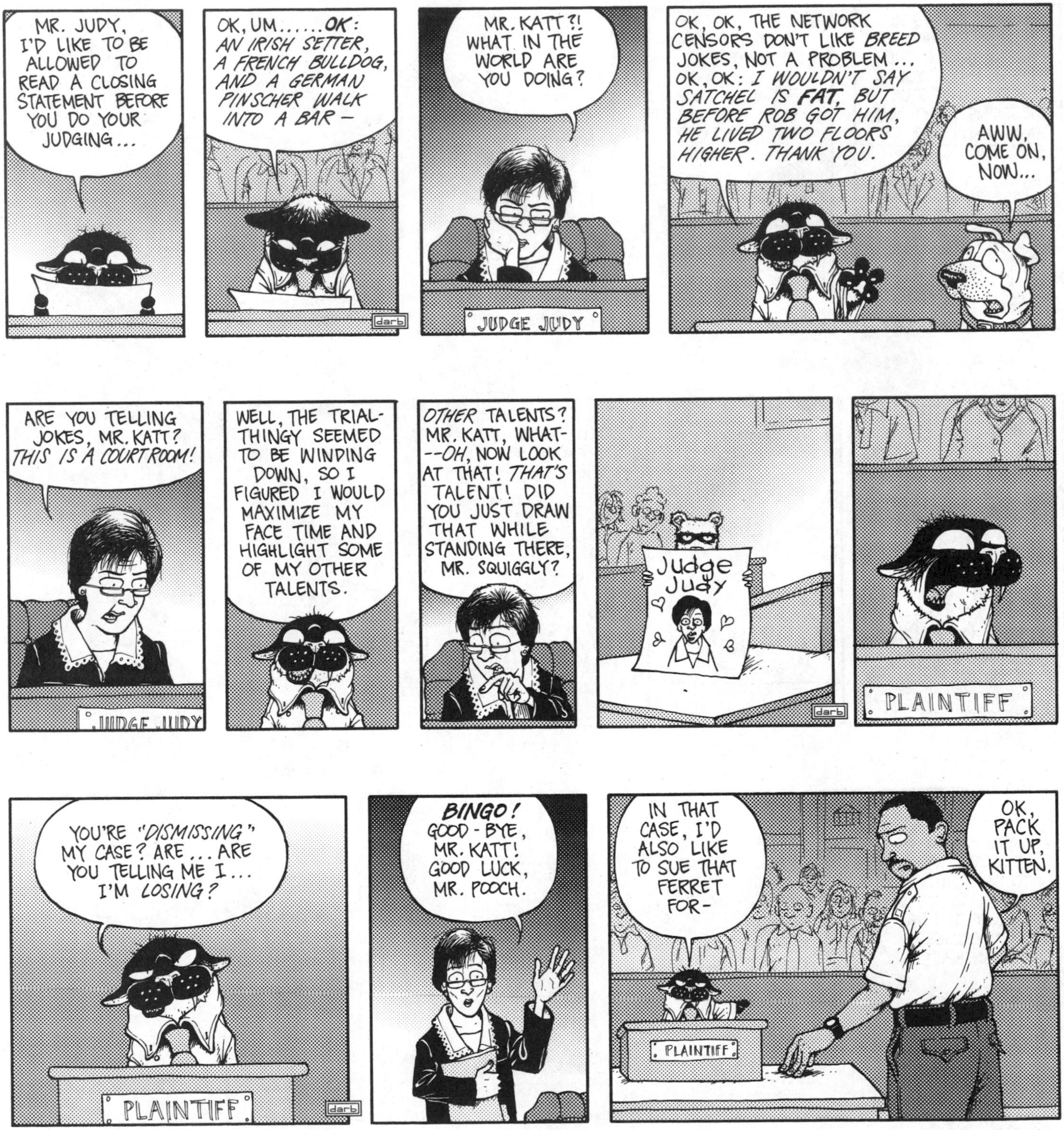

MR. JUDY, I'D LIKE TO BE ALLOWED TO READ A CLOSING STATEMENT BEFORE YOU DO YOUR JUDGING...
OK, UM......OK: AN IRISH SETTER, A FRENCH BULLDOG, AND A GERMAN PINSCHER WALK INTO A BAR–
MR. KATT?! WHAT IN THE WORLD ARE YOU DOING?
JUDGE JUDY
OK, OK, THE NETWORK CENSORS DON'T LIKE BREED JOKES, NOT A PROBLEM... OK, OK: I WOULDN'T SAY SATCHEL IS FAT, BUT BEFORE ROB GOT HIM, HE LIVED TWO FLOORS HIGHER. THANK YOU.
AWW, COME ON, NOW...
ARE YOU TELLING JOKES, MR. KATT? THIS IS A COURTROOM!
WELL, THE TRIAL-THINGY SEEMED TO BE WINDING DOWN, SO I FIGURED I WOULD MAXIMIZE MY FACE TIME AND HIGHLIGHT SOME OF MY OTHER TALENTS.
OTHER TALENTS? MR. KATT, WHAT--OH, NOW LOOK AT THAT! THAT'S TALENT! DID YOU JUST DRAW THAT WHILE STANDING THERE, MR. SQUIGGLY?
Judge Judy
PLAINTIFF
YOU'RE "DISMISSING" MY CASE? ARE... ARE YOU TELLING ME I... I'M LOSING?
PLAINTIFF
BINGO! GOOD-BYE, MR. KATT! GOOD LUCK, MR. POOCH.
IN THAT CASE, I'D ALSO LIKE TO SUE THAT FERRET FOR–
OK, PACK IT UP, KITTEN.
PLAINTIFF

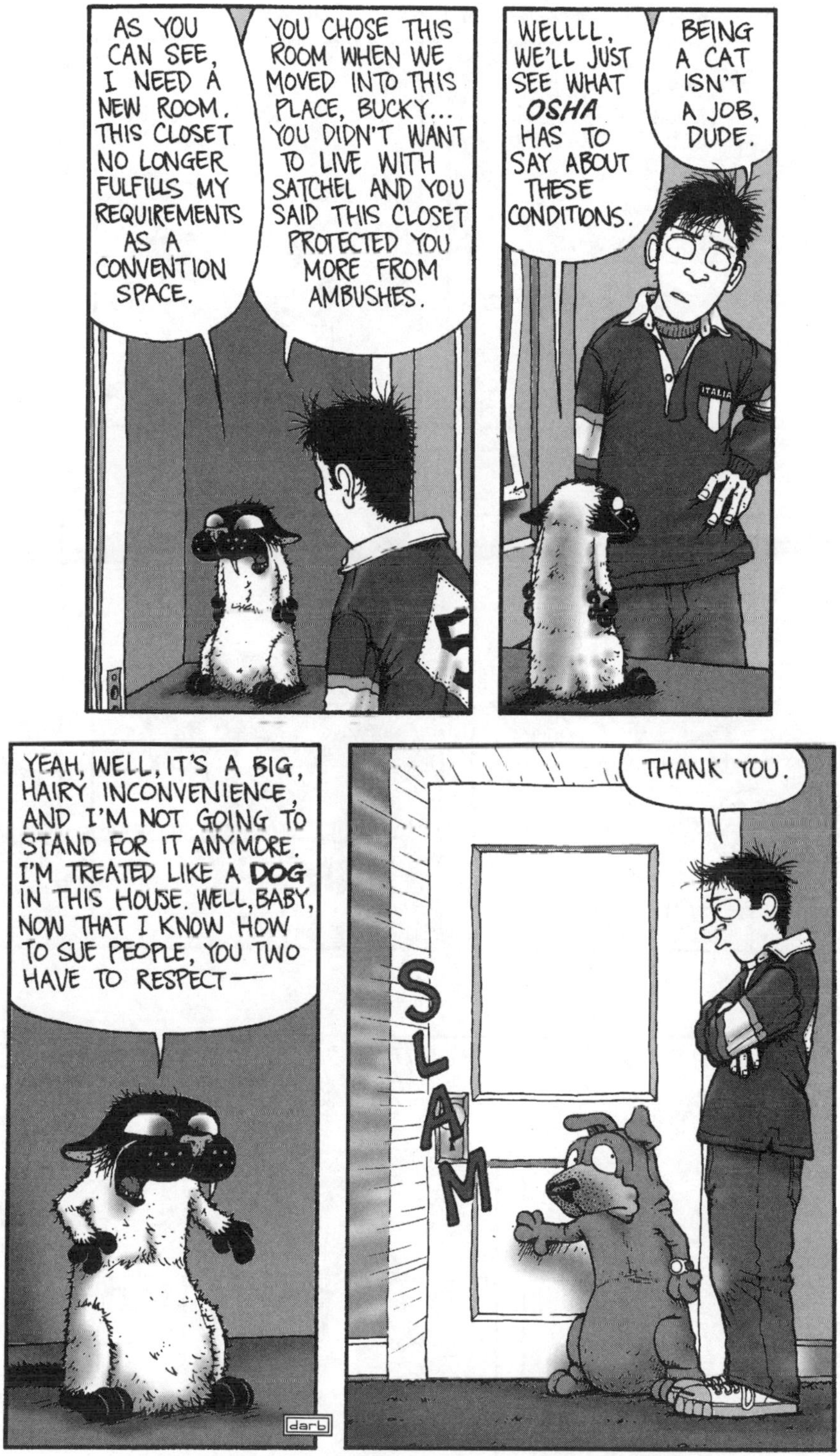
AS YOU CAN SEE, I NEED A NEW ROOM. THIS CLOSET NO LONGER FULFILLS MY REQUIREMENTS AS A CONVENTION SPACE.
YOU CHOSE THIS ROOM WHEN WE MOVED INTO THIS PLACE, BUCKY... YOU DIDN'T WANT TO LIVE WITH SATCHEL AND YOU SAID THIS CLOSET PROTECTED YOU MORE FROM AMBUSHES.
WELLLL, WE'LL JUST SEE WHAT OSHA HAS TO SAY ABOUT THESE CONDITIONS.
BEING A CAT ISN'T A JOB, DUDE.
YEAH, WELL, IT'S A BIG, HAIRY INCONVENIENCE, AND I'M NOT GOING TO STAND FOR IT ANYMORE. I'M TREATED LIKE A DOG IN THIS HOUSE. WELL, BABY, NOW THAT I KNOW HOW TO SUE PEOPLE, YOU TWO HAVE TO RESPECT—
darb
SLAM
THANK YOU.

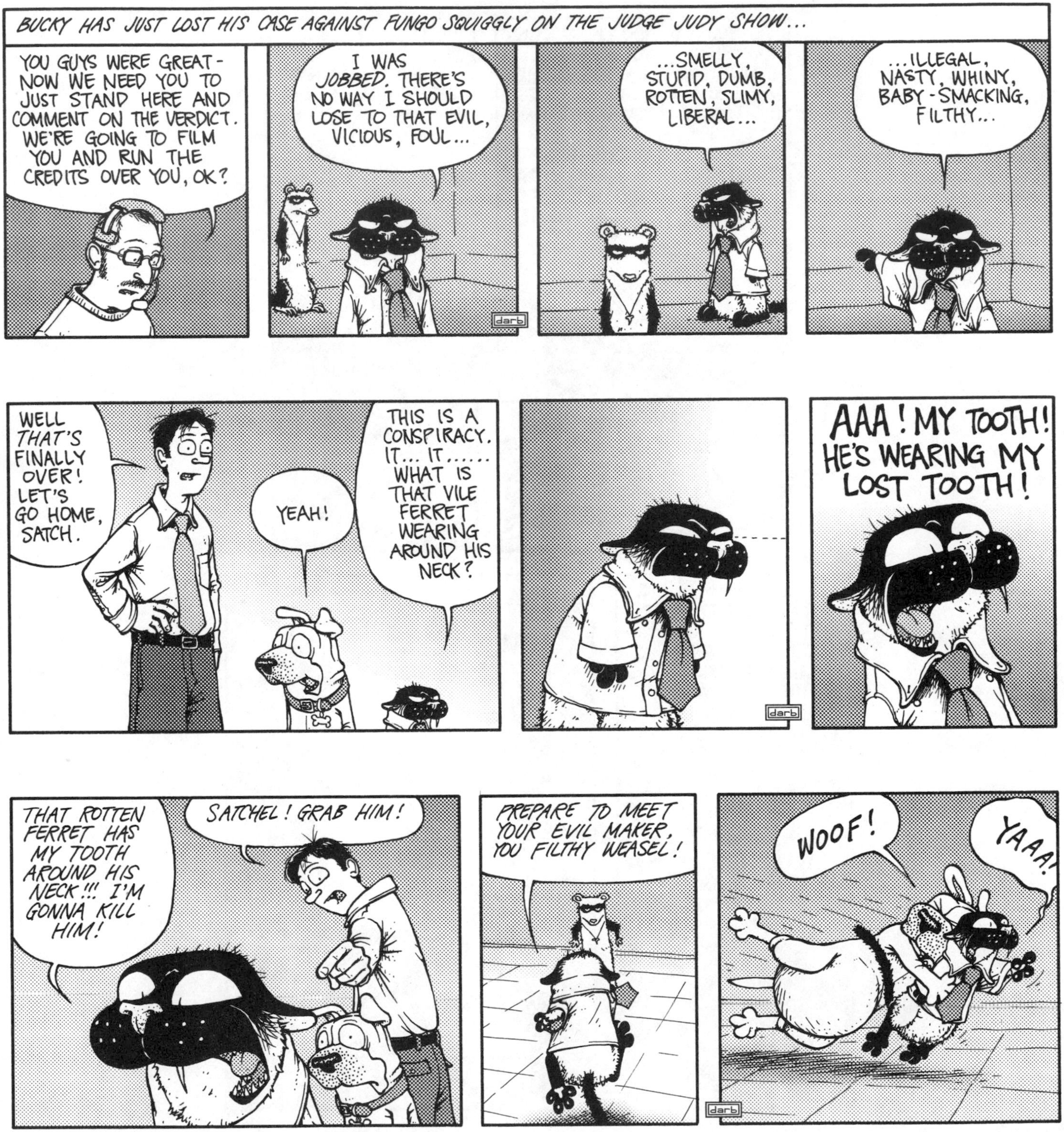
BUCKY HAS JUST LOST HIS CASE AGAINST FUNGO SQUIGGLY ON THE JUDGE JUDY SHOW...
YOU GUYS WERE GREAT - NOW WE NEED YOU TO JUST STAND HERE AND COMMENT ON THE VERDICT. WE'RE GOING TO FILM YOU AND RUN THE CREDITS OVER YOU, OK?
I WAS JOBBED. THERE'S NO WAY I SHOULD LOSE TO THAT EVIL, VICIOUS, FOUL...
...SMELLY, STUPID, DUMB, ROTTEN, SLIMY, LIBERAL...
...ILLEGAL, NASTY, WHINY, BABY-SMACKING, FILTHY...
darb
WELL THAT'S FINALLY OVER! LET'S GO HOME, SATCH.
YEAH!
THIS IS A CONSPIRACY. IT... IT...... WHAT IS THAT VILE FERRET WEARING AROUND HIS NECK?
AAA! MY TOOTH! HE'S WEARING MY LOST TOOTH!
darb
THAT ROTTEN FERRET HAS MY TOOTH AROUND HIS NECK!!! I'M GONNA KILL HIM!
SATCHEL! GRAB HIM!
PREPARE TO MEET YOUR EVIL MAKER, YOU FILTHY WEASEL!
WOOF!
YAAA!
darb

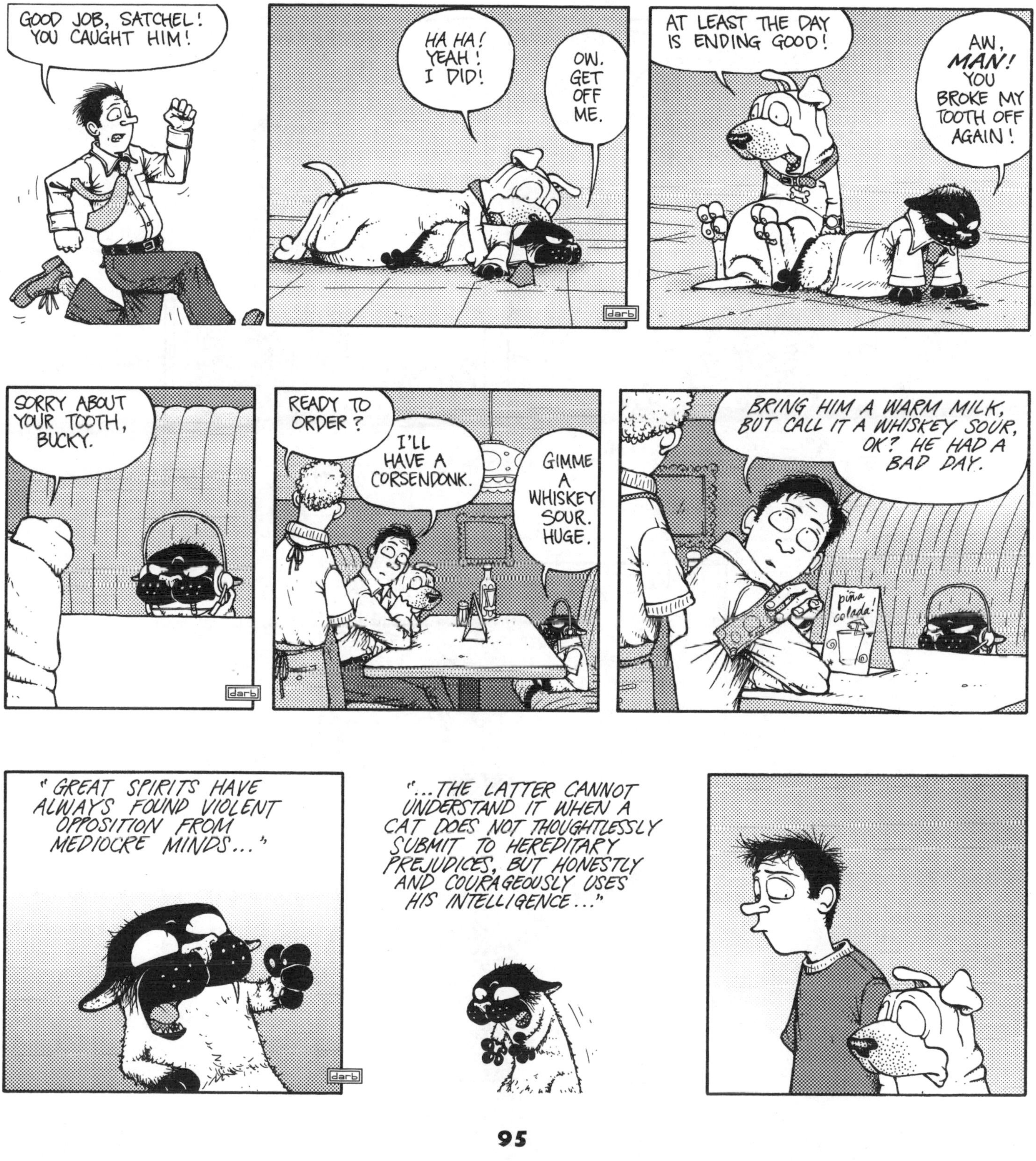
GOOD JOB, SATCHEL! YOU CAUGHT HIM!
HA HA! YEAH! I DID!
OW. GET OFF ME.
darb
AT LEAST THE DAY IS ENDING GOOD!
AW, MAN! YOU BROKE MY TOOTH OFF AGAIN!
SORRY ABOUT YOUR TOOTH, BUCKY.
darb
READY TO ORDER?
I'LL HAVE A CORSENDONK.
GIMME A WHISKEY SOUR. HUGE.
BRING HIM A WARM MILK, BUT CALL IT A WHISKEY SOUR, OK? HE HAD A BAD DAY.
piña colada!
"GREAT SPIRITS HAVE ALWAYS FOUND VIOLENT OPPOSITION FROM MEDIOCRE MINDS..."
darb
"...THE LATTER CANNOT UNDERSTAND IT WHEN A CAT DOES NOT THOUGHTLESSLY SUBMIT TO HEREDITARY PREJUDICES, BUT HONESTLY AND COURAGEOUSLY USES HIS INTELLIGENCE..."

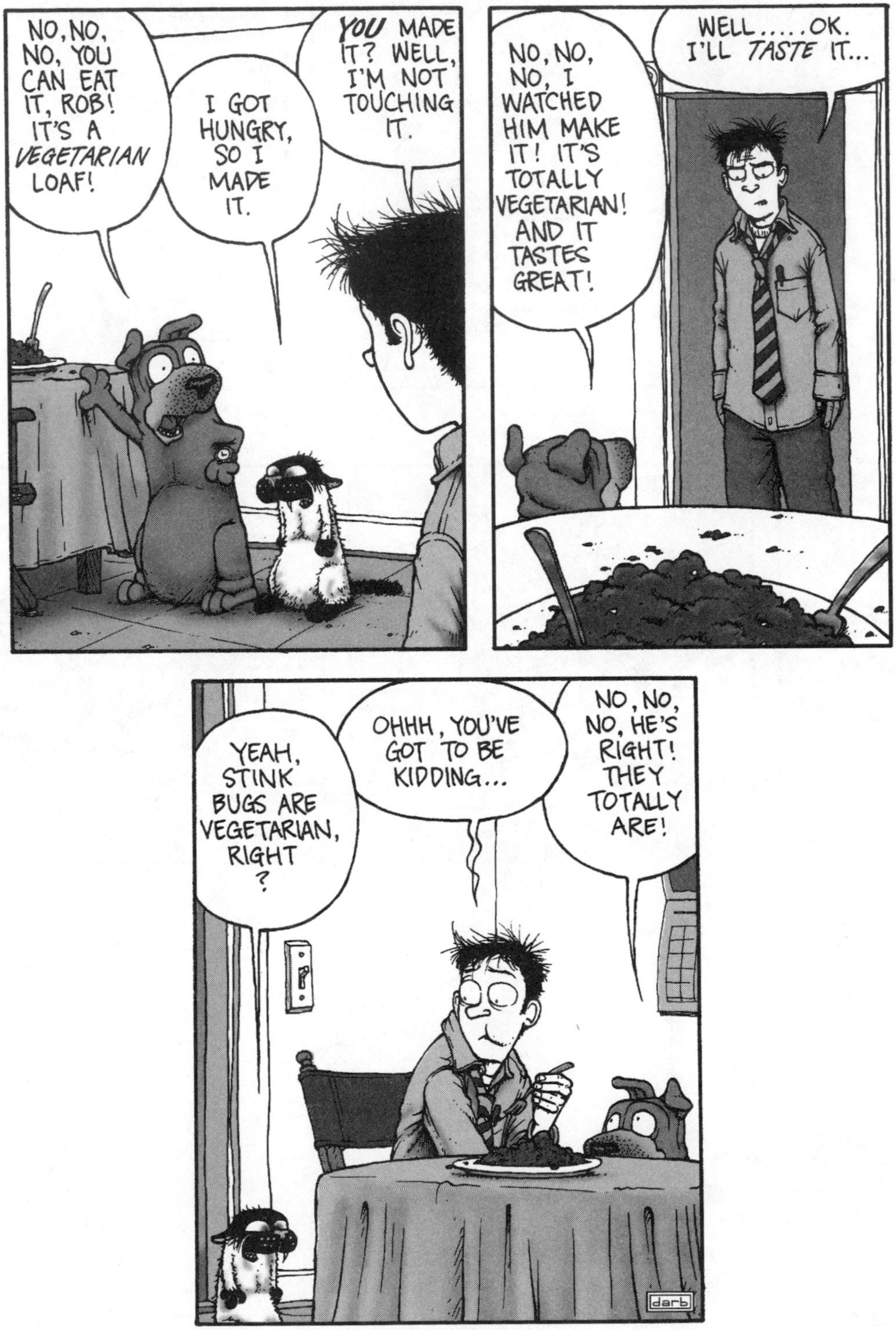
NO, NO, NO, YOU CAN EAT IT, ROB! IT'S A *VEGETARIAN* LOAF!
I GOT HUNGRY, SO I MADE IT.
YOU MADE IT? WELL, I'M NOT TOUCHING IT.
NO, NO, NO, I WATCHED HIM MAKE IT! IT'S TOTALLY VEGETARIAN! AND IT TASTES GREAT!
WELL.....OK. I'LL *TASTE* IT...
YEAH, STINK BUGS ARE VEGETARIAN, RIGHT?
OHHH, YOU'VE GOT TO BE KIDDING...
NO, NO, NO, HE'S RIGHT! THEY TOTALLY ARE!
darb

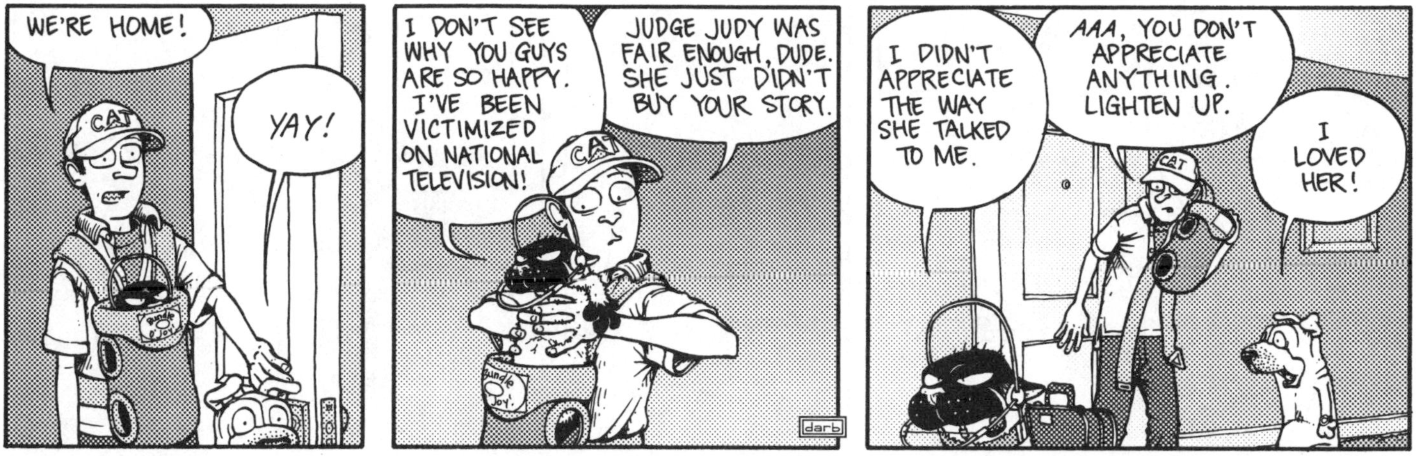
WE'RE HOME!
YAY!
I DON'T SEE WHY YOU GUYS ARE SO HAPPY. I'VE BEEN VICTIMIZED ON NATIONAL TELEVISION!
JUDGE JUDY WAS FAIR ENOUGH, DUDE. SHE JUST DIDN'T BUY YOUR STORY.
I DIDN'T APPRECIATE THE WAY SHE TALKED TO ME.
AAA, YOU DON'T APPRECIATE ANYTHING. LIGHTEN UP.
I LOVED HER!

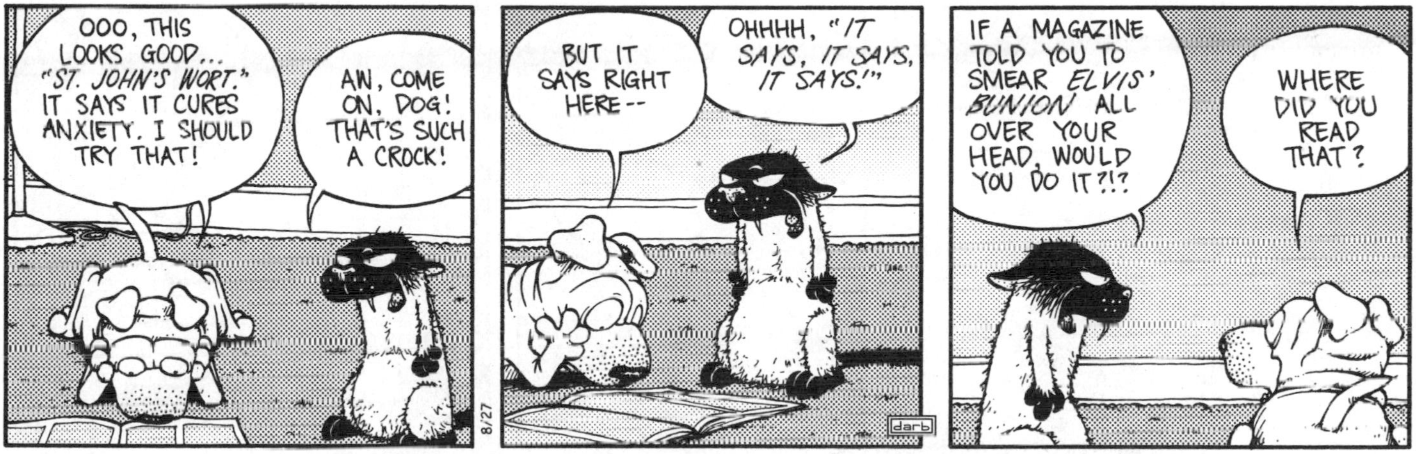
OOO, THIS LOOKS GOOD... *"ST. JOHN'S WORT."* IT SAYS IT CURES ANXIETY. I SHOULD TRY THAT!
AW, COME ON, DOG! THAT'S SUCH A CROCK!
8/27
BUT IT SAYS RIGHT HERE--
OHHHH, *"IT SAYS, IT SAYS, IT SAYS!"*
IF A MAGAZINE TOLD YOU TO SMEAR *ELVIS' BUNION* ALL OVER YOUR HEAD, WOULD YOU DO IT?!?
WHERE DID YOU READ THAT?

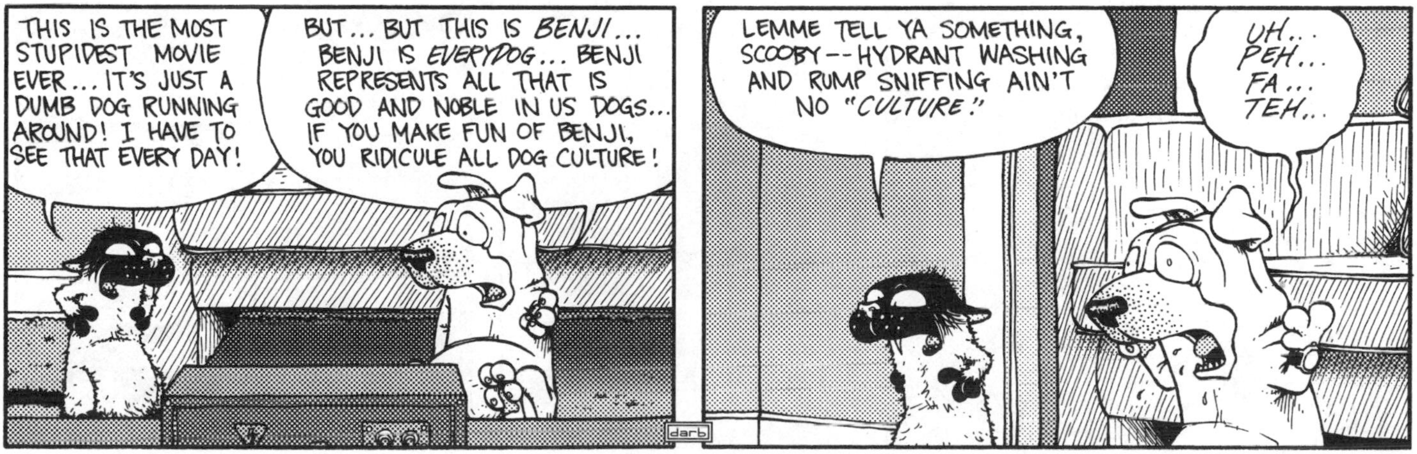
THIS IS THE MOST STUPIDEST MOVIE EVER... IT'S JUST A DUMB DOG RUNNING AROUND! I HAVE TO SEE THAT EVERY DAY!
BUT... BUT THIS IS *BENJI*... BENJI IS *EVERYDOG*... BENJI REPRESENTS ALL THAT IS GOOD AND NOBLE IN US DOGS... IF YOU MAKE FUN OF BENJI, YOU RIDICULE ALL DOG CULTURE!
LEMME TELL YA SOMETHING, SCOOBY--HYDRANT WASHING AND RUMP SNIFFING AIN'T NO *"CULTURE."*
UH... PEH... FA... TEH...

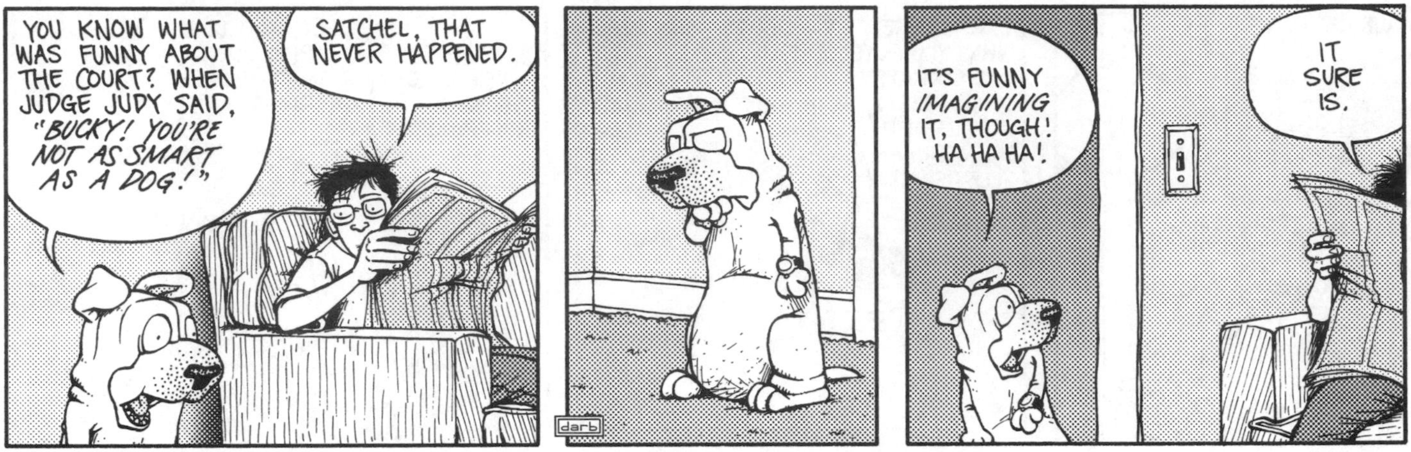
YOU KNOW WHAT WAS FUNNY ABOUT THE COURT? WHEN JUDGE JUDY SAID, *"BUCKY! YOU'RE NOT AS SMART AS A DOG!"*
SATCHEL, THAT NEVER HAPPENED.
darb
IT'S FUNNY *IMAGINING* IT, THOUGH! HA HA HA!
IT SURE IS.

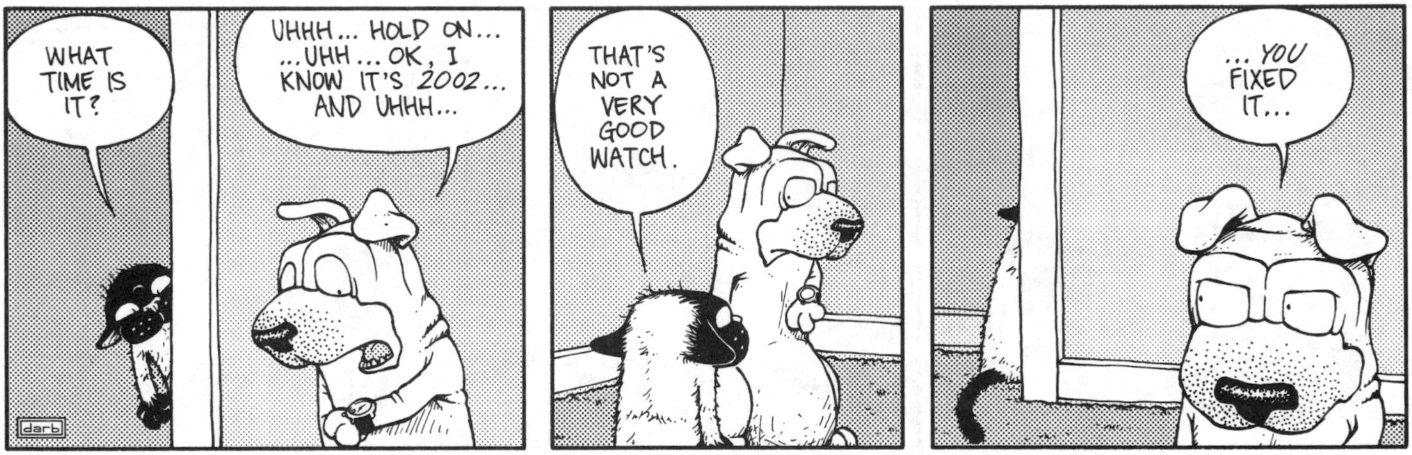
WHAT TIME IS IT?
UHHH... HOLD ON... ...UHH... OK, I KNOW IT'S *2002*... AND UHHH...
darb
THAT'S NOT A VERY GOOD WATCH.
... *YOU* FIXED IT...

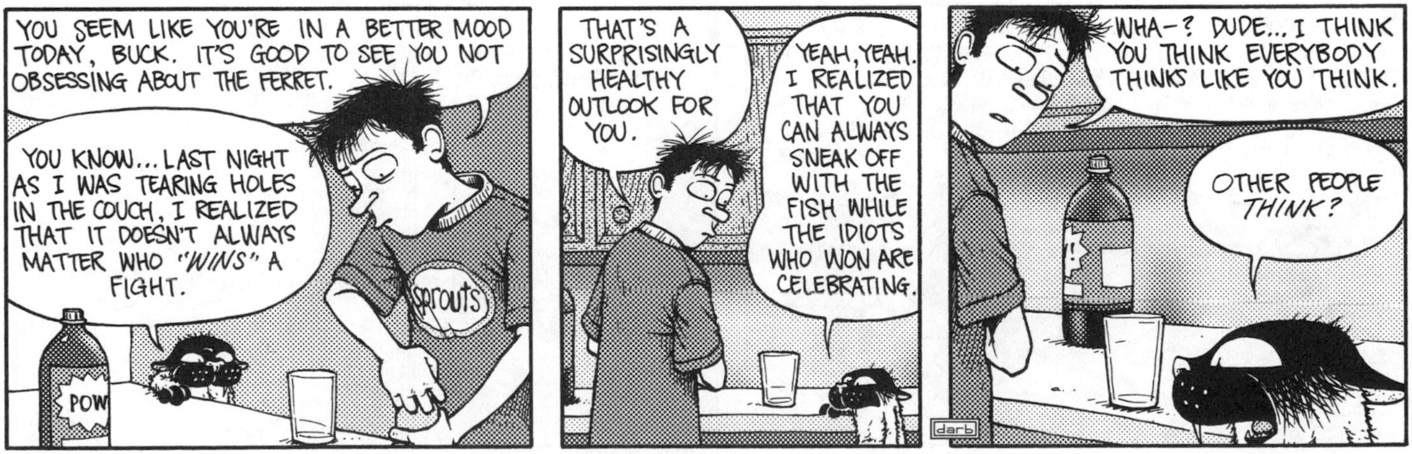
YOU SEEM LIKE YOU'RE IN A BETTER MOOD TODAY, BUCK. IT'S GOOD TO SEE YOU NOT OBSESSING ABOUT THE FERRET.
YOU KNOW... LAST NIGHT AS I WAS TEARING HOLES IN THE COUCH, I REALIZED THAT IT DOESN'T ALWAYS MATTER WHO *"WINS"* A FIGHT.
sprouts
POW
THAT'S A SURPRISINGLY HEALTHY OUTLOOK FOR YOU.
YEAH, YEAH. I REALIZED THAT YOU CAN ALWAYS SNEAK OFF WITH THE FISH WHILE THE IDIOTS WHO WON ARE CELEBRATING.
WHA-? DUDE... I THINK YOU THINK EVERYBODY THINKS LIKE YOU THINK.
OTHER PEOPLE *THINK?*
darb

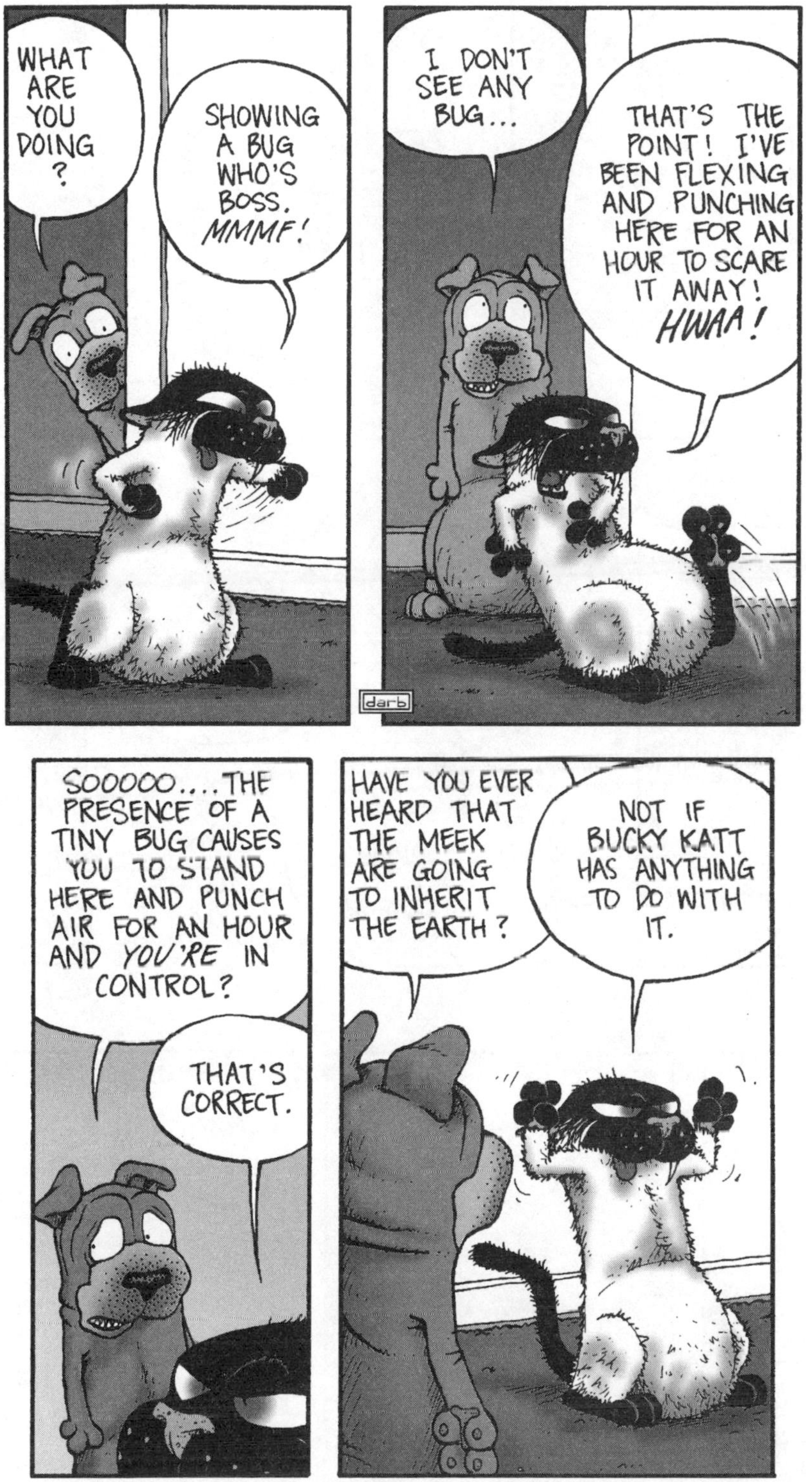

WHAT ARE YOU DOING ?
SHOWING A BUG WHO'S BOSS. *MMMF!*
I DON'T SEE ANY BUG...
THAT'S THE POINT! I'VE BEEN FLEXING AND PUNCHING HERE FOR AN HOUR TO SCARE IT AWAY! *HWAA!*
darb
SOOOOO.... THE PRESENCE OF A TINY BUG CAUSES YOU TO STAND HERE AND PUNCH AIR FOR AN HOUR AND *YOU'RE* IN CONTROL?
THAT'S CORRECT.
HAVE YOU EVER HEARD THAT THE MEEK ARE GOING TO INHERIT THE EARTH?
NOT IF BUCKY KATT HAS ANYTHING TO DO WITH IT.

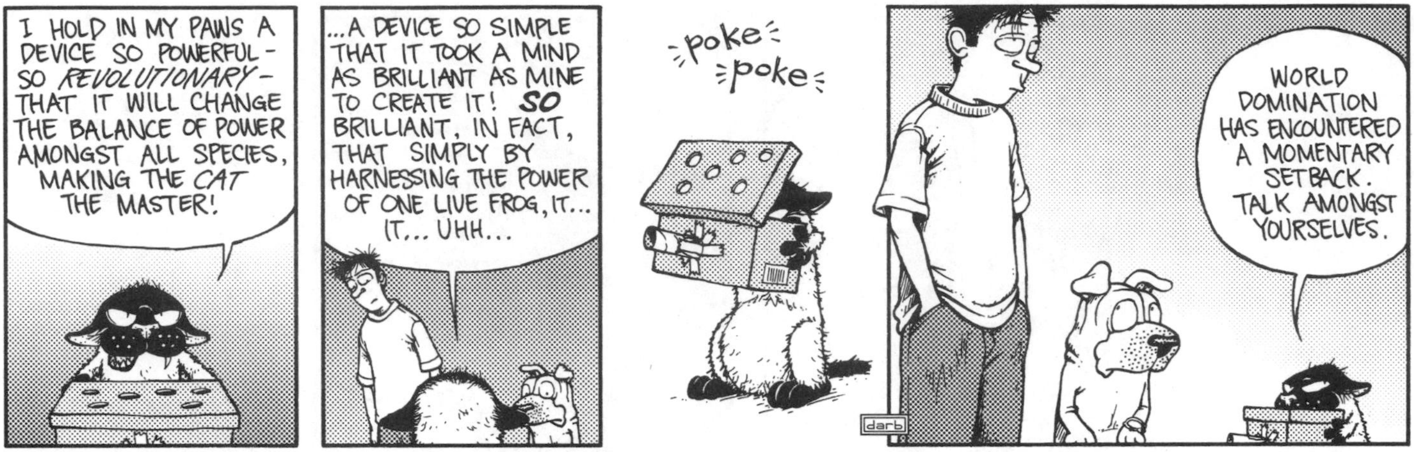
I HOLD IN MY PAWS A DEVICE SO POWERFUL - SO *REVOLUTIONARY* - THAT IT WILL CHANGE THE BALANCE OF POWER AMONGST ALL SPECIES, MAKING THE *CAT* THE MASTER!
...A DEVICE SO SIMPLE THAT IT TOOK A MIND AS BRILLIANT AS MINE TO CREATE IT! **SO** BRILLIANT, IN FACT, THAT SIMPLY BY HARNESSING THE POWER OF ONE LIVE FROG, IT... IT... UHH...
poke
poke
WORLD DOMINATION HAS ENCOUNTERED A MOMENTARY SETBACK. TALK AMONGST YOURSELVES.

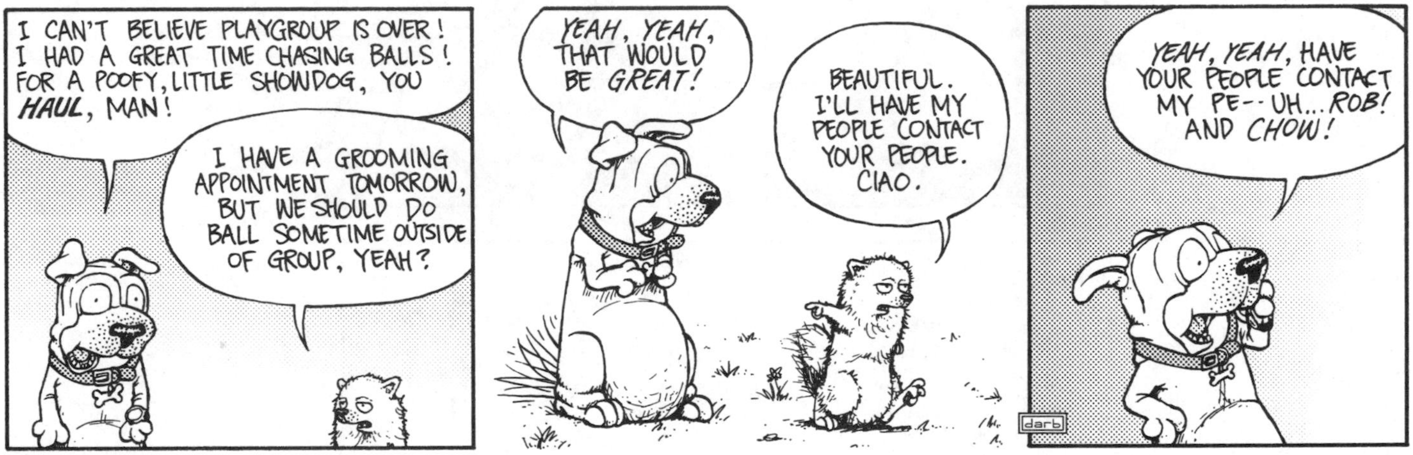
I CAN'T BELIEVE PLAYGROUP IS OVER! I HAD A GREAT TIME CHASING BALLS! FOR A POOFY, LITTLE SHOWDOG, YOU **HAUL**, MAN!
I HAVE A GROOMING APPOINTMENT TOMORROW, BUT WE SHOULD DO BALL SOMETIME OUTSIDE OF GROUP, YEAH?
YEAH, YEAH, THAT WOULD BE *GREAT!*
BEAUTIFUL. I'LL HAVE MY PEOPLE CONTACT YOUR PEOPLE. CIAO.
YEAH, YEAH, HAVE YOUR PEOPLE CONTACT MY PE-- UH... *ROB!* AND *CHOW!*

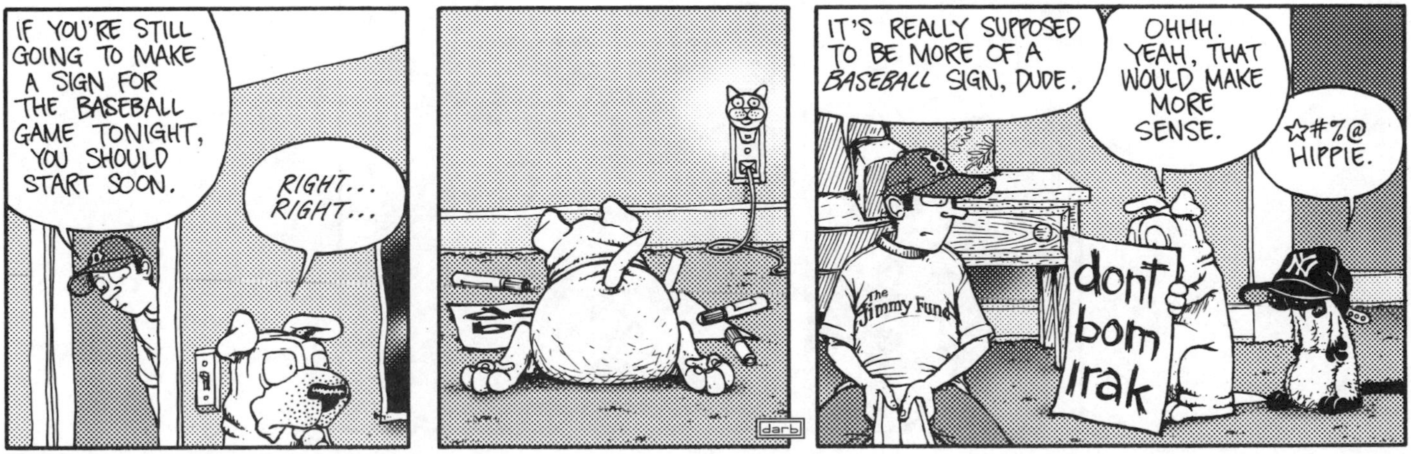
IF YOU'RE STILL GOING TO MAKE A SIGN FOR THE BASEBALL GAME TONIGHT, YOU SHOULD START SOON.
RIGHT... RIGHT...
IT'S REALLY SUPPOSED TO BE MORE OF A *BASEBALL* SIGN, DUDE.
OHHH. YEAH, THAT WOULD MAKE MORE SENSE.
☆#%@ HIPPIE.
The Jimmy Fund
dont bom Irak

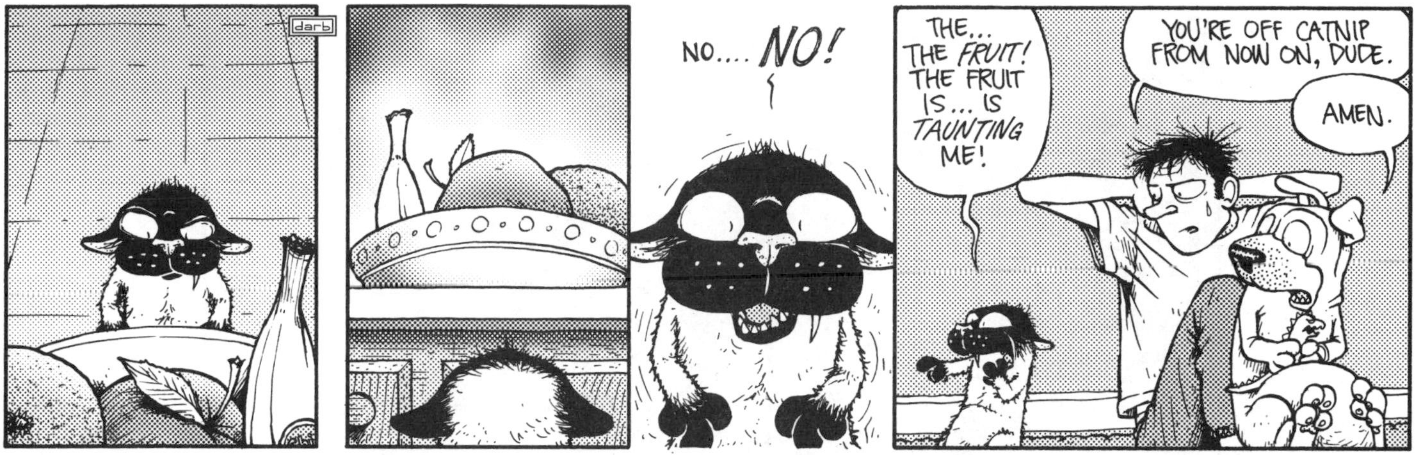
NO.... NO!
THE... THE FRUIT! THE FRUIT IS... IS TAUNTING ME!
YOU'RE OFF CATNIP FROM NOW ON, DUDE.
AMEN.

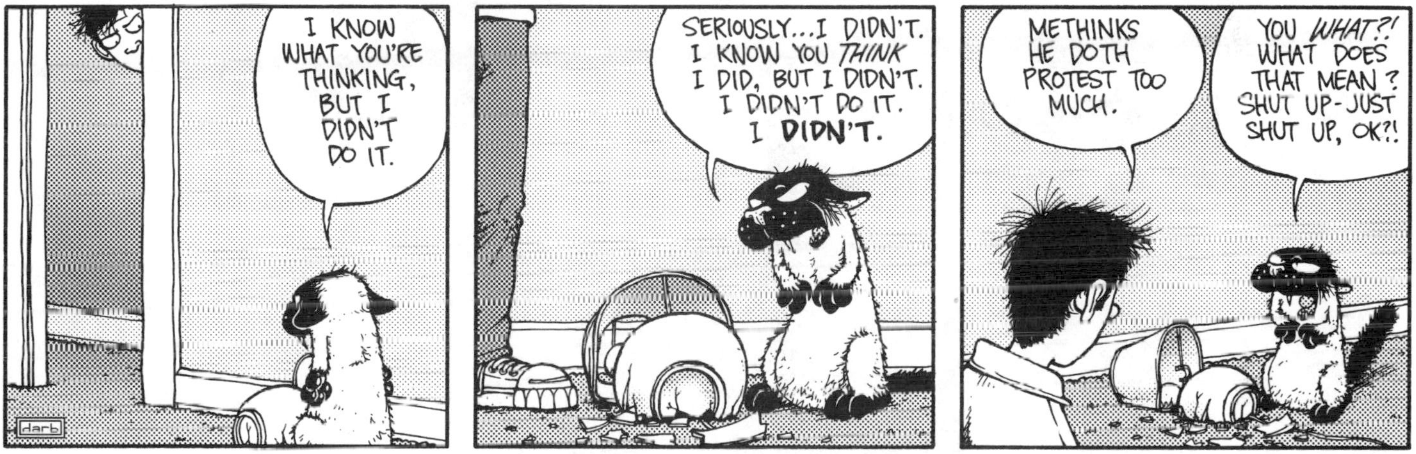
I KNOW WHAT YOU'RE THINKING, BUT I DIDN'T DO IT.
SERIOUSLY...I DIDN'T. I KNOW YOU THINK I DID, BUT I DIDN'T. I DIDN'T DO IT. I DIDN'T.
METHINKS HE DOTH PROTEST TOO MUCH.
YOU WHAT?! WHAT DOES THAT MEAN ? SHUT UP-JUST SHUT UP, OK?!

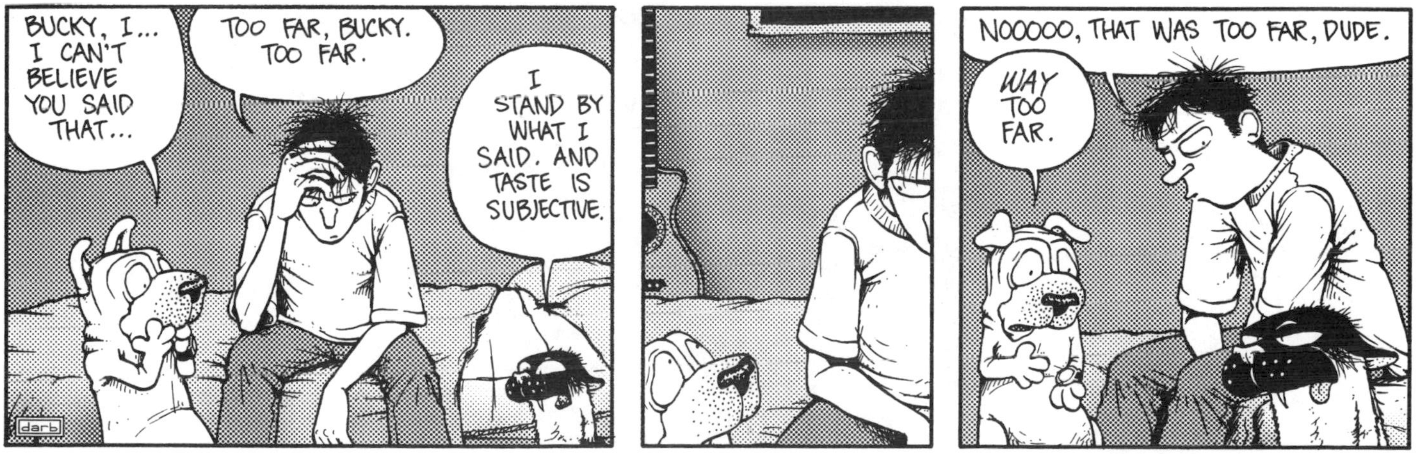
BUCKY, I... I CAN'T BELIEVE YOU SAID THAT...
TOO FAR, BUCKY. TOO FAR.
I STAND BY WHAT I SAID. AND TASTE IS SUBJECTIVE.
NOOOOO, THAT WAS TOO FAR, DUDE.
WAY TOO FAR.

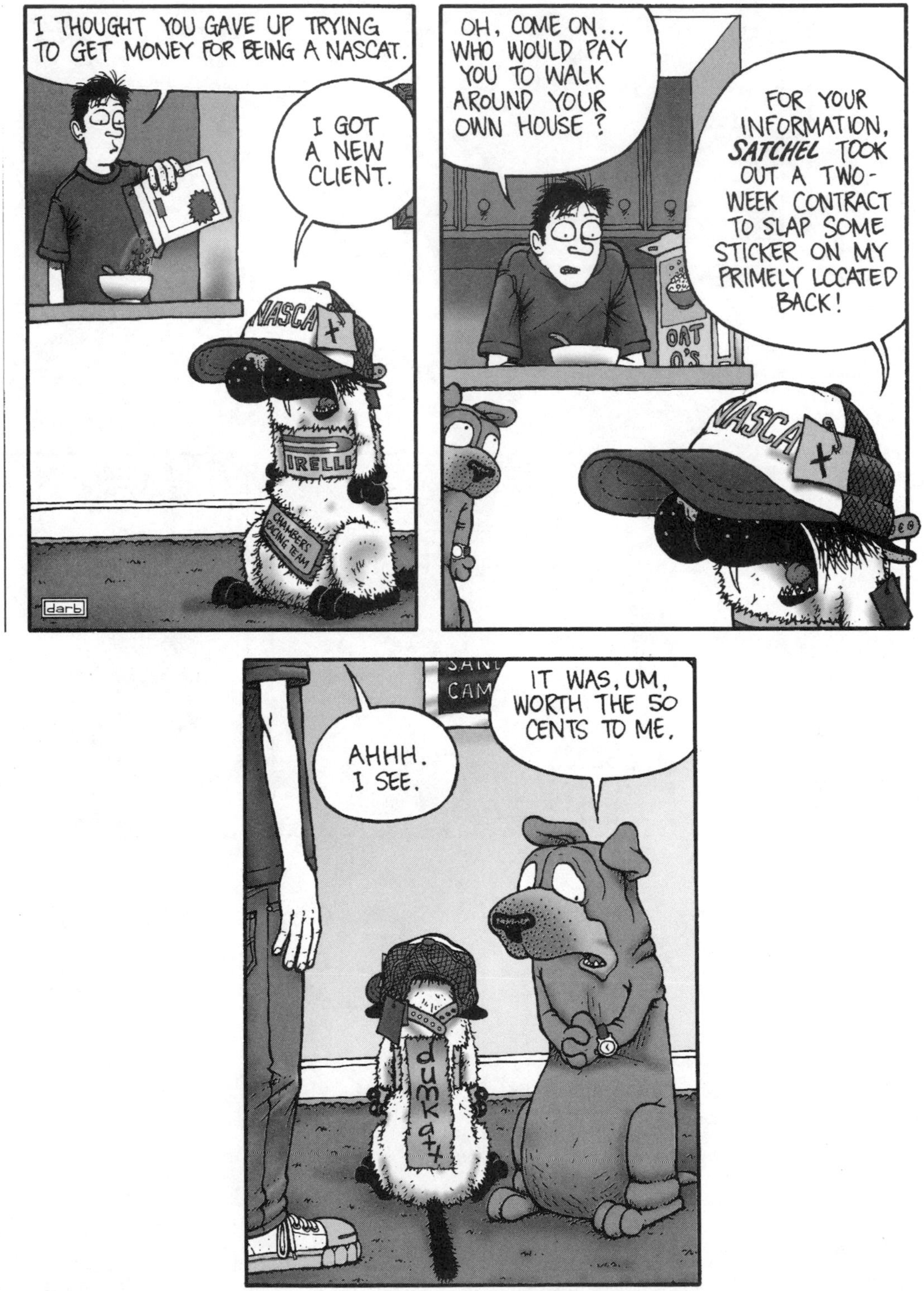
I THOUGHT YOU GAVE UP TRYING TO GET MONEY FOR BEING A NASCAT.
I GOT A NEW CLIENT.
NASCA
IRELLI
CHAMBERS RACING TEAM
darb
OH, COME ON... WHO WOULD PAY YOU TO WALK AROUND YOUR OWN HOUSE ?
FOR YOUR INFORMATION, **SATCHEL** TOOK OUT A TWO-WEEK CONTRACT TO SLAP SOME STICKER ON MY PRIMELY LOCATED BACK!
OAT O's
NASCA
AHHH. I SEE.
IT WAS, UM, WORTH THE 50 CENTS TO ME.
dumkatt

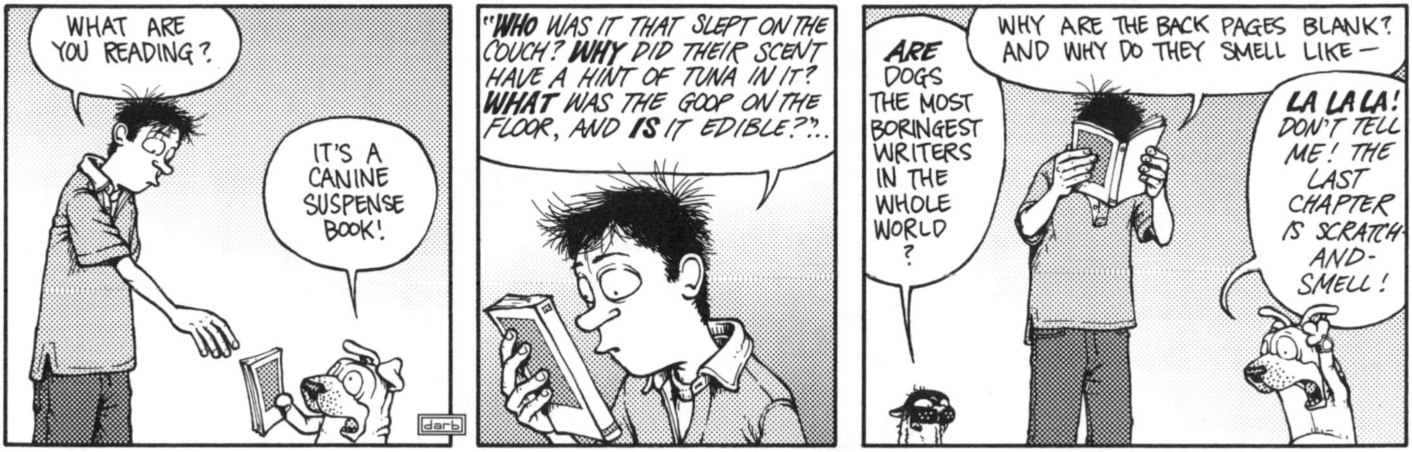
WHAT ARE YOU READING?
IT'S A CANINE SUSPENSE BOOK!
"WHO WAS IT THAT SLEPT ON THE COUCH? WHY DID THEIR SCENT HAVE A HINT OF TUNA IN IT? WHAT WAS THE GOOP ON THE FLOOR, AND IS IT EDIBLE?"...
WHY ARE THE BACK PAGES BLANK? AND WHY DO THEY SMELL LIKE—
LA LA LA! DON'T TELL ME! THE LAST CHAPTER IS SCRATCH-AND-SMELL!
ARE DOGS THE MOST BORINGEST WRITERS IN THE WHOLE WORLD?

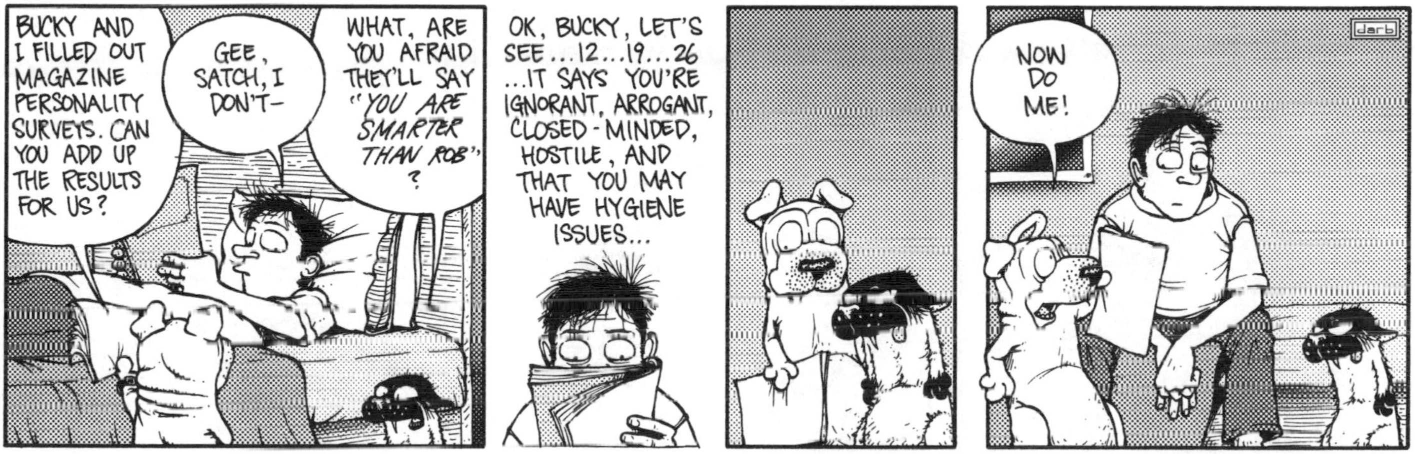
BUCKY AND I FILLED OUT MAGAZINE PERSONALITY SURVEYS. CAN YOU ADD UP THE RESULTS FOR US?
GEE, SATCH, I DON'T-
WHAT, ARE YOU AFRAID THEY'LL SAY "YOU ARE SMARTER THAN ROB"?
OK, BUCKY, LET'S SEE...12...19...26 ...IT SAYS YOU'RE IGNORANT, ARROGANT, CLOSED-MINDED, HOSTILE, AND THAT YOU MAY HAVE HYGIENE ISSUES...
NOW DO ME!

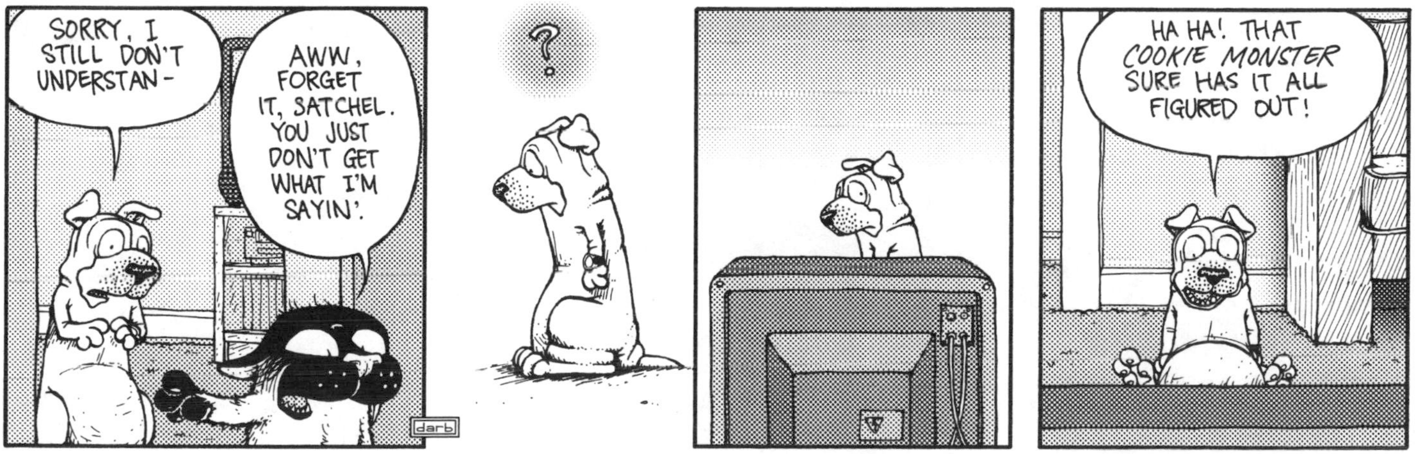
SORRY, I STILL DON'T UNDERSTAN-
AWW, FORGET IT, SATCHEL. YOU JUST DON'T GET WHAT I'M SAYIN'.
?
HA HA! THAT COOKIE MONSTER SURE HAS IT ALL FIGURED OUT!

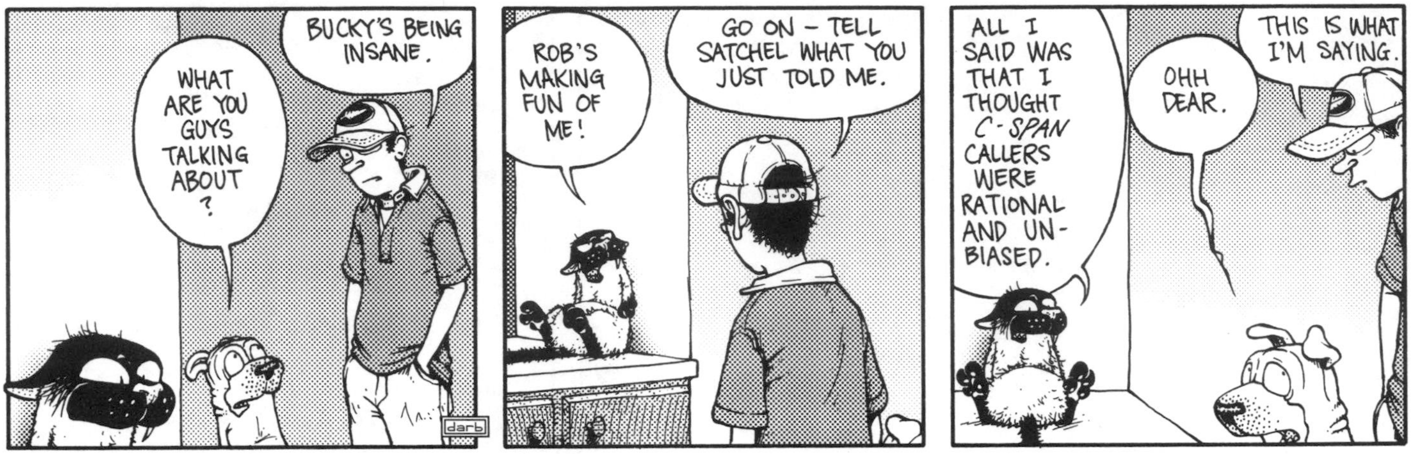
WHAT ARE YOU GUYS TALKING ABOUT?
BUCKY'S BEING INSANE.
ROB'S MAKING FUN OF ME!
GO ON – TELL SATCHEL WHAT YOU JUST TOLD ME.
ALL I SAID WAS THAT I THOUGHT *C-SPAN* CALLERS WERE RATIONAL AND UN-BIASED.
OHH DEAR.
THIS IS WHAT I'M SAYING.
darb

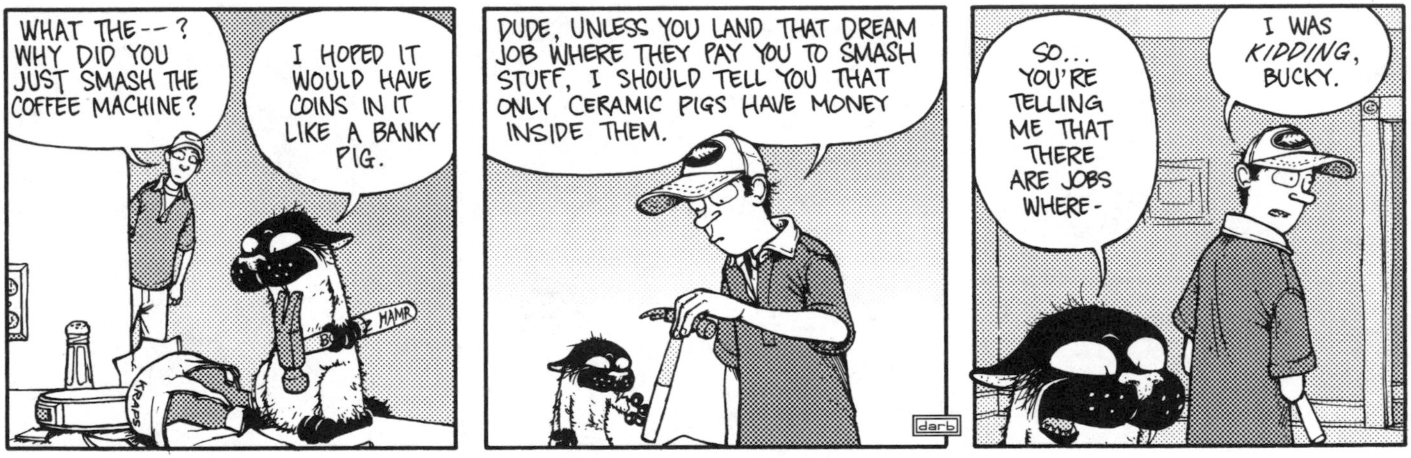
WHAT THE--? WHY DID YOU JUST SMASH THE COFFEE MACHINE?
I HOPED IT WOULD HAVE COINS IN IT LIKE A BANKY PIG.
HAMR
KRAPS
DUDE, UNLESS YOU LAND THAT DREAM JOB WHERE THEY PAY YOU TO SMASH STUFF, I SHOULD TELL YOU THAT ONLY CERAMIC PIGS HAVE MONEY INSIDE THEM.
SO... YOU'RE TELLING ME THAT THERE ARE JOBS WHERE-
I WAS *KIDDING*, BUCKY.
darb

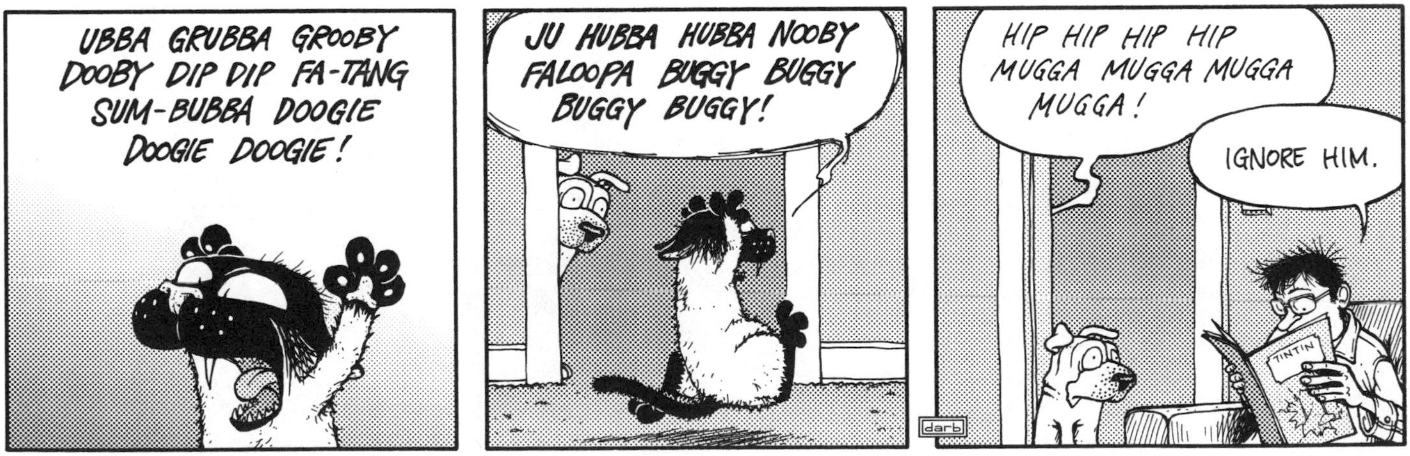
UBBA GRUBBA GROOBY DOOBY DIP DIP FA-TANG SUM-BUBBA DOOGIE DOOGIE DOOGIE!
JU HUBBA HUBBA NOOBY FALOOPA BUGGY BUGGY BUGGY BUGGY!
HIP HIP HIP HIP MUGGA MUGGA MUGGA MUGGA!
IGNORE HIM.
TINTIN
darb

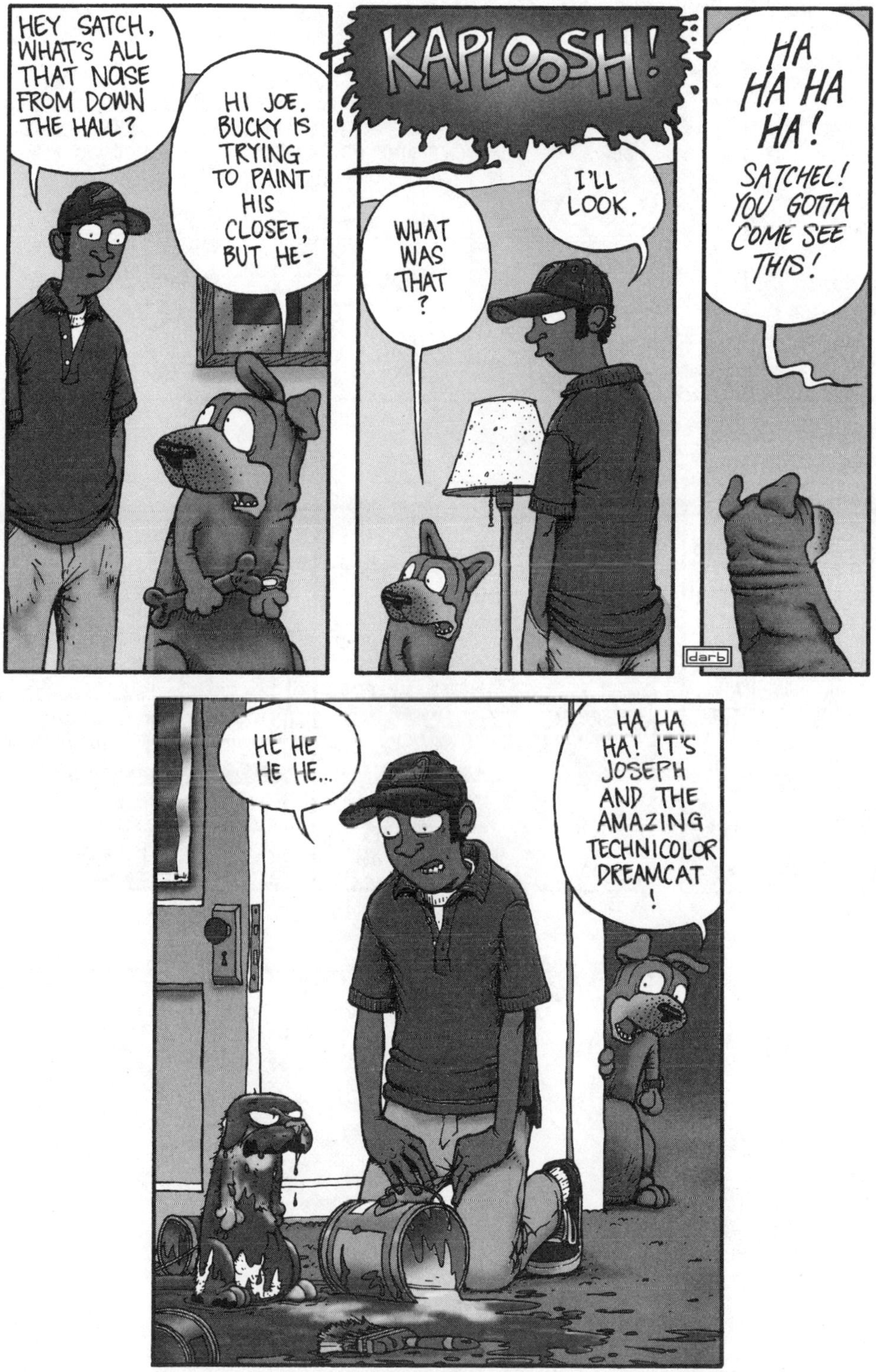
HEY SATCH, WHAT'S ALL THAT NOISE FROM DOWN THE HALL?
HI JOE. BUCKY IS TRYING TO PAINT HIS CLOSET, BUT HE-
KAPLOOSH!
WHAT WAS THAT?
I'LL LOOK.
HA HA HA HA!
SATCHEL! YOU GOTTA COME SEE THIS!
darb
HE HE HE HE...
HA HA HA! IT'S JOSEPH AND THE AMAZING TECHNICOLOR DREAMCAT!

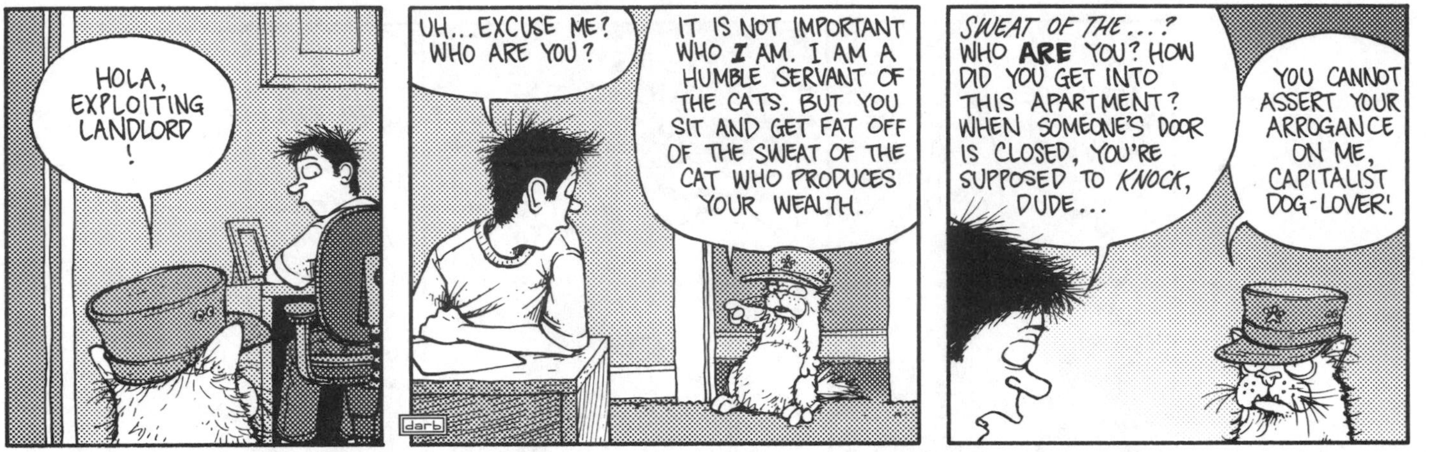
HOLA, EXPLOITING LANDLORD!
darb
UH... EXCUSE ME? WHO ARE YOU?
IT IS NOT IMPORTANT WHO **I** AM. I AM A HUMBLE SERVANT OF THE CATS. BUT YOU SIT AND GET FAT OFF OF THE SWEAT OF THE CAT WHO PRODUCES YOUR WEALTH.
SWEAT OF THE....? WHO **ARE** YOU? HOW DID YOU GET INTO THIS APARTMENT? WHEN SOMEONE'S DOOR IS CLOSED, YOU'RE SUPPOSED TO *KNOCK*, DUDE...
YOU CANNOT ASSERT YOUR ARROGANCE ON ME, CAPITALIST DOG-LOVER!

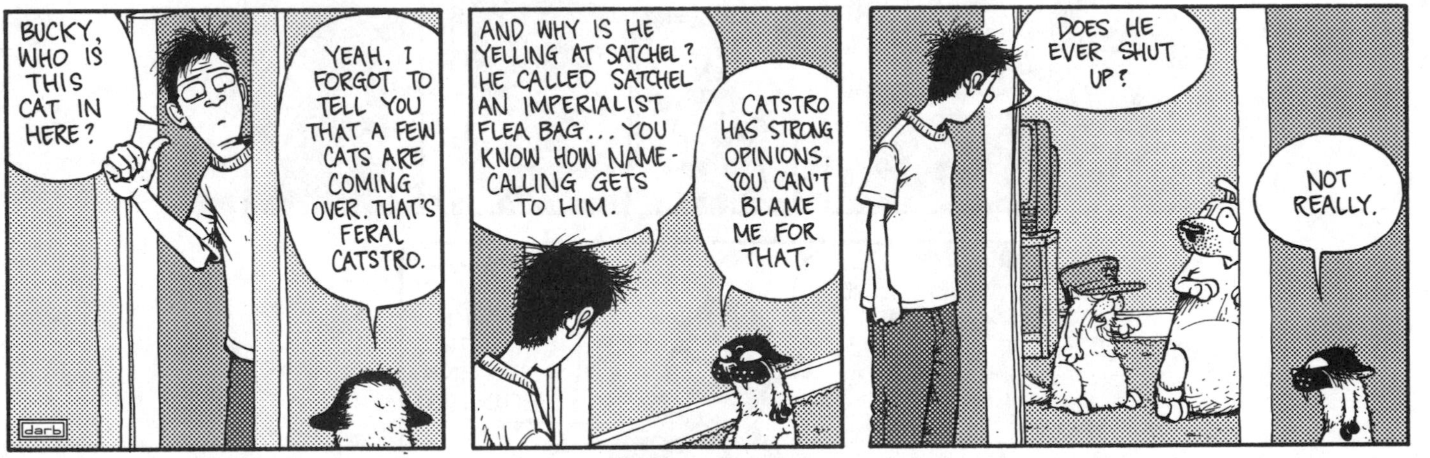
BUCKY, WHO IS THIS CAT IN HERE?
YEAH, I FORGOT TO TELL YOU THAT A FEW CATS ARE COMING OVER. THAT'S FERAL CATSTRO.
darb
AND WHY IS HE YELLING AT SATCHEL? HE CALLED SATCHEL AN IMPERIALIST FLEA BAG... YOU KNOW HOW NAME-CALLING GETS TO HIM.
CATSTRO HAS STRONG OPINIONS. YOU CAN'T BLAME ME FOR THAT.
DOES HE EVER SHUT UP?
NOT REALLY.

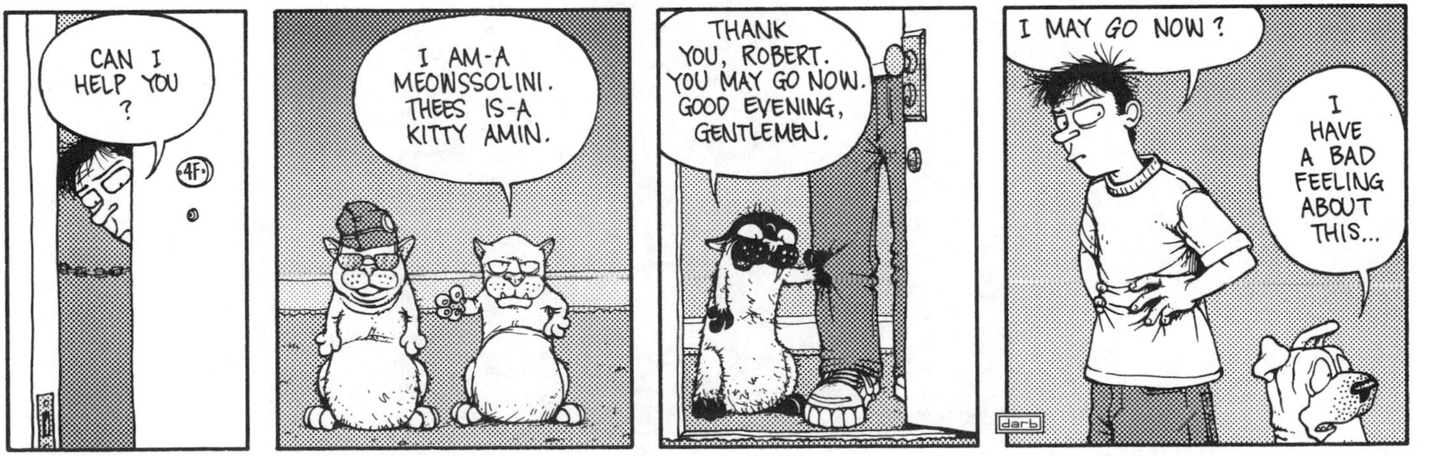
CAN I HELP YOU?
4F
I AM-A MEOWSSOLINI. THEES IS-A KITTY AMIN.
THANK YOU, ROBERT. YOU MAY GO NOW. GOOD EVENING, GENTLEMEN.
I MAY *GO* NOW?
I HAVE A BAD FEELING ABOUT THIS...
darb

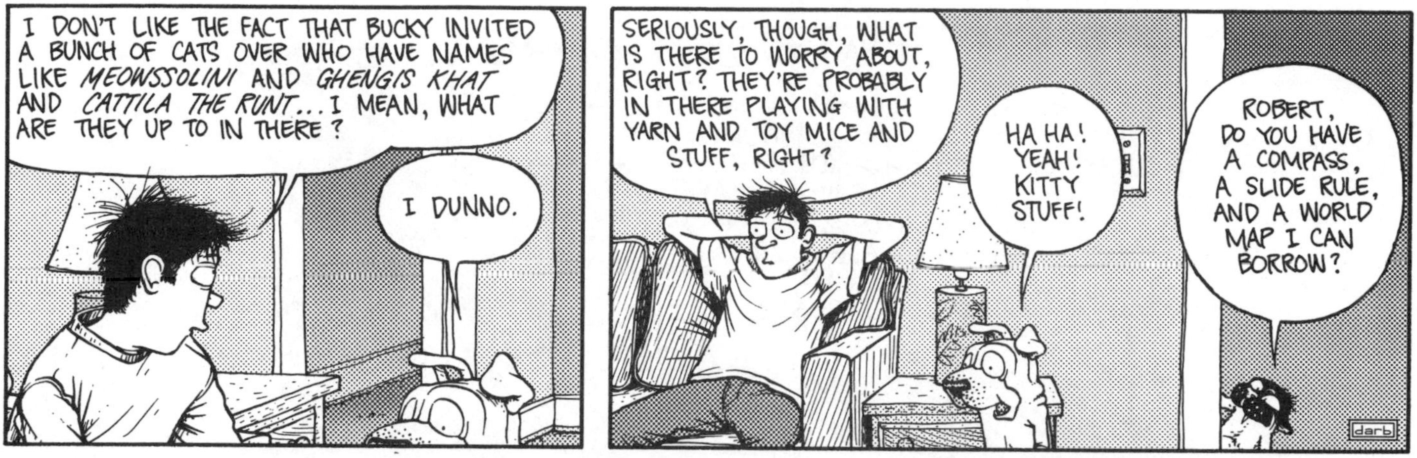
I DON'T LIKE THE FACT THAT BUCKY INVITED A BUNCH OF CATS OVER WHO HAVE NAMES LIKE *MEOWSSOLINI* AND *GHENGIS KHAT* AND *CATTILA THE RUNT*... I MEAN, WHAT ARE THEY UP TO IN THERE?
I DUNNO.
SERIOUSLY, THOUGH, WHAT IS THERE TO WORRY ABOUT, RIGHT? THEY'RE PROBABLY IN THERE PLAYING WITH YARN AND TOY MICE AND STUFF, RIGHT?
HA HA! YEAH! KITTY STUFF!
ROBERT, DO YOU HAVE A COMPASS, A SLIDE RULE, AND A WORLD MAP I CAN BORROW?
darb

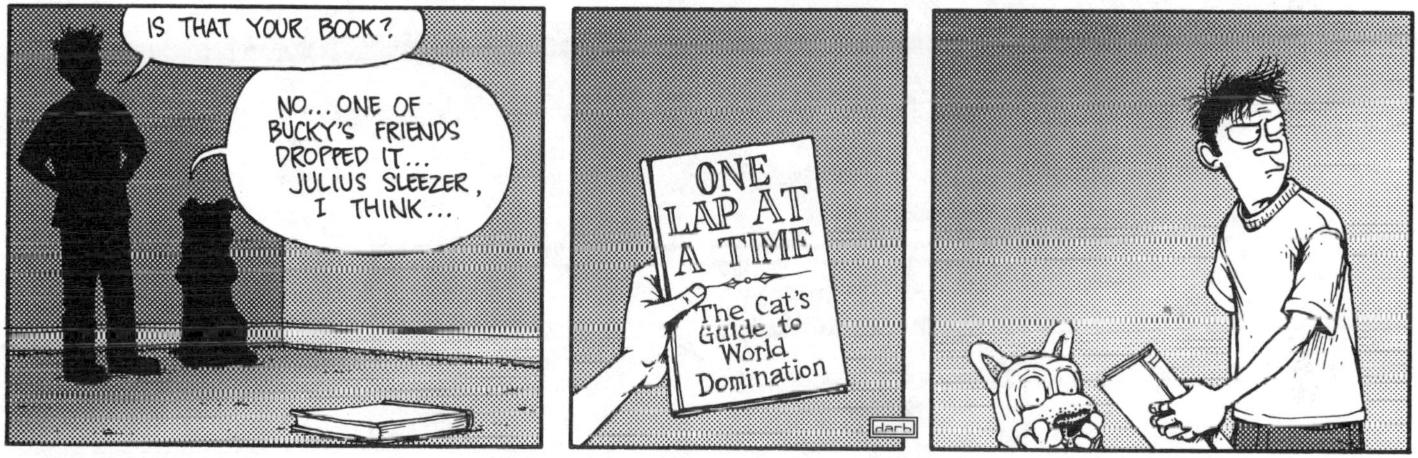
IS THAT YOUR BOOK?
NO... ONE OF BUCKY'S FRIENDS DROPPED IT... JULIUS SLEEZER, I THINK...
ONE LAP AT A TIME
The Cat's Guide to World Domination
darb

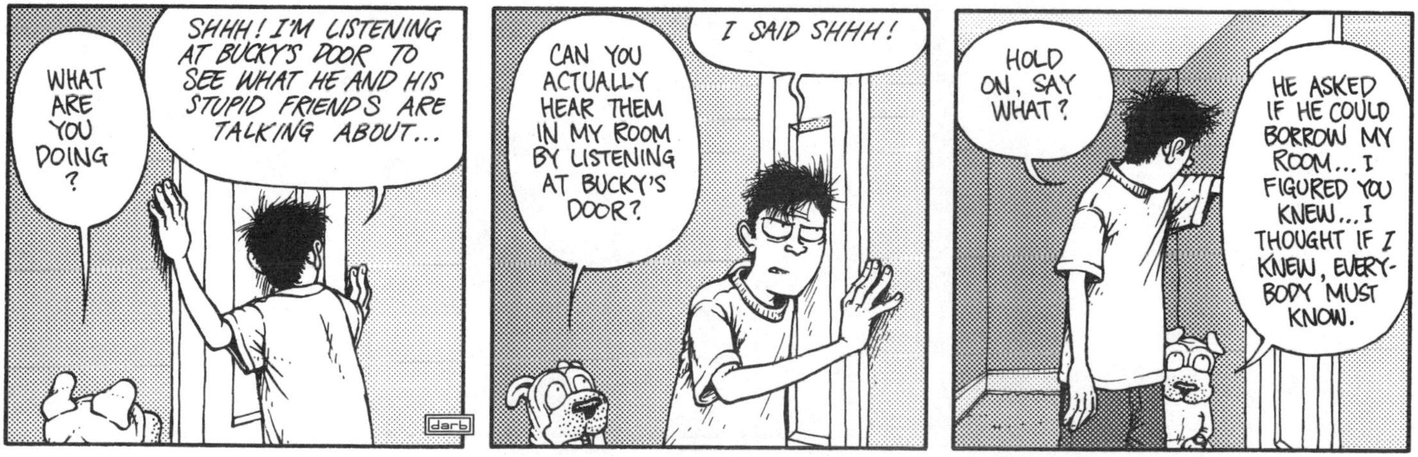
WHAT ARE YOU DOING?
SHHH! I'M LISTENING AT BUCKY'S DOOR TO SEE WHAT HE AND HIS STUPID FRIENDS ARE TALKING ABOUT...
darb
CAN YOU ACTUALLY HEAR THEM IN MY ROOM BY LISTENING AT BUCKY'S DOOR?
I SAID SHHH!
HOLD ON, SAY WHAT?
HE ASKED IF HE COULD BORROW MY ROOM... I FIGURED YOU KNEW... I THOUGHT IF *I* KNEW, EVERYBODY MUST KNOW.

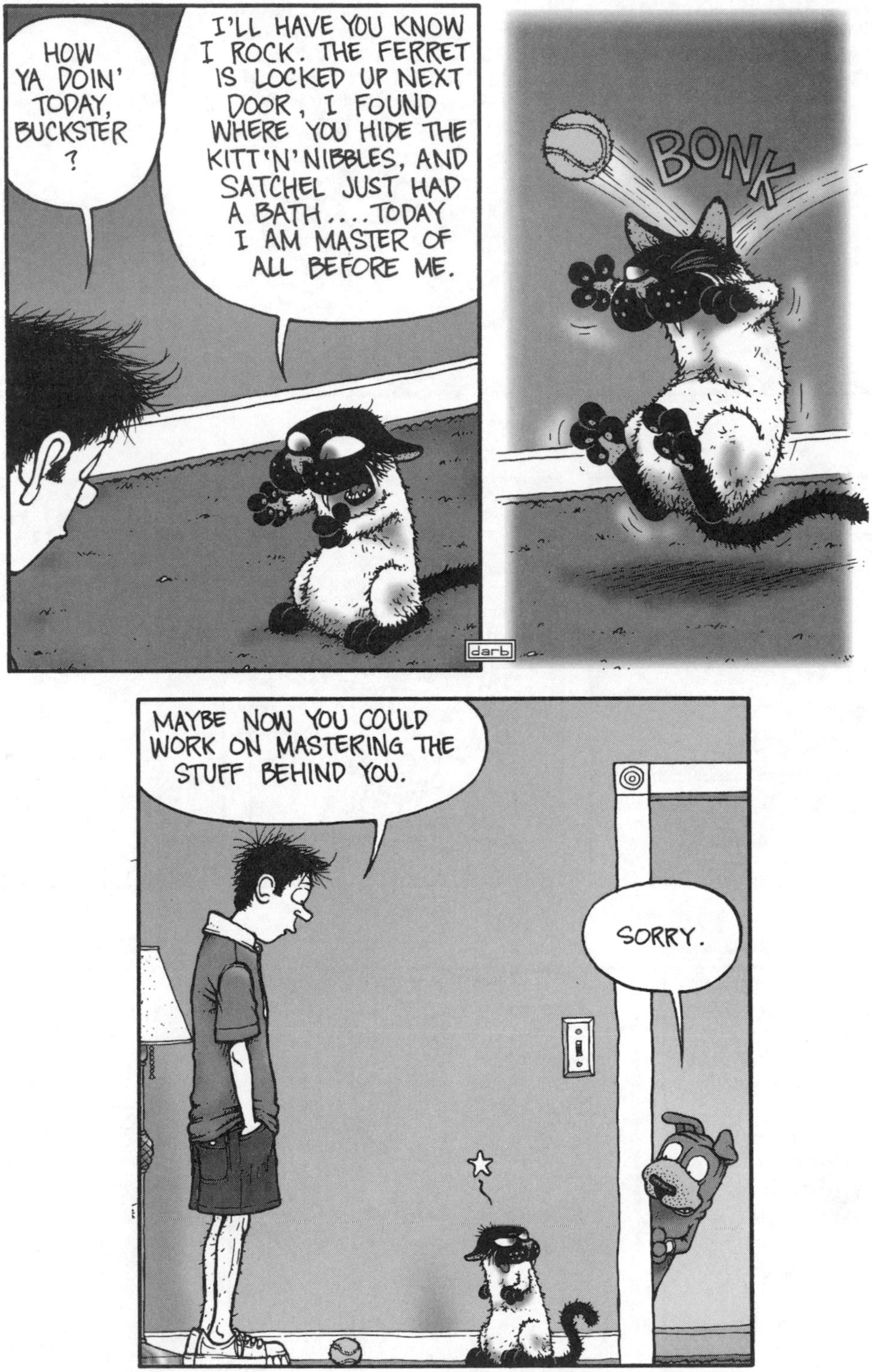
HOW YA DOIN' TODAY, BUCKSTER ?
I'LL HAVE YOU KNOW I ROCK. THE FERRET IS LOCKED UP NEXT DOOR, I FOUND WHERE YOU HIDE THE KITT'N'NIBBLES, AND SATCHEL JUST HAD A BATH.... TODAY I AM MASTER OF ALL BEFORE ME.
darb
BONK
MAYBE NOW YOU COULD WORK ON MASTERING THE STUFF BEHIND YOU.
SORRY.

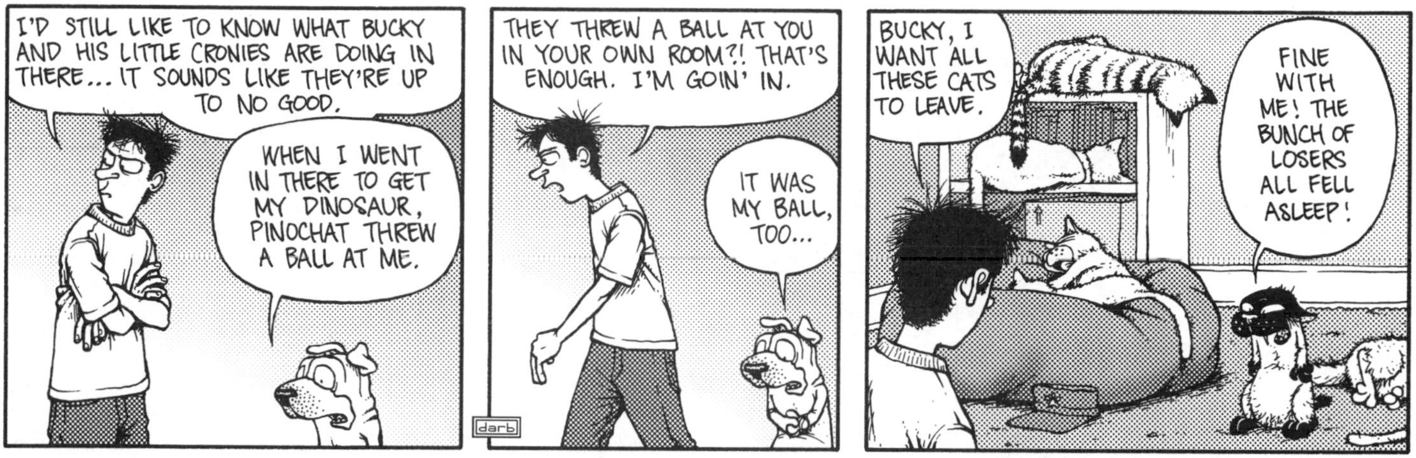
I'D STILL LIKE TO KNOW WHAT BUCKY AND HIS LITTLE CRONIES ARE DOING IN THERE... IT SOUNDS LIKE THEY'RE UP TO NO GOOD.
WHEN I WENT IN THERE TO GET MY DINOSAUR, PINOCHAT THREW A BALL AT ME.
THEY THREW A BALL AT YOU IN YOUR OWN ROOM?! THAT'S ENOUGH. I'M GOIN' IN.
IT WAS MY BALL, TOO...
darb
BUCKY, I WANT ALL THESE CATS TO LEAVE.
FINE WITH ME! THE BUNCH OF LOSERS ALL FELL ASLEEP!

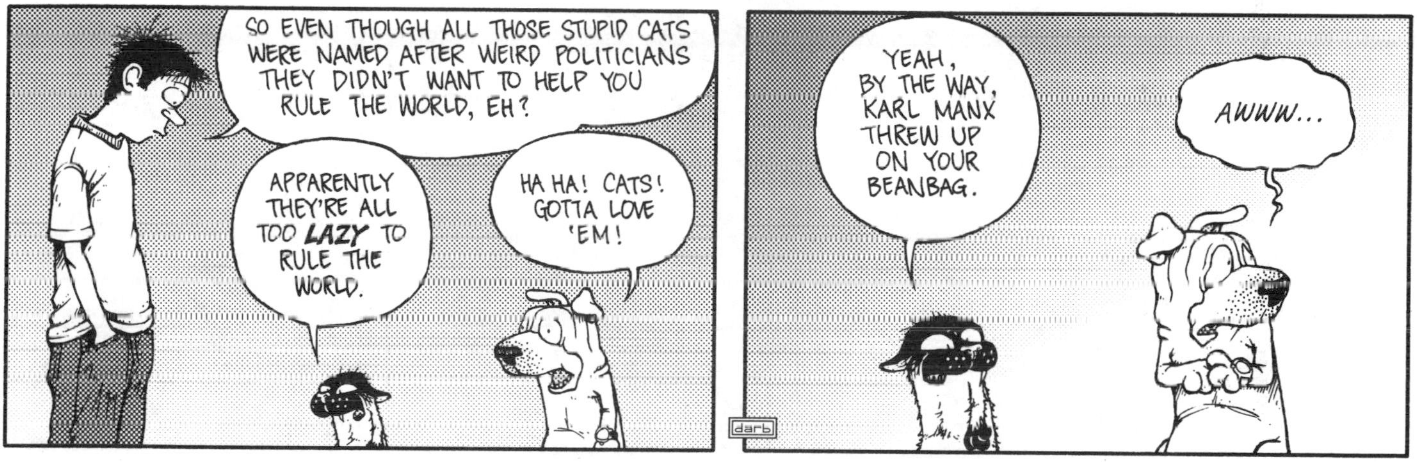
SO EVEN THOUGH ALL THOSE STUPID CATS WERE NAMED AFTER WEIRD POLITICIANS THEY DIDN'T WANT TO HELP YOU RULE THE WORLD, EH?
APPARENTLY THEY'RE ALL TOO LAZY TO RULE THE WORLD.
HA HA! CATS! GOTTA LOVE 'EM!
darb
YEAH, BY THE WAY, KARL MANX THREW UP ON YOUR BEANBAG.
AWWW...

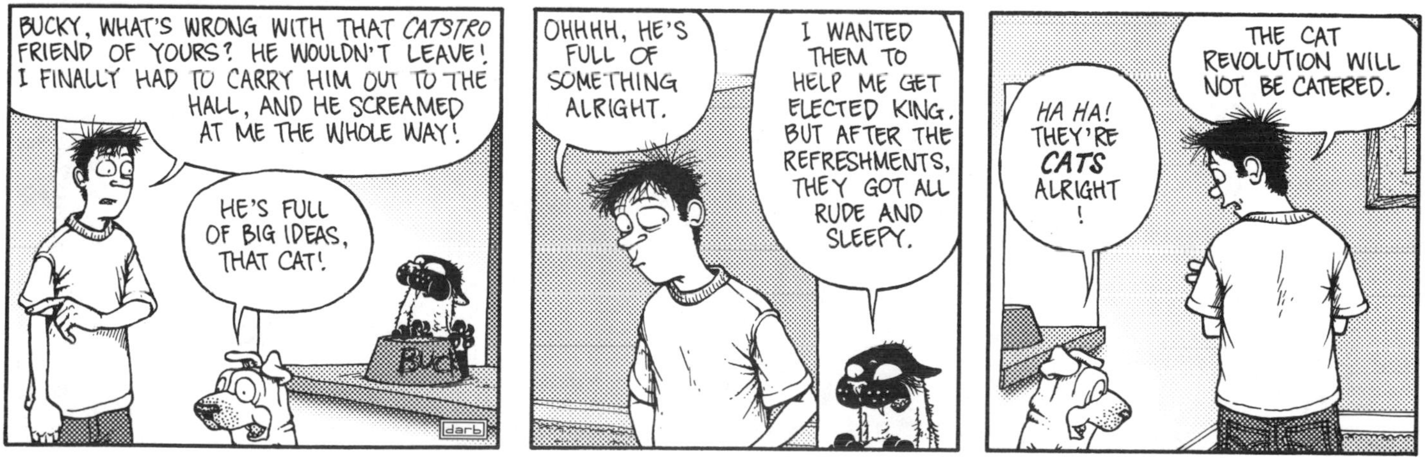
BUCKY, WHAT'S WRONG WITH THAT CATSTRO FRIEND OF YOURS? HE WOULDN'T LEAVE! I FINALLY HAD TO CARRY HIM OUT TO THE HALL, AND HE SCREAMED AT ME THE WHOLE WAY!
HE'S FULL OF BIG IDEAS, THAT CAT!
darb
OHHHH, HE'S FULL OF SOMETHING ALRIGHT.
I WANTED THEM TO HELP ME GET ELECTED KING. BUT AFTER THE REFRESHMENTS, THEY GOT ALL RUDE AND SLEEPY.
HA HA! THEY'RE CATS ALRIGHT!
THE CAT REVOLUTION WILL NOT BE CATERED.

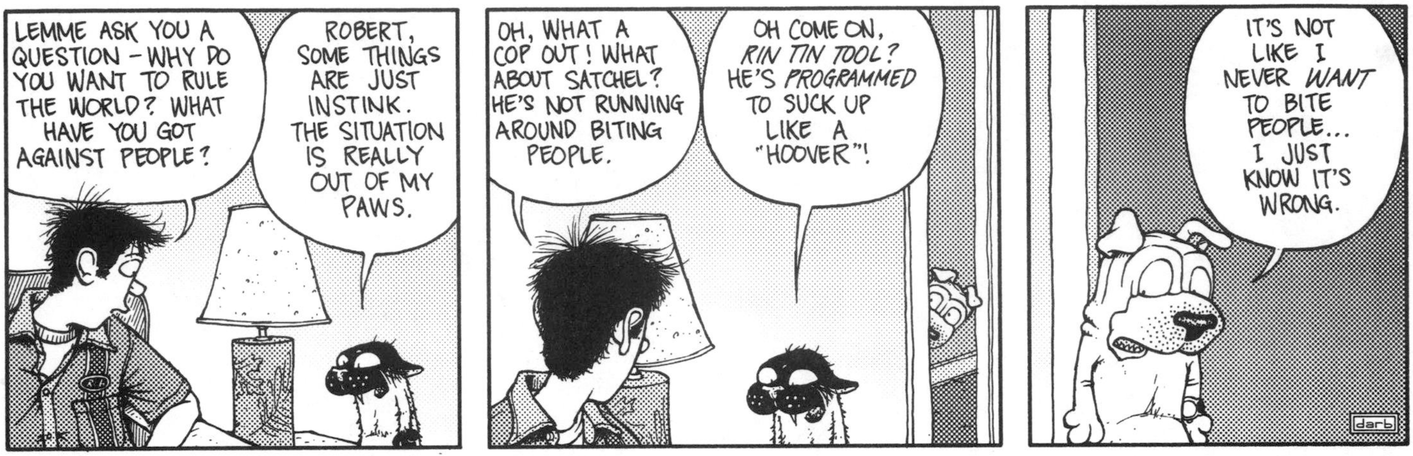
LEMME ASK YOU A QUESTION - WHY DO YOU WANT TO RULE THE WORLD? WHAT HAVE YOU GOT AGAINST PEOPLE?
ROBERT, SOME THINGS ARE JUST INSTINK. THE SITUATION IS REALLY OUT OF MY PAWS.
OH, WHAT A COP OUT! WHAT ABOUT SATCHEL? HE'S NOT RUNNING AROUND BITING PEOPLE.
OH COME ON, *RIN TIN TOOL?* HE'S *PROGRAMMED* TO SUCK UP LIKE A "HOOVER"!
IT'S NOT LIKE I NEVER *WANT* TO BITE PEOPLE... I JUST KNOW IT'S WRONG.
darb

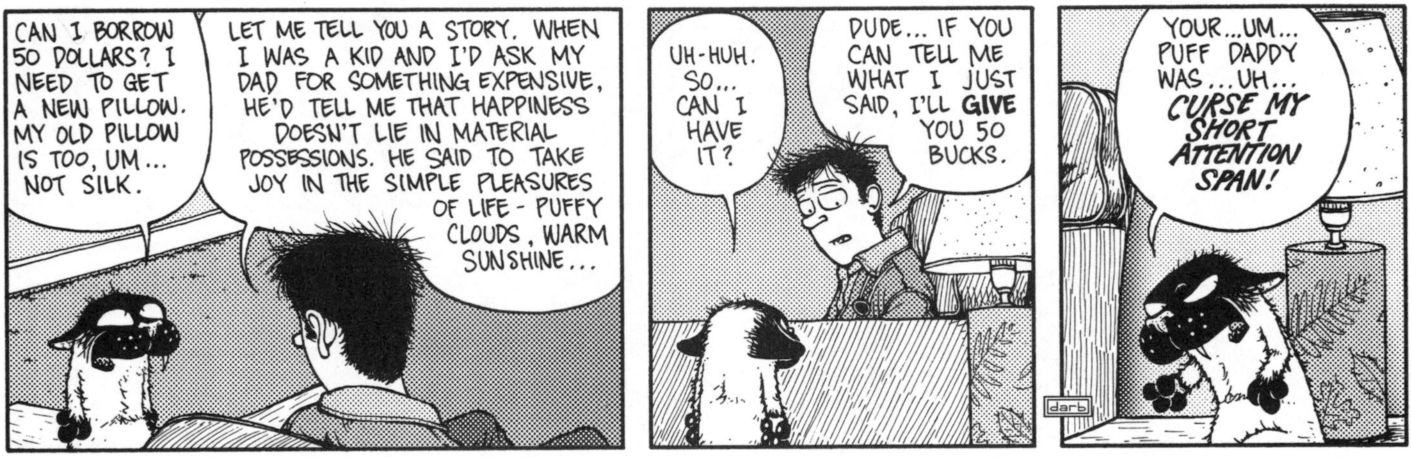
CAN I BORROW 50 DOLLARS? I NEED TO GET A NEW PILLOW. MY OLD PILLOW IS TOO, UM... NOT SILK.
LET ME TELL YOU A STORY. WHEN I WAS A KID AND I'D ASK MY DAD FOR SOMETHING EXPENSIVE, HE'D TELL ME THAT HAPPINESS DOESN'T LIE IN MATERIAL POSSESSIONS. HE SAID TO TAKE JOY IN THE SIMPLE PLEASURES OF LIFE - PUFFY CLOUDS, WARM SUNSHINE...
UH-HUH. SO... CAN I HAVE IT?
DUDE... IF YOU CAN TELL ME WHAT I JUST SAID, I'LL **GIVE** YOU 50 BUCKS.
YOUR...UM... PUFF DADDY WAS...UH... ***CURSE MY SHORT ATTENTION SPAN!***
darb

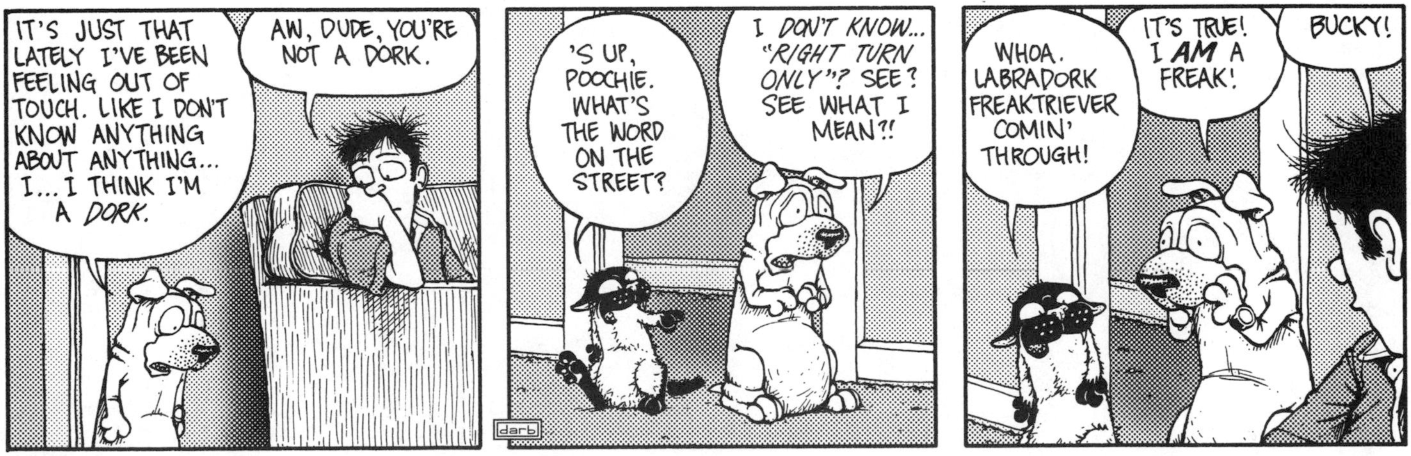
IT'S JUST THAT LATELY I'VE BEEN FEELING OUT OF TOUCH. LIKE I DON'T KNOW ANYTHING ABOUT ANYTHING... I... I THINK I'M A *DORK*.
AW, DUDE, YOU'RE NOT A DORK.
'S UP, POOCHIE. WHAT'S THE WORD ON THE STREET?
I *DON'T KNOW...* *"RIGHT TURN ONLY"*? SEE? SEE WHAT I MEAN?!
darb
WHOA. LABRADORK FREAKTRIEVER COMIN' THROUGH!
IT'S TRUE! I ***AM*** A FREAK!
BUCKY!

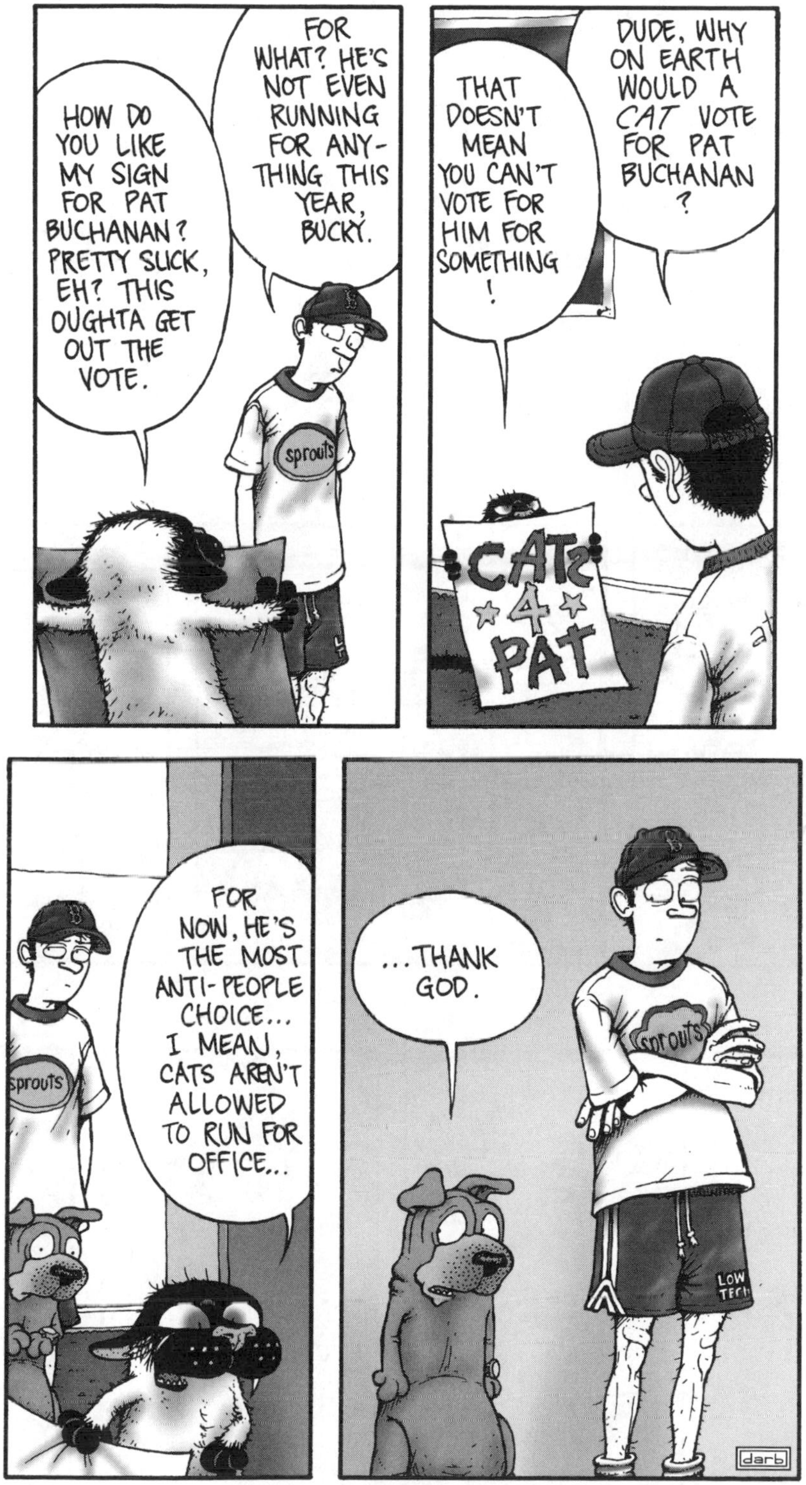
HOW DO YOU LIKE MY SIGN FOR PAT BUCHANAN? PRETTY SLICK, EH? THIS OUGHTA GET OUT THE VOTE.
FOR WHAT? HE'S NOT EVEN RUNNING FOR ANYTHING THIS YEAR, BUCKY.
THAT DOESN'T MEAN YOU CAN'T VOTE FOR HIM FOR SOMETHING!
DUDE, WHY ON EARTH WOULD A CAT VOTE FOR PAT BUCHANAN?
CATS 4 PAT
sprouts
FOR NOW, HE'S THE MOST ANTI-PEOPLE CHOICE... I MEAN, CATS AREN'T ALLOWED TO RUN FOR OFFICE...
...THANK GOD.
LOW TECH
darb

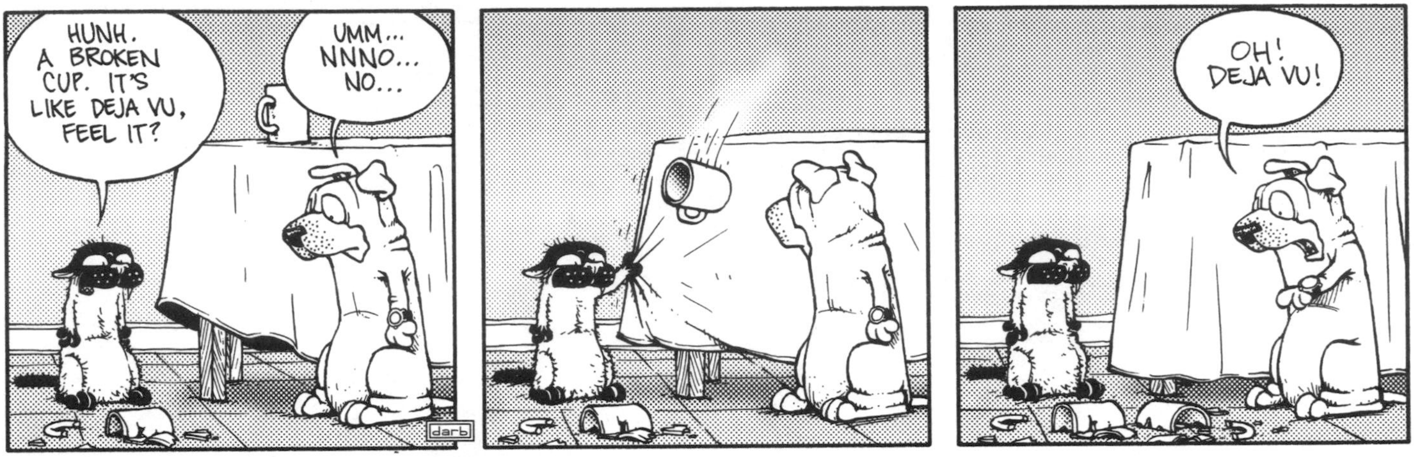
HUNH. A BROKEN CUP. IT'S LIKE DEJA VU, FEEL IT?
UMM... NNNO... NO...
OH! DEJA VU!

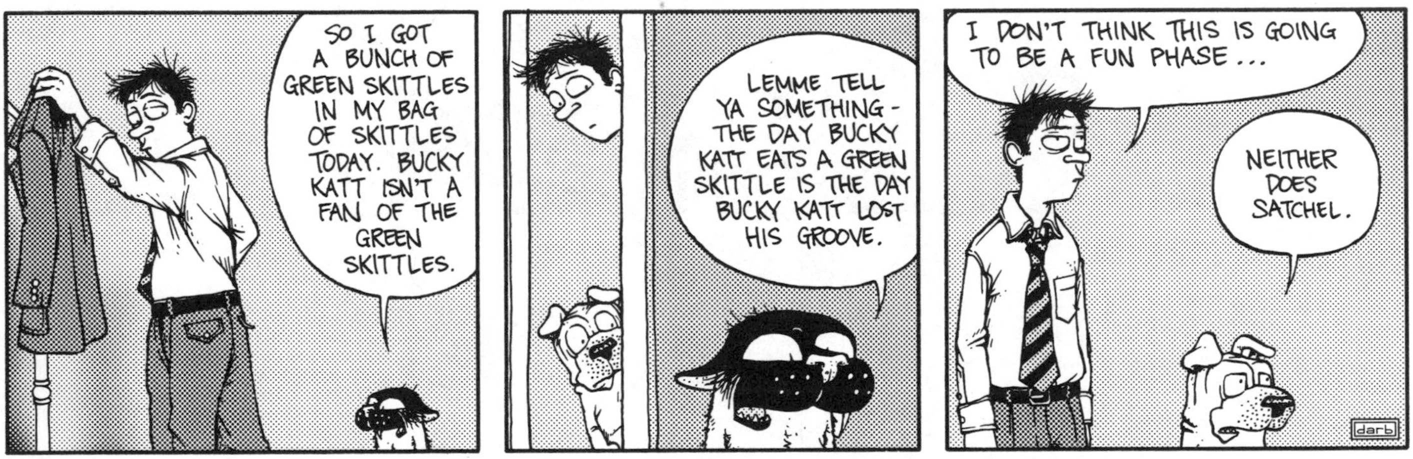
SO I GOT A BUNCH OF GREEN SKITTLES IN MY BAG OF SKITTLES TODAY. BUCKY KATT ISN'T A FAN OF THE GREEN SKITTLES.
LEMME TELL YA SOMETHING - THE DAY BUCKY KATT EATS A GREEN SKITTLE IS THE DAY BUCKY KATT LOST HIS GROOVE.
I DON'T THINK THIS IS GOING TO BE A FUN PHASE...
NEITHER DOES SATCHEL.

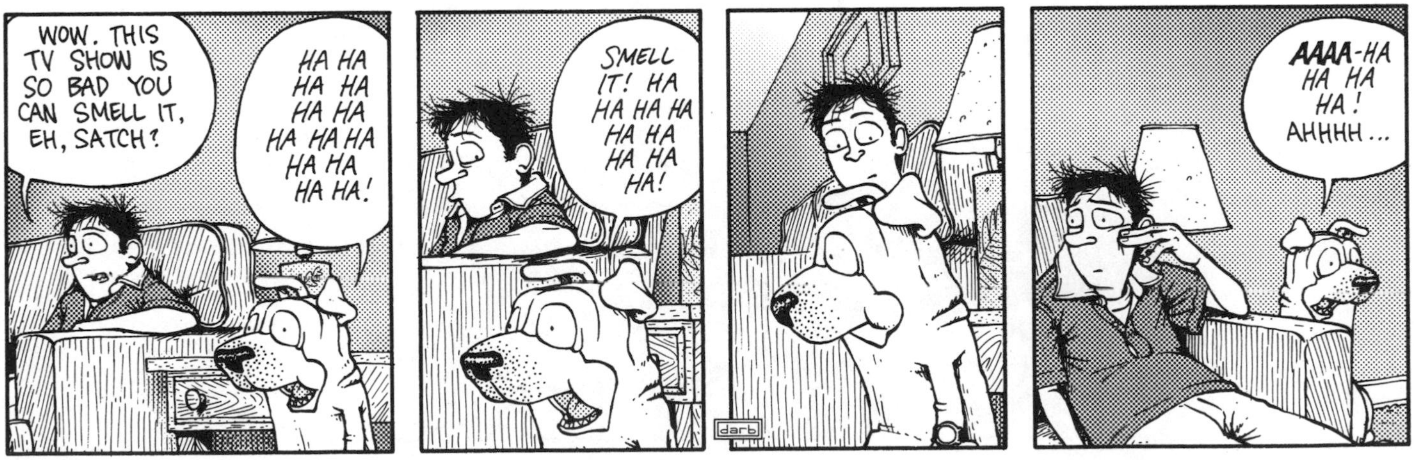
WOW. THIS TV SHOW IS SO BAD YOU CAN SMELL IT, EH, SATCH?
HA HA HA HA HA HA HA HA HA HA HA HA HA!
SMELL IT! HA HA HA HA HA HA HA HA HA!
AAAA-HA HA HA HA! AHHHH...

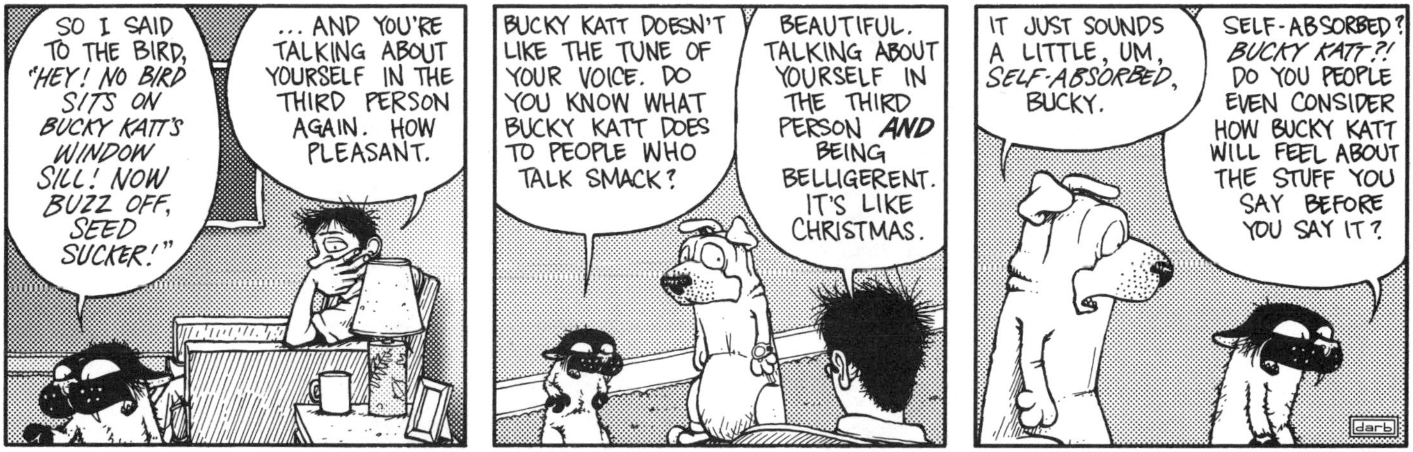
SO I SAID TO THE BIRD, *"HEY! NO BIRD SITS ON BUCKY KATT'S WINDOW SILL! NOW BUZZ OFF, SEED SUCKER!"*
... AND YOU'RE TALKING ABOUT YOURSELF IN THE THIRD PERSON AGAIN. HOW PLEASANT.
BUCKY KATT DOESN'T LIKE THE TUNE OF YOUR VOICE. DO YOU KNOW WHAT BUCKY KATT DOES TO PEOPLE WHO TALK SMACK?
BEAUTIFUL. TALKING ABOUT YOURSELF IN THE THIRD PERSON **AND** BEING BELLIGERENT. IT'S LIKE CHRISTMAS.
IT JUST SOUNDS A LITTLE, UM, *SELF-ABSORBED*, BUCKY.
SELF-ABSORBED? *BUCKY KATT?!* DO YOU PEOPLE EVEN CONSIDER HOW BUCKY KATT WILL FEEL ABOUT THE STUFF YOU SAY BEFORE YOU SAY IT?

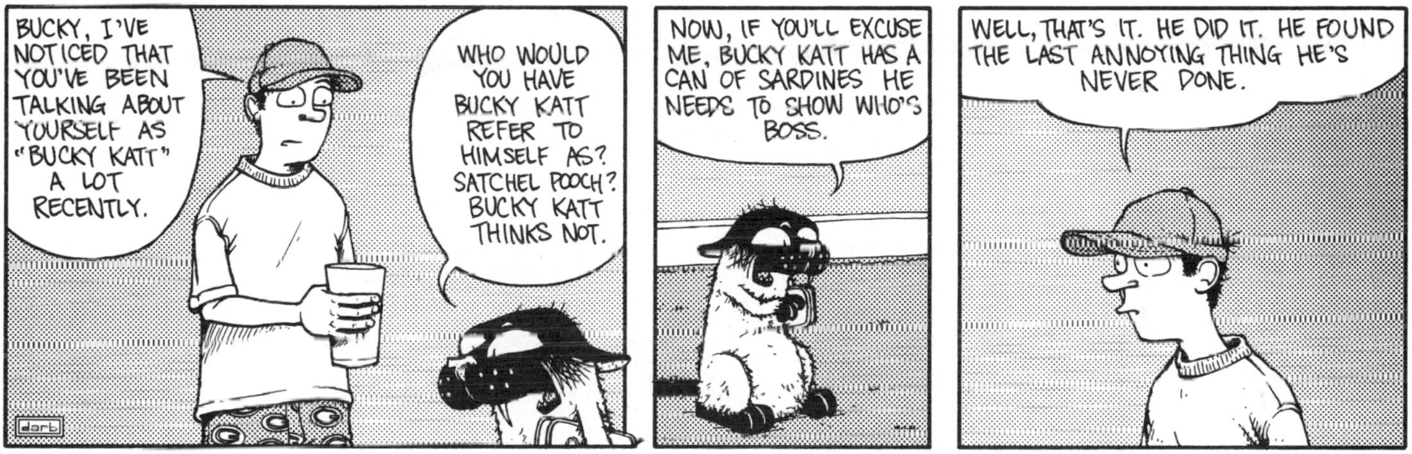
BUCKY, I'VE NOTICED THAT YOU'VE BEEN TALKING ABOUT YOURSELF AS "BUCKY KATT" A LOT RECENTLY.
WHO WOULD YOU HAVE BUCKY KATT REFER TO HIMSELF AS? SATCHEL POOCH? BUCKY KATT THINKS NOT.
NOW, IF YOU'LL EXCUSE ME, BUCKY KATT HAS A CAN OF SARDINES HE NEEDS TO SHOW WHO'S BOSS.
WELL, THAT'S IT. HE DID IT. HE FOUND THE LAST ANNOYING THING HE'S NEVER DONE.

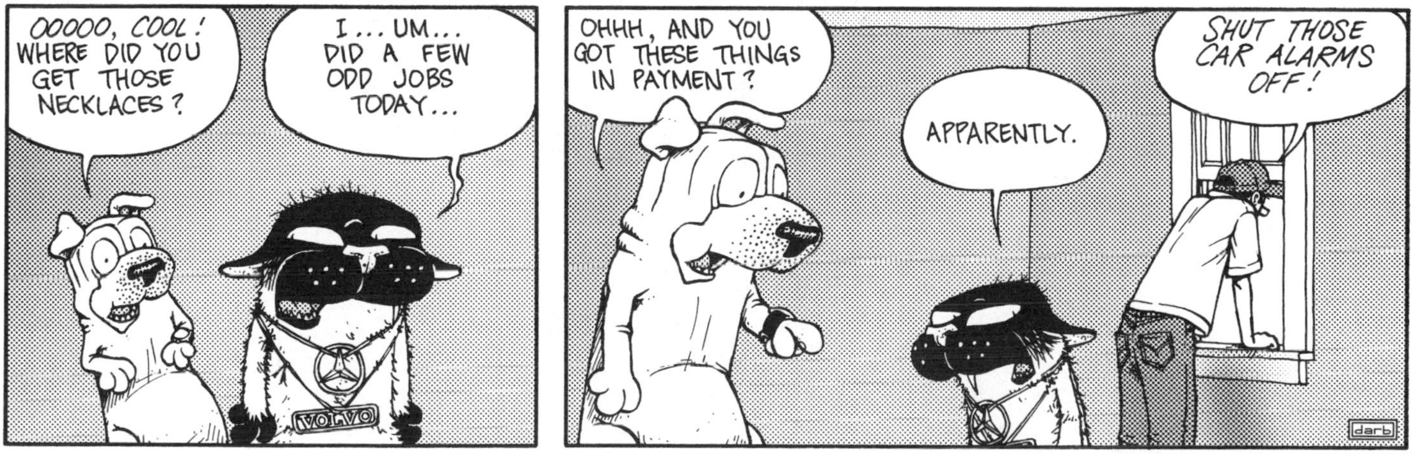
OOOOO, COOL! WHERE DID YOU GET THOSE NECKLACES?
I... UM... DID A FEW ODD JOBS TODAY...
VOLVO
OHHH, AND YOU GOT THESE THINGS IN PAYMENT?
APPARENTLY.
SHUT THOSE CAR ALARMS OFF!

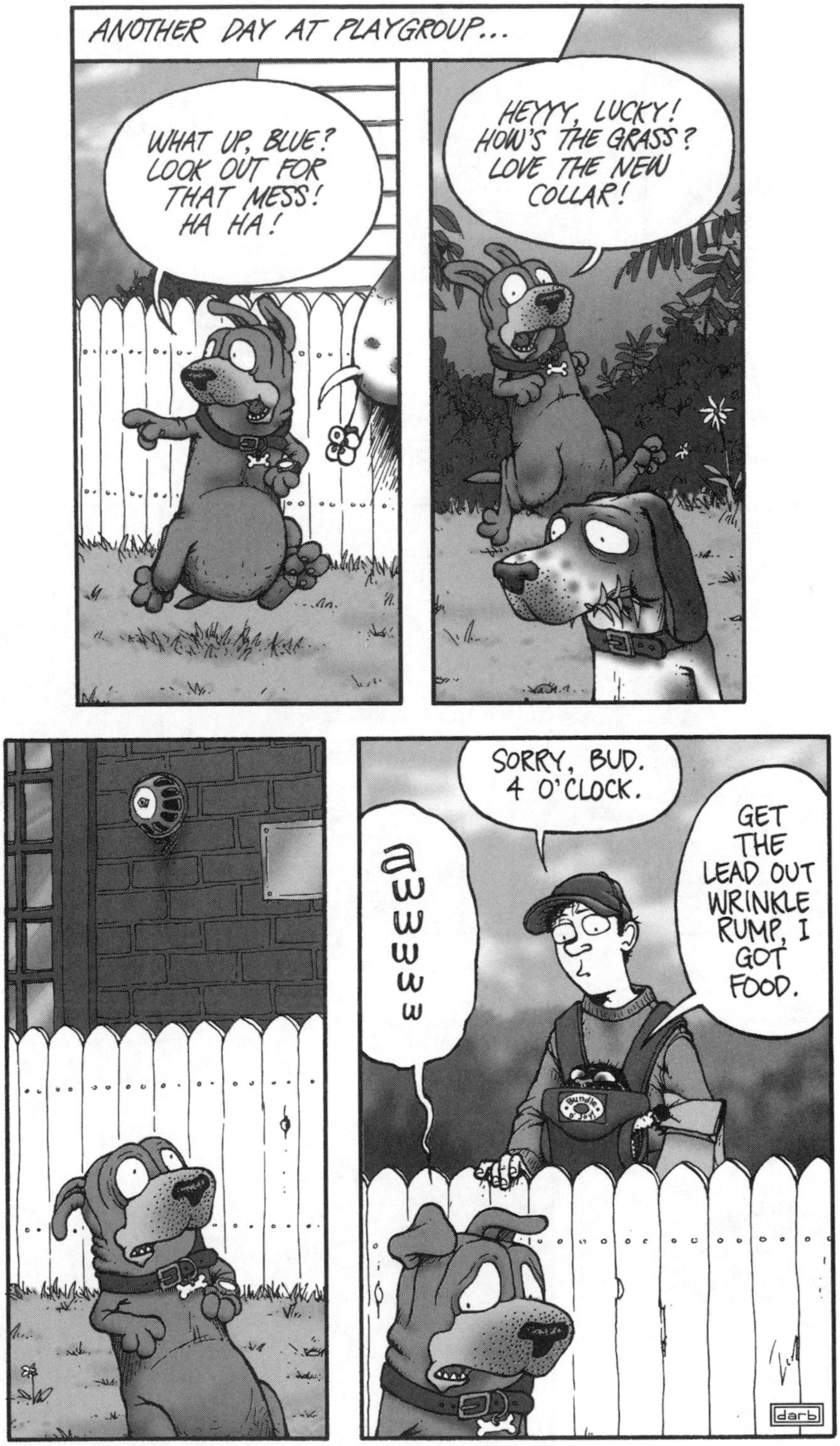
ANOTHER DAY AT PLAYGROUP...
WHAT UP, BLUE? LOOK OUT FOR THAT MESS! HA HA!
HEYYY, LUCKY! HOW'S THE GRASS? LOVE THE NEW COLLAR!
SORRY, BUD. 4 O'CLOCK.
aWWWWW
GET THE LEAD OUT WRINKLE RUMP, I GOT FOOD.
darb

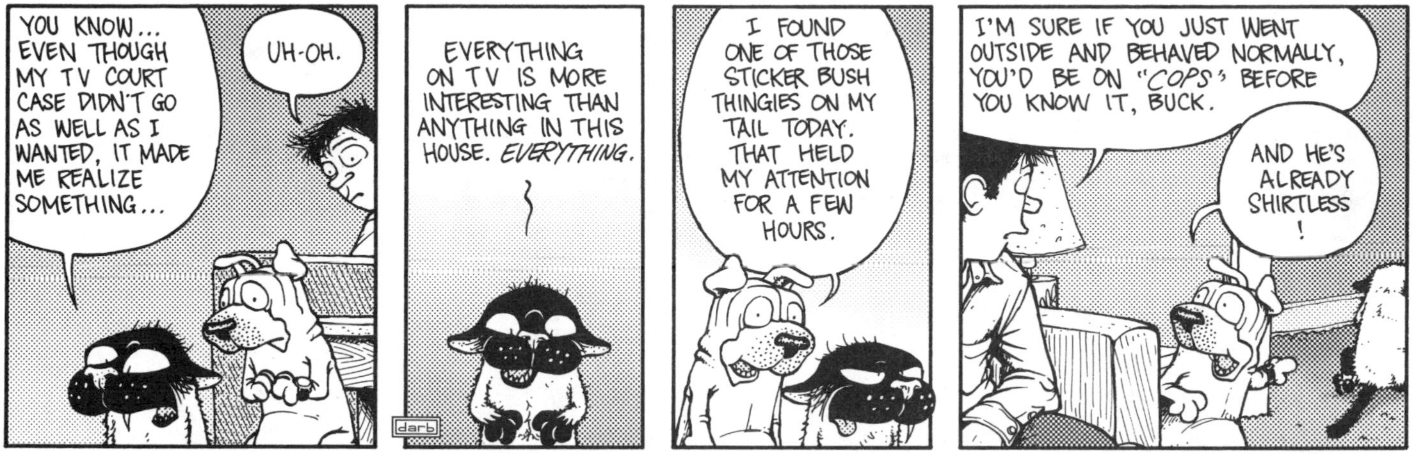
YOU KNOW... EVEN THOUGH MY TV COURT CASE DIDN'T GO AS WELL AS I WANTED, IT MADE ME REALIZE SOMETHING...
UH-OH.
EVERYTHING ON TV IS MORE INTERESTING THAN ANYTHING IN THIS HOUSE. EVERYTHING.
I FOUND ONE OF THOSE STICKER BUSH THINGIES ON MY TAIL TODAY. THAT HELD MY ATTENTION FOR A FEW HOURS.
I'M SURE IF YOU JUST WENT OUTSIDE AND BEHAVED NORMALLY, YOU'D BE ON "COPS" BEFORE YOU KNOW IT, BUCK.
AND HE'S ALREADY SHIRTLESS!
darb

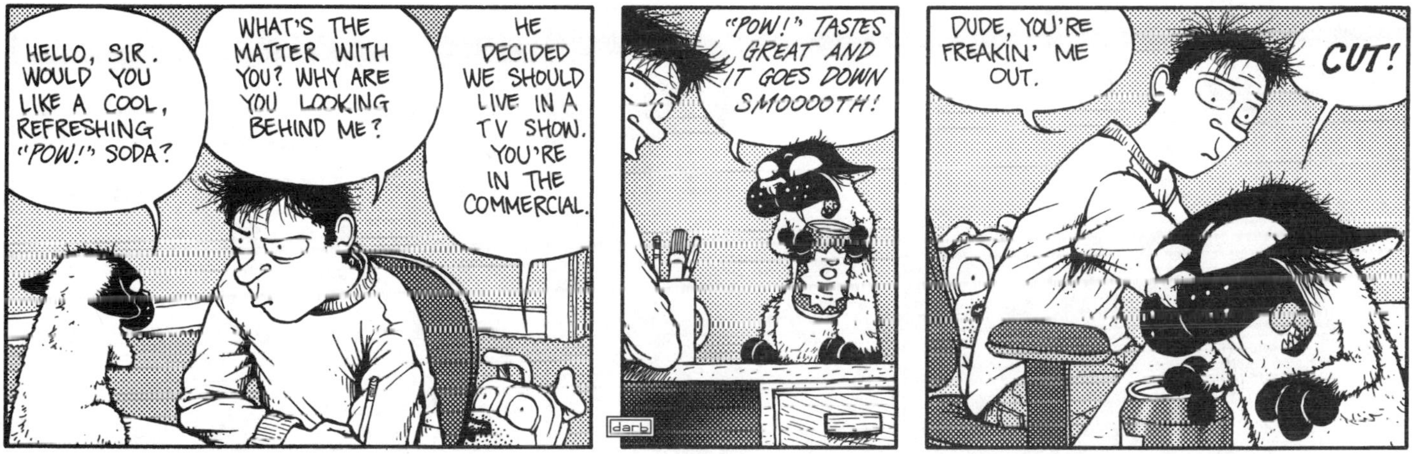
HELLO, SIR. WOULD YOU LIKE A COOL, REFRESHING "POW!" SODA?
WHAT'S THE MATTER WITH YOU? WHY ARE YOU LOOKING BEHIND ME?
HE DECIDED WE SHOULD LIVE IN A TV SHOW. YOU'RE IN THE COMMERCIAL.
"POW!" TASTES GREAT AND IT GOES DOWN SMOOOOTH!
DUDE, YOU'RE FREAKIN' ME OUT.
CUT!
darb

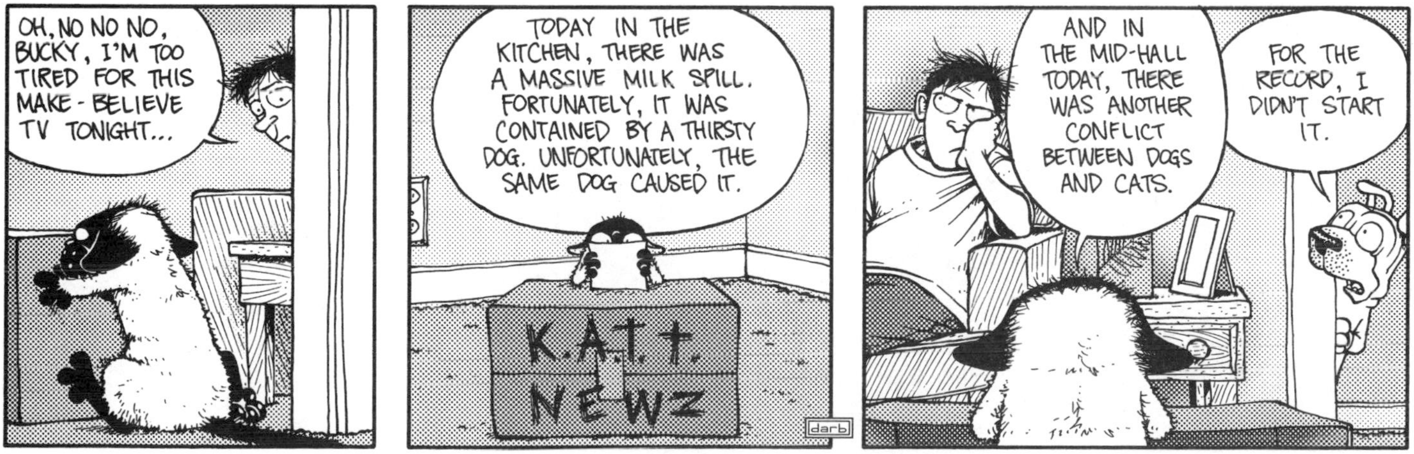
OH, NO NO NO, BUCKY, I'M TOO TIRED FOR THIS MAKE-BELIEVE TV TONIGHT...
TODAY IN THE KITCHEN, THERE WAS A MASSIVE MILK SPILL. FORTUNATELY, IT WAS CONTAINED BY A THIRSTY DOG. UNFORTUNATELY, THE SAME DOG CAUSED IT.
K.A.T.T. NEWZ
AND IN THE MID-HALL TODAY, THERE WAS ANOTHER CONFLICT BETWEEN DOGS AND CATS.
FOR THE RECORD, I DIDN'T START IT.
darb

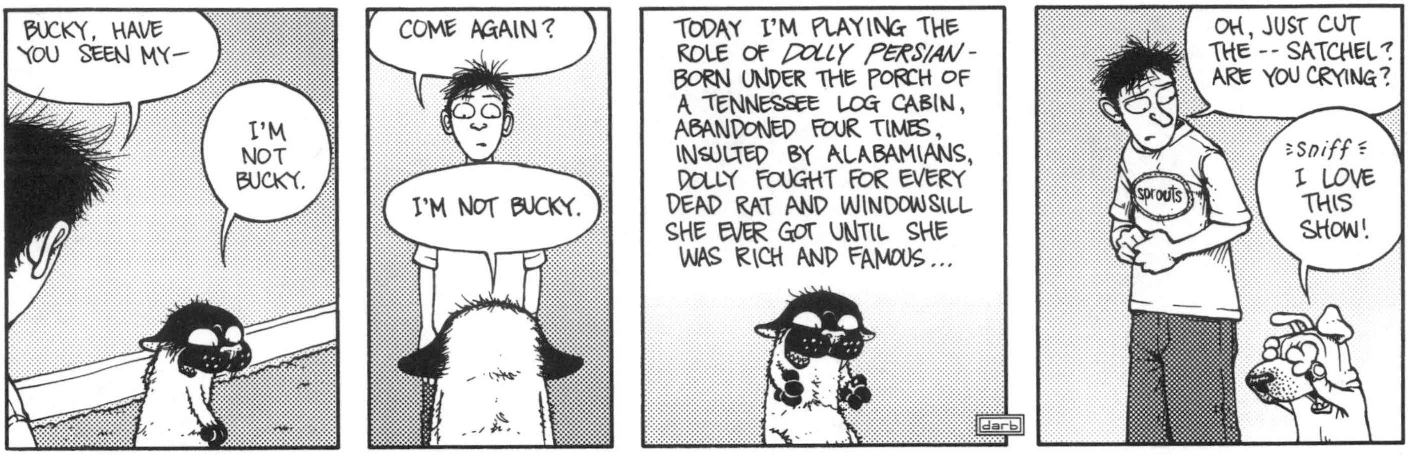
BUCKY, HAVE YOU SEEN MY—
I'M NOT BUCKY.
COME AGAIN?
I'M NOT BUCKY.
TODAY I'M PLAYING THE ROLE OF DOLLY PERSIAN - BORN UNDER THE PORCH OF A TENNESSEE LOG CABIN, ABANDONED FOUR TIMES, INSULTED BY ALABAMIANS, DOLLY FOUGHT FOR EVERY DEAD RAT AND WINDOWSILL SHE EVER GOT UNTIL SHE WAS RICH AND FAMOUS...
darb
OH, JUST CUT THE -- SATCHEL? ARE YOU CRYING?
sprouts
SNIFF I LOVE THIS SHOW!

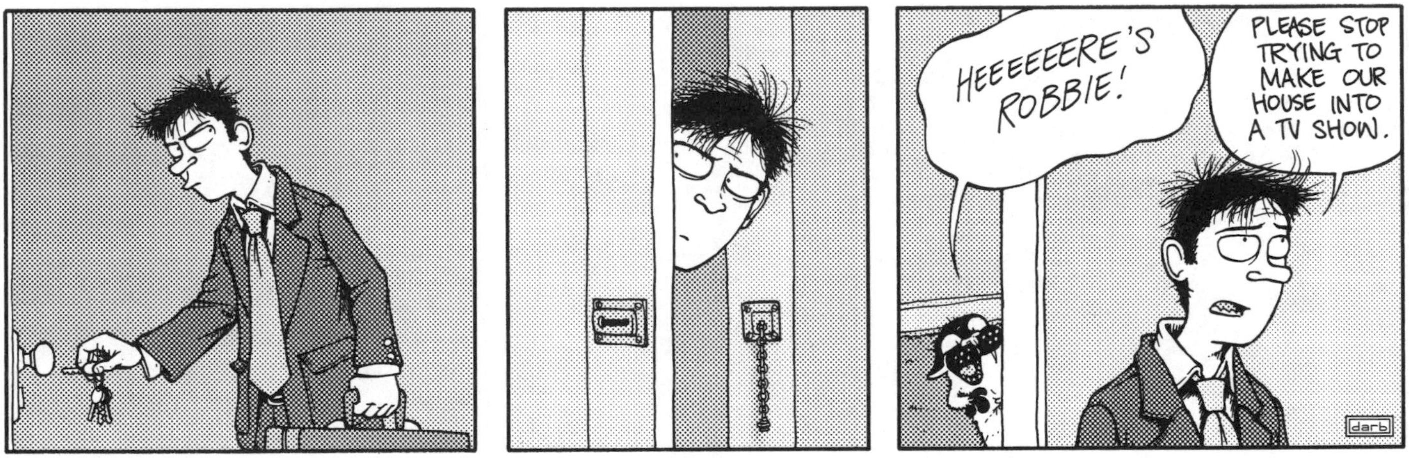
HEEEEEERE'S ROBBIE!
PLEASE STOP TRYING TO MAKE OUR HOUSE INTO A TV SHOW.
darb

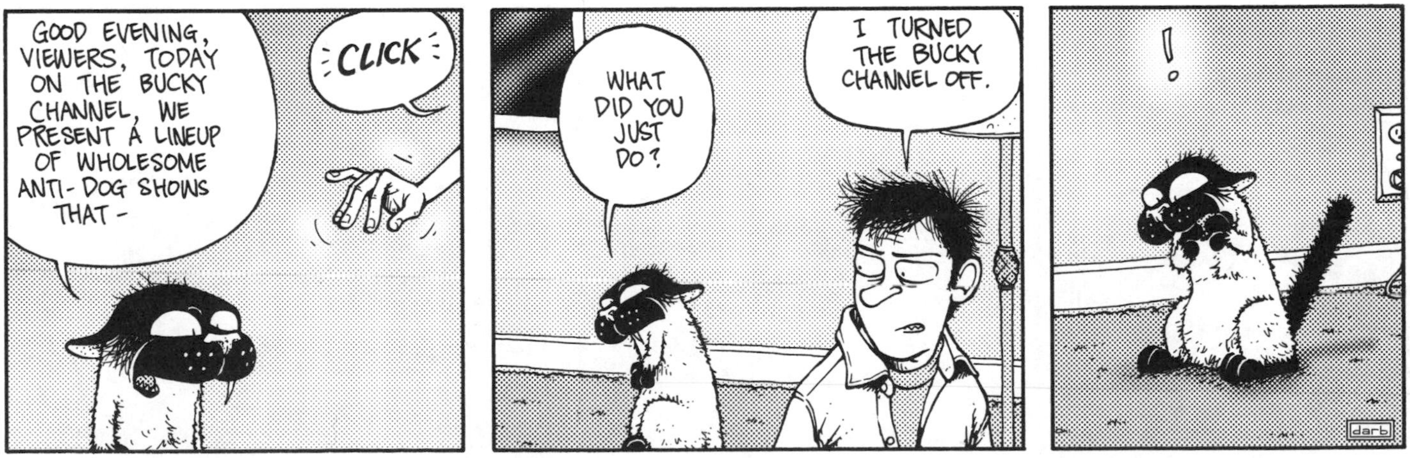
GOOD EVENING, VIEWERS, TODAY ON THE BUCKY CHANNEL, WE PRESENT A LINEUP OF WHOLESOME ANTI-DOG SHOWS THAT -
CLICK
WHAT DID YOU JUST DO?
I TURNED THE BUCKY CHANNEL OFF.
!
darb

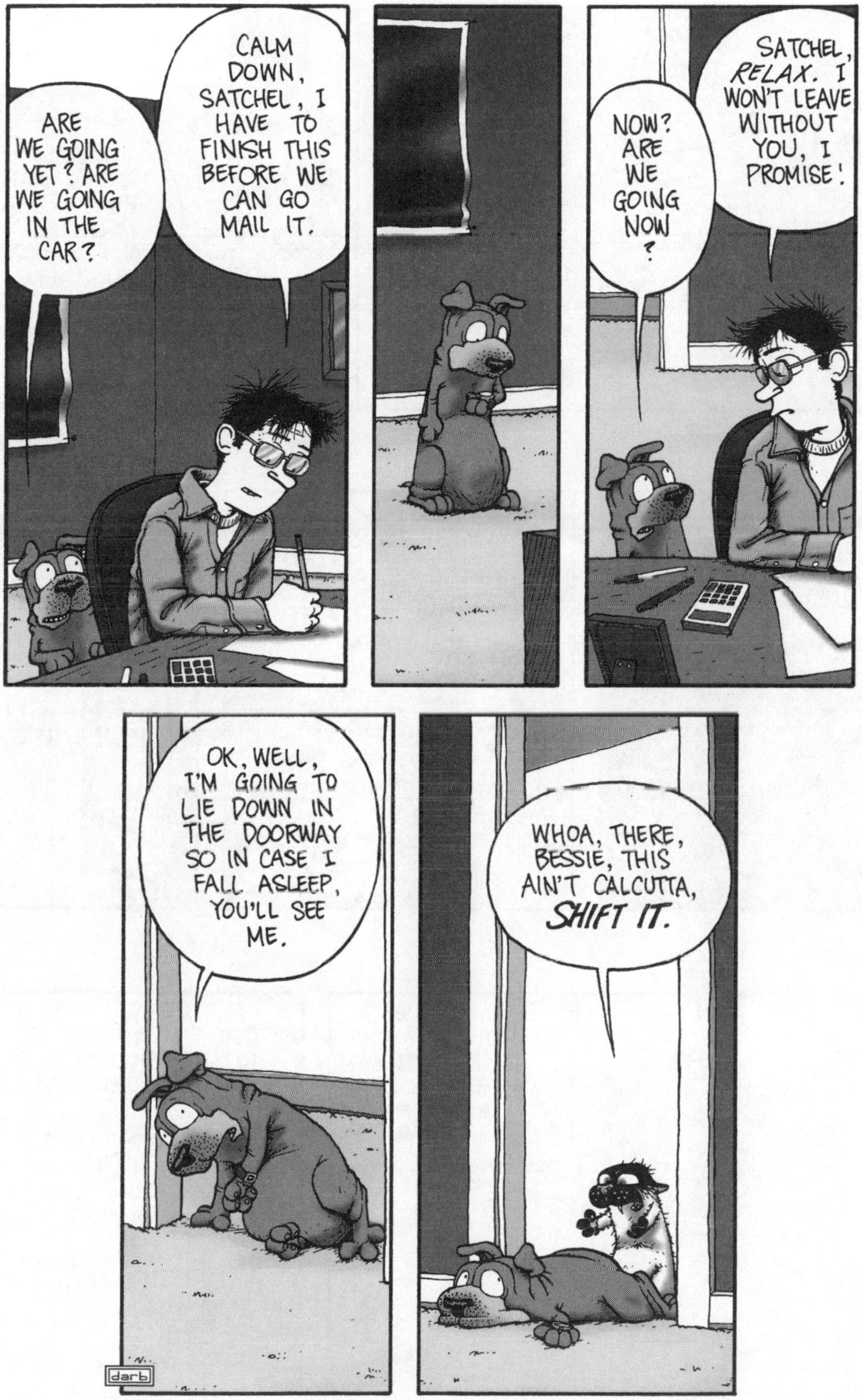
ARE WE GOING YET? ARE WE GOING IN THE CAR?
CALM DOWN, SATCHEL, I HAVE TO FINISH THIS BEFORE WE CAN GO MAIL IT.
NOW? ARE WE GOING NOW?
SATCHEL, RELAX. I WON'T LEAVE WITHOUT YOU, I PROMISE!
OK, WELL, I'M GOING TO LIE DOWN IN THE DOORWAY SO IN CASE I FALL ASLEEP, YOU'LL SEE ME.
WHOA, THERE, BESSIE, THIS AIN'T CALCUTTA, SHIFT IT.
darb

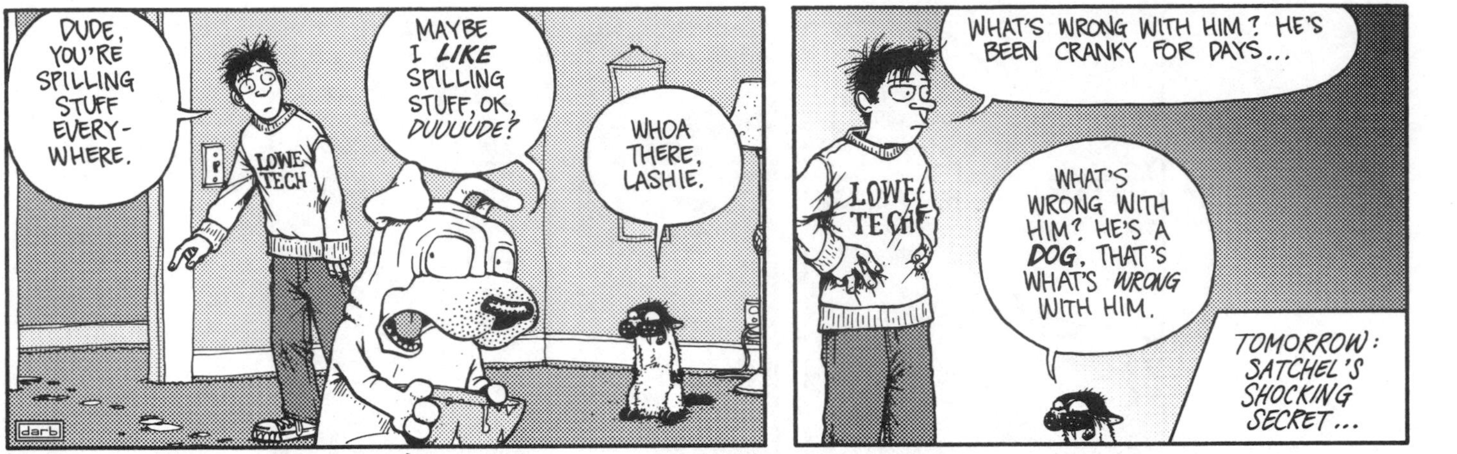
DUDE, YOU'RE SPILLING STUFF EVERY-WHERE.
LOWE TECH
MAYBE I ***LIKE*** SPILLING STUFF, OK, *DUUUUDE?*
WHOA THERE, LASHIE.
WHAT'S WRONG WITH HIM? HE'S BEEN CRANKY FOR DAYS...
WHAT'S WRONG WITH HIM? HE'S A **DOG**. THAT'S WHAT'S *WRONG* WITH HIM.
TOMORROW: SATCHEL'S SHOCKING SECRET...
darb

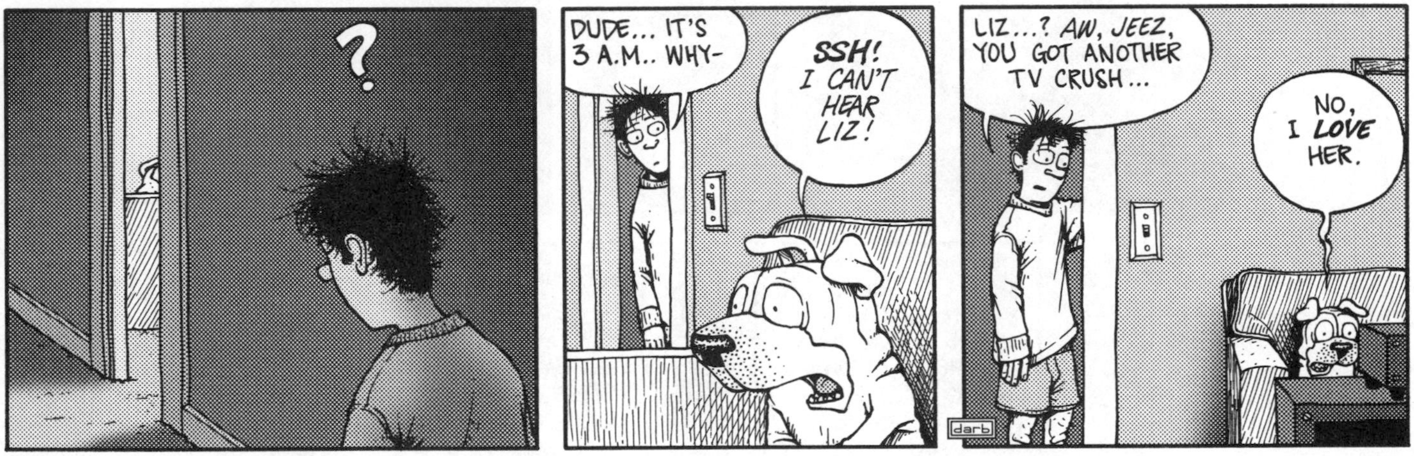
?
DUDE... IT'S 3 A.M.. WHY-
SSH! *I CAN'T HEAR LIZ!*
LIZ...? *AW, JEEZ,* YOU GOT ANOTHER TV CRUSH...
NO, I ***LOVE*** HER.
darb

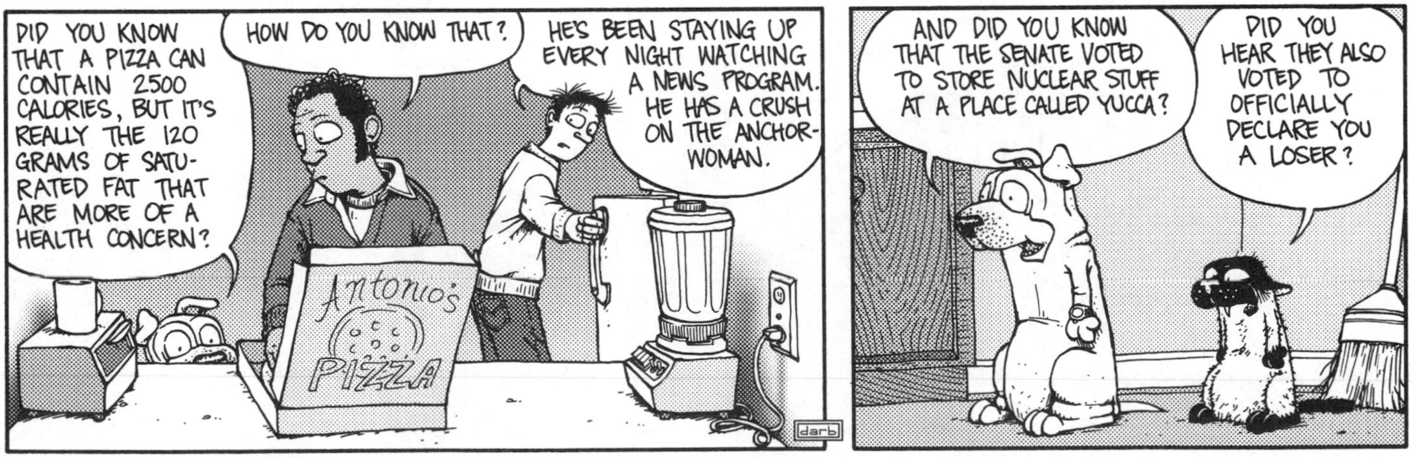
DID YOU KNOW THAT A PIZZA CAN CONTAIN 2500 CALORIES, BUT IT'S REALLY THE 120 GRAMS OF SATU-RATED FAT THAT ARE MORE OF A HEALTH CONCERN?
HOW DO YOU KNOW THAT?
HE'S BEEN STAYING UP EVERY NIGHT WATCHING A NEWS PROGRAM. HE HAS A CRUSH ON THE ANCHOR-WOMAN.
Antonio's PIZZA
darb
AND DID YOU KNOW THAT THE SENATE VOTED TO STORE NUCLEAR STUFF AT A PLACE CALLED YUCCA?
DID YOU HEAR THEY ALSO VOTED TO OFFICIALLY DECLARE YOU A LOSER?

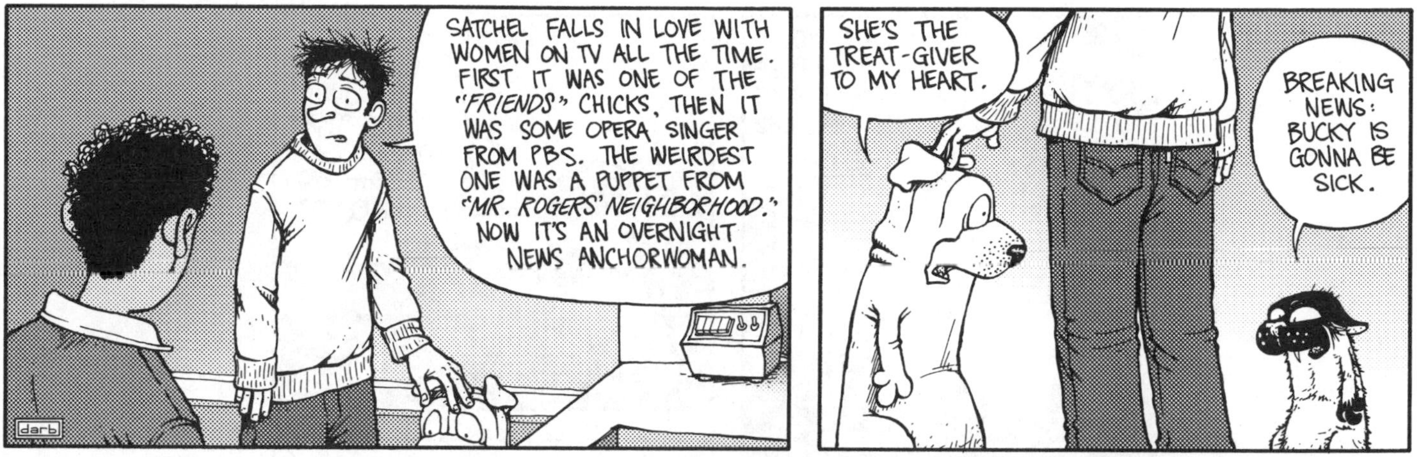
SATCHEL FALLS IN LOVE WITH WOMEN ON TV ALL THE TIME. FIRST IT WAS ONE OF THE "FRIENDS" CHICKS, THEN IT WAS SOME OPERA SINGER FROM PBS. THE WEIRDEST ONE WAS A PUPPET FROM "MR. ROGERS' NEIGHBORHOOD." NOW IT'S AN OVERNIGHT NEWS ANCHORWOMAN.
SHE'S THE TREAT-GIVER TO MY HEART.
BREAKING NEWS: BUCKY IS GONNA BE SICK.

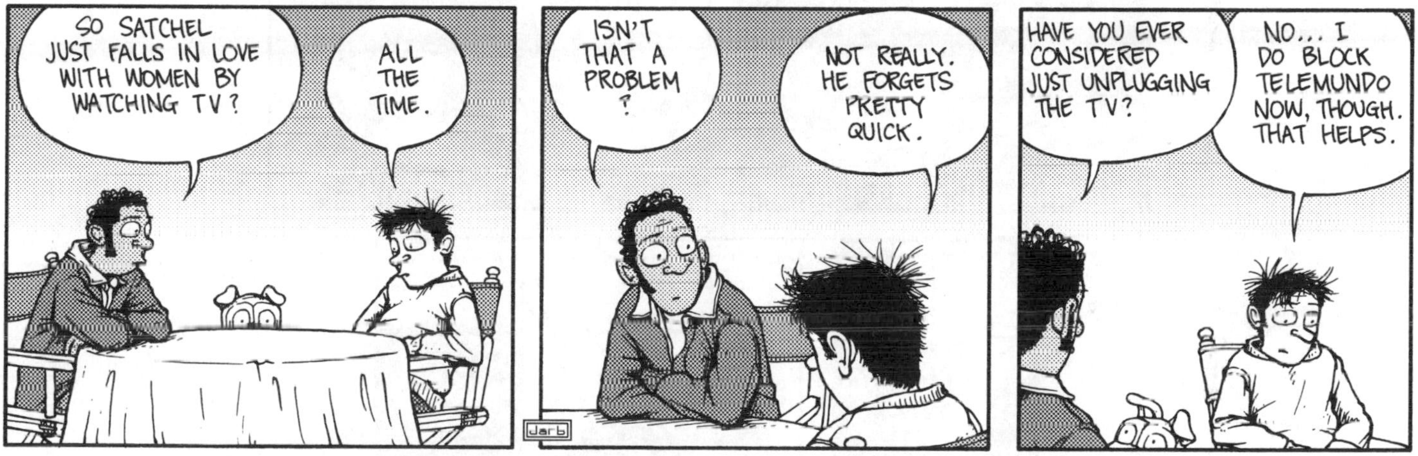
SO SATCHEL JUST FALLS IN LOVE WITH WOMEN BY WATCHING TV?
ALL THE TIME.
ISN'T THAT A PROBLEM?
NOT REALLY. HE FORGETS PRETTY QUICK.
HAVE YOU EVER CONSIDERED JUST UNPLUGGING THE TV?
NO... I DO BLOCK TELEMUNDO NOW, THOUGH. THAT HELPS.

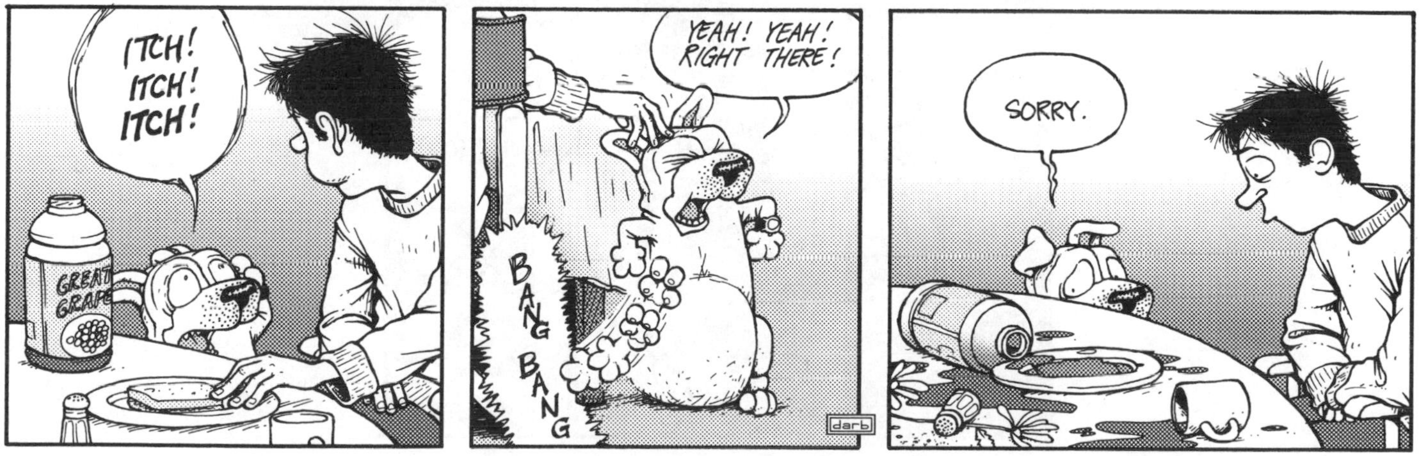
ITCH! ITCH! ITCH!
GREAT GRAPE
YEAH! YEAH! RIGHT THERE!
BANG BANG
SORRY.

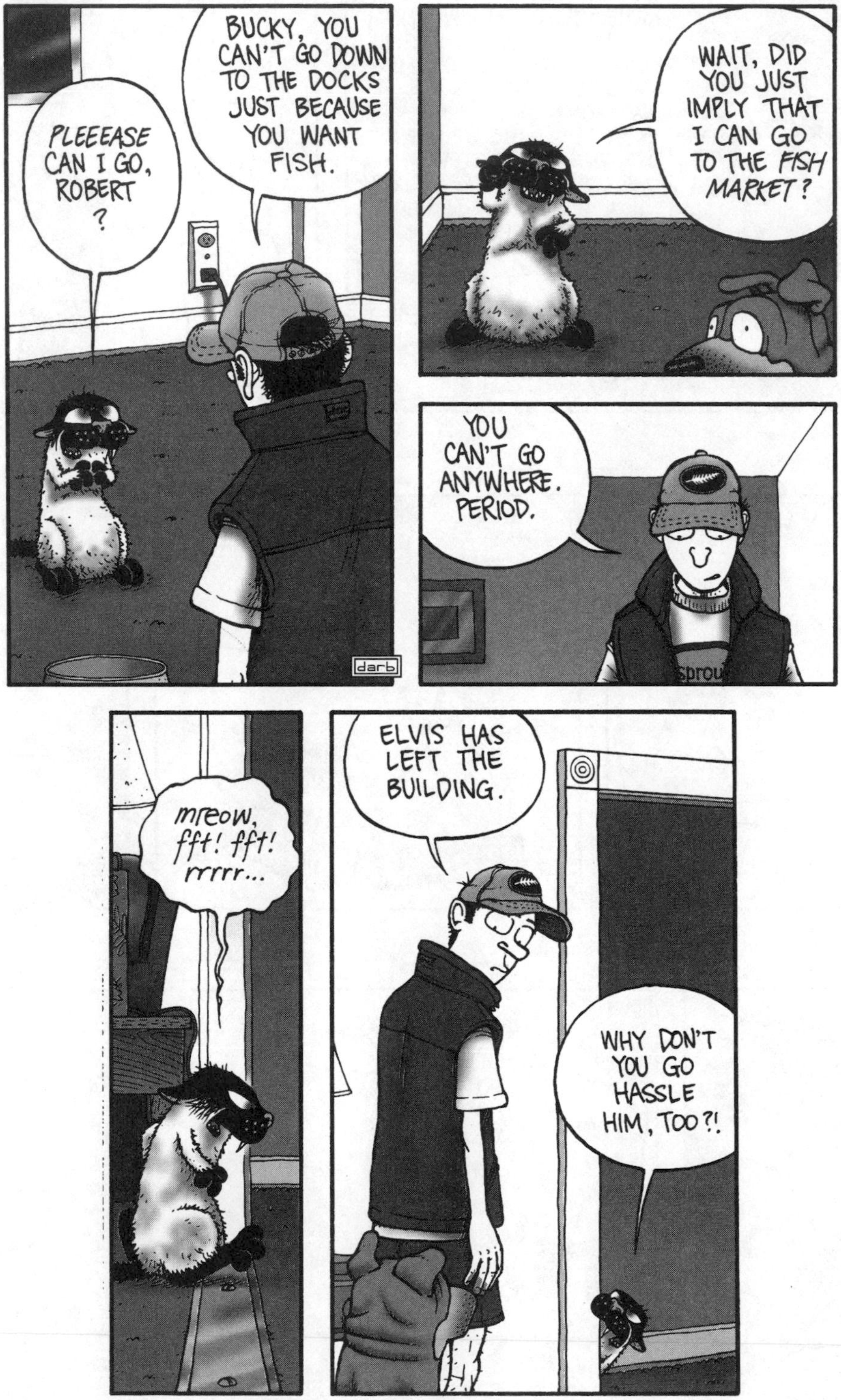
PLEEEASE CAN I GO, ROBERT ?
BUCKY, YOU CAN'T GO DOWN TO THE DOCKS JUST BECAUSE YOU WANT FISH.
darb
WAIT, DID YOU JUST IMPLY THAT I CAN GO TO THE FISH MARKET?
YOU CAN'T GO ANYWHERE. PERIOD.
mreow, fft! fft! rrrrr...
ELVIS HAS LEFT THE BUILDING.
WHY DON'T YOU GO HASSLE HIM, TOO?!

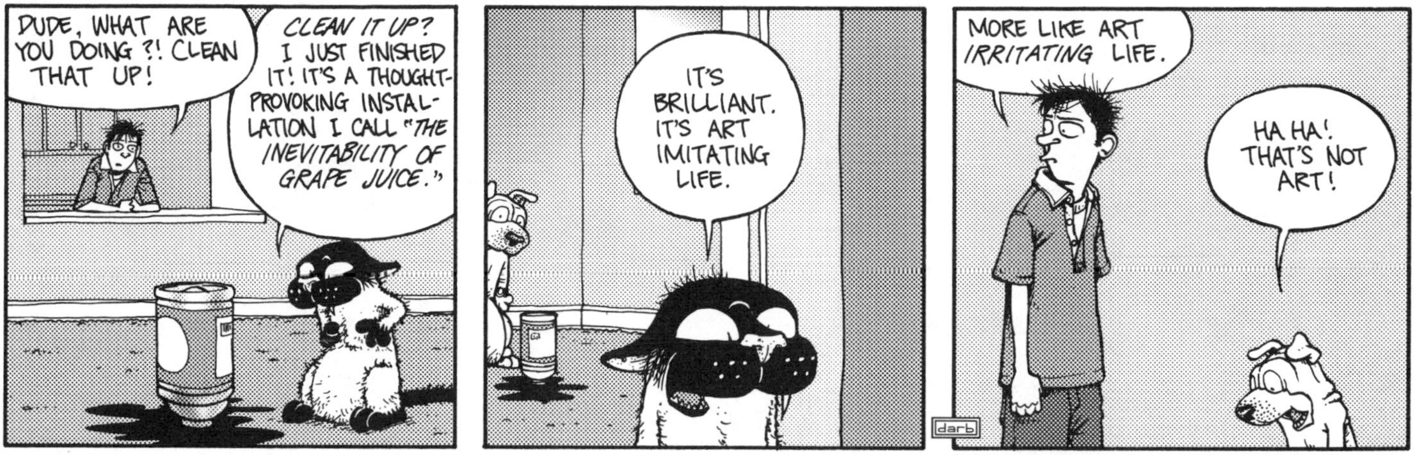
DUDE, WHAT ARE YOU DOING ?! CLEAN THAT UP!
CLEAN IT UP? I JUST FINISHED IT! IT'S A THOUGHT-PROVOKING INSTAL-LATION I CALL "THE INEVITABILITY OF GRAPE JUICE."
IT'S BRILLIANT. IT'S ART IMITATING LIFE.
MORE LIKE ART IRRITATING LIFE.
HA HA! THAT'S NOT ART!
darb

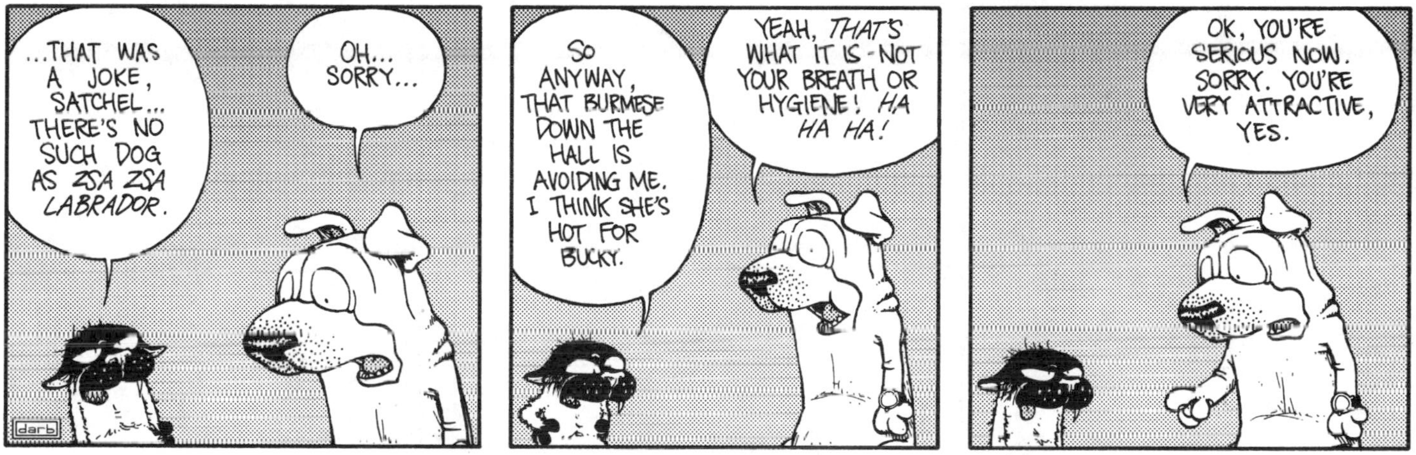
...THAT WAS A JOKE, SATCHEL... THERE'S NO SUCH DOG AS ZSA ZSA LABRADOR.
OH... SORRY...
darb
SO ANYWAY, THAT BURMESE DOWN THE HALL IS AVOIDING ME. I THINK SHE'S HOT FOR BUCKY.
YEAH, THAT'S WHAT IT IS - NOT YOUR BREATH OR HYGIENE! HA HA HA!
OK, YOU'RE SERIOUS NOW. SORRY. YOU'RE VERY ATTRACTIVE, YES.

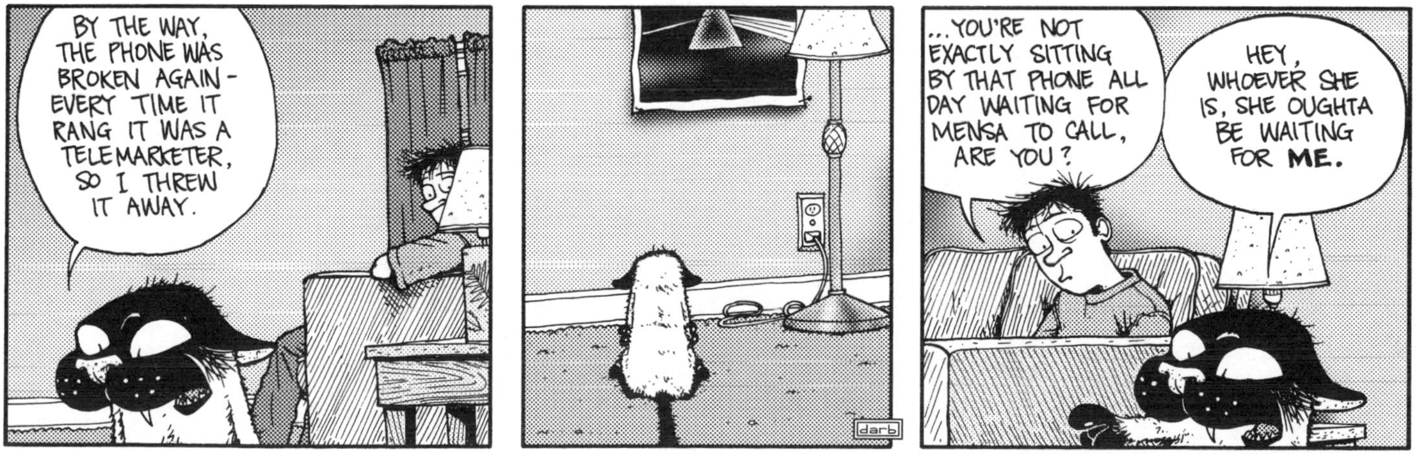
BY THE WAY, THE PHONE WAS BROKEN AGAIN - EVERY TIME IT RANG IT WAS A TELEMARKETER, SO I THREW IT AWAY.
darb
...YOU'RE NOT EXACTLY SITTING BY THAT PHONE ALL DAY WAITING FOR MENSA TO CALL, ARE YOU?
HEY, WHOEVER SHE IS, SHE OUGHTA BE WAITING FOR ME.

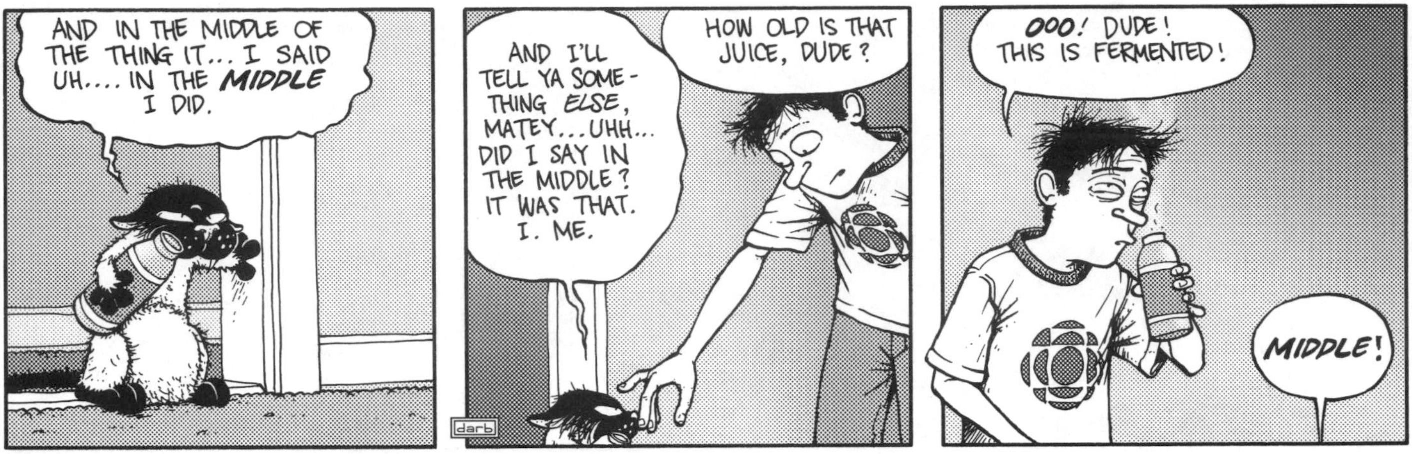
AND IN THE MIDDLE OF THE THING IT... I SAID UH.... IN THE MIDDLE I DID.
HOW OLD IS THAT JUICE, DUDE?
AND I'LL TELL YA SOME-THING ELSE, MATEY...UHH... DID I SAY IN THE MIDDLE? IT WAS THAT. I. ME.
OOO! DUDE! THIS IS FERMENTED!
MIDDLE!

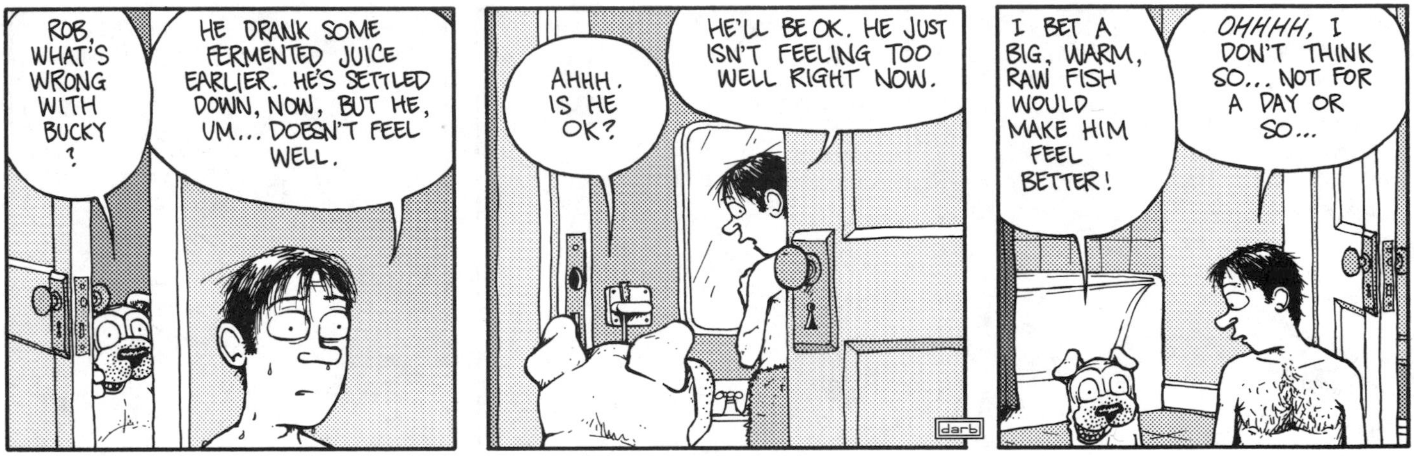
ROB, WHAT'S WRONG WITH BUCKY?
HE DRANK SOME FERMENTED JUICE EARLIER. HE'S SETTLED DOWN, NOW, BUT HE, UM... DOESN'T FEEL WELL.
AHHH. IS HE OK?
HE'LL BE OK. HE JUST ISN'T FEELING TOO WELL RIGHT NOW.
I BET A BIG, WARM, RAW FISH WOULD MAKE HIM FEEL BETTER!
OHHHH, I DON'T THINK SO... NOT FOR A DAY OR SO...

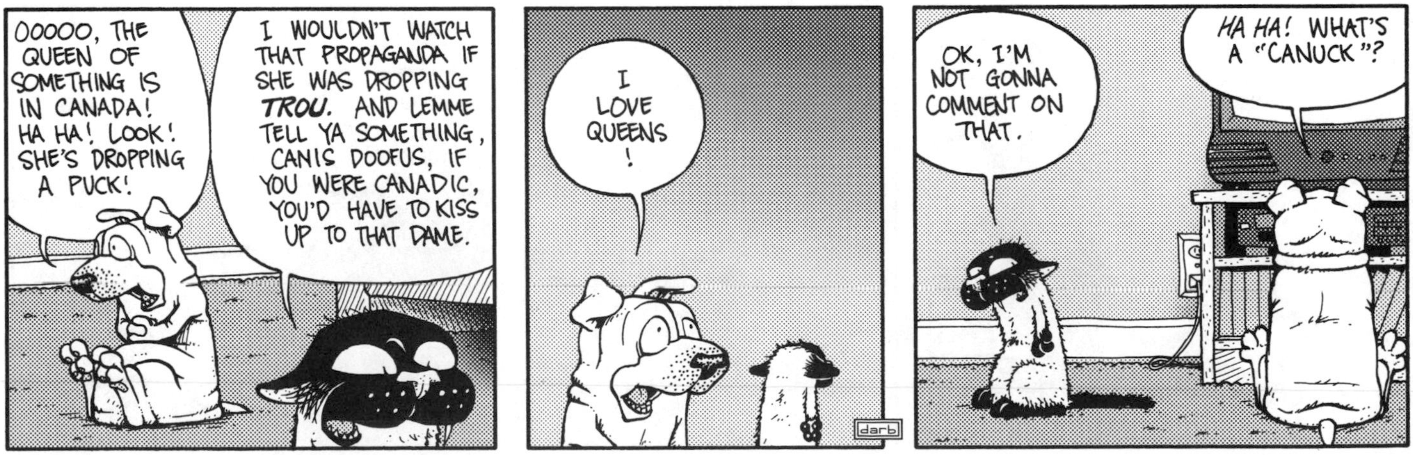
OOOOO, THE QUEEN OF SOMETHING IS IN CANADA! HA HA! LOOK! SHE'S DROPPING A PUCK!
I WOULDN'T WATCH THAT PROPAGANDA IF SHE WAS DROPPING TROU. AND LEMME TELL YA SOMETHING, CANIS DOOFUS, IF YOU WERE CANADIC, YOU'D HAVE TO KISS UP TO THAT DAME.
I LOVE QUEENS!
OK, I'M NOT GONNA COMMENT ON THAT.
HA HA! WHAT'S A "CANUCK"?

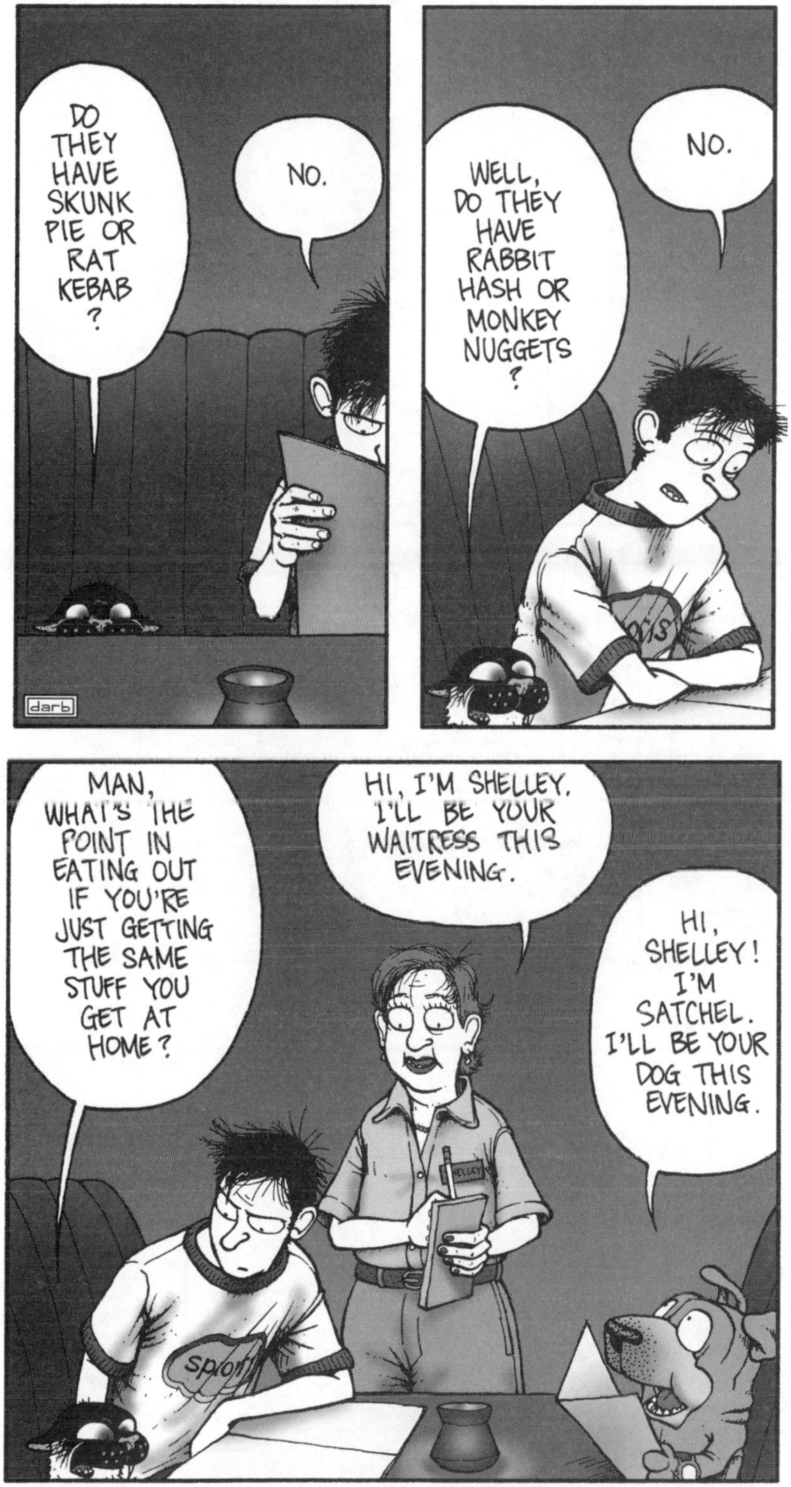
DO THEY HAVE SKUNK PIE OR RAT KEBAB?
NO.
darb
WELL, DO THEY HAVE RABBIT HASH OR MONKEY NUGGETS?
NO.
MAN, WHAT'S THE POINT IN EATING OUT IF YOU'RE JUST GETTING THE SAME STUFF YOU GET AT HOME?
HI, I'M SHELLEY. I'LL BE YOUR WAITRESS THIS EVENING.
HI, SHELLEY! I'M SATCHEL. I'LL BE YOUR DOG THIS EVENING.

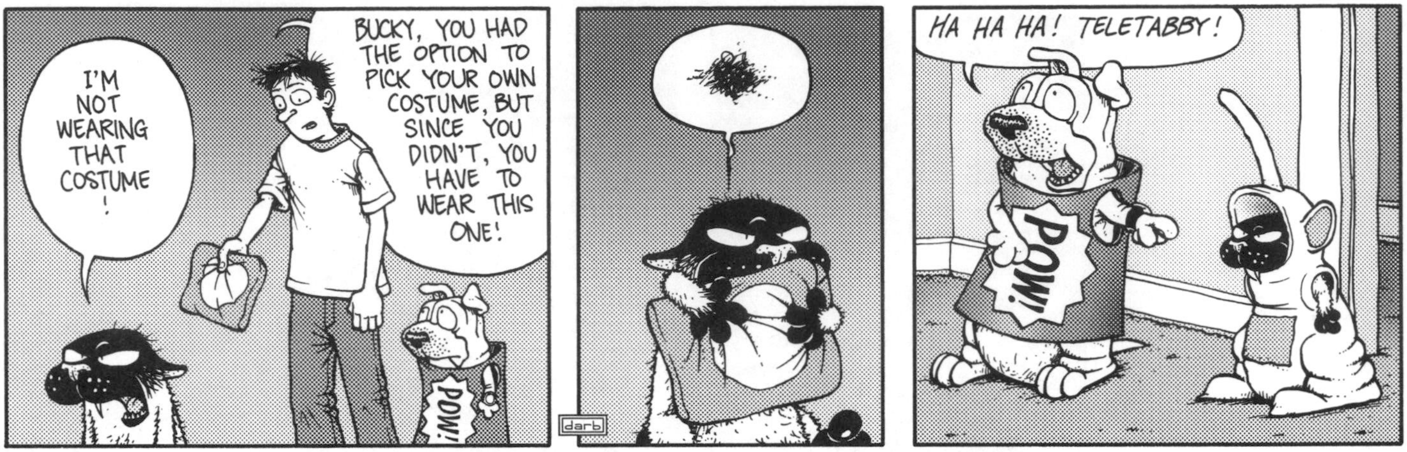
I'M NOT WEARING THAT COSTUME!
BUCKY, YOU HAD THE OPTION TO PICK YOUR OWN COSTUME, BUT SINCE YOU DIDN'T, YOU HAVE TO WEAR THIS ONE!
POW!
HA HA HA! TELETABBY!
POW!

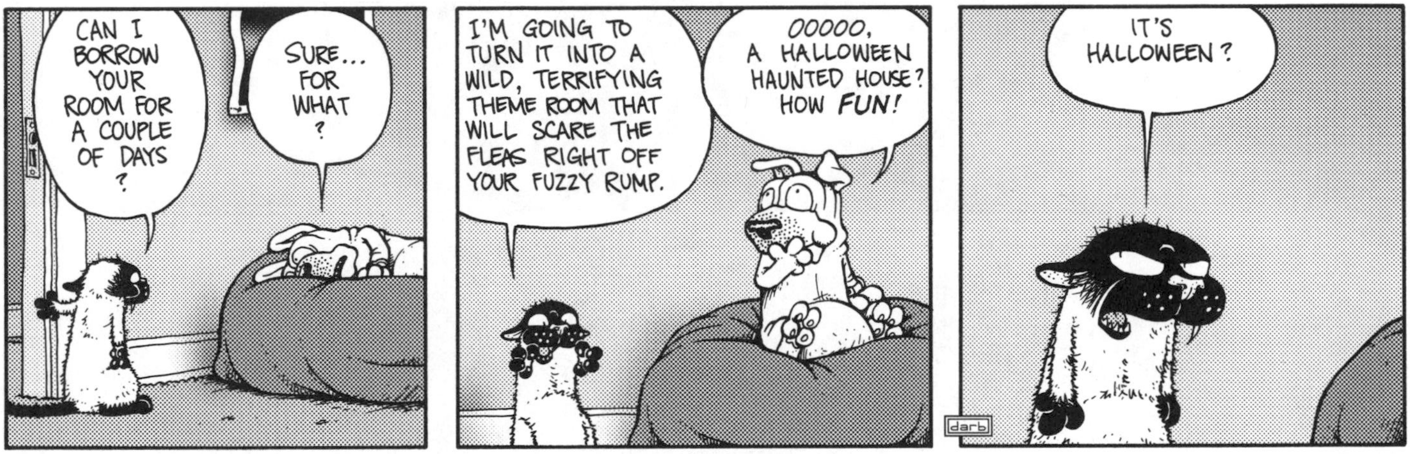
CAN I BORROW YOUR ROOM FOR A COUPLE OF DAYS?
SURE... FOR WHAT?
I'M GOING TO TURN IT INTO A WILD, TERRIFYING THEME ROOM THAT WILL SCARE THE FLEAS RIGHT OFF YOUR FUZZY RUMP.
OOOOO, A HALLOWEEN HAUNTED HOUSE? HOW FUN!
IT'S HALLOWEEN?

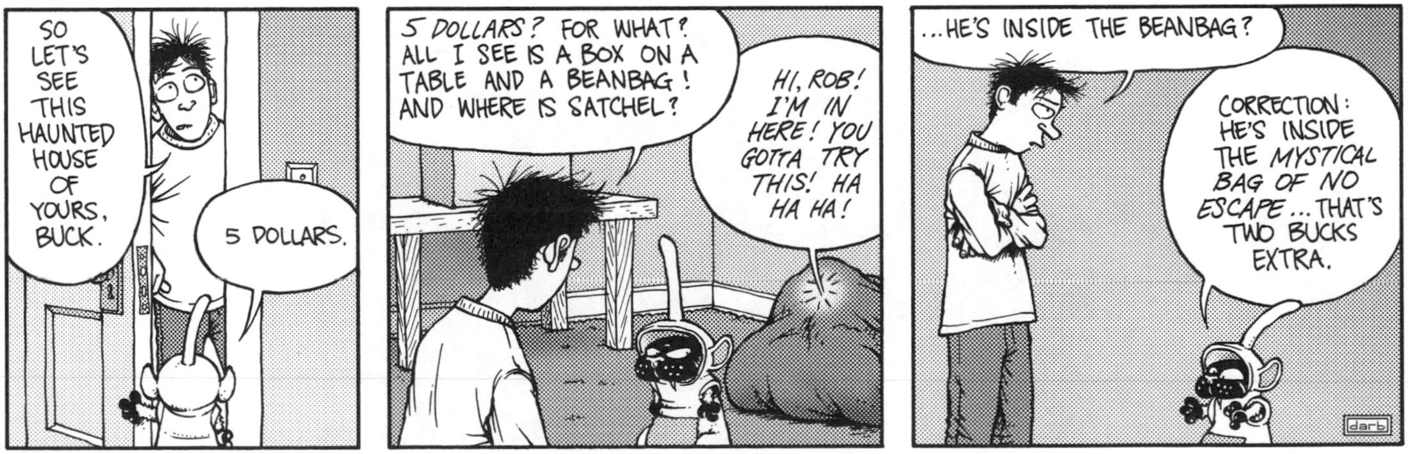
SO LET'S SEE THIS HAUNTED HOUSE OF YOURS, BUCK.
5 DOLLARS.
5 DOLLARS? FOR WHAT? ALL I SEE IS A BOX ON A TABLE AND A BEANBAG! AND WHERE IS SATCHEL?
HI, ROB! I'M IN HERE! YOU GOTTA TRY THIS! HA HA HA!
...HE'S INSIDE THE BEANBAG?
CORRECTION: HE'S INSIDE THE MYSTICAL BAG OF NO ESCAPE... THAT'S TWO BUCKS EXTRA.

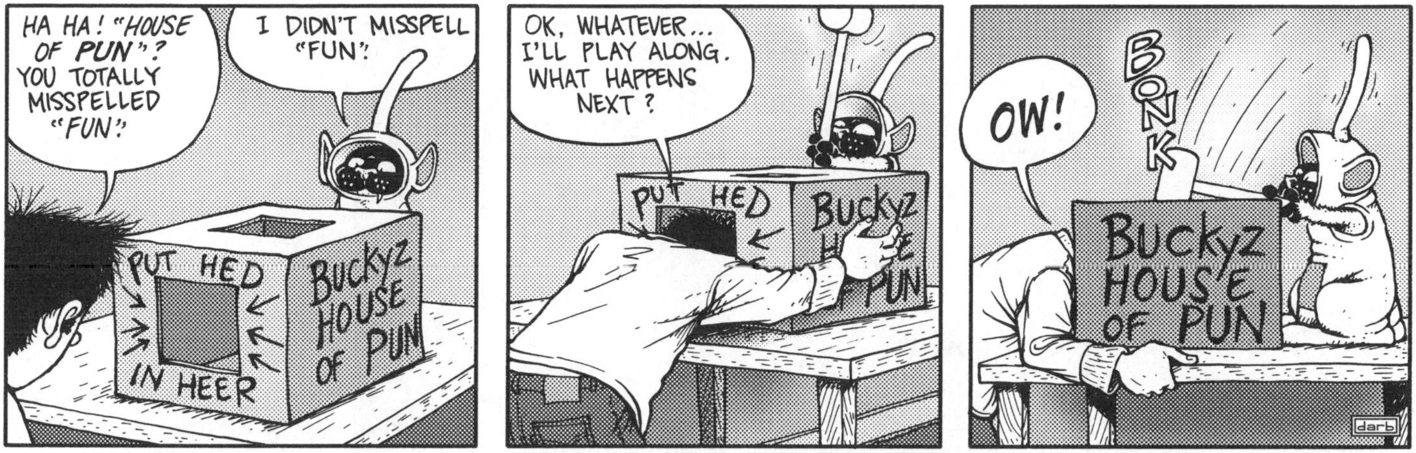
HA HA! "HOUSE OF PUN"? YOU TOTALLY MISSPELLED "FUN".
I DIDN'T MISSPELL "FUN".
PUT HED IN HEER
BUCKYZ HOUSE OF PUN
OK, WHATEVER... I'LL PLAY ALONG. WHAT HAPPENS NEXT?
OW!
BONK
darb

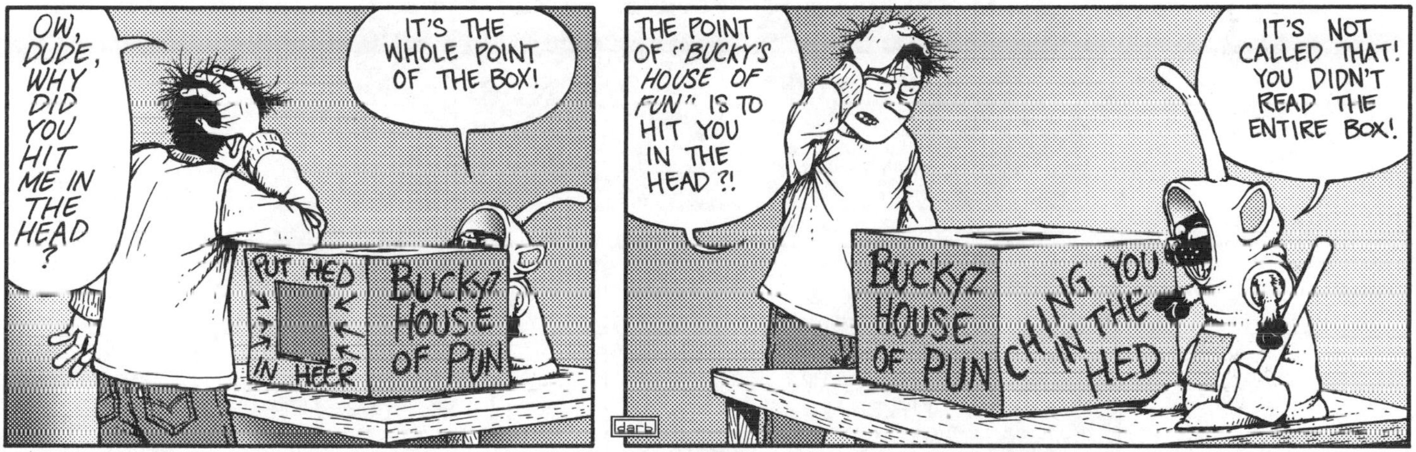
OW, DUDE, WHY DID YOU HIT ME IN THE HEAD?
IT'S THE WHOLE POINT OF THE BOX!
darb
THE POINT OF "BUCKY'S HOUSE OF FUN" IS TO HIT YOU IN THE HEAD?!
IT'S NOT CALLED THAT! YOU DIDN'T READ THE ENTIRE BOX!
BUCKYZ HOUSE OF PUNCHING YOU IN THE HED

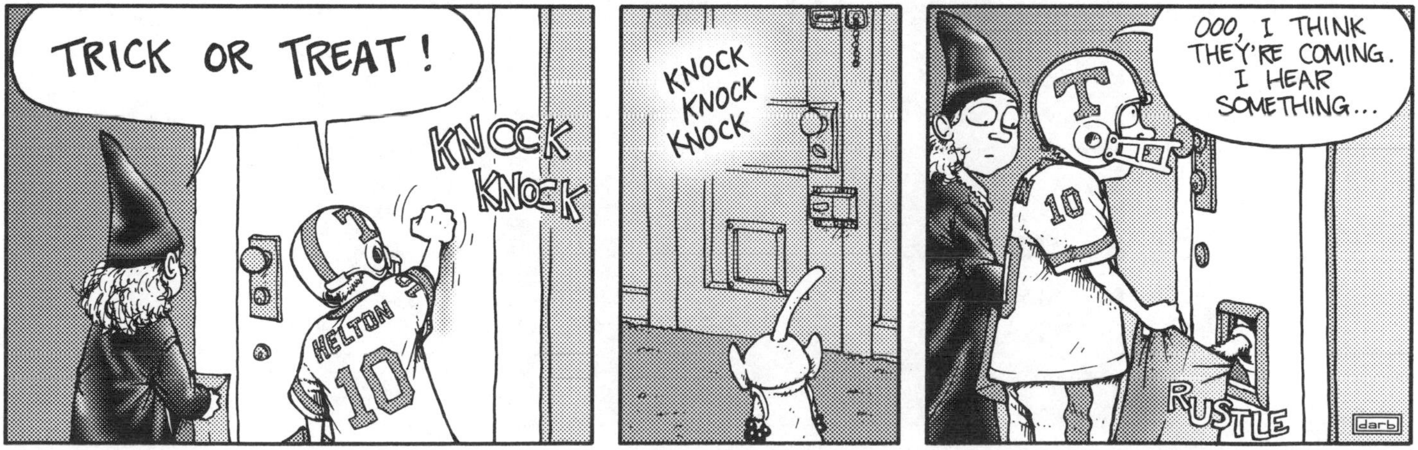
TRICK OR TREAT!
KNOCK KNOCK
HELTON 10
KNOCK KNOCK KNOCK
OOO, I THINK THEY'RE COMING. I HEAR SOMETHING...
RUSTLE
darb

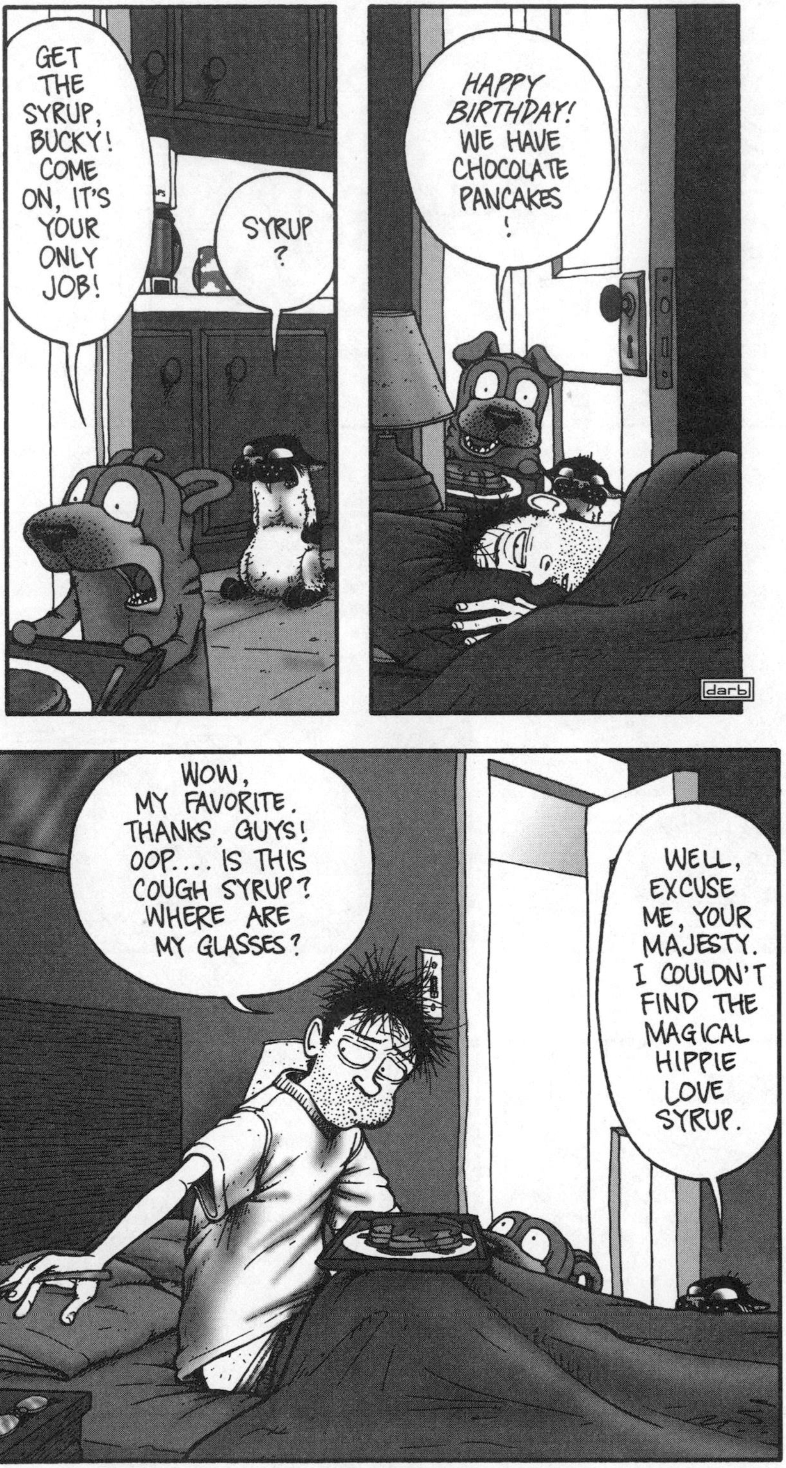
GET THE SYRUP, BUCKY! COME ON, IT'S YOUR ONLY JOB!
SYRUP?
HAPPY BIRTHDAY! WE HAVE CHOCOLATE PANCAKES!
darb
WOW, MY FAVORITE. THANKS, GUYS! OOP.... IS THIS COUGH SYRUP? WHERE ARE MY GLASSES?
WELL, EXCUSE ME, YOUR MAJESTY. I COULDN'T FIND THE MAGICAL HIPPIE LOVE SYRUP.

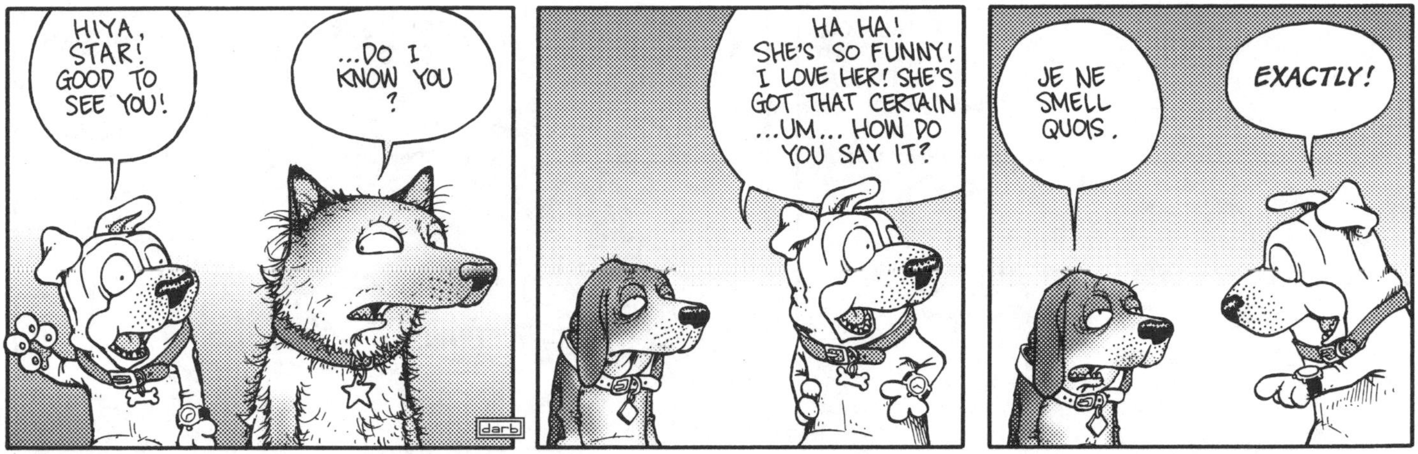
HIYA, STAR! GOOD TO SEE YOU!
...DO I KNOW YOU?
HA HA! SHE'S SO FUNNY! I LOVE HER! SHE'S GOT THAT CERTAIN ...UM... HOW DO YOU SAY IT?
JE NE SMELL QUOIS.
EXACTLY!
darb

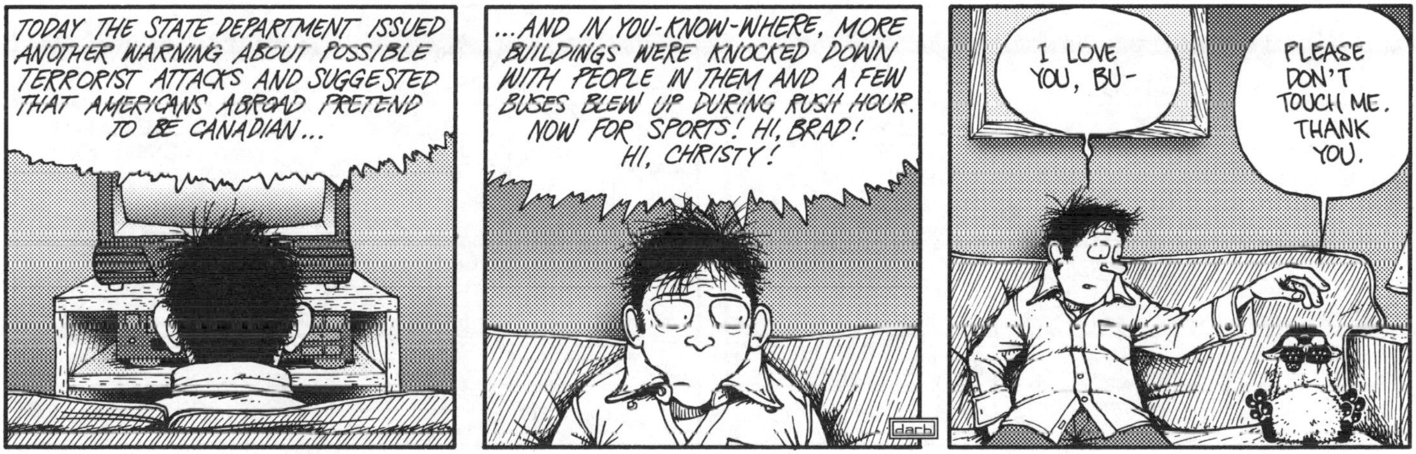
TODAY THE STATE DEPARTMENT ISSUED ANOTHER WARNING ABOUT POSSIBLE TERRORIST ATTACKS AND SUGGESTED THAT AMERICANS ABROAD PRETEND TO BE CANADIAN...
...AND IN YOU-KNOW-WHERE, MORE BUILDINGS WERE KNOCKED DOWN WITH PEOPLE IN THEM AND A FEW BUSES BLEW UP DURING RUSH HOUR. NOW FOR SPORTS! HI, BRAD! HI, CHRISTY!
darb
I LOVE YOU, BU-
PLEASE DON'T TOUCH ME. THANK YOU.

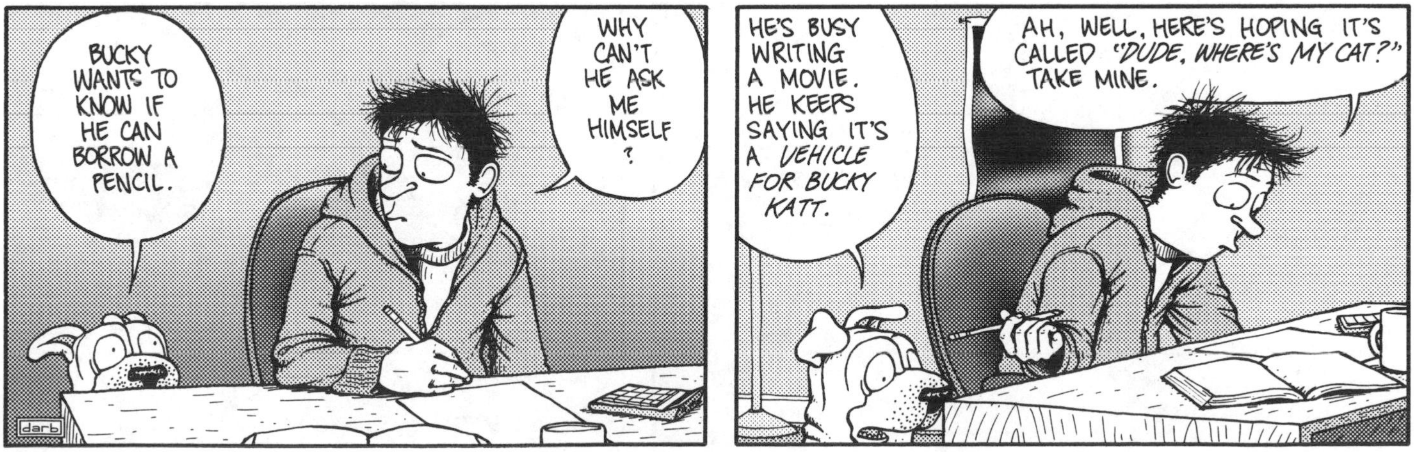
BUCKY WANTS TO KNOW IF HE CAN BORROW A PENCIL.
WHY CAN'T HE ASK ME HIMSELF?
darb
HE'S BUSY WRITING A MOVIE. HE KEEPS SAYING IT'S A VEHICLE FOR BUCKY KATT.
AH, WELL, HERE'S HOPING IT'S CALLED "DUDE, WHERE'S MY CAT?" TAKE MINE.

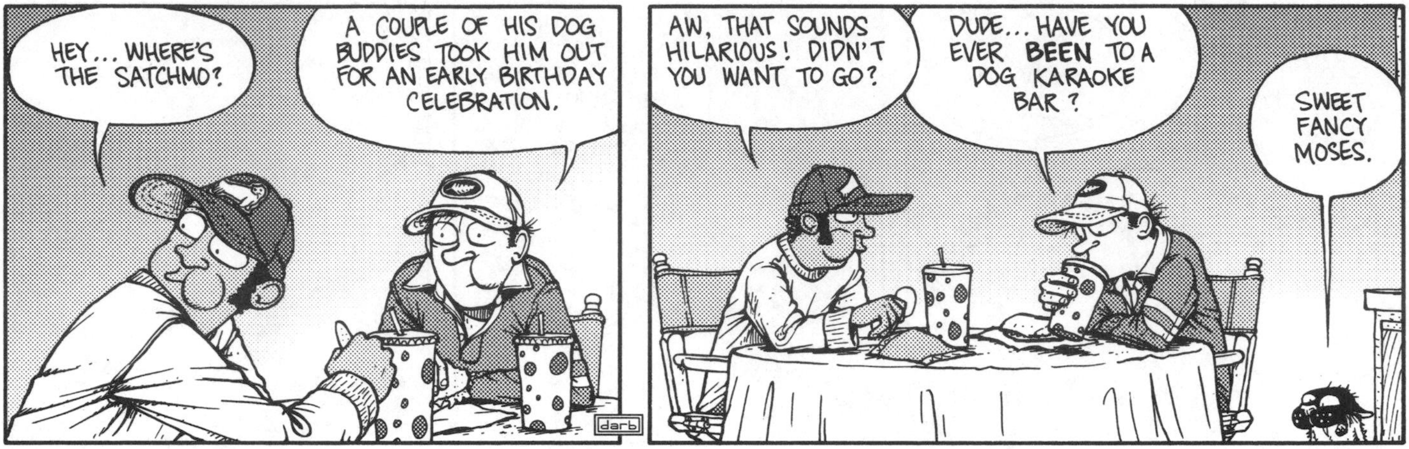
HEY... WHERE'S THE SATCHMO?
A COUPLE OF HIS DOG BUDDIES TOOK HIM OUT FOR AN EARLY BIRTHDAY CELEBRATION.
AW, THAT SOUNDS HILARIOUS! DIDN'T YOU WANT TO GO?
DUDE... HAVE YOU EVER **BEEN** TO A DOG KARAOKE BAR?
SWEET FANCY MOSES.
darb

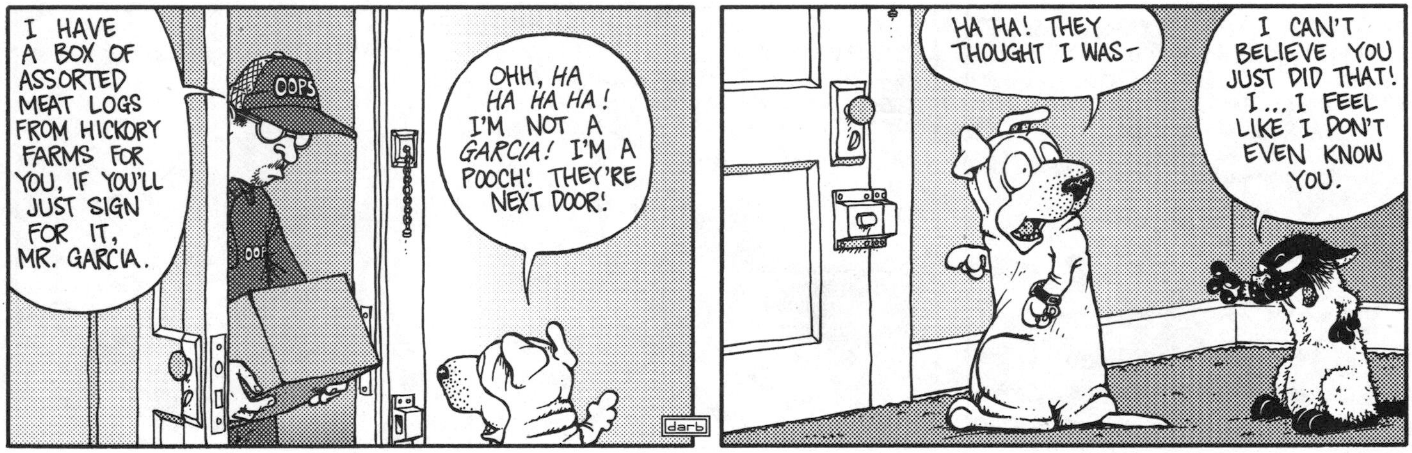
I HAVE A BOX OF ASSORTED MEAT LOGS FROM HICKORY FARMS FOR YOU, IF YOU'LL JUST SIGN FOR IT, MR. GARCIA.
OOPS
OHH, HA HA HA HA! I'M NOT A *GARCIA*! I'M A POOCH! THEY'RE NEXT DOOR!
darb
HA HA! THEY THOUGHT I WAS-
I CAN'T BELIEVE YOU JUST DID THAT! I... I FEEL LIKE I DON'T EVEN KNOW YOU.

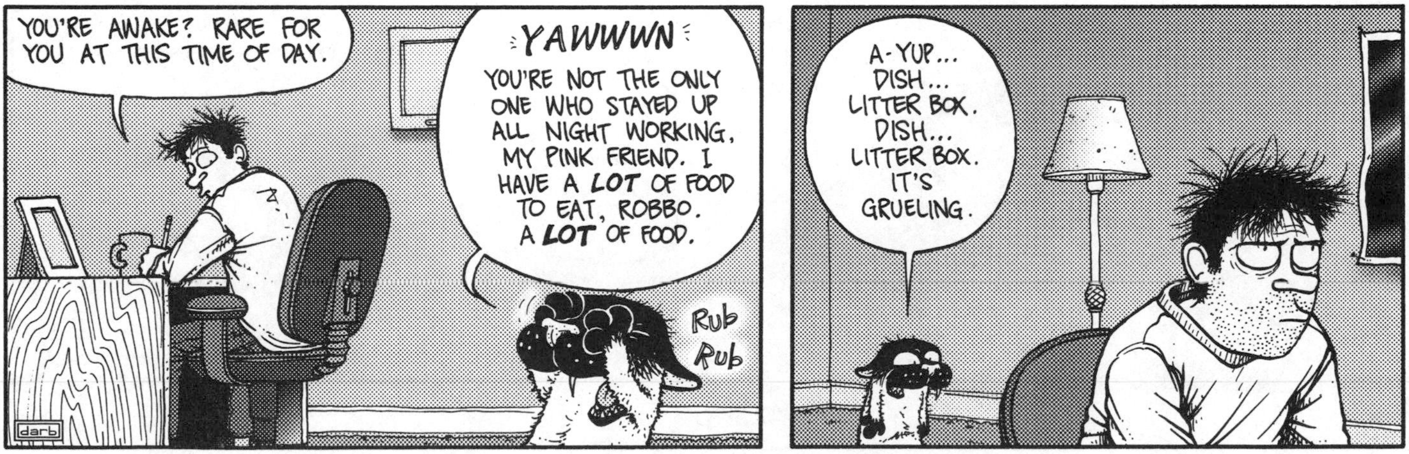
YOU'RE AWAKE? RARE FOR YOU AT THIS TIME OF DAY.
YAWWUN
YOU'RE NOT THE ONLY ONE WHO STAYED UP ALL NIGHT WORKING, MY PINK FRIEND. I HAVE A ***LOT*** OF FOOD TO EAT, ROBBO. A ***LOT*** OF FOOD.
Rub Rub
darb
A-YUP... DISH... LITTER BOX. DISH... LITTER BOX. IT'S GRUELING.